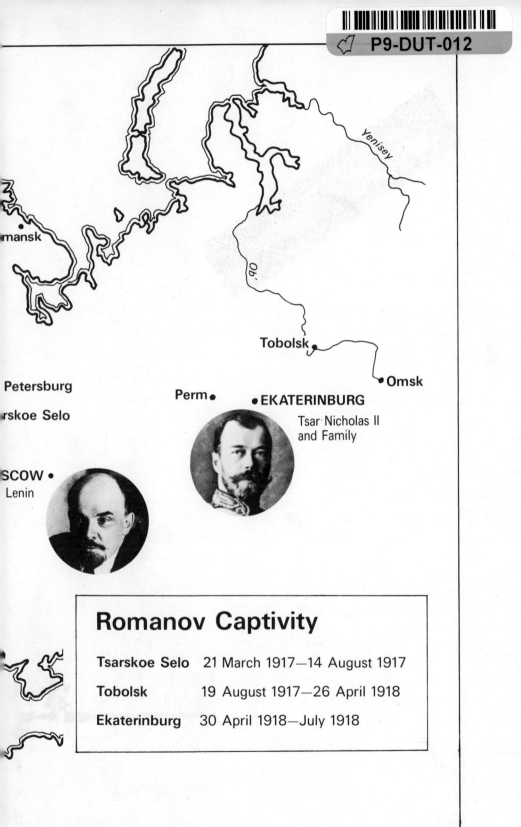

P9-DUT-012

Yenisey

Ob

mansk

Tobolsk

Omsk

Petersburg

Perm ● EKATERINBURG

rskoe Selo

Tsar Nicholas II
and Family

SCOW ●
Lenin

Romanov Captivity

Tsarskoe Selo   21 March 1917—14 August 1917

Tobolsk   19 August 1917—26 April 1918

Ekaterinburg   30 April 1918—July 1918

THE FILE ON THE TSAR

THE FILE ON THE TSAR

ANTHONY SUMMERS

TOM MANGOLD

HARPER & ROW, PUBLISHERS
New York, Hagerstown, San Francisco, London

FIRST U.S. EDITION

ISBN: 0-06-012807-0

LIBRARY OF CONGRESS CATALOG CARD NUMBER: 75-25050

77 78 79 80 81 10 9 8 7 6 5 4

for
Kenneth Allsop, who told me to write it,
and for Sean

A. S.

for
Valerie, Sarah and Abigail

T. M.

CONTENTS

Acknowledgements   13

Preface   17

Cast of Main Characters   21

PART ONE   *Disappearance*

1 The Empire Collapses   31
2 The Romanovs Disappear   41
3 Doubt and Disbelief   52
4 The File Is Found   59

PART TWO   *Investigation*

5 Signposts to a Massacre   65
6 The Sergeyev Investigation   80
7 The Whites Lose Patience   90

PART THREE   *Sokolov*

8   Sokolov Takes on the Case   101
9   The Suspect Telegram   106
10 The Key Guard Who Disappeared   118
11 Other Guards, Other Stories   130
12 Blood, Bullets, Fire and Acid   136
13 Professor Camps Reports   146
14 The Corpse of a Female Dog   161
15 The End of Sokolov   169
16 A Compendium of Lies   177

PART FOUR   *Pretenders*

17 The Claimants   187
18 Anna Anderson   198

PART FIVE *Cousins*

19 King George Slams the Door   243
20 The Jonas Lied Affair   253
21 The Yakovlev Mission   261
22 The German Connection   273
23 Moscow Barters with Berlin   291

PART SIX *Perm*

24 The End of Nicholas   307
25 To Perm and Beyond   321

Sources and Notes   357

Bibliography   395

Index   403

LIST OF ILLUSTRATIONS

The imperial family   *following page* 48
Imprisonment at Tsarskoe Selo, 1917   48
Grand duchesses at Tobolsk   48
The arrival at Ekaterinburg   48
The Ipatiev House, June 1918   48
The town of Ekaterinburg   *facing page* 49
The window of the "murder room"   49
The Ipatiev House, 1959 (by courtesy of Harrison Salisbury)   49
Yakov Yurovsky   96
Chaya Goloshchokin (*Soviet Encyclopaedia*)   96
Alexander Beloborodov   96
Pyotr Voikov (*Soviet Encyclopaedia*)   96
The Sokolov Dossier   97
The Mirolyubov Papers   97
Search for bodies near Ekaterinburg   128
"Murder room" interior   128
Nikolai Sokolov   129
Admiral Kolchak   129
Mikhail Diterikhs   129
Robert Wilton (by courtesy of *The Times*)   129
Pavel Bulygin   129
Coded telegram, and signatures of Chairman Beloborodov   144
Sir Charles Eliot and his report (*Illustrated London News*
   and Public Record Office)   144
German inscription   *following page* 144
Bullets from "murder room"   144
Corset stays   144
Newspaper fragments found at mine   144
Pumping operations at Ganin Shaft (by courtesy of
   Houghton Library)   144
The finger found at the mine   144
The denture found at the mine, and Dr Botkin—the
   alleged owner   144
The bones allegedly found   144
Professor Camps and Professor Simpson   *facing page* 145

The corpse of the dog "Jemmy", and General Domonto-
vich, who reported the find (Domontovich by courtesy
of George Gibbes) *facing page* 145
Anna Anderson, Berlin 1925 *following page* 208
Anna Anderson, U.S.A. 1928 208
Grand Duchess Anastasia, family snapshot 208
Anna Anderson, U.S.A. 1974 (by courtesy of Brien
Purcell Horan) 208
Franziska Schanzkowska, Polish factory girl *facing page* 209
Anna Anderson, in the Black Forest, during the fifties 209
Anna Anderson, in 1967, compared with Grand
Duchess Xenia, also in old age 209
King George V and his cousin Tsar Nicholas 256
Alexander Kerensky (by courtesy of Radio Times
Hulton Picture Library) 256
Sir George Buchanan (by courtesy of *Illustrated London News*) 256
Plan of Governor's House, Tobolsk (by courtesy of
George Gibbes) 257
Jonas Lied 257
Vassily Yakovlev 257
Kaiser Wilhelm with Tsar Nicholas (by courtesy of
Radio Times Hulton Picture Library) 288
Nicholas and Alexandra with the Grand Duke of Hesse 288
Telegram from Crown Princess of Sweden on survival of
the tsar's family (from the Broadlands Archives) 289
Count Alvensleben (by courtesy of Alvensleben family) 289
Prince Max of Baden 289
Lenin *following page* 336
Yakov Sverdlov 336
Karl Radek (by courtesy of Radio Times Hulton Picture
Library) 336
Major Homer Slaughter (by courtesy of the Slaughter
family) 336
Poul Ree (by courtesy of the Ree family) 336
Carl Ackerman (by permission of Associated Press) 336
The tsarina and her four daughters 336
The town of Perm *facing page* 337
Telegram requesting services of "Comrade Kostina" (by
courtesy of V. Alexandrov) 337
General Rudolf Gaida 337

DRAWINGS, MAPS AND PLANS

Position of Romanovs in "murder room"   74
Inscription on wall   76
Ekaterinburg and alleged route to Four Brothers   143
The Yakovlev Mission   265
Germany and the Romanovs   283
Perm   328
Alleged movement of Romanov family from July 1918   346

The authors acknowledge the help of George Gibbes in providing some of the photographs of the imperial family. Many photographs connected with the investigation are taken from the Slowo Verlag (Berlin) edition of Sokolov's *Ubiistvo tsarskoi sem'i* (1925). A large number of other photographs are prints from the collection of Ian Lilburn, in London.

ACKNOWLEDGEMENTS

For their guidance, and for reading the manuscript, our thanks to the late Sir John Wheeler-Bennett, former historical adviser to the Foreign Office and the Royal Archives, and Michael Glenny, Research Fellow at the Centre for Soviet and European Studies, Southern Illinois University at Carbondale.

Over four years, three people provided a unique fund of knowledge, unlimited access to rare research material, and guided us out of many blind alleys: Ian Lilburn, FSA (Scot.), research historian and the only observer to attend every session of the "Anastasia" appeal process; John O'Conor, lawyer, translator, and author of *The Sokolov Investigation* and an unpublished study of German Foreign Ministry papers connected with the Romanov case; and Clare Selerie, our researcher and translator of the hundreds of original Russian documents located and studied.

The following relatives of the Romanov family kindly gave us interviews or corresponded: HRH the Duchess of Brunswick, HH Prince Frederick of Saxe Altenburg, Lord Mountbatten of Burma, HH Princess Nikita of Russia, Prince Alexander Nikitich Romanov, HRH Prince Sigismund of Prussia, HM King Simeon of Bulgaria, HIH Grand Duke Vladimir of Russia, heir assumptive to the imperial throne, and HIM the Empress Zita of Austria.

We owe a special debt of gratitude to the BBC, which in 1971 allowed unprecedented time for research on the television programme *File on the Tsar*, and started us on the investigation. The corporation was generous in giving extended leave during the writing of this book, and we are grateful to John Tisdall, assistant head of television current affairs department, for his patience and for listening.

A host of professional journalists, academic bodies and friends have made the book possible. We thank them here, and apologize to any we have left out.

IN BRITAIN: Dr Tony Batchelor of Camborne School of Mining; John Bescoby-Chambers; Sheridan Besford; Broadlands Archives, where Lord Mountbatten gave us access to his family papers; Cambridge University Library; the late Professor Francis Camps, Home Office pathologist; Brian Clifford, BBC, photographic consultant; Richard Deacon, author on the world's secret services, and former foreign manager of the *Sunday Times*; Stephanie Dee; the British Foreign Office, and its historical adviser, Rohan Butler; David Green, photographic work; Lord Hardinge of Penshurst and his mother Lady Hardinge; Ralph Hewins, Scandinavian affairs specialist who led us to the Lied diary; Angela Holdsworth, researcher on the TV programme *File on the Tsar*; David Hunn of the *Observer*; Jan Kavan; Lady Violet Kirkpatrick; Dr Faina Kononenko; Captain Michael Laing; Judy Lowe, for her Danish translation work; Richard Luckett, of St Catherine's College, Cambridge; Marvin Lyons; the family of William Peer Groves; Sir Thomas Preston; Sir Francis Pridham; the Public Record Office, and especially Albert Harrington. Transcripts of Crown Copyright Records in the PRO appear by permission of Controller, HM Stationery Office; Linley Rowan, who drew the maps; the royal archivist, Robert Mackworth-Young; RAF Museum; Royal Geographical Society; Sir Anthony Royle, MP, former Undersecretary of State for Foreign Affairs; Professor Keith Simpson, Home Office pathologist; Anthony Smith, former editor of *24 Hours*, now at St Antony's College, Oxford; Jeremy Thorpe, MP, former leader of the Liberal Party; *The Times* archivist, Gordon Phillips; and Robert Webster, gemmologist. IN CANADA: William Rodney, professor of history, Royal Roads Military College, Victoria, BC; Peter Worthington, *Toronto Sun*. IN COSTA RICA: Jean-Pierre Bilodeau. IN DENMARK: Baron Paul Meyendorff; Ole Meyer; Prince Daniel Myschetzky. IN FRANCE: Dominique Auclères of *Le Figaro*; Mme Tatiana Botkin; the family of Joseph Lasies; William Stoneman, former correspondent of *Chicago Daily News* in Moscow. IN GERMANY: Moritz Furtmayr, police identification expert; Dr Erich Hüttenhain, authority on Russian codes; Frau Robert von Lerche. IN GREECE: Alan Trist. IN JAPAN: Robert Kearsley and Sachiko Kawana of BBC Tokyo. IN MALTA: the late Captain Robert Ingham; J. G. Vassallo. IN UNITED STATES OF AMERICA: Douglas Ackerman; Congressman John Ashbrooke; Clare Boothe Luce; Dr Wernher von Braun; Library of Congress; Sally Davis; Paul Dean of the *Arizona Republic*; Flora B. Frisch, daughter of Colonel Joe Boyle; Gretchen Haskin; Hoover Institution on War, Revolution and Peace, Stanford University, with special thanks to Ron Bulatoff; Houghton Library, Harvard University; Bayard L. Kilgour; Stephen Kosack of American Federation of Government Employees; Princess Marina Kropotkin; National Archives, with special thanks to Milton Gustafson, chief of Diplomat Branch, and Tim Nenninger of Old Military Branch; Prince Serge Obolensky; David Osterlund, who researched the "Chivers" papers in depth; William Philipps, House of Representatives Foreign Operations, Government Information Committee; Dr Edward Rich, of West Point; Mary Rose, who did research for us over four years; Jane Rosemond; Professor John E. Slaughter; David Sloan, teaching fellow in Slavic Studies at Harvard University, who helped disentangle the Sokolov dossier; Gregory Tschebotarioff; Professor Richard Ullman, of Princeton University; we had help from various US government agencies, including the Historical Office of the State Department and retired officials of the Department, R. F. Kelly and Loy Henderson; Department of Defense consultant historian, Professor Rudolf Winnacker, and archivist Charles McDonald; Eugene Rosenfeld, press attaché in London, was consistently helpful; we are grateful to officials at the CIA and the National Security Council, who prefer to remain anonymous.

All italics in the book are the authors'. Transliteration of Russian names and words is according to the system detailed on page 121 of Hart's *Rules for Compositors and Readers* (OUP), except where names are already so familiar that strictly academic rendering would make them look outlandish.

PREFACE

In July 1918 the entire imperial family of Russia—Tsar Nicholas II, his wife Alexandra, and their five children—disappeared while in Communist hands, and were never seen again. Officially, they were shot and bayoneted to death in the house at Ekaterinburg where they had been held prisoner by the Bolsheviks. But in the fifty-eight years since then, mystery and contradiction have grown around the case, blurring the truth, creating legends, compounding the confusion. The more serious devotees of Romanov mystery have spent years studying the woman, still alive today, who claims to be Anastasia, youngest daughter of the tsar, and sole survivor of her family's murder. Others have fostered fantastic tales about the "escape" of the whole family. Even so, the story of massacre in the cellar was generally accepted, and with good reason—none of the Romanovs had ever been reliably reported alive after the date of their disappearance. Today, as for earlier generations, the end of the Romanovs stands as a symbol of bloody revolution, and perhaps the most outrageous act of regicide in history.

But more than any other assassination of our time, from Sarajevo to Dallas, the Romanov case bore the mark of mystery from the very start. White Russian investigators, arriving within days of the family's disappearance and with a year to work at the scene of the crime, found not a single body, and no more damning evidence than a few bullet-holes and bloodstains, and some charred imperial clothing and jewellery. The detectives produced only one eye-witness who, allegedly, claimed he had seen the imperial corpses. When we started work on the case for a BBC documentary in 1971, we tried to tackle it with modern investigative techniques, treading though we were the borderline between dusty history and live journalism. Forensic scientists analysed the known material, cipher experts rechecked coded messages, and hand-writing specialists from Scotland Yard pondered over crucial signatures. Very slowly significant pieces of old evidence, submitted to a harsher analysis, began to show their flaws. The only recognizable remains ever found, those of a pet dog belonging to the imperial family, now appeared to have been planted. A crucial telegram had all the telltale signs of forgery. Yet though the case for the massacre was seriously challenged, our discoveries brought us no nearer to establishing the real fate of the Romanovs.

Backed by the resources of the BBC, we were able to travel worldwide, tracking down the handful of people still alive who might yet be able to explain the growing number of discrepancies. We searched also for the paper witnesses, the letters and reports, the testimony and memoranda, written half a century ago by kings and revolutionaries, prime ministers and peasants Over three years the dossier grew—a secret agent's despatch in Paris led to a Foreign Ministry file in Tokyo, a lead in Denmark dovetailed with an intelligence report in Washington. A private telegram from King George V in London to the tsarina's sister had to be weighed against a sudden flurry in British intelligence circles at the same date. A scrap of information about Lenin's mood on a certain day was measured against a report of what the German Kaiser said over breakfast. Supported by advice from specialist historians, the information confirmed our instinct that there really was a mystery to solve. But still we lacked a solution.

It was only late in the day that we located evidence we had sought from the start, but had despaired of ever finding. This was the original dossier of the White Russian investigators whose conclusions, published in the twenties, had given history its massacre. It was as though some future researcher into the killing of President Kennedy were suddenly to discover the full records of the Warren Commission, from which its official report had beeen compiled. What we found in the Romanov case were the seven volumes of original testimony, police reports and affidavits, all in Russian, which had been lost to scholars for decades. It was at once clear that whole areas of vital evidence had been deliberately suppressed. Inside the dossier was detailed evidence, as compelling as any that exists for the massacre version, which shows that most of the Romanov family were alive for many months *after* their historical "deaths".

The File on the Tsar offers a detailed unravelling of a unique mystery, and a glimpse of what may really have happened to Nicholas, Alexandra and their children in the momentous high summer of 1918.

A. S.
T. M.

CAST OF MAIN CHARACTERS

Romanov Family, the ruling house of Russia

Nicholas II, Emperor of Russia, 1894–1917.

Alexandra Feodorovna, the tsarina; born Princess Alix of Hesse.

Alexei, the tsarevich.

Olga
Tatiana } Daughters of Nicholas and Alexandra. All grand
Maria   duchesses.
Anastasia

Marie Feodorovna, Dowager Empress; Danish-born mother of
    Nicholas.

Xenia, Grand Duchess } sisters of Nicholas.
Olga, Grand Duchess

Andrei, Grand Duke; first cousin of Nicholas, who investigated
    the "Anastasia" case.

Nikolai Nikolayevich, Grand Duke; commander-in-chief
    Russian Armies in World War I.

Xenia Georgievna, Princess of Russia; second cousin to
    Anastasia.

Ackerman, Carl; *New York Times* foreign correspondent.

Alexeyev, S.; White official said to have arrested several key
    witnesses.

Alvensleben, Count Hans Bodo; senior German diplomat at
    Kiev, German-occupied Ukraine.

Anderson, Anna (also formerly known as Tschaikowsky,
    now Mrs Manahan); claims to be Grand Duchess
    Anastasia.

Avdeyev, Alexander; first commandant of Ipatiev House.

Balfour, Arthur; British foreign secretary.

Barbara, Duchess Christian Ludwig of Mecklenburg, Princess
    of Hesse and by Rhine, Princess of Prussia; defendant in
    suit to establish identity of Anastasia claimant.

Beloborodov, Alexander; chairman of Ural Regional Soviet.

Bessedovsky, Grigory; former Soviet diplomat; writer of fake memoirs.

Botkin, Dr Yevgeny; physician to imperial family.

Botkin, Gleb; son of Dr Botkin.

Botkin, Tatiana (married name Melnik), daughter of Dr Botkin.

Buchanan, Sir George; British ambassador in St Petersburg.

Bulygin, Captain Pavel; assistant to Sokolov, originally sent to investigate by tsar's mother.

Buxhoeveden, Baroness Sophie; lady-in-waiting to tsarina.

Bykov, Pavel; author of Soviet account of Ekaterinburg massacre.

Cecile, German Crown Princess; Kaiser's daughter-in-law, second cousin to Nicholas.

Chemodurov, Terenty; tsar's valet.

Chicherin, Georgy; People's Commissar for Foreign Affairs.

Christian X, King of Denmark; first cousin to tsar.

Demidova, Anna; tsarina's maid.

Derevenko, Dr Vladimir; physician assigned to the tsarevich.

Diterikhs, General Mikhail; staff officer in White Russian regime who directed Romanov enquiry from January 1919.

Dolgorukov, Prince Alexander; White Russian general in the Ukraine during the civil war.

Dolgorukov, Prince Vassily; aide-de-camp to tsar.

Eliot, Sir Charles; British high commissioner and consul-general for Siberia.

Ernst Ludwig, Grand Duke of Hesse; tsarina's brother.

Frederick, Prince of Saxe Altenburg: related to Romanovs, supporter of Anna Anderson.

Gaida, General Rudolf; Czech commander-in-chief of White army in Urals, instigated enquiry into presence of imperial survivors at Perm.

George V, King of Great Britain; first cousin to both Nicholas and Alexandra.

Gibbes, Sydney; English tutor to Alexei.

Goloshchokin, Chaya; member of the Ural Soviet and regional commissar for war.

Gorshkov, Fyodor; first witness to speak of Ipatiev House massacre.

Hardinge of Penshurst; Charles, 1st baron; permanent undersecretary at British Foreign Office.

Hoffmann, General Max; German Chief of Staff Eastern Front and negotiator at Brest-Litovsk peace talks.

Irene, Princess Heinrich of Prussia; tsarina's sister.

Janin, General Maurice; head of French military mission in Siberia.

Jemmy, Grand Duchess Tatiana's dog, allegedly found dead in mineshaft.

Jordansky, Valery; prosecutor who kept watching brief on enquiry for White civilian judiciary.

Karakhan, Lev; Bolshevik deputy foreign commissar.

Kerensky, Alexander; minister of justice, then prime minister, in 1917 Provisional Government.

Kharitonov, Ivan; tsar's cook.

Kirsta, Alexander; assistant head of White Military Control at Perm, made major discoveries in connection with presence of Romanov survivors in that town.

Kobylinsky, Colonel Yevgeny; in charge of Romanov garrison at Tobolsk.

Kolchak, Admiral Alexander; supreme ruler of White government at Omsk.

Kschessinska, Mathilde; ballerina, mistress of tsar before his marriage, later wife of Grand Duke Andrei.

Kutuzov, Alexander; public prosecutor at Ekaterinburg.

Lampson, Miles (later Lord Killearn); British chargé d'affaires at Peking.

Lasies, Commandant Joseph; French parliamentary deputy and special correspondent of *Le Matin*.

Lenin (Vladimir Ulyanov); first leader of Communist Russia.

Letemin, Mikhail; former Ipatiev House guard, later a Sokolov witness.

Leuchtenberg, Duke George of; cousin to tsar, later host to Anna Anderson.

Leuchtenberg, Duke Nicholas of; cousin to tsar, and former aide-de-camp.

Lied, Jonas; Norwegian summoned to London to advise on Romanov rescue.

Lloyd George, David; British prime minister.

Lvov, Prince Georgy; prime minister in Provincial Government 1917, imprisoned at Ekaterinburg 1918.

Magnitsky, N. N.; assistant prosecutor in charge of early searches at mineshafts.

Malinovsky, Captain; member of Officers' Investigating Commission.

Markov, Lieutenant Sergei; officer who contacted Romanovs at Tobolsk probably acting as courier for Grand Duke of Hesse.

Max, Prince of Baden; German general, later chancellor.

Medvedev, Pavel; former sergeant of Ipatiev House guard, key Sokolov witness.

Milyukov, Pavel; foreign minister in Provincial Government 1917.

Mirbach, Count Wilhelm; German ambassador in Moscow, assassinated 6 July 1918.

Mirolyubov, Professor Nikander; public prosecutor of Kazan Assize Court, ordered observation of Sokolov on behalf of civilian judiciary.

Mountbatten, Earl; tsar's nephew and now nearest surviving British relative.

Mutnykh, Natalya; nurse, key witness to presence of Romanov survivors at Perm.

Nametkin, Alexander; Examining Magistrate for Important Cases at Ekaterinburg, in charge of first civilian enquiry.

Nikiforov, Colonel; head of White Military Control at Perm.

Preston, Thomas (later Sir); British consul at Ekaterinburg.

Proskuryakov, Philip; Ipatiev House guard, later a Sokolov witness.

Radek, Karl; head of European Department of Bolshevik Foreign Commissariat, (German specialist).

Rasputin, Grigory; lay preacher and peasant, gained tsarina's confidence through apparent ability to heal the tsarevich.

Ree, Poul; Danish vice-consul at Perm.

Riezler, Dr Kurt; senior counsellor at German embassy, Moscow.

Sednev, Leonid; kitchen-boy with Romanovs at Ekaterinburg.

Sergeyev, Judge Ivan; in charge of second civilian enquiry at Ekaterinburg, fired by General Diterikhs.

Sheremetevsky, Lieutenant Alexander; pumped out mines in early searches.

Sigismund, Prince of Prussia; tsarina's nephew.

Slaughter, Major Homer; military intelligence officer with US forces in Siberia.

Sokolov, Nikolai; Court Investigator for Specially Important Cases, took over Romanov enquiry, and produced accepted version of massacre.

Storozhev, Father; priest who visited Romanovs at Ipatiev House.

Sverdlov, Yakov; chairman of Soviet Central Executive Committee, and first Communist head of state.

Thomas, Arthur; assistant to British consul, Ekaterinburg.

Trupp, Alexei; footman to imperial family.

Trotsky, Lev; People's Commissar for war.

Utkin, Dr Pavel; testified that he treated Anastasia in autumn 1918 at Perm.

Valdemar, Prince of Denmark; tsar's uncle.

Varakushev, Alexander; former Ipatiev guard, statement suppressed by Sokolov.

Victoria, Marchioness of Milford Haven; tsarina's sister.

Voikov, Pyotr; commissar for supply at Ekaterinburg.

Wilhelm II; German Emperor.

Yakimov, Anatoly; former Ipatiev House guard, later Sokolov witness.

Yakovlev, Vassily; "special commissar", removed Romanovs from Tobolsk.

Yermakov, Pyotr; military commissar for Verkh-Isetsk (Ekaterinburg suburb).

Yurovsky, Yakov; last commandant of Ipatiev House.

Zahle, Herluf; Danish minister in Berlin charged by Danish royal family with enquiry into Anastasia case.

Zinoviev, Grigory; member Politburo of Russian Communist Party, and of Central Executive Committee.

"Truth: An ingenious compound of
desirability of appearance."
—Ambrose Bierce: *The Devil's Dictionary*

PART ONE

Disappearance

I

THE EMPIRE COLLAPSES

". . . . nobody in your family will remain alive for more than two years. They will be killed by the Russian people."

(Rasputin: Warning to the tsar, December 1916)

EARLY EVENING ON 16 July 1918, in the mining town of Ekaterinburg, Russia. At the end of a hot, cloudless day Arthur Thomas, an assistant to the British consul, was strolling home. While he walked he could hear the boom of artillery, as anti-Communist troops continued their advance on the town. Just before he reached the consulate Thomas had to pass a large mansion called the Ipatiev House. Inside it was the Russian imperial family, the former tsar, Nicholas, the tsarina, and their five children. They were prisoners, guarded by a detachment of Red Guards. Tonight something out of the ordinary seemed to be going on; the sentries ordered Thomas to walk on the other side of the street. Later, as night came, his colleague, Thomas Preston, the British consul, sat at his window observing the Ipatiev House. He saw passers-by being diverted, and new machine-gun posts being erected near the prison of the imperial family. Ekaterinburg was under curfew and the streets were soon deserted.

Around midnight Viktor Buivid, a peasant living in the building immediately opposite the Ipatiev House, woke up feeling sick. He went into the courtyard to vomit. Suddenly he heard muffled volleys, followed by individual shots, coming from somewhere inside the Ipatiev House. Frightened, he hurried back to bed, and his room-mate asked him:

"Did you hear?"

He answered: "I heard shots."

"Did you understand?"

"I understood," said Buivid—and the two men fell silent.

Both of them believed the shots to have been the final epilogue to 304 years of Romanov rule in Russia. Their few, frightened words are the first recorded reaction of the outside world to the most notorious act of regicide in contemporary history: the murder by shooting of Tsar Nicholas II, his wife Alexandra, his little son Tsarevich Alexei, and his four daughters, the Grand Duchesses Olga, Tatiana, Maria and Anastasia. That instant assumption by two Russian peasants has been endorsed by the historians of half a century. It is how the world now accepts the time, place and manner of the end of the Romanovs.

Thirty-seven years earlier, Nicholas had watched another tsar die. As a little boy in a sailor suit, he stood at the foot of the imperial bed as his grandfather, Emperor Alexander II, lay bleeding to death. That tsar had been the victim of a terrorist bomb thrown in a St Petersburg street. With both legs ripped off, his lower stomach torn open, and his face terribly mutilated, the fifteenth Romanov tsar had been carried into the Winter Palace to die, dripping gobbets of blood on the marble stairs and corridors.

For Nicholas, then aged thirteen, that day in 1881 was a glimpse of a savage birthright; more than anyone could know, it signposted the road to his personal tragedy, and the mightiest political earthquake the world has known. The reign of his grandfather had seen the birth of an unstoppable historical force, changes that made a nonsense of the ancient definition of the tsar, "by nature like any other man, but in power and office like the highest God". Ironically, Alexander II had seen the writing on the wall; he had become the "Tsar Liberator" freeing the serfs, reforming the judiciary, and making education available for all. But reform is not revolution, and it swiftly boomeranged on Tsar Alexander. Before his reign was out, leading revolutionaries were preaching the total destruction of the Romanov dynasty.

From now on, removal of the autocracy was a keystone of revolutionary policy. The young men Alexander II had educated worked tirelessly to kill him, and eventually succeeded with the grenade in St Petersburg. Nicholas's father now became Tsar Alexander III, and began as he was to continue, unleashing a wave of repression to crush all political opposition. A month after the assassination, five young terrorists who had committed it were publicly hanged in front of a huge crowd, massed troops, churchmen and foreign diplomats. Hundreds of political activists were sent to exile in Siberia, press censorship was imposed, and many of Alexander's reforms were rescinded.

Meanwhile the nobility was strengthened, with new laws to ensure that their vast estates remained intact, and that the aristocracy had a clear supremacy in regional government. In St. Petersburg, high society was allowed to indulge in luxury and extravagance on a scale unparalleled since Versailles. The tsar ruled as he had declared he would, with "faith in the power and right of the autocracy".

Nicholas, now heir to the throne, was taught by his tutor that "among the falsest of political principles is the principle of the sovereignty of the people . . . which has unhappily infatuated certain Russians". Some of those infatuated Russians soon tried to kill Alexander III as his father had been killed. When some young university students were caught with a makeshift bomb hidden inside a medical textbook, all five were summarily executed. It was an unimportant, abortive effort, but it was made significant by the identity of one of the plotters. He was Alexander Ulyanov, the elder brother of a man the world was later to know as Lenin. Although few thought so, as the nobility danced their way through the gala seasons of St Petersburg, the Romanovs were now firmly set on a collision course with history.

In 1894, kidney disease did for Alexander III what assassins had failed to do. He died very suddenly, aged only 49, when everyone expected him to rule for another twenty years. And so a retiring young man of 26 became Tsar Nicholas II. He was armed only with a knowledge of languages, a love of military ceremonial, and the reactionary creed dinned into him by his political tutor. His father had neglected to teach him anything at all about affairs of state. Yet now he abruptly became Emperor and Autocrat of all the Russias, ruler of 130 million subjects, and a territory which covered one-sixth of the earth's surface. Nicholas was aghast, exclaiming within hours of his father's death: "I am not prepared to be a tsar. I never wanted to be one. I know nothing of the business of ruling. What is going to happen to me—to all of Russia?"

What did happen all the world now knows. Slowly but inexorably over a reign of 23 years, Nicholas, and Russia with him, stumbled towards calamity and chaos. It was a time heavy with symbolism from the start. During the coronation ceremony in 1896 the heavy chain of office slipped from the young tsar's shoulders and thudded noisily to the floor. The few who had seen the incident were sworn to secrecy so that the public would not take it as a bad omen. There was no hiding the disaster of the next day, when hundreds of people were killed and thousands injured as a crowd stampeded on the way to a traditional open-air feast. Nicholas's first reaction was to call off further festivities in sympathy with the victims, but for the first of many times he listened to bad advice. That evening he and his young bride danced as planned at a reception in the tsar's honour. It was the first propaganda gift to Nicholas's political enemies. The bride was Alexandra of Hesse, the German princess whom Nicholas had insisted on marrying against his parents' wishes. Their wedding occurred within a month of his father's funeral, and even then there were murmurs of resentment against "the German woman" who "has come to us behind a coffin". Yet Alexandra, and the five children she bore, were the one constant source of happiness to Tsar Nicholas. At first the tsarina restricted herself to the role of wife and mother, and the couple were devoted to each other. Nicholas was in theory the richest man in the world with eight magnificent palaces, a staff of 15,000 and crown property estimated at between eight and ten billion pounds. But in spite of their opulent surroundings, and in spite of the decadence of the aristocracy, Nicholas and his family lived a life of ordered simplicity.

As tsar, Nicholas genuinely tried to rule well, and was prepared to work hard for what he saw as the good of the people. But he was a solitary figure, cut off from his people and hopelessly blinkered by the precept that autocracy was, and would remain, the only workable system of government for Russia. Within a year of coming to the throne he gave this answer to one mild appeal for democratic change: "Certain people . . . have permitted themselves to be carried away by the senseless dream of participation by elected regional representatives in internal government. Let all know that, in devoting all my strength on behalf of the welfare of my people, I shall defend the principles of autocracy as unswervingly as my deceased father."

With hindsight, what followed was utterly predictable. Demonstrations against Nicholas and his government became frequent and widespread. The regime answered with increased police severity, which alienated moderate liberals along with the extremists. Terrorism increased and neither Nicholas nor his ministers were ever safe from assassins. When the Romanov family travelled, two identical imperial trains were made up for each trip, travelling the same route but a few miles apart —all to confuse potential bombers.

In January 1905, thousands of ordinary citizens made a massive but peaceful march to present a petition to the tsar for full civil and political freedom, and a constituent assembly. As they approached the Winter Palace police and troops fired into the crowd in cold blood, killing and wounding hundreds. This was St Petersburg's "Bloody Sunday", and although Nicholas had not been in the city at the time, it was he who was blamed. From now on, the tsar was not the "Little Father" to whom the people could turn in distress. He was "Nicholas the Bloody", "soul-murderer of the Russian empire". Soon, as unrest spread across the nation, the bewildered Nicholas was at last persuaded to give Russia a form of constitution, which provided for an assembly *(Duma)* and a cabinet system. This did lay the foundations of parliamentary democracy in Russia, but the tsar still had sweeping powers to suspend the constitution at will.

But even as Nicholas took the first faltering steps towards a more progressive form of government, the seeds of ultimate disaster were taking root in what he held most dear, his own family. After four daughters, the empress had at last given him a son, Alexei. But the heir was cursed with "the royal disease" —haemophilia—which Alexandra had inherited through her grandmother, Queen Victoria. Haemophilia prevents the blood clotting, and means that the slightest bump or bruise can cause unstoppable bleeding and intense pain. Throughout his childhood, Alexei was to lurch from crisis to crisis, with the imperial doctors fluttering around powerless to help. In the midst of her despair, Alexandra found Rasputin, a mystic from Siberia reputed to have miraculous powers of healing and prophecy. Time after time, even when the doctors had given up all hope of recovery, Rasputin would pray and little Alexei would rally. The empress, always intensely religious and superstitious, believed that he had been sent by God to save her son.

Nicholas too accepted Rasputin as a holy man and felt that through him he was in touch with the peasant millions of Russia. But outside the palace, Rasputin drank and whored his way through the high society of St Petersburg. Quickly rumours spread that the empress and her daughters were among his mistresses. It was nonsense, but the story spread across Russia, embroidered and exaggerated out of all proportion. Worst of all, Alexandra came to rely on Rasputin's advice in matters other than the health of her son. If he told her that a certain minister or general was pursuing policies contrary to the will of God, Alexandra faithfully passed on the advice to her husband. Incredibly, in the face of dozens of warnings, Nicholas listened, and often acted accordingly. Rasputin's pernicious influence over Alexandra was to last until the end of Nicholas's reign.

Nevertheless, the Romanovs rode out the first decade of the twentieth century, and imperial life continued as though there were no threat, no danger of imminent change. Regularly each spring the imperial household migrated south to a palace in the Crimea, in high summer they moved up to their villa on the Baltic, then on to a hunting lodge in Poland and back to St Petersburg for the winter.

In 1909 the tsar travelled to England, and saw his cousin and friend, the Prince of Wales, the future King George V. The Romanovs arrived in style aboard the imperial yacht, to attend Regatta Week at Cowes in the Isle of Wight. Nicholas was welcomed with a salute from the Royal Navy, the crash of cannon, and bands playing both "God Save the Tsar" and "God Save the King". In 1912 another relative, the head of the Hohenzollern dynasty, visited Russia to see the Romanovs. Kaiser Wilhelm II, a passionate believer in absolute monarchy, had for years behaved paternally towards his Russian cousin, deluging him with compliments and political advice. The yachts of the two emperors were moored side by side for three days, while the bands played, the champagne flowed and the families exchanged priceless presents.

In 1913, as if all were well and would remain so indefinitely, Russia celebrated the tercentenary of Romanov rule in a spectacular display of pageantry. Vast crowds cheered Nicholas and Alexandra as they rode in state through the streets of their capital. For Alexandra, it proved that her husband's ministers were foolish to worry about social upheaval. "They are constantly worrying the emperor with threats of revolution," she said, "and here we need merely to show ourselves and at once their hearts are ours."

A year later, when the first world war broke out, it seemed initially to prove Alexandra right. A huge multitude listened with approval before the Winter Palace as the tsar, simply dressed in infantry uniform, swore he would never make peace while the enemy remained on Russian soil. Not for 100 years had there been a cause to unite the Russian people so suddenly and spontaneously under the emperor. Nobody, least of all Nicholas, remotely imagined the cataclysm that was to follow. 1915 was a year of defeats which ended with four million Russian soldiers dead on the battlefield. As a mood of despair spread across the land, Nicholas made a fatal mistake. He decided the tsar should be seen to be at the head of his troops, dismissed an excellent commander-in-chief, and departed for field headquarters. Recently, Alexandra had advised him: "Be more autocratic, my very own sweetheart . . . be the master and lord, you are the autocrat." But now, with the tsar far away from the capital, the real power passed more and more into the hands of the empress and Rasputin. A mediocre, unknown conservative, of German origin, Boris Stürmer, was appointed prime minister at Rasputin's recommendation. Ministers who offended Rasputin, or questioned imperial policy, were forced out of office. Thus, at a crucial time, the best men in Nicholas's government were discarded, ignored or insulted. The tsar, of course, had to rubber-stamp these changes, but he was impossibly remote and allowed himself to be guided by an endless stream of letters and telegrams from his wife.

Just before Christmas 1916 Rasputin was killed by a group of right-wing assassins, but it was too late to stem the onrush of events. Conditions in the country had reached breaking point. The cost of living had risen 300 per cent. Hundreds of thousands of workers were idle. In the cities, food was in desperately short supply. Every morning, long queues of hungry, poor people formed outside the bakeries. Russia was ripe for revolution, and everyone seemed aware of it—except Tsar Nicholas. By mid-January 1917, he was being warned by senior members of his own family, by foreign diplomats, and by loyal members of the Duma, that his overthrow was imminent. But Nicholas seemed to be sleepwalking towards disaster. He rejected all approaches, and the Romanov family withdrew into a closed world of their own.

In early March, Nicholas left the capital and returned to army headquarters. Behind him the administration swiftly disintegrated, and St Petersburg erupted first into riots and then army mutinies. Nicholas was informed, but seemed to have no idea how serious things were. When at last he tried to return to the capital, the way was blocked by dissident troops. The imperial train diverted to Pskov, headquarters of the northern front, and there, on the deserted station, the tsar bowed to the unanimous advice of his generals. On the evening of 15 March 1917, seated alone in his private railway compartment, Nicholas abdicated.

He signed away the throne in favour of his brother, Grand Duke Mikhail, who himself renounced it a day later. A Provisional Government was formed, the result of a shaky compromise between the rump of the old Duma and the new revolutionary leaders of the Left. It was the formal end of the Romanov dynasty, and the beginning of a long trauma for the imperial family.

The tsar came home to find he was to be a prisoner in one of his own palaces. With Alexandra and the children, and a tiny remnant of his retinue, Nicholas was confined in the fairytale palace at Tsarskoe Selo, a few miles south of St Petersburg. The Romanovs were told it was for their own safety, and it was a genuine explanation. The press, now freed from censorship, was whipping up public hatred of the tsar and tsarina, who were both now accused of plotting to regain the throne by betraying Russia to the Germans. The allegations were completely false, for Nicholas was fiercely patriotic, and after his abdication hoped fervently that under new leadership the army would be able to defeat Germany. But the danger to the family was real. In the St Petersburg Soviet, the council of revolutionary workers and soldiers—soon to give its name to a whole new system of national government—there was talk of vengeance for generations of oppression. The extremists were calling for Romanov blood, and the Soviet demanded that the tsar and his wife be shut up in a common prison. But the new minister of justice, Alexander Kerensky, rejected such talk, exclaiming: "I will not be the Marat of the Russian Revolution. The Russian Revolution does not take vengeance." While Kerensky lasted, the Romanovs were safe. Through the spring and summer of 1917, the family adjusted to captivity remarkably well. In the part of the great park they were allowed to use, they dug up the lawn and planted a vegetable garden (*see plate* 7). The tsar, who had always been keen on physical exercise, worked hard sawing and stacking firewood. For Nicholas in particular, this was, however ironically, the moment he had yearned for all his life. He had never wanted to be tsar in the first place, and now that nightmare was over. He had always envied the quiet industrious life of an English country squire, had longed for time to be with his children, and captivity seemed to offer both. The future was to provide no such solace.

While the Romanovs were digging their garden, two political exiles had been making the long-awaited journey home. Lenin and Trotsky were back in St Petersburg. It was fourteen years since the key section of the Russian revolutionary movement had split into two—the Bolsheviks, or Majority, led by Lenin, and the Mensheviks, the Minority, usually supported by Trotsky. That decision had been made by a ragtag group of exiles meeting in 1903 at a rundown church in London; now, in St Petersburg, Lenin was working feverishly from Bolshevik headquarters set up in a mansion seized from the tsar's first love, a prima ballerina. Trotsky had joined with him in the common cause, the entire overthrow of the old system. They preached that the real revolution was yet to come, and demanded the overthrow of the Provisional Government.

Kerensky, now prime minister, warned Nicholas, "The Bolsheviks are after me and then they will be after you." In

August 1917 the government arranged to move the imperial family to the relative safety of Tobolsk, in far-off Siberia. And so the Romanovs made the journey on which they had sent so many thousands of their own political enemies in the past. At Tobolsk they were installed in the Governor's House, where at first life continued to be tolerable. Then the "October Revolution" brought the Bolskeviks—and Lenin—to power, marking the end for ever of all the tsar stood for. Gradually the royal confinement began to take on the grimmer realities of prison life (*see plate 8*). A high stockade was built round the entrance of the house, and in the bitter cold of the Siberian winter food ran short; the imperial family were issued ration cards and placed on soldiers' rations.

Eight uncomfortable months later, after increasing pressure from left-wing extremists in the prison guard, and much talk about escape plots, the family was suddenly transferred again —this time to Ekaterinburg in the Ural mountains. On 30 April 1918, as the closely guarded train pulled into the station, the emperor murmured: "I would have gone anywhere but to the Urals. Judging from the local papers the workers there are bitterly hostile to me."

It was at Ekaterinburg that the Romanov family disappeared. It is there that our investigation begins.

2

THE ROMANOVS DISAPPEAR

"No cause for apprehension . . ."
(Ekaterinburg cable to Bolshevik head of state, 4 July 1918)

IN EKATERINBURG THE tsar and his entourage were handed over to the chairman of the Executive Committee of the Workers' and Peasants' Soviet of the Ural Region, and a bizarre official receipt was issued, itemizing acceptance of:

1. The ex-Tsar Nicholas Romanov
2. The ex-Tsarina Alexandra Feodorovna Romanova
3. The ex-Grand Duchess Maria Nikolayevna Romanova.
For detention under surveillance in the town of Ekaterinburg.

Signed for like a load of groceries the former emperor of all the Russias was hustled with his wife and daughter into the Ipatiev House (*see plate 9*). A senior member of the Ural Soviet, Chaya Goloshchokin, ushered him in with the ironic greeting: "Citizen Romanov, you may enter". The tsarina marked the date of arrival on the wall by the window of her new room; above the date she pencilled a swastika, which in 1918 was still a symbol of good luck. But the crooked cross brought little fortune to the Romanovs.

An aide-de-camp, Prince Vassily Dolgorukov, who arrived with the emperor, was at once packed off to the common jail. The other three Romanov daughters, Olga, Tatiana, and Anastasia, did not arrive till three weeks later, bringing with them their brother Alexei, whose latest haemophiliac crisis had delayed the rest of the imperial retinue. When they reached Ekaterinburg, more staff were dispatched to prison: another aide, General Tatishchev, two female retainers, and the empress's manservant. Another group of retainers were allowed to stay in Ekaterinburg, but not at the Ipatiev House. They included Alexei's physician Dr Derevenko, the foreign tutors

Sydney Gibbes and Pierre Gilliard, and Baroness Buxhoeveden, a lady-in-waiting. For the tsar the transition from power to prisoner was now complete. Ekaterinburg was the Romanovs' third place of confinement in a year, and May marked their fifteenth month in captivity.

Ironically it was the workers of this town who had once laboured to reproduce the tsar's image by the million. The imperial mint had been situated at Ekaterinburg, the centre of a mining area rich in gold and precious minerals. Before the revolution the mines and the fur markets had made the local merchants rich, and Ekaterinburg boasted dozens of large white mansions with grand facades and plate-glass windows. It was the poor workers from the local factories who were chosen to guard the family, and the house of one of these rich merchants was peremptorily commandeered to house them. Professor Nikolai Ipatiev was given a few hours to get out, and wisely took to his country dacha and stayed there.

Today the Ipatiev House is still there. It is a two-storey brick house, faced with white stucco, near the centre of the town (*see plate 13*). When Tsar Nicholas and his family were there it looked out on a wide boulevard, Voznesensky Avenue. The mansion was built on an incline so that the ground floor on one side of the house formed a semi-basement. In the front an imposing stone archway led into a courtyard. Behind was a terrace overlooking a scrappy garden. The Communists re-christened the house ominously, "The House of Special Purpose". Even before the tsar arrived, a wooden palisade had been constructed close against the facade (*see plate 10*); later a second fence was erected, blocking off the courtyard and the main entrance to the house.

Some 50 men did guard duty, manning sentry boxes at the main entrances, and watching the courtyard and the garden. Machine guns were mounted in the attic window and in commanding positions downstairs. Upstairs, the interior guards lounged around all day outside the Romanovs' quarters.

The tsar, his family and remaining servants were crowded into six upstairs rooms, with the four grand duchesses crammed into just one of them. The tsar and tsarina shared another room with the sick tsarevich. The windows were soon white-washed over, to prevent the prisoners looking out and the curious peering in. Despite the stifling summer heat, there were orders, at first anyway, to keep all the windows closed. There was only one entrance to the Romanovs' rooms, and outside this was another sentry and a command post for the guard commander and several comrades. "The House of Special Purpose" was now a secure armed fortress.

The tsar turned 50 during the Ekaterinburg imprisonment. It was one of the Ipatiev guards, Anatoly Yakimov, who later provided this last description:

> The tsar was no longer young, his beard was getting grey. I saw him wearing a soldier's shirt with an officer's belt buckled round his waist. The shirt was khaki, the same colour as his trousers and his old worn-out boots. His eyes were kind and he had a truly gentle expression. I got the impression that he was a kind, simple, frank and talkative person. Sometimes I felt that he was going to speak to me. He looked as if he would like to talk to us.

The tsarina, Alexandra, celebrated her 46th birthday in the Ipatiev House. Describing her, the guard Yakimov reflected the deep dislike of many Russians for the German-born tsarina:

> The tsarina was not at all like him. She was severe looking and had the appearance and ways of a haughty, grave woman. Sometimes we used to discuss them amongst ourselves, and we decided Nicholas Alexandrovich was a modest man, but that she was different and looked exactly like a tsarina. She seemed older than the tsar. Grey hair was plainly visible on her temples, and her face was not that of a young woman.

Alexandra, obsessed with her religion, and herself suffering from heart trouble, was constantly preoccupied with her son, still chronically ill.

Fourteen-year-old Alexei was now a virtual cripple. Another guard more sympathetic to the monarchy said of him: "Poor Alexei stayed in bed all day. His father helped to carry his cot from one room to another. His face was waxen and transparent and his eyes were sad like an animal pursued by wolves. Yet he smiled at me and joked when I gave him a deep bow." Almost all the grand duchesses had mid-summer birthdays. In June Maria was nineteen. She was by far the prettiest of the four girls, with thick golden hair and blue eyes. Years before she had caught the eye of her English cousin, Prince Louis of Battenberg, now Lord Mountbatten, when he had visited the imperial family at St Petersburg. He keeps a photograph of her in his bedroom to this day. Tatiana, who came of age in Ekaterinburg, was most like her mother. A thin, imperious girl, she was the natural leader of the five youngsters—although not the eldest. Olga, a year older, was a quiet girl who loved painting and playing the piano, and like her mother was extremely religious. Also in June, the youngest of the girls, Anastasia, was seventeen. A month or two earlier, in Tobolsk, she had been unflatteringly described as short and too stout—the ungraceful member of the family. By way of compensation, Anastasia also had the reputation of being the family comedian.

And in the Ipatiev House the Romanovs needed all the humour they could find. Life was very tough indeed for a family used to the very best in life. The tsar's personal valet, the elderly Chemodurov, who was in the house for part of the time, survived Ekaterinburg. He later described an average day: "In the morning, the family would drink tea together, served with black bread left over from the day before. At about two o'clock lunch was sent over from the local Soviet: thin meat broth and a roast, or more often rissoles . . . We all ate at the same table, by order of the emperor."

But slowly the numbers were diminishing. Two more servants were taken away to the local jail, leaving the Romanovs with the family doctor Yevgeny Botkin, a maid Anna Demidova, a cook Ivan Kharitonov, a servant Alexei Trupp, and a kitchen boy Leonid Sednev. The two servants taken to jail were subsequently shot—but not before they passed on the story of how life was deteriorating:

The guards started pilfering, first valuables, then the linen and shoes. The tsar couldn't put up with it, and flew into a rage. He was told roughly that he was a prisoner, and no longer the one who gave the orders. Every day things got worse. At first they were given twenty minutes to go walking, but then the time was reduced to five minutes. Physical jerks were banned. The tsarevich was ill . . . the attitude of the guards was especially shameful towards the grand duchesses. They weren't allowed to go to the lavatory without permission, or without being accompanied by a Red Guard. In the evening they were forced to play the piano.

To reach the lavatory, the Romanovs had to leave their quarters and walk across the landing. On the way they passed two sentries who would taunt the women crudely, asking them where they were going, and what for. The guards scrawled obscene doggerel on the walls of the house, and the Romanovs must have seen some of it. One specimen read:

> Our Russian Tsar called Nick
> was pulled off his throne by his prick.

Given the relative allure of the girls and the coarseness of their guards, it is not surprising to find there were unpleasant sexual undercurrents in life at the Ipatiev House. Olga and Tatiana were forced to play the piano, and the tunes requested were a little outside their drawing-room repertoire. Amongst the guards' favourite songs was one called "Let's Forget the Old Regime" and "You Fell as a Victim in the Struggle".

It was the guard commander, Alexander Avdeyev, who was largely responsible for the bad treatment initially inflicted on the Romanovs. A 35-year-old fitter, he had earlier led the workers' takeover of a munitions factory, and recruited many of the Ipatiev House guards from friends at work. He was described by one guard as "a real Bolshevik", who took delight in haranguing the comrades on how the Communists had destroyed the rich bourgeoisie, and seized power from "Nicholas the Bloody". A bully and a braggart, Avdeyev used to invite selected friends into the house to show off his imperial prisoners, and to have a drink at the command post. He also joined the family and their servants at meal times, and once, according to an outraged Chemodurov, he jabbed the tsar in the mouth with his elbow while reaching for food across the table.

Outside "The House of Special Purpose", in an atmosphere of growing tension, the two foreign tutors, the Englishman Gibbes and the Swiss Gilliard, along with the lady-in-waiting, Baroness Buxhoeveden, were trying to do something for their masters. They trooped along repeatedly to the British consulate, just along the road from the Ipatiev House, begging Thomas Preston to bring pressure to bear on the Bolshevik authorities.

Today, Preston says he did intercede with the local Communists as far as he could: "Our only hope was diplomatic pressure. I used to visit the Soviet daily . . . saying that the British government was interested in the situation of the imperial family. They always assured me they were in perfectly good health, well treated, and they were certainly in no danger."

Concern for the family's welfare was often counter-productive, because it tended to irritate the local authorities. The two tutors and the baroness were eventually ordered out of town, but the physician to the tsarevich, Dr Derevenko, remained in Ekaterinburg, and was several times allowed into the Ipatiev House to see young Alexei. As a result of these visits word was sent to the local convent of the poor diet in the Ipatiev House. From the middle of June, two nuns were allowed to make regular deliveries of fresh milk, eggs and butter, even extra meat and pastries. Also in June, a priest was admitted to say mass for the family. Father Storozhev, from the local cathedral, went to the house with a deacon, and held a simple Russian Orthodox service. The priests' visits provide rare first-hand accounts of what was happening in the house in the last crucial month, and of the behaviour of the imperial prisoners. Storozhev says he found the tsar wearing a khaki tunic and trousers, high boots and the Cross of St George; the girls had on dark skirts and white blouses and were looking cheerful. Their hair had been cut short at the back. Alexei was lying down on a camp bed. The priest was struck by the ardour with which everyone took part in the mass; the girls sang enthusiastically and the tsar chimed in too—with a deep bass. But through it all Avdeyev, the guard commander, stood in the corner watching silently. Apart from the priests and Dr Derevenko, the family were now cut off from the outside world.

During June there were press rumours that the tsar had been shot. These were denied in Moscow, and the outside world received independent confirmation that Nicholas was safe and well. A French intelligence officer got through Red lines from Ekaterinburg and reported as much to the Foreign Ministry in Paris.

But in the Ipatiev House life was becoming intolerable, as Avdeyev's loutish behaviour worsened. His drinking bouts became more frequent. Once when the chairman of the Ural Soviet called to see him, the guard commander had passed out drunk in one of the downstairs rooms. His friends covered up for him, and said he was out. Pilfering was reaching a climax. The emperor's belongings were being filched by the sackload, to be taken away on horse-back and even by motor car. At the end of June, Avdeyev blamed his deputy for the theft of a gold crucifix belonging to the tsar. Then suddenly, on 4 July, Avdeyev himself was summoned by phone to the local Soviet and abruptly fired. Immediately afterwards the senior local Communists descended on the house and made a thorough inspection. As they were leaving the chairman of the Soviet, Alexander Beloborodov, explained to the guards that Avdeyev and his deputy had been arrested. Then he sent this message to Moscow: ". . . no cause for apprehension. Avdeyev removed. His assistant Moshkin arrested. In place of Avdeyev Yurovsky. Internal guard entirely replaced by others. Beloborodov."

The new guard commander, Yakov Yurovsky, was a member of the local Soviet, and the regional commissar for justice. History has always credited him with being the Romanovs' chief assassin—a ruthless fiend appointed specifically to murder the imperial family. Yet what we know of his behaviour before and during his assignment hardly suggests a man of violence. Aged about 40, Yurovsky had first been a watch-maker and then opened a small photographic shop in Ekaterinburg. During the war he had trained at the army medical school and become an orderly in the infantry; he showed his medical knowledge during a visit to the Ipatiev House a few weeks before his appointment as guard commander, when he commented on a swelling on the tsarevich's leg while the boy was being treated by Dr Derevenko. He suggested it might help to

put the boy's leg in plaster. Yurovsky was later described by
another Ekaterinburg doctor who had known him since 1915,
when Yurovsky had worked under him as a surgeon's assistant.
The doctor spoke of his respect for the man: "Yurovsky proved
to be an efficient, honest and conscientious worker . . . He was
educated and well-read enough to stand out among his colleagues and friends for his knowledge . . . Yurovsky was kind
to me, and often visited me when I fell ill . . ."

In reality then, Yurovsky appears to have been a gentler and
more responsible sort of man than Avdeyev. Moscow no longer
had to rely on the uncontrollable whims of a man capable of
doing away with the Romanovs in a drunken rage. In fact, as
soon as Yurovsky took over command discipline was quickly
restored. The pilfering stopped at once. On the very day he
arrived, Yurovsky discovered that some close friends of
Avdeyev were still on duty indoors. They were instantly removed, and ten of Yurovsky's own hand-picked men sent in to
replace them. The new guards received preferential treatment;
they alone ate with Yurovsky in the command post, and they
alone had sleeping quarters inside the house, on the ground
floor. All the former guards were now kept away from the
family, and at night they slept across the street in a separate
house. Their sentry duties were restricted to guarding the outside of the Ipatiev House, and they were expressly forbidden to
go upstairs.

Most of the privileged newcomers were not even really
Russians. Avdeyev's guards lumped them together as "Letts"
—soldiers from the Baltic provinces of north Russia. The men
from the Lettish divisions were known for their fine physique
and as well-trained disciplined fighters—a vital part of the
Bolshevik army. One British agent called them the backbone
of Bolshevism. But all the new guards were not Letts. From
graffiti on the walls, it is clear that one at least was Hungarian,
and another Austrian. In July 1918, thousands of Austro-
Hungarian prisoners-of-war were fighting on the Bolshevik
side in the Ekaterinburg area.

Apart from organizing this change of personnel Yurovsky
quickly tightened up on security. When the nuns arrived with
food, he wanted to know who had authorized such deliveries
and where the nuns were from. He cut the deliveries down to

THE IMPERIAL FAMILY

1 Olga

2 Tatiana

3 Maria

4 Nicholas and Alexandra

5 Anastasia

6 Alexei

7 Spring 1917—prisoners in their own palace at Tsarskoe Selo, the Romanovs try their hand at growing vegetables. Two of the tsar's daughters carry turf, the emperor leans on a spade. But confidence of early exile in England soon vanished.

8 Tobolsk—the Romanovs' second place of imprisonment. (*Left to right*) Olga, Tatiana and Anastasia on the terrace of the Governor's House. With them is the maid Demidova (*centre*). Outside, extremists and moderates are already squabbling about what to do with them.

9 April 30 1918—the Romanovs arrive at Ekaterinburg, and are handed over to the local Bolsheviks (*Soviet artist's impression*).

10 The Ipatiev House in June 1918, after the tsar's arrival—a second outer palisade was built in the first week of July.

11

12

11 Ekaterinburg in 1918.

12 The south side of the Ipatiev House—the barred window (*right*) is that of the alleged murder room.

13 The front of the Ipatiev House, where the tsar and his family entered forty-one years earlier, photographed in 1959 by an American journalist.

13

just the milk which had been prescribed for Alexei. He increased the number of guard posts—a second machine gun in the attic and a new sentry in the backyard. Yurovsky himself was only in the house in the day time, but his assistant Nikulin was always there during the night.

Yurovsky and his men had one thing in common: all had come to the Ipatiev House from the local Cheka—the secret, police. Cheka headquarters were in the Hotel America, and during July the four top Communists in the town met there regularly, usually in Room 3, Yurovsky's room. There was Beloborodov, chairman of the Ural Soviet, the man who had received the Romanovs in the first place; his deputy, Chutskayev, the man who had been dealing with the British consul; and in the second week of July they were rejoined by Chaya Goloshchokin, the regional commissar for war. Goloshchokin was a veteran revolutionary who had been in exile with Lenin, and in early July it was he who had been summoned to Moscow for consultations on the military situation, and what was to be done about the Romanovs. By 14 July he was back in Ekaterinburg, armed with the leadership's instructions. He arrived to face a major military crisis: anti-Communist White Russian troops, spearheaded by two crack Czech divisions, were gradually encircling the city. Communist forces were falling back in disorder, and as the commissars in Room 3 talked far into the night, they could hear the sound of battle creeping inexorably towards Ekaterinburg.

The Czech offensive was one new thread in Russia's tangled military situation that summer. The Czechs had been on their way out of Russia, via the Far East, to join the Allies fighting Germany on the western front. Under pressure from Germany, the Bolsheviks had tried to disarm the Czechs—and failed. The Czechs had turned around, allied themselves to the Whites, and were now fighting their way westwards to link up with another White Russian army. By 14 July the fall of Ekaterinburg was only a matter of time. The men in Room 3 knew it and had to take some fast decisions. One was to determine the fate of the Romanovs.

14 July was a Sunday, and that morning Father Storozhev and his deacon had again visited the Romanovs to hold a service. Their report of the visit was to be the last detailed

account by outside observers of conditions inside the Ipatiev
House. The priests donned their robes in the command post
just outside the imperial family's living quarters. Commissar
Yurovsky enquired after Storozhev's health and the priest
mentioned that he had just had pleurisy. Yurovsky confided
that he too had trouble with his lungs. Then they went in to
the imperial family. This time Alexei was sitting in an arm-
chair, pale, but not as pale as the priest remembered him from
a previous visit. The tsarina looked brighter too. All the
family was dressed as before; but there was a noticeable oddity:
the emperor looked different—his beard seemed shorter and
narrower, as if he had shaved around it. And there was something else. The grand duchesses's hair, which the priest recalled as cut short at the back only six weeks previously,
seemed now to have grown right down to their shoulders.
According to Storozhev, there was something strange about
the service too:

> Just after the liturgy of the low mass, there's a point where
> we read the following prayer: "May the souls of the dead
> rest in peace with the saints." For some reason the deacon,
> instead of reading it, began to chant. I did the same, a little
> annoyed by his forgetting the routine, but hardly had we
> begun than behind me I heard all the members of the
> family falling on their knees . . . As I was leaving, I walked
> past the grand duchesses, and I heard a faint "thank you".
> I'm sure I wasn't mistaken. The deacon and I departed in
> silence. Suddenly, near the School of Fine Arts, the deacon
> said to me: "Do you know, something has happened to
> them in there." Since these words expressed my very own
> thoughts, I stopped and asked him why he thought that.
> "Yes, definitely, it's as if they were all somehow different.
> Why, nobody even sang!"

The following day, Monday 15 July, Yurovsky sent the little
kitchen boy, Leonid Sednev, out of the Ipatiev House to live
with the guards across the street. That day also the local labour
union sent in four women to clean the floors of the Ipatiev
House. The grand duchesses, they said later, seemed very
cheerful, and helped them move the beds. One of the women

overheard Yurovsky chatting to Alexei, asking after his health. When the nuns came with their milk, Yurovsky asked for milk for the following day plus 50 eggs in a basket. He also passed a note from one of the emperor's daughters, asking for thread. Early on the morning of Tuesday, 16 July, the sisters delivered the thread, and the milk and eggs. Two guards later testified that they saw the imperial family in the afternoon exercising as usual. That evening, as the anti-Communist forces drew closer and closer to Ekaterinburg, there was an early curfew.

According to the history books, this was the night the Romanovs vanished from the face of the earth.

3

DOUBT AND DISBELIEF

"The family of Romanov has been taken to another
and safer place."
(Communist poster in Ekaterinburg, 20 July 1918)

THE FOLLOWING MORNING, shortly after sunrise, Sisters
Antonina Trinkina and Maria Krokhaleva, two novices from
the convent, set off as usual through the waking streets of
Ekaterinburg to deliver fresh milk at the Ipatiev House. But
nothing was as usual when they reached "The House of
Special Purpose".

Sister Antonina said:

We arrived, and we waited and waited, but nobody took
our provisions. We asked the sentries where the commandant
was. They said, "He's eating". "What, at seven o'clock in
the morning?" we asked. They went in and out of the house
several times and then they said, "Go away. Don't bring
things any more." And that day they didn't even take our
milk.

Yurovsky does appear to have been out. His assistant,
Nikulin, was there though, together with some of the Letts.
Other guards said they looked preoccupied and depressed. For
the first time in weeks, members of the exterior guard were
allowed to go upstairs in the Ipatiev House. Lying on the table,
in the commandant's room, were valuables belonging to the
imperial family. One guard said:

The door leading to the rooms used by the imperial family
was closed as before, but there was nobody in the rooms; not a
single sound was heard. Formerly, sounds of life were always
heard in these rooms. There was no life there now. Only their
little dog was standing near the door, waiting to be let in.

The dog, a spaniel called Joy, had been Alexei's pet since before the tsar's abdication. Now it defected to one of the guards.

Eight hundred miles away in Moscow, the diplomatic corps had some time since left town in fear of either the new Communist regime, or of a possible German invasion. But the British consul-general, Robert Bruce Lockhart, remained, living alone in the Elite Hotel, playing a lonely game of tight-rope diplomacy. On Wednesday, 17 July, Lockhart took a phone call from Lev Karakhan, a deputy foreign commissar. Karakhan told him the tsar had been executed. A laconic entry in Lockhart's diary for that day reads: "Order out by Trotsky that no officers belonging to the British or French are allowed to travel on account of their counter-revolutionary tendencies . . . news that the emperor has been shot at Ekaterinburg." The consul may have been the first non-Russian to hear the news.

There had of course been rumours before, but this seemed to be the real thing. The following day, Thursday, 18 July, the news became official. The official Communist press bureau published a statement by the chairman of the All-Russian Executive Committee:

Chairman Sverdlov announced receipt by direct wire of advice from the Ural Oblast Soviet of the shooting of former Tsar Nicholas Romanov. In recent days, the danger of approach of Czechoslovak bands posed a serious threat to Ekaterinburg, the capital of the Red Urals. At the same time, a new plot of counter-revolutionaries was exposed, which aimed at tearing the crowned executioner from the hands of the Soviet government. In view of all these circumstances, the Presidium of the Ural Soviet decided to shoot Nicholas Romanov, and this was carried out on 16 July. The wife and son of Nicholas have been sent to a safe place. Documents concerning the plot have been sent to Moscow by special courier . . . It had recently been proposed to put the former tsar on trial for all his crimes against the people. But current events prevented this court being convened. After the presidium had discussed the reasons that pushed the Ural Soviet to take the decision to shoot Romanov, the

Central Executive Committee, in the form of its presidium, voted to accept the decision of the Ural Oblast Soviet as correct . . .

When this official statement appeared in the Moscow newspapers the people reacted with a yawn of indifference. Bruce Lockhart noted: "Their apathy was extraordinary."

The news was first flashed to the outside world by radio —from a broadcasting station at Tsarskoe Selo, near the old imperial palace. Lockhart hurried to send telegram No. 339: "Following for Foreign Office. Ex-Emperor of Russia was shot on the night of 16 July by order of Ekaterinburg local Soviet in view of approaching danger of his capture by Czechs. The Central Executive at Moscow has approved action." But the telegram took ten days to reach London, and the outside world had only the Communist radio version to go on. After the weeks of rumour, Europe's foreign ministries hedged, and the newspapers hesitated for a few more days.

In Ekaterinburg there was still a guard on the Ipatiev House, although there was apparently no one left to guard. Commandant Yurovsky had by now returned several times, authorizing wages for the sentries and supervising the clearing up. On 19 July he ordered a horse-drawn cab and left for the railway station. His baggage included seven pieces of luggage, one of them a black leather suitcase, sealed with wax.

Two full days after Moscow had announced the emperor's execution, the people of Ekaterinburg were still in the dark. But there were now more urgent things to worry about as the anti-Communist forces closed in. The Soviet tried to seize all foreign residents as hostages. Prosperous Russian citizens were forced to go to the front to dig trenches, while in Ekaterinburg the executions of "counter-revolutionaries" became a nightly orgy of kangaroo courts and summary killings. Rival factions fought running gun battles in the streets.

On 20 July, while forward enemy patrols moved into the woods surrounding the town, Moscow cleared the line for crisis consultations. We know what was said from the telegraph tape, filed at the post-office and later retrieved by the victorious Whites. The Communists at Ekaterinburg explained, with a note of desperation, that they could not hold on much longer—the city was certain to fall. They also discussed the publication of a text which had been discussed with Moscow in advance, and which appeared to be about the Romanovs. Moscow replied: "At the session of the Central Executive Committee of the 18th it was resolved to accept the decision of the Ural Regional Soviet. You may publish your text."

So, at a workers' meeting in the city theatre, the people of Ekaterinburg were at last given some news about the tsar. Commissar Goloshchokin did not try to hide the hopeless military situation: "The Czechs, the hirelings of British and French capitalists, are close at hand. The old tsarist generals are with them; Cossacks are coming too—and they all think they will get their tsar back again. But they never shall. We have shot him!" The commissar noticed that there were no cheers, only an ominous silence. He swung into revolutionary rhetoric, reminding his listeners that Nicholas had been the "Palach"—executioner. He proposed a resolution that "the execution of Nicholas the Bloody is a reply and a stern warning to the bourgeois monarchist counter-revolution which is trying to drown the workers' and peasants' revolution in blood". Still there were no roars of approval, only a pervasive atmosphere of disbelief. From the audience came cries of "Show us the body!" but Goloshchokin had neither body nor anything else to show. He did add that the tsar's family had been taken away from Ekaterinburg—but then he was interrupted by an unseen voice offstage, and the meeting abruptly ended. As the crowd dispersed people seemed, in the words of one commentator, to feel "there was something left unclear, vague, something left unsaid" about the announcement.

Even before the meeting in the theatre, contradictory rumours were spreading about the disappearance of the imperial family. A day or two before, the barber at Ekaterinburg central station, Fyodor Ivanov, had had a curious conversation with an important Bolshevik, Rail Commissar Gulyayev. The Commissar moaned about having too much work to do, and then explained it was because "Today we are sending away Nicholas". Later, pressed for details, Gulyayev said the tsar had been taken to Ekaterinburg Station 2, some distance outside the town, but would not say what his destination was. The day after that Ivanov talked with both the rail commissar and

a senior military commissar, Kucherov, and got the impression
this time that Nicholas had perhaps been killed. When he next
met them, it was just after the announcement of the tsar's
execution, and as Ivanov testified later: "In general there was
a great secret among all of them about the fate of Nicholas II
and they were all very disturbed during those days. None of
them said anything about the family of the former tsar, and I
was afraid to ask."

Within hours of the proclamation in the theatre, the tsar's
execution notice was posted up on walls around the town. The
last paragraph stated: "The family of Romanov has been sent
away from Ekaterinburg to another and safer place." Then,
just a short while afterwards, squads of Communist soldiers
were to be seen rushing about the streets, tearing the posters
down again.

Before Ekaterinburg fell two of the women who had washed
the floors of the Ipatiev House the day before the family's
disappearance, went back to pick up their wages. When they
found no one in charge they questioned soldiers nearby, and
they explained the house was empty because "everybody has
been taken towards Perm". Perm, 200 miles away, was the
next major stronghold on the Bolshevik line of retreat.

By 25 July, when Ekaterinburg finally collapsed, even before
the Communists were out, the first whispers of doubt had
begun to circulate.

As the war moved on and away from Ekaterinburg, to the
north-west, the Whites began to investigate what had happened to their fallen tsar and his family. Their enquiries were
to last twelve months, until the tide of battle turned again,
and the Communists retook Ekaterinburg.

A detective's dream is a short, sharp enquiry, beginning
immediately after the crime, involving objective witnesses,
warm trails, and an unspoiled scene of the crime for the
forensic experts to study. Speed is of the essence. Another re-
quirement is a minimum of interference from outside authorities. Where there are political considerations, the investigator
can be severely hampered by top brass breathing down his neck.

It is an understatement to say that the White Russian investigations into the fate of the Romanovs suffered all the

nightmares of subjective witnesses, a trampled scene of the crime, and chronic political interference. Although the detective work on the ground ended after a year, another six years passed before the conclusions were published. Control was to pass through the hands of no less than five separate sets of investigators, and much of their work was to be coloured by political in-fighting, plain bickering, and inefficiency. To be fair, the Whites faced abnormal handicaps. There was a savage war going on, and communications were appalling; forensic expertise was minimal, and many amateur sleuths became involved. Even so, it was still a ludicrous, indefensible way to run a multiple murder enquiry, especially one of such major political importance.

In the first crucial months after the disappearance of the Romanovs it was open season for investigators at Ekaterinburg. Every train into town seemed to bring one more determined amateur detective. Apart from the various White teams, foreigners arrived to conduct their own private hunts; and there were the royal envoys, sent by relatives of the imperial family, like the tsar's mother, then still living in south Russia, and the tsar's cousin, King George V of England. There was no central authority to control this battalion of investigators, each working to his own brief, each jealous of his own discoveries, each anxious to prove his ability.

In Ekaterinburg, that stifling July of 1918, it was the White military who took the first steps in setting up an investigation, mainly because civilian justice was still disorganized after the recent fighting. The local commandant set up a commission comprising in part men from the St Petersburg Military Academy—Russia's Sandhurst—which had been transferred to the town by the Communists. Many of its officers had survived, and remained in Ekaterinburg to fight with the Whites. The army also ordered its Criminal Investigation Division to pursue separate enquiries. Apart from these two sets of investigators, and perhaps to give its Officers' Commission the stamp of democracy, the army asked the local justice department to provide a court investigator to work alongside the military. The Ekaterinburg prosecutor was out of town but his deputy quickly appointed Alexander Nametkin, Examining Magistrate for Important Cases. Then, a few days later when the city prosecutor returned, he decided there should be a completely separate civilian enquiry, and Nametkin was ordered to run it. So there were in effect three separate sets of investigators working at once.

Those first months after the capture of Ekaterinburg were all confusion, a town of some 70,000 people seething with rumour and counter-rumour. There was the Ipatiev House, with its abandoned, forlorn rooms, and its sinister, unanswered questions. At this stage many even doubted that the tsar himself had been shot, whilst everyone accepted that the ex-empress and all the children were still alive and had indeed been "evacuated under guard", just as the Bolsheviks had publicly announced. In all probability, that theory was perfectly correct.

4

THE FILE IS FOUND

"Get those papers . . . No-one can rebuild the truth
once it's out."

(William Burroughs, jnr)

W<small>E</small> HAVE DISCOVERED new evidence which clearly
indicates that the Romanovs were not all massacred in the
Ipatiev House. It suggests that, at most, only two members of
the family were killed at Ekaterinburg. This evidence was deliberately suppressed at the time, and has lain hidden for nearly
60 years. The new material explains why no bodies were ever
found, why so little *prima facie* evidence of massacre was ever
produced. Analysis of the enquiry also shows how, at the
height of the civil war, it became more convenient for the
White authorities to "prove" a massacre of all the family at
Ekaterinburg, whether the hard evidence supported it or not.
For propaganda reasons it was more profitable to show that
everyone, including the helpless children, had died together as
martyrs at the hands of the brutal Bolsheviks. This end was
achieved at the expense of integrity, by turning a blind eye to
key testimony, and almost certainly by the planting of false
clues.

We uncovered the fresh evidence from official White
Russian records which were kept secret but never destroyed.
The original documents of the investigation were never made
public; they have been missing since the early twenties, not
necessarily for purely conspiratorial reasons but because time
passed, men died, and files went astray. Over the last four
years we have managed to trace some of the records, from dusty
attics in Paris to unsorted archives in California.

The one source accepted as authoritative and honest, in-
disputable in its conclusions, is not a report, but a book,
written by Nikolai Sokolov, a monarchist, and the last of the
investigators to be in charge of the enquiry. His book, *Judicial*

Enquiry into the Assassination of the Russian Imperial Family, has become the basis for history's version of the fate of the Romanovs. During the writing of our own book, however, it became clear that we needed much more than Sokolov's published work. We also needed to see what the investigator had *not* published, how he had selected his material. That meant finding the original seven-volume dossier which Sokolov brought out of Russia, and the search turned out to be as exhausting an operation as investigating the fate of the Romanovs themselves.

The negatives of photographs taken during the investigation had turned up in the attic of a Paris antique dealer in 1962. They were found abandoned and a little the worse for wear, but still neatly ordered and numbered, in two wooden boxes, marked "N. Sokolov", in Russian cyrillics. But the mass of documentation that should have been with them was missing. General Pozdnyshev, an ancient tsarist officer in Paris, said the original dossier had been stolen by the Germans during the second world war. But there was another set, and that was still safe—"in the hands of neutrals". He would not say more.

As Sokolov was leaving Siberia in 1919, with the Whites about to be routed and his own life in danger, he entrusted one copy of the testimony and evidence collected in Russia to a British journalist, Robert Wilton of *The Times*. Because we were based in London, we decided to chase Wilton's copy. First we went to Paris, where he had died. His last known address was, naturally, the only demolished building in the street. We did find Wilton's old landlady but she could not help. Next we advertised in the personal column of his old newspaper, appealing for relatives to come forward. Several replied, and one told us that Wilton's widow had auctioned the dossier at Sotheby's in 1937. Sotheby's could not help, but suggested we might find the purchaser by checking their old records in the British Museum. We did, and discovered the dossier had been sold to Maggs Brothers of Mayfair, dealers in rare books and manuscripts; even though half-a-century had passed since the disappearance of the Romanovs, Maggs Brothers would not tell us who had bought the dossier from them. They did however agree to write to the purchaser on our behalf and get clearance to give us the information. It turned out that their customer had died, but his widow, a Mrs Duschnes, was still alive. She told us her late husband had sold the papers for a four-figure sum to Bayard Kilgour, a retired chairman of the Cincinnati Bell Telephone Company. When we located him sick in bed in California, he said he had donated the dossier to the Houghton Library, at Harvard University. We wrote to Houghton and at last received the reply we needed: "Your sleuthing is correct in its assumption." We had found the Sokolov dossier (*see plate 18*).

That dossier, the raw material from which he wrote his authoritative book, turns out to be a vital new source of material for historians. Study of the papers shows that Sokolov was indeed highly selective. He meticulously included all the evidence that supported his premise that the entire imperial family had been massacred at the Ipatiev House, but he omitted evidence that hinted, or stated categorically, that something else had happened.

Corroboration for the new evidence also emerged from another untapped source, in papers that came to light in all the aura of mystery and melodrama that has consistently surrounded the Romanov affair.

In 1936, a foreigner walked into the reception area of the Tower Building of the Hoover Institution on War, Revolution and Peace, at Stanford University in California. He carried with him a black cloth bag, sewn shut with thread, and asked a bemused archivist if he could donate the contents to the institution, on the condition that they remained sealed in the bag: "not to be opened until 1 January 1950". He then hurried away and never returned. The condition was honoured by the librarians, and the bag was indeed held, with a restriction label on it, until as late as 1960. When the bag was opened it was found to contain a mass of papers, many written in longhand in outdated Russian script, concerning the investigation into the disappearance of the Romanovs (*see plate 19*). Until we came across these records, no one appears to have studied them; they turned out to be the files of Nikander Mirolyubov, a Russian professor of criminology who had been public prosecutor at Kazan, which administered the Ekaterinburg area. Mirolyubov maintained a judicial watching brief on the Romanov investigations, and had the right to summon depositions and review expenditure. There are two folders of Mirolyubov papers. One contains Sokolov's expense accounts and some correspondence. The other contains a series of letters on the case exchanged between Mirolyubov and his own man in the area, Prosecutor Jordansky. Those letters include further vital testimony never published by Sokolov.

Before evaluating all this new evidence, assessing its implications and placing it in context, it is necessary to return to Ekaterinburg in the sweltering summer of 1918, and the start of the search for the missing imperial family.

PART TWO

Investigation

5

SIGNPOSTS TO A MASSACRE

"The world will never know what we did with them."
(Commissar Voikov, Ekaterinburg, July 1918)

FOUR DAYS AFTER the fall of Ekaterinburg a White Russian officer, Lieutenant Andrei Sheremetevsky, reported to the commander of the 8th Military District in the suburbs of the city. He carried with him a disquieting assortment of articles —a Maltese cross with emeralds, a small buckle bearing the imperial coat of arms, burnt pieces of corsets, buttons with pearls in them, and buckles from men's suspenders and braces.

The lieutenant told a strange story. He said he had been hiding out in the woods, dressed in civilian clothes, near the village of Koptyaki, some thirteen miles from Ekaterinburg. Starting at dawn on 17 July 1918, the village had been disturbed by a series of mysterious events. A peasant family—Nastasya, Nikolai and Maria Zykov—had set out by wagon on their way to sell fish in Ekaterinburg, when they suddenly came upon a small Red Army detachment, soldiers on horseback and foot, and some with carts. As soon as the peasants were spotted, two Red horsemen rode towards them shouting: "Turn back!" To show they meant it, one of them pulled out a revolver and brandished it over the heads of the terrified peasants. The Zykovs turned around so quickly that their own wagon nearly overturned, but still the soldiers hustled them down the road at gunpoint, shouting "Don't look back! We'll shoot!"

News of all this caused a stir in Koptyaki, and other villagers set out to discover what was going on, accompanied by the disguised White officer, Lieutenant Sheremetevsky. The party got as far as the junction to an abandoned iron mine—the Ganin Pit—when they too were halted and turned back by a Red Army soldier armed to the teeth. He told the peasants there was going to be training in grenade throwing at the mine;

and sure enough, during the next two days the villagers heard the sound of explosions, and the mine area remained cordoned off. This was a part of the woods called the Four Brothers, after some lone pine trees that had once grown there. It was a name that was shortly to ring around the world, like Ekaterinburg and the Ipatiev House, as part of the death-knell for the imperial family.

It was not till a week later, after the fall of Ekaterinburg to the Whites, that the peasants returned to the mine. They found obvious signs of bonfires, and the debris of burned clothing that had clearly belonged to wealthy people. There was also broken jewellery. Everybody knew that the Romanovs had been imprisoned at Ekaterinburg, and the peasants immediately feared the worst. One is said to have turned his eyes to the sky and exclaimed: "Merciful Christ, can they have burned the whole family alive?"

One of the peasants was lowered on a rope into the nearby Ganin mineshaft, and found sticks, charred logs, bark, planks and pine needles floating on the water. Lieutenant Sheremetevsky collected some of the more sinister debris found lying openly on the earth around the shaft, and took it to the military in Ekaterinburg. Next day, 30 July, he guided an official inspection party to the Four Brothers—members of the Officers' Commission and Nametkin, the civilian court investigator. With them went Chemodurov, the tsar's former valet, and Dr Derevenko, Alexei's physician, both of whom had survived the Bolshevik occupation. Nametkin found a charred lady's handbag close to the shaft, and not far away burnt rags, lace, and a torn piece of dress material. The material smelt strongly of paraffin. And there were jewels, fragments of emerald and pearl, and "a dirty stone, the colour of water, of considerable size, with a flat centre in a white setting with small sparks, which on examination by an expert jeweller was afterwards found to be a diamond of great value". It was obvious that these objects all came from the same sources. The valet and the doctor were there to confirm it. The priceless debris scattered around the mineshaft and in the ashes had belonged to the imperial family.

The first serious doubts now began to grow about the Bolshevik announcement that while the tsar was dead, the rest of the family was safe. The same day, in Ekaterinburg itself, a form of evidence given to Assistant Public Prosecutor Kutuzov seemed to confirm the fears aroused by the evidence at the mine. Citizen Fyodor Gorshkov testified that the entire Romanov family had been murdered at the Ipatiev House. He said his information came "from the Court Investigator Tomashevsky, who in his turn had learned it from someone who was either an eye witness or a person close to the Soviet authorities". Gorshkov's story was at best third-hand but it was nevertheless shattering; it remains to this day the basis of the historically accepted version. He testified:

> The whole of the imperial family was assembled in the dining-room where they were informed that they were going to be shot, and shortly after this the Letts fired at the imperial family, and they all fell down on the floor. After this, the Letts began to make sure that they were all killed, and discovered that the Grand Duchess Anastasia Nikolayevna was still alive, and when they touched her, she screamed dreadfully; she was hit on the head with a rifle butt, and stabbed thirty-two times with bayonets.

This statement, from a Communist source, was formally supplied to Investigator Nametkin by the prosecutor's office as "The basis on which to begin the preliminary enquiry".

Nametkin began work, as one might expect of a professional, by making a minute inspection of the Ipatiev House. He was accompanied by Captain Malinovsky of the Officers' Commission, and again by Chemodurov and Dr Derevenko. Together they made a painstaking inventory of all that seemed to be left of the Romanovs—the pathetic flotsam of what had once been the mightiest family in the world.

At the top of the stairs outside the imperial quarters, Nametkin found empty saucers bearing the emperor's monogram "N.II", and a stove filled with empty paper and glass. Scrawled on the wallpaper were the words "Commissar of the House of Special Purpose Avdeyev". In the bathroom were dirty pillow slips, long towels with the imperial crown and initials "T.N:1911", a grey-blue collar, knitted pants, and, in the left-hand corner, on the linoleum near the water pipes, short pieces of hair cuttings.

The lavatory was a mess. Someone had written a sign: "Please be so kind as to leave the seat as clean as you found it." And someone else had scrawled graffiti on the walls. In the vestibule outside the imperial quarters there were empty medicine bottles, a broken spirit lamp, books and magazines, more strands of hair, and six pages from the English newspaper *Daily Graphic* dated 21 November 1914. And curiously, even more hair—this time a box with cut hair of four different colours. Chemodurov later identified the hair as coming from the four grand duchesses.

In Yurovsky's room there was a bottle of scent, a set of draughts belonging to the tsarevich, and beneath the divan, a rosary of cypress wood. The valet said it had belonged to the empress.

In the reception room there were eau-de-cologne bottles, four pieces of paper with French text written in the tsarevich's handwriting, a blue-lined envelope with the inscription "Jewels belonging to Anastasia Nikolayevna," and a picture postcard of the tsarina.

In the dining room, the clock had stopped at three minutes to ten; the empress's wheel chair still stood mournfully in a corner; there was a wine bottle marked "Court Wine Cellar".

In the grand duchesses' room there was a New Testament, a book of Psalms in Russian, an elaborate picture of the Virgin —the crown, once topped by a star of precious stones, now torn off—a book, Tolstoy's *War and Peace*, and notes for an English play acted by the children in Tobolsk; in the stove, ashes of picture frames, icons, and medallions.

The tsar and tsarina had shared a room with Alexei. Here there were books—the works of Chekhov and *Stories for Convalescents*. There was a bottle of English perfume, cold cream, nail-scissors and vaseline, water still standing in a carafe. There was also a wall calendar, torn off only as far as the date 23 June; the Romanovs were probably still using the old style date system, which was thirteen days behind the western European calendar. But even so, this meant the calendar was last attended to on 6 July, ten days before the Romanovs' disappearance. The trunks and wardrobes in the apartments were all empty. There was a complete absence of clothes and shoes. Dr Belogradsky, a member of the inspection party, said: "The general impression the house gave me was that of a house abandoned by its owners and invaded by strangers who had destroyed various objects of different sizes and left only insignificant things."

First conclusions, after a meticulous six-day search at the Ipatiev House and one day at the mine, came from Captain Malinovsky of the Officers' Commission. His judgement, formally logged and found by us in the official dossier, comes as a jolt to the subsequent version of a massacre. The captain testified:

As a result of my work on this case I became convinced that the imperial family was *alive*. It appeared to me that the Bolsheviks had shot someone in the room in order to *simulate* the murder of the imperial family, had taken them away in the night along the Koptyaki road, also with the purpose of simulating a murder, changed them into peasant clothing, then taken them from there to some other place, and burned their clothing. These were my impressions as a result of my observation and considered thought. It seems to me that the German Imperial House could in no way permit such evil. It could not allow it. That is how I thought, and it also seemed to me that everything I had observed during the investigation was a simulation of murder.

Malinovsky's assessment of the evidence is important, partly because he was on the scene when the trail was still really fresh. He felt convinced he was in the presence of a put-up job, was not prepared to fall for it, and said so formally. His reference to the "German Imperial House" is strangely prophetic; he was referring to Kaiser Wilhelm II, and there were indeed clues to suggest that Germany had a hand in the events at Ekaterinburg. As our investigation develops, that country will gradually emerge as a vital factor. But to the White officials who eventually took over the enquiry, Captain Malinovsky's theories were heresy. Nothing that associated the imperial family in a positive way with the wartime enemy, Germany, was permissible; and any hint of doubt about the massacre, even from a respectable source, was to be suppressed. Until today that has been the fate of the Malinovsky statement, and we publish it here for the first time. Nor did the world ever hear the opinions of the captain's civilian colleague, Investigator Nametkin. Before he had time to assemble the evidence, let alone draw any formal conclusions, he was summarily fired.

Years later the last White investigator, Sokolov, was to smear Nametkin as a coward, implying that he had been afraid to pursue the clues in the woods because Bolshevik troops were still around. Indeed Nametkin had every reason to be scared, for a large Communist force tried to retake Ekaterinburg just after the enquiry started, and Red units roamed the woods around the town for some time. Yet it is absurd to accuse the first investigator of cowardice, for he went to the Four Brothers on a day White intelligence reported Communist elements in that specific area. The White patrol which accompanied Nametkin's inspection party was actually on a search-and-destroy mission at the time. Nametkin was also later accused of laziness and carelessness, but that is unjustified; in his few days on the assignment he crammed in the painstaking inventory at the Ipatiev House as well as the forest expedition —an inventory so well prepared that Sokolov was eventually to quote many pages of it verbatim.

Nametkin was never able to clear his name, for he became the first of many to die violently during the Romanov enquiry. The White version was that he was "caught by the Bolsheviks and executed for investigating the murder of the tsar and his family". One last point about Nametkin. Before he was sacked, like his military colleagues, he had been pursuing other leads, including evidence that the imperial family had left Ekaterinburg alive.

During August some surviving members of the scattered imperial suite, those with the most pressing personal reasons for finding out what had happened, began to arrive at Ekaterinburg. One of the first was Gleb Botkin, son of the tsar's doctor. He had been left behind in Tobolsk when the family were moved away, and now he rode into Ekaterinburg on a munitions train, anxious for news, above all of his father.

The first man he met was Dr Derevenko, the one member of the imperial household whom the Bolsheviks had allowed to remain free in Ekaterinburg, and make regular visits to the imperial prisoners. Derevenko welcomed the young Botkin warmly, saying rather apologetically: "The Reds must have forgotten me." When Botkin asked after the imperial family, Derevenko replied that the Ipatiev House was now empty, its cellar stained with blood and other traces of slaughter. But curiously, he insisted that this was only a ruse and that the imperial family had not been murdered. A puzzled Botkin went off to see the garrison commander of the White occupation forces, Prince Kuli-Mirza. The prince expressed the firm belief that the family were still alive, and showed Botkin several secret reports "according to which the imperial family had first been taken to a monastery in the province of Perm, and later sent to Denmark".

It was in this atmosphere, and with the growing realization that this was going to be no simple enquiry, that the Ekaterinburg prosecutor, Kutuzov, now found himself looking for a new man to run the Romanov case. From amongst the few investigating magistrates left after the period of Bolshevik rule, he had to find a man with no violent political bias for or against the monarchy, and experienced enough to deal with a very sensitive case. Kutuzov decided it was a job for a fully-fledged judge, made a short-list of three, and left the final selection to a ballot of the Ural Regional Court. The man chosen was Judge Ivan Sergeyev, and his assignment was now given the title of "Investigation of Special Importance". Little is known about Sergeyev personally, but he was no monarchist. The judge was apparently a middle-of-the-road democrat who had supported the Provisional Government. One Ekaterinburg assistant prosecutor who was present as Sergeyev was sworn in described him later as "the most talented member of the regional court".

It was now 7 August 1918, still only 21 days since the Romanovs had vanished, so the new investigator picked up a trail still relatively warm. Judge Sergeyev, who was to be in charge for the next six months, has been more or less ignored by history, but his stewardship was a vital period; it was he who collated almost all the material evidence that ever was found, and he who interviewed dozens of key witnesses. Because Sergeyev, like his predecessor, was also to be dismissed and to vanish in mysterious circumstances, we have an incomplete picture of his time in office. But enough remains to trace his progress and record his surprising conclusions.

Sergeyev's takeover from Investigator Nametkin seems to have been orderly and amicable. While Nametkin finished documenting his inventory of the upper storey of the Ipatiev House, the judge picked up where he had left off. Since another court official was already at work with the military investigators out at the Four Brothers mine, Sergeyev now began a thorough, week-long study of the ground floor of the Ipatiev House. He had fifteen rooms to examine, rooms which had been the living quarters for the "Lettish" guards in the last weeks of the Romanovs' imprisonment; several storerooms, and a hall with a main staircase connecting with the Romanovs' quarters upstairs. Sergeyev examined all these, but it was a room at the side of the house, on Voznesensky Street, which drew the greatest attention and held most of the macabre clues. This was the room which was to become notorious as the "murder cellar" where according to history the entire Romanov family and their servants were shot and bayoneted to death by Yurovsky and his brutal assistants.

In fact the room is not a cellar at all. Because the Ipatiev House stands on a fairly steep hill, the ground-floor rooms at the front of the house are indeed almost completely underground, with their windows just peeping above the surface. But the three rooms at the side of the house are much more exposed, and the middle one, the "murder room", is almost entirely above ground. Sergeyev found a room with a vaulted ceiling, a wooden floor of yellow-painted boards, and walls decorated with striped wallpaper and lined in parts with thin wood planking. On one wall were crude pornographic drawings, featuring the tsarina in sexual poses with Rasputin. The drawings had almost certainly been done by the Russian interior guard, some of whom had lived on the ground floor in the early days, while Avdeyev was commandant. There was one barred window in the wall facing the street (*see plate 12*), and only one entrance, through double doors leading from a lobby. In the wall facing the entrance there was another door leading to a storeroom, but there was no way of going beyond the store—it was a dead end. If the Romanov family had been brought to the downstairs room they had no possible exit apart from the way they had come in. Sergeyev found that the room measured seventeen feet by fourteen, and it is worth pausing to consider those dimensions. According to testimony produced by the eventual White investigators, 23 people are supposed to have crammed into that space—eleven victims and twelve killers; that would mean the Romanovs and their executioners standing at uncomfortably close quarters, without allowing for the fact that several of the victims were allegedly seated on chairs and taking up even more space (*see plan over page*). These would be cramped conditions for a cocktail party, let alone a mass execution. In the panic and confusion of a massacre the murderers themselves would have been at real risk from flying bullets. But then as we shall see, Judge Sergeyev did not believe all the imperial party had been killed in the room.

Nevertheless the room did contain evidence of violence, vital evidence which the judge catalogued with care (*see plate 21*). It is worth emphasizing that he took five days doing so, because he was later to be accused of missing important details. This raises a question-mark over exactly when some of the evidence appeared; part of it seems to have "arrived" during Sergeyev's time in office. In the walls, doors and floor, the judge is alleged to have found a total of 27 bullet holes, many with bullets still in them. There was a bullet hole in each of the double doors leading into the storeroom, and matching holes in the facing wall of the storeroom itself, suggesting that bullets had been fired straight through the door and embedded themselves in the wall opposite. There were also six holes in the floor, and two more in the wall beneath the window. Sergeyev had portions of the wall and floor removed, and sure enough found bullets (*see plate 30a*). Some were still in the floor, and others had slipped down between the plank wall-lining and the plaster behind. Sergeyev's meticulous plotting of the bullet holes provided information about the situation in which they had been fired. Two matching holes in the door and its frame showed that the door into the hall-way had been open when at least one of the bullets was fired. But by far the greatest cluster of bullet holes was in the wall opposite the door; there were sixteen, and only three were more than two feet above the floor. In other words if the bullets which made these holes had first passed through bodies,

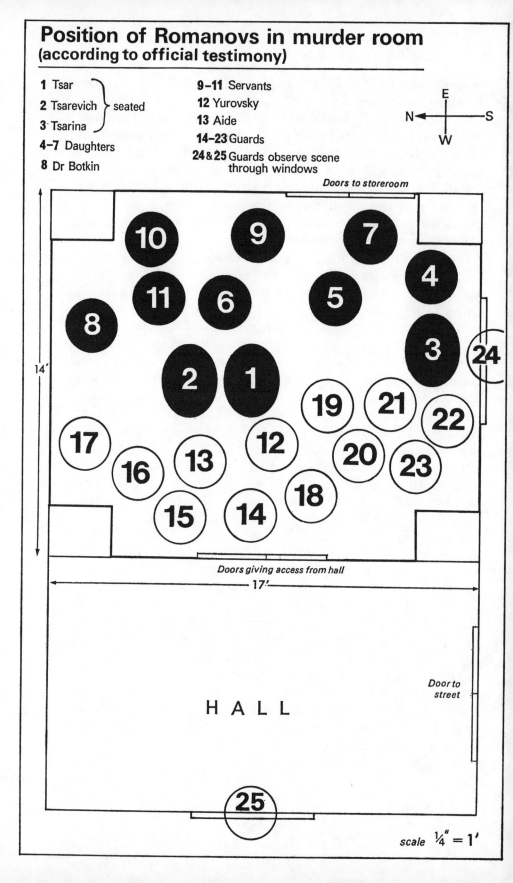

then the victims must either have been kneeling, sitting, or even lying, on the floor.

Judge Sergeyev's inspection left him little doubt that there had indeed been victims. He observed that the floor in both the "murder room" and in the hall outside appeared to have been washed, and his report stated: "It bears visible traces of washing, notably irregular and zig-zag marks, formed by particles of sand and chalk, which on drying have stuck firmly to the floor. On the skirting boards there are thicker layers of the same mixture of dried sand and chalk." Ominously the judge added: "On the surface of the floor, you can make out stains of a reddish colour." Unfortunately there is no clear record of just how many "stains of a reddish colour" Sergeyev found. But chemical tests carried out on five pieces of wood did establish conclusively that the marks were indeed made by human blood. Certainly there was blood in the murder room, but there is a significant divergence of testimony about how much, or when it got there, a point we shall examine along with the final White conclusions.

The mute testimony announced only too clearly that people had been shot in the sinister ground-floor room at the Ipatiev House. In the circumstances it was easy to conclude that it was the Romanovs who had been the victims. But just in case the point might be in doubt, somebody had obligingly left a message on the wall by the window. Sergeyev found two lines from a German poem (*see plate 29*):

> Belsatzar ward in selbiger Nacht
> Von seinen Knechten umgebracht.

This is an adapted quotation from the German poet Heinrich Heine, and means: "On the same night, Belsatzar was killed by his slaves." The original poem stemmed from the Old Testament story of the writing on the wall, and how King Belshazzar, who had scorned the God of the Jews, was murdered by his own men. The writer of the murder-room quote has tinkered with the original verse, making it more positive, and apparently punning on the German form of the name "Belsazar", by turning it into "Belsa*tz*ar".

This piece of literary graffiti remains one of the greater

curiosities in a very curious case. What sort of person wrote this? He would need to have been educated with a fair know-ledge of German poetry. If the Bolsheviks went to so much trouble to hide what had happened, why advertise the murder —and specifically regicide—on the wall of the murder room? Why commit the murders at dead of night, scrub the floors in an attempt to remove the bloody traces, get rid of the bodies —and then leave a signpost describing exactly what you have done?

And there is a further point in the selection of this particular quotation. Much was eventually to be made of the fact that several of the Ekaterinburg Bolsheviks were Jews. Heine, the poet who wrote the original verse, was a Jew, and the poem is about a Gentile sovereign who offended Old Testament Israel. So was the writing on the wall produced by a Jew boasting about the murder of the tsar, or was it written by someone deliberately wanting the Jews to be blamed for the death of the imperial family?

On the same wall there was yet another enigma. Just above the level of the planking, was a second odd inscription com-prising four symbols which have never been satisfactorily interpreted:

In the British Museum there is a curious little booklet called *Sacrifice*, devoted entirely to deciphering these signs. The author, a scholar writing in 1923 under the pseudonym of Enel, decided that three of the symbols were the letter "L" in its Greek, Hebrew and Samaritan versions. Since these were the three languages of Jewish history, Enel deduces that the writer was a Jew. He would also have us believe that the symbols were written from above, with the arm extended downwards, as though the writer was writing with his back to the wall. Perhaps Enel had his back to the wall too, as he struggled to interpret the symbols. They remain, alas, meaningless to the contemporary investigator.

When Sergeyev finished his work in the murder room, he had photographs taken inside the Ipatiev House, and set up his working headquarters in the Ekaterinburg Palace of Justice. Evidence of one kind and another continued to stream in, some of it ominous, some suggesting the family was still alive. All of it came to Sergeyev, and he apparently found none of it conclusive. He was receiving regular reports on progress on the other main search area—the Four Brothers mine. The shafts in the area were flooded, and the Officers' Commission spent weeks pumping out all the water from the suspect shaft. These operations, and a search of the ground around, brought in more debris to add to the evidence produced by the very first visits to the mine. Sergeyev catalogued the finds:

one man's finger
two pieces of epidermis [skin]
one earring
some artificial teeth
pieces of a hand-grenade
one necktie holder
bones of a bird
pieces of a small glass bottle
one iron plate from the heel of a man's boot
collection of buttons
one iron shovel.

By now the tutors to the imperial children, Pierre Gilliard and Sydney Gibbes, had returned to Ekaterinburg. Together with Chemodurov and Derevenko, they now gave Judge Sergeyev formal confirmation that much of the mineshaft material had indeed belonged to the imperial household. Derevenko identified the finger as being the ringfinger of his colleague, Dr Botkin. Chemodurov identified a piece of cloth as having been cut from the tsarevich's knapsack, and Gilliard

offered an explanation of how the jewels probably got into the
mineshaft.

He said that the empress and her daughters had held on to
their personal jewellery in prison, even after the Romanovs ran
short of funds. After arriving at Ekaterinburg, the empress had
been so alarmed by Avdeyev's searches that she had sent a
letter to her daughters, still at Tobolsk, warning them by pre-
arranged code to conceal the family jewels. The word "medicine" in the letter was the code for "jewellery", and the grand
duchesses had been told to "dispose of the medicines as agreed".
"As agreed" meant inside their clothes, and before leaving the
girls and their maids spent days sewing jewels into their bodices,
into their hats, and even into their buttons. Olga apparently
carried a satchel round her neck containing gems, and wore
ropes of pearls on her neck but hidden under her clothes.
Money and jewels were also sewn into cushions and Demidova,
the maid, had carried one of these to Ekaterinburg. Gibbes,
the English tutor, estimated the total value of this jewellery at
£100,000.

If the bodies of the family had been taken to the Four
Brothers mine, the jewels could have fallen out of the clothes
when they were being searched or ripped open by the murderers; a plausible enough explanation if you accept that the
dead bodies were inside the clothes found at the mine. But
many weeks of searching by a highly organized team of
foresters, miners, and volunteers had failed to produce any
sign of Romanov corpses. To account for eleven bodies there
was only the anonymous human finger, the minute fragment
of skin, and the false teeth. Since Dr Botkin had worn false
teeth, and since the finger was believed to be his, it was a fair
assumption that he was dead. But as far as Judge Sergeyev was
concerned, the presence of tell-tale jewels and family effects
did not by any means prove that the actual bodies of the
imperial family had been at the Four Brothers; and in all
the White searches that followed over the coming year, no
Romanov remains were ever found. This is one of the most
important aspects of the entire case.

Within weeks of starting work Sergeyev also had a mass of
verbal testimony to sift. He had known the traditional version of
the Ipatiev House massacre from the start, as it had been told

as early as 30 July by the first man to retail the story, Fyodor Gorshkov. That evidence was third-hand, and the original source was allegedly one of the former Ipatiev House guards, Anatoly Yakimov. According to his sister, Yakimov had come home on 17 July looking shocked and scared, and had told her that the whole imperial family had been killed the previous night. He had said he had "seen the scene of the murder", but as we shall see in testimony later, that did not mean he had seen the bodies, but only the suspect downstairs room. This lone hearsay evidence was insufficient to convince Judge Sergeyev that there had been a massacre; for he had simultaneously been receiving repeated testimony, and reports, which said that some, possibly all, of the Romanovs had been transferred from Ekaterinburg alive. From information collected by undercover agents working behind Communist lines, the judge now had varying accounts of the removal operation. Some of the reports specified the route travelled and the means of transport used; they matched both the earliest rumours in Ekaterinburg and the Bolsheviks' own public announcement—that they had taken the family to a place of safety after the execution of the tsar.

Sergeyev remained puzzled, and open-minded. No good detective can close a case until the overwhelming weight of the evidence points to one conclusion. In October, three months after the disappearance of the Romanovs, that was by no means the situation. Nor was the judge alone in his doubts. He was soon to find himself in distinguished company.

6

THE SERGEYEV INVESTIGATION

"I do not believe that all the people, the tsar, his
family, and those with them, were shot there."
(Judge Sergeyev, commenting on the Ipatiev House,
December 1918)

"On 17 July a train with the blinds down left Ekaterinburg for an unknown destination and it is believed that
the surviving members of the imperial family were in
it."
(Sir Charles Eliot, British High Commissioner,
October 1918)

THE DOUBTS AND rumours circulating in Ekaterinburg
were now being reflected in London, where the tsar's cousin,
King George, had a special personal concern to know what
had happened to his relatives. Buckingham Palace had
accepted long since that the tsar himself was dead, and had
gone into formal mourning after the Bolshevik execution
announcement in mid-July. But British intelligence reports on
the fate of the rest of the family had caused some confusion in
London. The first had reached Whitehall on 29 August when
a Polish officer of the Czech general staff made his way in
disguise through Bolshevik lines to Allied headquarters at
Archangel in north Russia. This was Captain Voitkevich, who
brought military-situation reports in code from the British,
French and American consuls at Ekaterinburg. Voitkevich
also brought something no one else in the outside world could
boast of at that time—the first eye-witness account of the scene
at the Four Brothers. He had been with the Nametkin search
party which first visited the mine, and like some of his colleagues the Pole had not been convinced by what he saw. As
passed on to London his report stated: "It was believed that
the empress and her children are at Verkotur[ye], north of Ye

[*Ekaterinburg*] in which region Bolsheviks were still supreme."
But two days later, on 31 August, a completely different conclusion reached the Director of Military Intelligence, also from
north Russia. As passed on to King George at Windsor Castle,
it read:

> I think I ought to let you know at once for His Majesty's
> information that we have just received a very distressing
> telegram from the intelligence officer serving under General
> Poole at Murmansk to the effect that there is every prob-
> ability that the Empress of Russia, her four daughters, and
> the tsarevich, were all murdered at the same time as the late
> tsar. The information reached the intelligence officer from a
> source which he had no reason to doubt. I am very much
> afraid therefore, that the news is only too likely to prove
> true.

This message was given more weight than Captain Voitkevich's report. Within hours, the king sat down to write to the
tsarina's sister, the German-born Marchioness of Milford
Haven, mother of the present Lord Mountbatten. Until now
she had thought that Alexandra and her daughters had all
survived Ekaterinburg, and she had been pressing friendly
states to negotiate asylum for them. Now she received this
letter from the king:

> My dear Victoria,
>   I am sending this letter by Louise who goes to you to-
> morrow as the posts are impossible. The enclosed is a copy
> of a letter I received from Lord Milner last night. I fear the
> sad news it contains will be a great shock to you as well as
> great sorrow. The source from which the information comes
> I am afraid leaves little doubt that it is true. May [*Queen
> Mary*] and I feel most deeply for you in the tragic end of
> your dear sister and her innocent children. But perhaps for
> her, who knows, it is better so; as after dear Nicky's death
> she could not have wished to live. And the beautiful girls
> may have been saved from worse than death at the hands
> of these horrible fiends . . . My heart goes out to you in
> this terrible tragedy and we pray that God may give you

comfort. May sends you her best love and all our sympathy. If I hear anything more I will of course let you know. I remain,

Your very affectionate cousin,
George.

It was the royal valedictory on the Romanovs. On the strength of one apparently well-informed intelligence report Buckingham Palace, at any rate, had accepted the death of all the Russian imperial family. But a fortnight later Whitehall received a third message, this time from its own man in Ekaterinburg, Consul Preston. His report, sent on 16 September, still held out hope:

. . . on 16 July at a meeting of Ural Provisional Government of Soldiers' and Workmen's Delegates it was decided to shoot the tsar and this was communicated to him and sentence carried out same night by Lettish soldiers. No trace of the body however has ever been found. And then immediately after this, the rest of the members of the imperial family *were taken away to an unknown destination* . . .

Early autumn thus found the Foreign Office in London still unsure of the true fate of the Romanovs. The conflicting reports, and Moscow's continued silence on the subject of the empress and the children, now prompted London to appoint its own investigator, a tried man of such talents and trustworthiness that his report would be as definitive and accurate as the circumstances permitted.

The man chosen was Sir Charles Eliot, high commissioner and consul-general for Siberia—one of the two senior British diplomats in Russia. He had been appointed to this post in August 1918, and moved to Russia from Hong Kong, where he was vice-chancellor of Hong Kong University. At 56, Sir Charles was already a veteran diplomat with worldwide experience. His career had been based on a formidable intellect and extraordinary linguistic capabilities. At Balliol College, Oxford, and then as a Fellow of Trinity, he had mastered Russian, Turkish, Chinese, Finnish, and all the conventional European languages. He was knighted in 1900, after serving with British embassies in Washington, the Balkans, the Pacific and Russia. By 1918 he had retired to take up the academic post in Hong Kong, but he readily accepted the invitation to return to active diplomacy—especially in Russia. His very first posting had been to St Petersburg, and he had spent months exploring uncharted areas of the Russian empire, travelling across Siberia to the remote frontiers with China. His appointment as high commissioner made him joint head of the British diplomatic service in Russia, with a roving commission taking in a vast area from his headquarters at Vladivostok in the Far East all the way to the borders of European Russia. Sir Charles's primary task was to keep a finger on the pulse of the civil war, and on a new development—Allied intervention. Since the summer the British had been landing troops in northern and far-eastern Russia, an initiative that was to lead to a build-up of thousands of British, American, Japanese and French troops. This was the clumsy attempt to help the Whites against the Bolsheviks which was to succeed in doing little more than prolonging the misery of the civil war. Sir Charles's base at Vladivostok was the eastern bridgehead for the Allied landings, and the high commissioner's office became a bastion of efficiency amidst the military chaos. Sir Charles became known as a stickler for detail, and for his impenetrable silences; his juniors nicknamed him "The Sphinx". This then was the man selected by London in late September 1918 to take advantage of a fact-finding mission in Siberia to clarify what had happened to the Romanovs.

Sir Charles arrived in Ekaterinburg by train, travelling in the first-class Wagon-Lit carriage in which he lived and worked. He of course met Thomas Preston, the British consul, and seems to have bowled him over; to this day Sir Thomas remembers him as "the most erudite man I have ever met". Sir Charles had long talks with Judge Sergeyev, and quickly arranged a visit to the Ipatiev House. Neither Sir Charles nor the judge recorded what they thought of each other, but we can assume a degree of mutual respect. They had something in common, for among his myriad distinctions Sir Charles was qualified in public law. One incident must have impressed Sergeyev. During the visit to the Ipatiev House, Sir Charles noticed some wall scribblings in Yiddish which had so far baffled the investigators' efforts to decipher them. The high commissioner obliged with an instant translation into perfect Russian. We can also deduce that Sir Charles approved of Sergeyev's work. He had been sent with a firm brief to see for himself and make his own assessment of progress on the case, and one might assume that his report to London would have reflected any professional criticism of the judge himself, or any disagreement with his conclusions. On 5 October, Sir Charles sent off a first interim cable to London. It made it quite clear that, as far as he and Judge Sergeyev were concerned, nothing about the alleged murders was clear at all:

> Mystery surrounds the fate of the tsar, who is stated by the Bolsheviks to have been shot here on the night of 16 July, and some of the highest and best informed officials cling to the belief that His Imperial Majesty was not murdered but removed and placed in German custody, story of murder being invented to explain his disappearance.
>
> Officer appointed by present government to investigate crime showed me over house where imperial family were confined and where His Imperial Majesty is supposed to have been shot. He dismissed as fabrications all stories respecting discovery of corpse, confessions of soldiers who had taken part in the murder, and on the other hand all narratives of persons who declared that they had seen the emperor after 16 July . . .

It is very significant that Judge Sergeyev firmly believed the "confessions of soldiers" were fabrications. The story he had heard of the killings in the Ipatiev House—as told by the guard Yakimov to his sister—was identical to the version that has since come to be accepted as gospel. Although this story was later to be repeated by other captured guards, it is important to know that in October 1918 Sergeyev had not only heard it, but actually considered it to be an invention.

After the interim message had gone off to London in code, Sir Charles sat down to write a full fifteen-page report, in his own hand, addressed directly to the foreign secretary, Mr Balfour. It remains to this day the only independent account from a legally-trained observer, made on the spot and before the trail was completely cold. He began by warning London straightaway not to hold out much hope for the tsar himself; he described the emperor's disappearance as a "singular mystery", but quoted Judge Sergeyev as saying the chances were four to three that Nicholas had indeed been killed. Then, after summarizing what was known of the family's conditions in captivity, he recorded his personal impressions of the Ipatiev House and in particular of the notorious downstairs room:

It was quite empty; . . . On the wall opposite the door and on the floor were the marks of seventeen bullets or, to be more accurate, marks showing where pieces of the wall and floor had been cut out in order to remove the bullet holes, the officials charged with the investigation having thought fit to take them away for examination elsewhere. They stated that Browning revolver bullets were found and that some of them were stained with blood. Otherwise no traces of blood were visible. The position of the bullets indicated that the victims had been shot when kneeling and that other shots had been fired into them when they had fallen on the floor. Mr Gibbes thought that for religious reasons the tsar and Dr Botkin would be sure to kneel when facing death. There is no real evidence as to who or how many the victims were but it is supposed that they were *five*, namely the tsar, Dr Botkin, the empress's maid and two lackeys. No corpses were discovered, nor any trace of their having been disposed of by burning or otherwise, but it was stated that a finger bearing a ring believed to have belonged to Dr Botkin was found in a well.

On 17 July a train with the blinds down left Ekaterinburg for an unknown destination and it is believed that the surviving members of the imperial family were in it.

It will be seen from the above account that the statement of the Bolsheviks is the only evidence for the death of the tsar, and it is an easy task for ingenious and sanguine minds to invent narratives giving a plausible account of His Imperial Majesty's escape. It must indeed be admitted that since the empress and her children, who are believed to be still alive, had totally disappeared, there is nothing unreasonable in supposing the tsar to be in the same case.

The marks in the room at Ekaterinburg prove at most that some persons unknown were shot there and might even be explained as the result of a drunken brawl. But I fear that another train of thought is nearer the truth . . . There is some evidence that they [the Bolsheviks] were much alarmed by an aeroplane flying over the garden of the house and I fear it is comprehensible that in a fit of rage and panic they made away with His Imperial Majesty.

It is the general opinion in Ekaterinburg that *the empress, her son and four daughters were not murdered but were despatched on 17 July to the north or west.* The story that they were burnt in a house seems to be an exaggeration of the fact that in a wood outside the town was found a heap of ashes, apparently the result of burning a considerable quantity of clothing. At the bottom of the ashes was a diamond and as one of the grand duchesses is said to have sewn a diamond into the lining of her cloak, it is supposed that the clothes of the imperial family were burnt here. Also hair, identified as belonging to one of the grand duchesses, was found in the house. *It therefore seems probable that the imperial family were disguised before their removal. At Ekaterinburg I did not hear even a rumour as to their fate, but subsequent stories about the murder of various grand dukes and grand duchesses cannot but inspire apprehension.*[1]

I have the honour to be with the highest respect

Sir,

Your most obedient,
humble servant.
C. Eliot.

When Sir Charles Eliot's report reached London, it was given priority treatment. A Foreign Office official first suggested it should be summarized and then sent to the king, but somebody senior to him then decided "This should go to the king in original."

Consul Preston, who has always been an outspoken supporter of the massacre version, told us in 1971 that he was perplexed by the Eliot report. He wondered whether Sir Charles "may have got information from other sources". But unlike the high commissioner Preston had no specific brief to investigate the fate of the Romanovs, and does not appear to have taken a keen personal interest. He admits today that he never even bothered to visit the Ipatiev House, although it was just along the street from his consulate.

Sir Charles Eliot's despatch was the first and last considered report by a distinguished and qualified British observer. If he was right about just some of the doubts he raised, then the accepted version of the end of the Romanovs is blown apart. The case for the alternative he postulated is arguably stronger, and a more sure-footed interpretation of the known facts, than the case for a wholesale massacre. Hindsight, and new evidence now available, suggest that Eliot was right in his hunch that the Romanov women were removed from Ekaterinburg, alive and in disguise, to a new location. The clues he found so impressive are worth re-examination.

First, the evidence of disguise. In fact, there was even more hair found in the Ipatiev House than Eliot mentioned. He referred to hair identified as belonging to *one* of the grand duchesses, but the investigators had actually found lengths of hair of four different colours. There was so much, and it was so distinctive, that the valet Chemodurov positively identified it as coming from each of the four grand duchesses. This had all been in a box outside the imperial quarters in the vestibule at the top of the stairs. And that had not been all—there had been other "strands of hair" lying around in the same vestibule, but not in the box. There were also the "short pieces of hair cuttings" which had been found lying on the linoleum in the bathroom. Now it is possible the Romanovs all had their hair cut at the same time, for routine reasons. Yet the visiting priest had noticed the girls with "hair right down to their shoulders", and that was only 48 hours before their disappearance. The haircuts do seem to have coincided oddly with the moment of their disappearance. And there was also the question mark about the tsar's beard. Colonel Rodzyanko, an officer serving with the British Mission, wrote in his account: "Also part of the tsar's beard was found in the chimney. It has all been kept." This seems to be confirmed by the evidence of the priest, who noticed that Nicholas appeared to "have cut around his beard". Had the tsar got halfway to taking off his whole beard when the priest saw him? Many men begin a total beard-shave by stages, rather than hacking off the whole thing at once.

Nicholas' beard was as distinctive in 1918 as Fidel Castro's is amongst statesmen today. Both would be publicly unrecognizable without them. Certainly the shaving of the tsar's beard and the cropping of the daughters' hair, fits neatly into the hypothesis that there was an effort to change the appearance of these well-known public figures for a secret transfer operation. It would not, however, mean that they escaped—merely that the Bolsheviks may have wanted to move them without advertising the fact to a highly volatile population. It has always been suggested that the Bolsheviks used the curfew on the night of 16 July as cover for the removal of corpses. It could equally well have been used to move live people.

The plane Sir Charles Eliot referred to, flying over the house shortly before the family vanished, remains unexplained. Both sides in the civil war did have some aircraft and the Czechs could have used one for reconnaissance during the advance on Ekaterinburg. It is unlikely to have played any part in the removal of the Romanovs. The train mentioned, however, is of much greater significance. It is reminiscent of the testimony about the two Bolshevik commissars discussing removal by train at Ekaterinburg station, and it runs like a thread through much of the testimony we have yet to examine; even those who later became disciples of the "cellar massacre" version believed for months that surviving Romanovs had been taken away by rail.

So by Christmas 1918 Judge Sergeyev had been working on the case for four months, and the case remained open. There are two contradictory versions of what he believed towards the end of his time in his office, as the evidence continued to come in; the first, and more well-known, is Sokolov's. He said: "My predecessor, Sergeyev, on handing the case over to me, had no doubt about the fact that the entire imperial family had been massacred in the Ipatiev House along with those living with them. In his report No. 106, sent to the Supreme Command on 1 February 1919, and delivered to General Diterikhs, he stated this quite categorically." We cannot locate any such report in the Sokolov dossier, which is supposed to be the complete record of White investigations in Russia. In the light of the dubious integrity of the later White investigators, it is perhaps just as well that Judge Sergeyev expressed his opinion separately in a newspaper interview given as late as December 1918.

One of the few western journalists to reach Ekaterinburg and report the Romanov story was Herman Bernstein, an American writing for the *New York Tribune*. This is his account of his meeting with Sergeyev:

He [*the Judge*] took from his desk a large blue folder which bore the inscription "The Case of Nicholas Romanov", and said: "Here I have all the evidence in connection with the Nicholas Romanov case . . . I examined the lower storey of the building where the royal family lived and where the crime was supposed to have been committed. I do not believe that all the . . . people, the tsar, his family, and those with them, were shot there. It is my belief that the empress, the tsarevich and the grand duchesses were not shot in that house. I believe, however, that the tsar, Professor Botkin, the family physician, two lackeys and the maid, Demidova were shot in the Ipatiev House."

Judge Sergeyev was saying flatly that only one member of the imperial family, the tsar, had been shot in the famous downstairs room.

About a month later, on 23 January 1919, Sergeyev was fired. He disappeared from the scene some weeks later, and is said to have been "executed by the Bolsheviks".

7

THE WHITES LOSE PATIENCE

"When in doubt, win the trick."
(Edmund Hoyle on whist)

THE CIRCUMSTANCES surrounding the decision to dismiss Judge Sergeyev were extraordinary and unethical, and the motives behind it highly suspect. It was an order that came from Government House in the city of Omsk, 400 miles east of Ekaterinburg, capital of the Siberian plain and headquarters of the White military dictatorship formed to unite the various anti-Communist forces. This White regime claimed to be the rightful government of "all the Russias", and indeed at one point during the coming year nine-tenths of Russia was to be in either White or foreign hands. The Bolsheviks were on the run in the Urals, and it was the time of greatest hope for a successful counter-revolution. The "Supreme Ruler" who headed the Omsk government was Admiral Kolchak, and it was with his knowledge that Sergeyev was ordered off the Romanov investigation.

But the man who actually issued the order was Lieutenant-General Mikhail Diterikhs, the senior member of the high command who was from now on to be in overall charge of the enquiry. He ordered Sergeyev to send all the case documents, and all the portable evidence, to him at headquarters. This caused an immediate outcry from the civilian judiciary, who were outraged by the forcible army takeover. Ostroumov, an assistant public prosecutor at Ekaterinburg, later described it angrily as "the illegal interference in the case of the military power". But the row went far higher than that. Within a week of Sergeyev's dismissal, Kolchak's own minister of justice, Starynkevich, sent a blistering message to General Diterikhs: ". . . I beg you to inform me on whose authority you undertook this removal of the documents, which infringes the laws of the country and complicates the conduct of the enquiry—which is the specific concern of the Russian judiciary. I beg you to return the documents to the investigator Sergeyev."

Diterikhs took no notice, and the civilian judiciary fell back on appointing a new official prosecutor, Valery Jordansky, to keep an eye on the next stage of the investigation. Although his role seems to have been merely symbolic as far as headquarters in Omsk was concerned, he did keep a watching brief, and some of his surviving documents have been helpful in our own investigation. But just like Sergeyev and Nametkin, he did not last the course. Like them, he is said to have been caught and killed by the Bolsheviks for his part in the Romanov investigation.

But why did the White leaders, men who were preoccupied with the life and death struggle against the Bolsheviks, suddenly give urgent attention to changing the course of the Romanov investigation? Why replace the judge in the middle of his enquiry? The army tried to justify their takeover by alleging that the investigation had not been formally accredited to the Omsk government. That excuse is patently absurd, since the Omsk government did not even exist until long after Sergeyev had been appointed. The enquiry could have been legitimized at the stroke of a pen. To seek the real motives for firing Sergeyev, we must take a close look at the see-saw between public belief and disbelief in the murders at the moment of his dismissal—the beginning of 1919.

It was by then six months since the disappearance of the Romanovs, and there were still persistent reports that the assassination had been a hoax. Some presented wildly improbable alternatives—like the story that one of the tsar's aides-de-camp, General Tatishchev, had heroically stood in for Nicholas on the night of execution. Ironically, this tale seems to have been spread by Grand Duke Kyril, the tsar's first cousin, who was later to claim the throne in exile on the assumption that the tsar was dead. But all the survival stories reflected the feeling that the Ekaterinburg evidence was unconvincing and that the real fate of the family remained hidden. It was a doubt shared by observers who cannot be lightly dismissed.

The tsar's mother, 71-year-old Empress Marie, was still living in south Russia, steadfastly refusing to leave, even with the Bolsheviks fast approaching. In November 1918 she was visited there by Colonel Joe Boyle, a senior operator in Allied intelligence, and he found her adamant about staying on until she received firmer news about the fate of her son and his family. Boyle himself had been receiving despatches from his own undercover men in Ekaterinburg, and considered the evidence inconclusive. As for the Dowager Empress, she was still telling British officers that the imperial family had survived when she finally left aboard a British warship sent by King George V in April 1919. On reaching Malta, she said she had positive information on the matter, and knew where the family were.[2]

At Christmas 1918, top diplomats and journalists were also sceptical about the massacre story. On 5 December the American ambassador in Rome, Nelson Page, had sent a cable to the secretary of state in Washington: "For your confidential information. I learned in highest quarters here it is believed that the tsar and his family are all alive." "Highest quarters" meant the Italian royal family. We discovered a letter written by the ambassador's wife a day after that cable was sent. In it Mrs Page mentioned that the Queen of Italy had asked privately for word to be passed to the President of the United States about various matters, including the fate of the tsar. The ambassador's wife wrote: "When I asked [the Queen] if she believed the tsar had been executed she said she did not, nor did she believe that anyone of the royal family had been killed, indeed she thinks they are all of them alive." Italy was at that time a functioning monarchy, and the royal family had relatives both in Russia and Germany. Two of the queen's sisters were married to Russian grand dukes. They were also closely related by marriage to Prince Louis of Battenberg, the German father of the present Lord Mountbatten.

The Page telegram spurred Washington into asking London for the latest official opinion there. The reply from the Foreign Office now referred to "apparently truthful reports that tsar and son were killed, but opinion is reserved as to veracity of reports regarding death of empress and her daughter" [misprint for "daughters"].

While the diplomats kept their options open, the first journalists were now filing from Ekaterinburg. We are aware of only four who made it to the town specifically to cover the Romanov story. In 1918 reporters could not simply hop aboard a jet plane to the Urals; because of the war, they had first to travel around the world by boat to the eastern seaboard, and then make a hazardous overland journey across 3,000 miles of Siberia. One who did was Carl Ackerman of the *New York Times*, who had been recalled from vacation and assigned to the story as soon as news came through that the Bolsheviks had announced the execution of Nicholas. Ackerman, later to become dean of the Columbia School of Journalism, was a respected political correspondent. He was sceptical enough to file a series of major stories expressing doubt about the alleged murder at the Ipatiev House. On 28 November under the headline, "Find No Proof Of Execution Of Tsar And Family", Ackerman reported what he called the "meagre evidence of tragedy", and summed up his personal reaction:

> After my investigation I am of the opinion of most people here that there is not sufficient evidence to prove that the family were executed. There is circumstantial evidence that they may still be alive. The question of the tsar's fate is a conundrum to which even the judicial commission has not found the answer. The tsar may be alive, or he may be dead. Who knows?

Thus, as 1918 ended, there were still as many reports suggesting survival as there were of massacre. But suddenly, as the doubts turned into real disbelief in the murders, the White Russian government at Omsk started a deliberate campaign to have the world believe all the Romanovs were dead. Just before the dismissal of Judge Sergeyev, White officials there began pouring out a series of massacre versions—all at least as wild as any of the survival reports.

On 29 December 1918 the French foreign minister, M. Pichon, gave the French parliament "definitive" information about the massacre of the imperial family. He quoted as his source Prince Georgy Lvov, former prime minister of the first Provisional Government, who had been held prisoner in Eka-terinburg at the same time as the tsar. He had been released by the Bolsheviks, and then spent some time with the White leaders in Omsk before travelling to Paris. The French foreign minister stated:

Prince Lvov was in a cell next to the one the members of the imperial family were in . . . They brought them together into the one room, and having made them sit down in a row, they spent the entire night inflicting bayonet blows on them, before finishing them off next morning, one after the other, with revolver shots; the emperor, the empress, the grand duchesses, the tsarevich, the lady-in-waiting, the empress' female companion, and all the people with the imperial family, so that according to what Prince Lvov has told me, the room was literally a pool of blood.

In spite of its distinguished source, the story had some embarrassing flaws. Prince Lvov had indeed been imprisoned at Ekaterinburg, but he was in the city jail, more than four miles away from the Ipatiev House. And there were no cells as such in the house. A friend of Prince Lvov, who had also been at Ekaterinburg, was to explain later that the French foreign minister had "obviously misunderstood" the former Russian prime minister. But the unfortunate prince seems to have made a habit of being misunderstood. The *New York Times* reported him declaring both in Vladivostok and Japan, while on his way to Europe, that he and the tsar had indeed "been kept in the same prison and had the same jailers". Prince Lvov did not have a reputation as a buffoon—yet even after M. Pichon's Paris announcement, he continued enthusiastically volunteering further "evidence" that appeared to seal the fate of the imperial family. He now said he had learned details of the massacre from "a judge who had made an investigation of the deaths", who had told him: "the chances are ninety-nine out of a hundred that the imperial family was massacred" and that "he had found the marks of 35 revolver bullets in the walls of the room where the family had been confined". This was all a little strange, since we know from Sergeyev's interview with Bernstein, a meeting held after Lvov saw the judge, that the investigator did not in fact believe more than one of the Romanovs had died at the Ipatiev House.

Piecing together the various statements about the murder of the Romanovs, we find that the source invariably leads not to Ekaterinburg, but to White headquarters in Omsk. It seems that irrespective of what Sergeyev thought the White regime now wanted the world to believe in the massacre of all the imperial family—and hard facts were apparently of no importance. On 5 December 1918 the French Secret Service filed this bloodcurdling account, drawing on Omsk government sources:

They [the White sources] affirm that first the prisoners were tied to their chairs, after which the soldiers abused them, especially the grand duchesses . . . The young girls had been abused and raped, and the tsar, in chains, was obliged to watch this scene. After the young girls had been killed, the tsar begged that the tsarina should at least be killed without further outrage.

On 29 January 1919, just six days after Sergeyev had been ordered off the case, the French General Janin, heading the French Military Mission in Siberia, sent off a long report about the assassination; once again, he quoted high sources in Omsk, and now the horrific details multiplied:

Nicholas II was killed with revolver and rifle shots by several men directed by a Lett called Biron who fired first. The tsarevich was sick and hardly conscious of what was going on around him, according to certain descriptions. On top of this, he was stupefied to see his mother and sisters killed before his very eyes. The empress and her daughters, whose attitude in their last moments was very dignified, were killed after having been raped over several days, on several occasions and in various different ways . . . The Lett, on rushing out, is supposed to have said to several witnesses: "Now I can die, I have had the empress . . ."

This fanciful account was sent to the French minister of war in Paris, with a request that it be forwarded to Washington, and communicated to the world diplomatic corps. Since General Janin himself sent the message, and without reservation, it is probable that his source in Omsk was close to the very top in the White regime. What we know of the political tensions in that government goes some way to explaining the sudden stream of clumsy propaganda stories about mass murder in the Ipatiev House. It matters, because after the departure of Sergeyev, the enquiry was set on a course that was never to change—the course that led inexorably from those first crude stories into the more sophisticated but similar version now usually accepted as historical fact.

The supreme ruler, Admiral Kolchak, was a professional officer of no specific political colour, motivated mainly by what he saw as his duty to his country. He had been a loyal officer in the imperial navy, and was anti-Bolshevik, but that did not mean he now stood for the restoration of tsardom. He had been appointed leader with the unenviable task not only of fighting the Bolsheviks, but of welding together hopelessly divided White political groupings. The myriad factions ranged from the Social Revolutionaries on the left to reactionary monarchists who wanted a restoration of the old regime. Mutual anti-Bolshevism was the only thing such opposites had in common, and it was not enough to unite them—internal squabbling was in the end to be fatal to the White cause. With all this to cope with, Kolchak would probably have let the existing Romanov enquiry run its course, if it had not been for intervention from the right-wing. For Admiral Kolchak decision-making meant running with the tide which currently most favoured an effective military campaign, and in early 1919 the reactionary monarchist generals were in the ascendant.[3] General Mikhail Diterikhs, the man who ordered Judge Sergeyev off the case, was one of those generals, and the briefest sketch of his character shows why his intervention spelt the end of objectivity for the Romanov investigation.

Diterikhs, whatever his military qualities, was imbued with religious and monarchist fanaticism, and believed he had a personal divine mission to save Russia from ruin. His nickname amongst his officers was "The Maid of Orleans in Riding-breeches". General Diterikhs lumped together Socialists and Jews as being the root of all evil, and considered them traitors, synonymous with Bolsheviks, even when they were fighting on the anti-Communist side. When Diterikhs' book on the Romanovs appeared in 1922, it was considered too bigoted to be published in England, and today parts of it read like a fascist pamphlet. Diterikhs was obsessed with Reds and Jews under the White bed, and was committed to tracking them down.

THE EKATERINBURG COMMUNISTS

14 Yakov Yurovsky, Commandant of the Ipatiev House—did he fire the shot that killed the tsar?

15 Commissar Chaya Goloshchokin—a secret mission to Moscow days before the Romanovs vanished.

16 Alexander Beloborodov, Chairman of the Regional Soviet—was it really his signature on the coded telegram?

17 Commissar Pyotr Voikov—a drunken "confession", or a faked memoir?

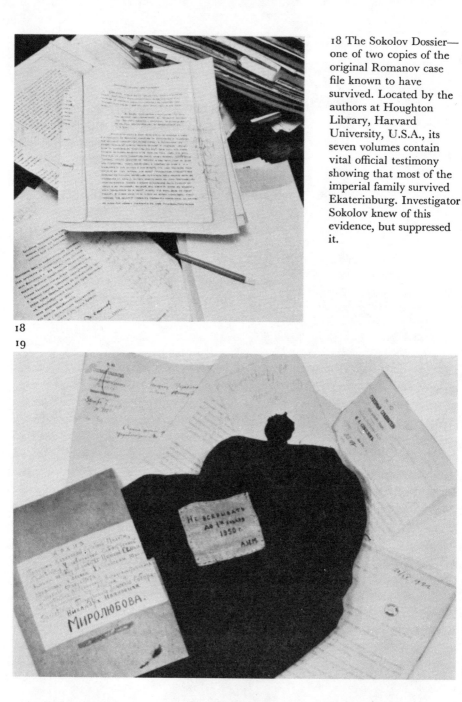

18 The Sokolov Dossier— one of two copies of the original Romanov case file known to have survived. Located by the authors at Houghton Library, Harvard University, U.S.A., its seven volumes contain vital official testimony showing that most of the imperial family survived Ekaterinburg. Investigator Sokolov knew of this evidence, but suppressed it.

18

19

19 The Mirolyubov Papers—two folders of documents, many throwing new light on the Romanov case, mysteriously deposited at the Hoover Institution on War, Revolution and Peace at Stanford University, U.S.A. In 1936 a stranger delivered the papers, sewn inside the black cloth bag, which bears the instruction: "Not to be opened until January 1st. 1950".

It is not very surprising to find that in order to justify the sacking of Judge Sergeyev Diterikhs fell back on the personal smear. First he accused him of being a bad investigator, and when he found no hard evidence to back up the accusation, attacked the judge not as an investigator but as a man. Diterikhs wrote: "Sergeyev, although baptized, was all the same a Jew, a Jew in blood, flesh and soul, and therefore could not refuse his fellow brethren. He fully realized that the heads of the Soviet activities in Ekaterinburg were Jews . . ." Diterikhs suggested that Sergeyev was a left-winger who actually went out of his way to warn the Bolsheviks how the investigation was going, by advertising in the press asking for anyone with relevant information to get in touch with him. Diterikhs added that Sergeyev had failed to find vital witnesses, and accused him of "idleness and criminal negligence". This is nonsense, for as has been seen, it was during the judge's period in office that almost all the key witnesses were interrogated.

The character assassination of Sergeyev makes more sense if we consider the likely feelings of reactionaries like Diterikhs about the Romanov mystery. For some time after the disappearance of the imperial family, loyalists had spread the legend that the tsar was still alive—presumably on the principle that the idea of a living tsar would rally people to the cause. But by Christmas 1918 that story had worn thin; half a year had gone by since the family vanished, and common sense now seemed to indicate that the tsar would have shown up if he were still alive. If the Whites now needed some alternative way of making political capital out of the missing Romanovs, Judge Sergeyev was certainly not providing it. In spite of all he had found out, he was still talking about fabricated evidence, and the theory that most of the Romanovs had left the Ipatiev House alive.

The White generals, including Diterikhs, appear to have lost patience. On the assumption that the family had in fact died, it was now a waste of time worrying about the niceties of conflicting evidence. It was clearly in the White interest to accept that all the family had indeed been killed in the Ipatiev House. As propaganda, this served the double purpose of exposing the Bolsheviks as vicious murderers of helpless women and children, and at the same time elevating the Romanovs to the status of martyrs. The silly statements dished out to Prince Lvov and General Janin may have been the first clumsy efforts to get this black propaganda off the ground. But unproven horror-comic stories would convince nobody for long; what was needed was an official enquiry which began with a definite premise—that all the Romanovs died at Ekaterinburg—and which could be firmly dominated from Omsk.

In 1974 our research led us to Los Angeles, and an elderly Russian emigré called Gregory Ptitsin. In 1918 he was a White officer, with duties that took him regularly to Admiral Kolchak's headquarters at Omsk. Ptitsin clearly remembers the rebuff he got when he attempted to report intelligence information that raised doubts about the Ipatiev House massacre: "I reported what I had learned to the commanding admiral, who said we were all to assume that the tsar had been killed, and hoped that would stop all the jerks searching for him. We were told to tell everyone he was dead, and that's what we continued to do."

It was not an auspicious atmosphere for the final phase of White enquiries at Ekaterinburg. But on 7 February 1919, General Diterikhs announced the appointment of the third and last official investigator, who was to work directly to him from now on. The new man was Nikolai Alexeyevich Sokolov. More than six months after the events at Ekaterinburg, he was now asked to begin "Preliminary Enquiries".

PART THREE

Sokolov

8

SOKOLOV TAKES ON THE CASE

"I here set forth the results of a successful judicial investigation. At its basis lies the law, the conscience of a judge, and the demands of the search for the truth."

(Nikolai Sokolov, 1924)

Nikolai Sokolov was a small, intense man, 36 years old when he began his investigation. He had dark thinning hair above a high forehead. His pale, rather weary face was given an unbalanced look by the alarming contrast between one eye, bright and attentive, and the other, blank and expressionless. In fact it was an artificial glass eye, the result of a hunting accident, and it looked even stranger because it was cracked as well. He had a lopsided moustache which he was forever tugging and biting. He was very nervous, and, when speaking, would rather disconcert his audience by swaying from side to side and constantly rubbing his hands. But at conferences he spoke quietly and deliberately, weighing every word, hunched almost double in his chair.

Sokolov had read law at Kharkov, in the Ukraine, and had gone on to become a "Court Investigator for Specially Important Cases". After the Bolsheviks seized power in his area, Sokolov had left his home and family to avoid service under the Communists, and made his precarious way to Siberia disguised as a peasant. He is said to have walked a large part of the way, and was so proud of his exploits that he had himself photographed, dressed in his peasant garb, against a rustic studio backdrop.

Sokolov was, according to Kerensky, a "staunch, extreme monarchist". He was to write in the foreword to his interim report: "The time will come when a national leader will raise the banner for the honour of the emperor. He will need all the material collected during the enquiry."

He was to be joined in his work by another monarchist, Captain Pavel Bulygin, a young officer who had actually been in Ekaterinburg in the month of the tsar's disappearance—on a mission to rescue him. According to Bulygin in his memoirs, he had been arrested by the Bolsheviks in Ekaterinburg, but talked his way out of prison and then travelled south to the Crimea, arriving in the autumn of 1918. There he reported to the tsar's mother, Dowager Empress Marie, and became commander of her personal guard until December, when the empress sent him back to Ekaterinburg "to make another attempt to find out what had become of the imperial family". Bulygin made his way to Siberia by a devious route half way round the world—the only safe route then from south Russia. At Omsk he reported to Admiral Kolchak and General Diterikhs—apparently by arrangement—because Bulygin records that they were expecting him. Bulygin was quickly appointed Sokolov's assistant and bodyguard, and was to stay at his side for the rest of the investigation. Like Bulygin, Sokolov himself had been involved in earlier attempts to have the tsar rescued, and so it was two committed tsarists who were to work together on the Romanov case.

After a while Sokolov was also joined by an Englishman. This was Robert Wilton of *The Times*. In 1917, as correspondent in St Petersburg, he had incurred the wrath of both the local and foreign press corps. They had protested formally about his reactionary bias, and his personal involvement with tsarist officials. He then returned to England before the Bolshevik revolution, but went back to Russia in late 1918 with a group of White Russians travelling to Siberia. From the start his role was ambiguous—ostensibly he was simply working as a *Times* correspondent, but the truth was certainly more complex. Wilton's staff file, still preserved at *The Times*, shows that he travelled with the co-operation of British Military Intelligence and the approval of the American secretary of state. Brigadier-General Cockerill, at the War Office, wrote to the editor of *The Times* that "the object of his journey is political", and Foreign Office files show that whilst in Siberia Wilton was sent £1,100 through government channels. One of the most famous British agents in Russia, Brigadier George Hill, was to say later that Wilton was indeed a British agent. It is now accepted that at this period, one in four *Times* correspondents were in intelligence. If Wilton was, he clashed swiftly with top officers of the British Military Mission in Russia, so much so that two generals were sufficiently incensed to ask London to recall him. General Knox, the British representative at Allied headquarters in Siberia, was so angry at Wilton's interference in political and military affairs that in June 1919 he cabled London: "I must ask definitely that Mr Wilton be recalled". A Foreign Office communication described Wilton as "inaccurate as to facts", and a *Times* memorandum even labelled its own employee as "not quite up to *The Times* standard either from the point of view of political judgement or style".

Wilton was deeply involved with White Russian politics, and wrote before leaving for Siberia: "I am in touch with a certain Russian organization . . . and thanks to this fact I would enjoy exclusive channels of information." While he clashed with the British command, Wilton openly leaped on the White Russian bandwagon, becoming a *de facto* assistant to none other than General Diterikhs. The two men shared a mutual hatred of Bolshevism and Germany, and above all of Jews, a hatred encapsulated in one sentence of the book Wilton was to write about the fate of the Romanovs: "The murder of the tsar, deliberately planned by the Jew Sverdlov (who came to Russia as a paid agent of Germany) and carried out by the Jews, Goloshchokin, Syromolotov, Safarov, Voikov, and Yurovsky, is the act not of the Russian people, but of this hostile invader." Wilton quickly became a vociferous supporter of the Ipatiev House assassination story, long before the enquiry was over. His journalistic objectivity is best summed up in a well-authenticated conversation he had with Commandant Joseph Lasies, a deputy in the French parliament who travelled to Siberia with the French Military Mission. He also made enquiries into the Romanov case, and strongly doubted the theory of death in the cellar.

On 18 May 1919, the two men had a heated argument on Ekaterinburg station, during which Lasies expressed scepticism over the fact that no corpses had been found. Wilton appeared nonplussed, went away for a while and then returned to explain that all the bodies really had been destroyed—with fire and acid. Lasies remained unconvinced, but Wilton became even more impatient and amazed his listeners by exclaiming: "Commandant Lasies, even if the tsar and the imperial family are alive, *it is necessary to say that they are dead!*" The discussion ended rancorously, with Wilton promising that he, at any rate, was going to make quite sure that the world believed in the assassination story, by publishing articles about it in his newspaper, *The Times*. He was as good as his word. In 1920 the paper published a long series of articles on the massacre at the Ipatiev House—articles studded throughout with virulent anti-Bolshevik and anti-semitic comments in a style of subjective reporting that would never get into print today. In his definitive book on war reporting, Phillip Knightley of the *Sunday Times* writes of Wilton: ". . . he compromised any claim to objective reporting by joining the staff of one of the White Russian generals . . . it is clear that his part in the intervention on behalf of various White Russian elements made his value as a war correspondent virtually nil." But in 1920 Wilton's articles on the Romanov massacre had the full authority of Printing House Square and carried considerable weight. The articles, and the later book based on them were major factors in establishing the orthodox assassination version in Britain. Wilton himself was to work closely with Sokolov until long after the war.

So it was in this atmosphere and company that Sokolov worked in Ekaterinburg. Yet he always saw himself as an honourable and independent investigator who went about his work in the correct ethical fashion. One of his first formal acts was to ask for more staff and for the appointment of some respected independent figure, like a veteran senator, to direct the enquiry. He wanted the investigation to have the correct image of legality—the image that had been lost once General Diterikhs wrested it from Judge Sergeyev. Unfortunately the White military granted neither of Sokolov's requests; the enquiry received only limited funds and later, when he ran out of money altogether, it was saved only by a grant from the tsar's mother, Empress Marie. Although Sokolov worked formally to the civilian Ministry of Justice at Omsk, there was never to be any doubt that in practice the hand of the army, in the shape of General Diterikhs, remained firmly on his shoulder.

Perhaps unaware of the complex political currents into which he was wading, Sokolov, dressed in khaki jacket and felt boots, started work in spring 1919 in the green third-class railway carriage, No. 1880, which was to be his base and working head-quarters for the coming months. Parked in a cluttered siding at Omsk, he began by going over all the paperwork amassed so far, as handed over to him by General Diterikhs.

When he finally published his findings, five years later in exile, Sokolov was to make this high judicial claim for his own work: "I here set forth the results of a successful judicial in-vestigation. At its basis lies the law, the conscience of a judge, and the demands of the search for the truth." Yet we now know that Sokolov actually made up his mind about the ulti-mate fate of the imperial family *before* he even started work. Pierre Gilliard visited Sokolov at Omsk within two days of his appointment, and before he had left for Ekaterinburg. He kept this startling record:

It was at this moment that I became acquainted with M. Sokolov. From our first discussion I realized that his mind was firmly made up and that he no longer had any hope. As for myself, I could not believe in so many horrors.

"But the children, the children?" I cried.

"The children suffered the same fate as their parents. I don't have a shadow of doubt about it."

"But the bodies?"

"It's in the clearing that we must look for them, it is there that we must look for the key to the mystery . . .

So, 400 miles away from the scene of the crime, before inter-viewing a single witness, the impartial investigator knew what had happened, and how he was going to prove it.

Seven months after the disappearance of the Romanovs, with many people still convinced that most of the family had survived, the investigation was now headed by a man deter-mined to provide history with its massacre at Ekaterinburg.

9

THE SUSPECT TELEGRAM

"Tell Sverdlov family suffered same fate as head"
(Alleged Bolshevik telegram, 17 July 1918)

SOKOLOV'S HISTORICAL testament has always been the one authoritative source for the belief that the entire Romanov family was shot by the Bolsheviks in the cellar of the Ipatiev House, and their bodies later destroyed. It took the form of the book called *Judicial Enquiry into the Assassination of the Russian Imperial Family*.[4] From the very title the reader is left in no doubt as to Sokolov's conclusion, and the book contains only the collected evidence for the massacre. The fact that Sokolov omitted the mass of material in his dossier pointing to a very different conclusion can be charitably explained in only one way. We must assume that the investigator saw himself as a prosecutor, who therefore had no interest in presenting evidence contrary to his case. That case rests on five pillars of evidence, each of which, taken separately, seems damning. Taken together, they appear unshakeable:

(1)   A captured telegram in which the Bolsheviks themselves confirm the murder of the entire family.

(2)   The testimony of an eye-witness who said he saw all the Romanovs dead minutes after their execution.

(3)   A large collection of jewellery, clothing and personal effects, found at the alleged scene of the massacre, all of which were positively identified as having belonged to the Romanovs.

(4)   The dead body of Tatiana's pet dog, Jemmy, found at the same place.[5]

(5)   The simple fact that none of the Romanovs was ever seen alive again.

If Sokolov's work is to be seriously questioned, then each of these five pillars must be shown to be hollow. And if they are, then history's version of the massacre at Ekaterinburg collaspses with them.

First—the keystone piece of evidence—the telegram. It was in code, and said to have been left behind by the retreating Bolsheviks at Ekaterinburg Post Office—one of a batch of messages, most of which had nothing to do with the Romanov case. But according to Sokolov this one, when deciphered, turned out to be a message from Ekaterinburg to the Soviet leadership in Moscow, sent on 17 July, the day following the disappearance of the imperial family. Unpunctuated, the message read: "Tell Sverdlov family suffered same fate as head officially family will die in evacuation".

Sokolov produces a photograph of the telegraph form, apparently showing that the message was signed, in ink, by the chairman of the Regional Soviet, Alexander Beloborodov (see plate 27). The preamble, which is not in code, says the addressee in Moscow was Gorbunov, secretary of the Council of Peoples' Commissars. The decoded text shows that Gorbunov is to pass on the information to Sverdlov, the chairman of the All Russian Central Committee.

On the face of it, this telegram is damning proof of the murder of all the Romanovs. Here in black and white is the information that the entire family has suffered the same fate—execution—as the head, the tsar himself. For Sokolov, the telegram exposed a big Bolshevik lie, designed to cover up the execution of helpless women and children. The investigator produced this clincher at the very end of his book. It arrives like a *deus ex machina* to dispose of any lingering doubts about conflicting evidence or unconvincing witnesses. If Sokolov had been praying for one single fact to fit his theory then his prayer had been handsomely answered.

That telegram matters, and we must put it under the microscope, as closely as an intelligence officer would scrutinize an enemy document that has fallen into his hands just a little too miraculously. The Russian language version of the decoded text runs: "Peredaite Sverdlovu Chto Vsyo Semeistvo Postigla Ta Zhe Uchast Chto I Glavu Ofitsialno Semya Pogibnet Pri Evakuatsii." Much may turn on the word, "Ofitsialno": "officially". John O'Conor, an American lawyer who pioneered the re-examination of Sokolov in his book *The Sokolov Investigation*, emphasizes that the word is first and foremost significant because it indicates that the Bolsheviks were involved in a deception. O'Conor suggests the deception is more complex than the one suggested by Sokolov, and wonders why the sender of the telegram did not simply say to Moscow: "Tell Sverdlov whole family executed"; he suggests the word "fate" was in fact a code within a code, previously agreed between Moscow and Ekaterinburg to deceive even the curious code clerks, and anyone else who might read the message. If that were so, and some or all the Romanovs had in fact been removed alive, according to a pre-arranged plan, then "fate" becomes a mere *double-entente*, indicating that the family had been taken to the same place as the tsar. O'Conor extends this idea and postulates that the reason for so much secrecy and communicating in riddles could be that what really happened to the Romanovs was so politically embarrassing and sensitive that it could never be revealed. Perhaps, for example, the Romanovs had been safely escorted out of Ekaterinburg by the Bolsheviks and handed over to the Germans—a possibility mooted by Sir Charles Eliot in his report. That would have been deeply humiliating for both the Bolsheviks and the tsar, and therefore secret.

But even if we adhere to Sokolov's interpretation of the telegram, there is something very odd about Ekaterinburg *needing* to inform Moscow that all the family had been killed as well as the tsar. Even Sokolov admits that Moscow knew in advance what was in store for the Romanovs, pointing out that "the fate of the imperial family was settled in Moscow between the 4th and 14th July, when Goloshchokin was staying in Sverdlov's house". It is generally accepted that Goloshchokin returned bearing Moscow's decision telling Ekaterinburg what to do with the Romanovs. If that were so, what was Ekaterinburg doing, on 17 July, suggesting a cover story to Moscow?

Some historians have suggested that the "extremists" of Ekaterinburg took matters into their own hands, and murdered all the Romanovs without Moscow's knowledge or approval, leaving Moscow with little alternative but to rubber-stamp the execution of the tsar, and then stall over the fate of the tsarina and the children. All the evidence is against this. On the contrary there is ample evidence that Chairman Beloborodov,

who signed the telegram, never took a decision without con-
sulting Moscow first—even on minor details about far less
important prisoners than the tsar and his family. It also seems
inconceivable, given the political trade-in value of any one
member of the family, that Moscow would have allowed
Ekaterinburg to throw away the whole royal flush without at
least agreeing in advance.

If then Moscow did know about the plan in advance, and if
it was important to keep it secret, why did Beloborodov have
to send such a detailed message? Whether the Romanovs had
been killed or removed alive, it would have been simpler and
safer simply to send a message on these lines: "Romanov
operation completed as agreed". This in turn leads to the next
crucial question. If the Bolsheviks wanted to keep their actions
so secret, why was the cold proof of the whole ruthless deed
left lying around in the post office for the Whites to pick up?
This question applies equally to other bits of allegedly damning
evidence in the Romanov case, and it is a question Sokolov
anticipated. He wrote disarmingly:

People who don't understand investigatory procedure always
see things the same way—the simplest crime appears
mysterious until it is solved, and the most mysterious crime
seems remarkably simple after it has been solved. You always
come up against the objection—"How could the criminals
have left such a vital piece of evidence undestroyed? Is this
genuine?"

Sokolov is ready with an explanation for the tell-tale telegram:

The Bolsheviks are human beings like other human beings,
capable of the same weaknesses and the same mistakes. We
must give them credit where it is due. They disposed of the
bodies as carefully as possible. They lied cleverly. But the
Bolsheviks could not help making some mistakes. And the
point is that they overestimated the effectiveness of their
precautions.

That statement contains the seeds of its own destruction.
If the Bolsheviks did kill the family, they did not dispose of

the evidence as carefully as possible—they left a wealth of material at the mine-shaft leaving no one in any doubt about whose bodies had apparently been destroyed there. They also left overt signs of shooting at the Ipatiev House—complete with bullet holes and bloodstains. The telegram fits neatly into the various signposts left all around Ekaterinburg pointing in only one direction—the one which Sokolov and General Diterikhs decided was the right road to travel.

In all, 65 messages were found at the post office, several of them in code. Yet this famous telegram does not read quite like the others—it has an almost literary quality. Because it stands out for so many reasons, because history's version of the assassination depends upon it, we decided to trace it back to its roots.

In the French edition of his book, Sokolov notes that of all the messages seized this one immediately caught his eye because it was despatched at 9.00 pm on 17 July—within 24 hours of the alleged murders. He was also struck by the fact that Ekaterinburg had asked Moscow for an acknowledgement of its safe arrival. Sokolov continues:

It was obvious, just from a superficial examination, that Beloborodov gave this telegram a special importance. He had written the text himself on the typewriter, had signed it by hand, and had not entrusted it to his administrative people to record it in the outgoing cables book . . . it took much time and work to decipher this message. . . . It delayed my departure from Omsk to Ekaterinburg, which caused a whole series of difficulties for my investigation. On the 24 February 1919, I sent it to a specialist at general headquarters, and on the 28th, to a specialist at the Ministry of Foreign Affairs. The results were pathetic. In August 1919, I went to General Janin, commander-in-chief of the Allied forces, asking him to have it deciphered. His efforts were in vain. When I reached Europe, I had the good luck to meet a Russian whom I had known long since to be particularly competent. Before the revolution he had worked in the government code department for many years. I gave him the telegram on 25 August 1920. He returned it to me deciphered on 15 September. He had not had the code-key previously. That is why, given the vital importance of this document, I must say how the deciphering was possible. On 25 August 1920 I was absolutely certain that the entire imperial family had been killed and the corpses destroyed. The Bolsheviks stated that the tsar had been shot and that his family had been evacuated. In public, they were lying. But amongst themselves, they had to say the truth. If, in this indecipherable telegram, they were speaking of the crime, they must indubitably have used words expressing their fundamental thought. When giving this telegram to the specialist to whom I gave the decoding job, I told him, to make his work easier, that he would probably find in it the words: "family" and "evacuation". This man, being endowed with exceptional faculties, and with considerable experience in the business, managed to decipher the message.

So Nikolai Sokolov, the man who predicted even before he went to Ekaterinburg that the whole family had been executed, now emerges as a seer. Faced with an indecipherable telegram, the contents of which are utterly unknown to him, he is able to guess that the words "family" and "evacuation" will be found in the contents. And miraculously, they are.

Now the odds on predicting the word "family" from that jumbled mass of figures are remote, although one could accept this as a clever hunch which paid off. But predicting the word "evacuation" strains credibility to breaking point. Why should this key word appear in an unknown telegram? Sokolov again anticipates this question, and in giving us the answer to his prescience he ties himself up in a further knot. He explains modestly that as the Bolsheviks themselves used the expression "family has been evacuated" he was able to anticipate the use of the word "evacuation" when offering his helpful suggestions. However, we can find no record of the Bolsheviks ever using that precise word. The nearest the word "evacuation" ever came to being used in a Bolshevik pronouncement was the public statement which read: "Wife and son of Nicholas *sent to* a safe place."

We submitted the coded telegram and Sokolov's explanations to a code expert, Dr Erich Hüttenhain. For 33 years he was employed by the German government as Head of Analytical

Cryptoanalysis, and he has extensive knowledge of Russian and European code systems. He is now retired and lectures in the history of code going back several centuries. He too was surprised by Sokolov's remarkable prophecy: "If Sokolov told the code expert that he would probably find the two words 'family' and 'evacuation' in the decoded text, then he must already have known the whole content of the telegram in advance." But Dr Hüttenhain also expressed considerable bewilderment over Sokolov's claim to have been unable to get the mystery message decoded for nearly two years—between early 1919 when he obtained it, and September 1920 when at last, he says, he managed to have it deciphered. This seemed odd to Dr Hüttenhain because:

> The general key system itself had been known for a long time, several centuries in fact. We call it the "Polyalphabetical Substitution" system . . . It seems to me out of the question that either the White Russians or the French would not have been able to decipher the telegram in 1919, especially as other code messages were available in the same key, and that key is quite systematically constructed.

Given the growing inconsistencies surrounding this crucial document, we began to wonder if it were possible that the telegram had been fabricated in 1920, as a late and desperate measure to put the final "convincing" touch to an otherwise shaky case. The mechanics of this would have been fairly simple. But we were wrong. A check in the Sokolov dossier suggests that the telegram was, amongst others, provided by the Ekaterinburg post office to Judge Sergeyev on 20 January 1919. And, just as Sokolov says, there is an entry showing that copies of the coded telegrams were submitted a month later to the chief of White Russian Military Intelligence, Colonel Zlobin. A few days after that, again as Sokolov says, the telegrams were sent on to A. N. Kulkov, chief of the code department at the White Russian Ministry of Foreign Affairs. Sure enough, both Zlobin and Kulkov seem to have had trouble with the messages, and they tell Sokolov the job will take them a long time. There is no record that Sokolov submitted the messages to General Janin. We also discovered the identity of

Sokolov's successful code-breaker. Writing from London to: "My dear Nikolai Alexeyevich," the expert wrote: "All of the telegrams which you sent me can be deciphered. But only one of them relates to the matter of interest to you, and it is precisely the one which you thought would be such, i.e. the telegram of 17 July." The expert signed himself "A. Abaza", and a Lieutenant Abaza was the assistant naval attaché at the White Russian embassy in London in 1920. He succeeded where all the professionals had failed, leaving unanswered the question why earlier efforts to decipher the telegram, efforts which should have been so simple, all led nowhere.

We now considered a further possibility surrounding this mysterious telegram. Could Sokolov have been duped by others who were prepared to go to great lengths to create the "proof" of the massacre of all the Romanovs? Once again, we returned to the Sokolov book for yet another analysis of the chapter on telegrams. We discovered that the Russian language edition published in 1925, a year after the French edition from which we have quoted so far, had been heavily edited. In the French edition, Sokolov had specified when the telegram had been handed over to Judge Sergeyev—20 January 1919. But in the Russian edition this date was omitted. Furthermore, the section in which Sokolov made his forecast about the two words that would "probably" appear in the message—"family" and "evacuation"—had vanished completely from the Russian edition. Instead, in the revised and doctored Russian edition it is now the code-breaker himself who comes up with the word "family"—which is of course what one would have expected in the first place.

By the time the Russian edition went to press in Germany in 1925, Sokolov had been dead for months. Someone else, usually identified as his patron, Prince Orlov, had by that time edited the book at various points. One can safely assume that Sokolov's amazingly successful prediction on "family" and "evacuation" was considered a story that would not stand the test of time—and was excised. That seemed an understandable thing to do. But why remove that date—the date the telegram had originally turned up in Ekaterinburg—20 January 1919? What sense was there in that? Assuming Sergeyev's and Sokolov's honesty about the telegram, but acknowledging there is much about it that doesn't ring true, it is always possible that the telegram was a fake deliberately planted by somebody else. If this theory were to hold water, the *timing* of the plant becomes crucial. The date 20 January, was within three days of the order to Judge Sergeyev to "transfer the investigation and *all material evidence*" to General Diterikhs. During this transfer there was a judicial vacuum between Sergeyev and Sokolov. If there was any tinkering with evidence, then this would have been the time to do it, with the dossier—including the telegrams—temporarily in the hands of the White leadership.

If the telegram was a plant, it was a fake, and if it was a fake one must look for the flaws. It was Sokolov himself who drew our attention to one. He noticed that, strangely, Beloborodov had signed the telegram by hand. Now this is odd, because on all the other telegrams of which copies have been preserved, Beloborodov's signature is *typewritten*. Sokolov implied that this crucial telegram had been signed by hand simply because it was so important. We decided to try to test the authenticity of Beloborodov's signature, and found one other one—on another Sokolov exhibit. The chairman of the Soviet had signed the receipt given for the imperial family when they first arrived in Ekaterinburg. A simple comparison of the two signatures (*see again plate 27*) shows even the unpractised eye that they are quite different. But it is not a simple question of one "Beloborodov" being the genuine article, and the other being a fake.

In February 1918 the Bolsheviks introduced a revised Russian alphabet, in which some letters used in tsarist days became obsolete. The first Beloborodov signature, written in late April 1918, is written in old-style script. The second, on the telegram, was allegedly written eleven weeks later, on 17 July, and is in the new-style script. Would Beloborodov have changed his writing style between those two dates? Perhaps, as chairman of the regional Soviet, he felt he should belatedly set a good example and comply with the new hand-writing edict ordered by Moscow. Alternatively, would he have bothered with such a tiresome detail while caught up in the turmoil of the civil war? Perhaps, though, it was *assumed* by any forger that Beloborodov had changed styles.

We submitted the two documents with their signatures to

Maxwell Fryd, ARCS, FRIC, for six years the head of documents' division of the Metropolitan Police Forensic Science Laboratory. Mr Fryd is one of the world's top handwriting experts. After examining the two Beloborodov signatures, Mr Fryd sent us his professional judgement on a detailed comparison. He reported:

> I have examined these. In the first instance I compared solely the name "Beloborodov" which is appended to the coded portion of the telegram in document 1 [the coded message] and the signature "A or L Beloborodov" which appears immediately below in the document 2 [*the receipt for the Romanovs*]. On the basis of the very limited amount of material available, *in my opinion there is no evidence that the writer of either one of these names wrote the other*. Further I find no evidence that any resemblance between the writing of the names is greater than might be expected between the writings of any two literate Russians of the early part of the twentieth century.

So it looks as though the two signatures were written by different men.

But Fryd was not yet finished. He pointed out that in the two documents that we submitted, there was "no evidence sufficient to suggest that the name 'Beloborodov' on the original of document 1 was a simulation or copy of the signature 'A or L Beloborodov' on the original of document 2". In other words, there did not seem to have been any attempt to forge one signature using the other as a model. And yet, if the two signatures were done by different men, there must have been fakery of some sort. Maybe then the "receipt" signature was false, and the "telegram" signature genuine. Perhaps a clerk at the post office had written the "signature" on the coded telegram merely to identify the name of the sender. But Sokolov insists in the book that Beloborodov really had "signed it with his own hand".

Next, Fryd pointed out a potential flaw in the typewritten text of the coded telegram. His report states:

> This consists of six lines of typing, of which the lower five were typed on one occasion. The upper line, however, is out

of vertical alignment with the rest. Therefore either the roller of the machine was released, and the paper moved between the typing of the first line and that of the remainder, or the paper was removed at some point, and re-inserted in the same or another machine.

You can see what Fryd is getting at by looking yet again at *Plate 27*; the first digit of the coded message—the figure 3—is beneath neither the "M" nor the "O" of the word in the first line. This could only have occurred if the paper had been moved in the typewriter, or removed altogether before the coded part of the message had been typed.

There seems no routine reason for doing this. It is just possible that the post office clerk typed the preamble in clear, and then removed it from the machine for Beloborodov or someone else to add the coded part of the message. However, in view of the discrepancies over the signature on the cable, one must now allow for the possibility that a forger obtained a telegraph blank, perhaps with the preamble already written, and then added his own coded message.

Sokolov notes, rather naïvely, that Beloborodov prepared this message himself to avoid it being seen by inquisitive code clerks. But if that were the case, it would have been non-sense to saunter out of the post office leaving the vital document lying around for any code clerk or White investigator to pick up.

One final point. Sokolov obtained the outgoing cables book, and claims to have found that the famous telegram was not entered in it. He interpreted this as reinforcing the fact that the telegram was top secret. But that seems a rather facile explanation. Beloborodov frequently sent secret messages, these messages were always registered in the outgoing cables book, and that did not mean they lost their secrecy. It would have stood out a mile if this famous telegram had been despatched and not entered in the book. Once again, why omit the telegram from the book and then leave it lying around?

There is a more plausible explanation as to why that telegram was unnumbered and never entered in the outgoing cables book. If the telegram were a later forgery, it would have been impossible to enter it because there would have been no available space; the next cable would have taken up the next line in the log, and an attempt to interfere with that sequence would have stood out for what it was—an addition after the event.

The "Beloborodov" telegram was submitted by Sokolov in his report as a vital plank of the evidence showing that all the Romanovs were murdered in the Ipatiev House, and that the Ekaterinburg Soviet and Moscow were responsible first for the massacre, and secondly for the cover-up. Historians have never questioned this document, but clearly an investigation of its authenticity suggests at best that the document is too suspect to stand up as evidence on its own; at worst it could be a forgery. It should now take a diminished role in any debate on the fate of the Romanovs. It is bad evidence—if indeed it is evidence at all.

10

THE KEY GUARD WHO DISAPPEARED

"He lies like an eye-witness."
(Old Russian saying)

ON 11 FEBRUARY 1919, four days after Sokolov took over the case, a White official called Alexeyev made a dramatic arrest near the town of Perm, 200 miles north-west of Ekaterinburg. He made a long report of what his Bolshevik prisoner had allegedly said, and set off to Ekaterinburg with his captive in chains. The prisoner had been a guard at the Ipatiev House, and this is part of what he is supposed to have said about the night the Romanovs disappeared:

> When I entered the room all the prisoners were lying on the ground, in various positions, in the midst of enormous pools of blood. All were dead, except for Alexei, who was still moaning. Before my eyes, Yurovsky gave him two or three shots with his Nagant revolver and he stopped moaning. The sight of this massacre affected me so much that I felt sick and went out . . . I saw the following people dead: the former emperor, his wife Alexandra, his son Alexei, his four daughters, Dr Botkin, the cook, his assistant and a maid.

These words were allegedly uttered by Pavel Medvedev, a 31-year-old factory worker and the former leader of the Russian exterior guard at the Ipatiev House. People in Ekaterinburg remembered him as tall and thickset, with a distinctive ginger moustache. His testimony, if true, seals the fate of the Romanovs. Three other guards also gave evidence, but their testimony is all second hand. As the only person who claimed to have actually seen the bodies, Medvedev became Sokolov's star witness, and the statement must be taken seriously. We publish here the greater part of it, as allegedly given on 12 February 1919 to his captor, Alexeyev. Although in his book Sokolov converted Medvedev's statement into the first person singular, the original version was written down as reported speech by the arresting officer. It appears here as it does in the dossier, omitting only sections irrelevant to the murder itself.

On 16 July 1918, towards seven o'clock in the evening, the commandant, Yurovsky, ordered him, Medvedev, to collect the revolvers from all the guards who were on duty round the house. There were twelve revolvers in all, all of them of the Nagant type. Having collected the revolvers he delivered them to the commandant Yurovsky at the office in the house, and put them on the table. Earlier that day, in the morning, Yurovsky had given instruction for the boy who was the waiter's nephew to be taken from the house to the guards' quarters next door, the Popov House. Yurovsky did not give him any reason for all this, but shortly after he had delivered the revolvers to Yurovsky, the latter said to him: "Today Medvedev, we are going to shoot the whole household," and ordered him to warn the guards on duty that if they heard shots they were not to be alarmed. He suggested that he should warn the sentries about this at about ten o'clock in the evening. At the appointed time, he, Medvedev, warned the guards about this, and then went back to the house. At about twelve midnight, Commandant Yurovsky started to wake up the imperial family. Nicholas II himself, all his family and also the doctor and servants, got up, dressed, washed, and about an hour later all eleven people left their rooms. They all looked calm, and as if they did not suspect the slightest danger. From the upper storey of the house they came down the stairs leading from the outside. Nicholas II himself carried his son, Alexei, in his arms. When they were downstairs, they entered the room at the end of the main part of the house. Several had brought a pillow with them, and the maid was carrying two pillows. Then Commandant Yurovsky ordered chairs to be brought in. Three chairs were brought. By this time two members of the Cheka had arrived at the "House of Special Purpose"; one of them, as he found out later, was Yermakov (he didn't know his first names) from Verkh-Isetsk Plant, and the other was a complete stranger to him. The first of these, Yermakov, was small, dark, looked about 30, clean-shaven, with a black moustache. The other was tall, blond, and looked about 25 or 26. Comandant Yurovsky, his assistant and these two people came downstairs, where the family was already. Of the guards downstairs in the room where the imperial family was, seven were Letts; and the other three Letts were also downstairs, but in a special room. The revolvers had already been distributed by Yurovsky to the seven Letts in the room, to the two Cheka members, to his assistant, and to Yurovsky himself. In all, eleven revolvers were given out, and Yurovsky allowed him, Medvedev, to take one revolver back. Besides this, Yurovsky had a Mauser revolver. Thus there were twenty-two people gathered together in the room downstairs, eleven who were to be shot and eleven men with weapons, all of whom he had summoned. Seated on the chairs in the room were the wife of Nicholas II, Nicholas II himself, and his son. The others remained standing by the wall. All were calm. A few minutes later, Yurovsky came out to him, Medvedev, in the adjoining room, and said to him: "Go outside Medvedev, and see if there are any unauthorized people about, and listen whether the shots can be heard or not." He, Medvedev, went out to the other side of the fence, immediately heard gunshots, and went back into the house to tell Yurovsky that the shots could be heard. When he entered the room where the imperial family was, they had all been shot already and were lying on the ground in various positions; beside them was a mass of blood, which was thick, like liver. With the exception of the tsar's son Alexei all seemed to be already dead. Alexei was still moaning. In his, Medvedev's, presence Yurovsky shot Alexei two or three more times with a Nagant, and then he stopped moaning. The appearance of the victims so affected him, Medvedev, that he began to feel sick and left the room. Yurovsky then ordered him to run over to the guardpost and tell them not to be worried if they had heard shots. As he went over to the post, two more shots came from the house, and he met the corporals of the guard, Ivan Starkov and Konstantin Dobrynin, running across from the guardpost. Meeting him in the road near the house, these two asked him: "You will have to be able to say that they have really shot Nicholas II and not someone else in his place—you saw him often enough." At this he told them that he had personally seen only too well that they had been shot, that is Nicholas II and his family, and he told them to go to the guardpost and calm the guards so that they would not get excited. Thus he, Medvedev, saw that the following people had been shot—the former Emperor Nicholas II, his wife Alexandra Feodorovna, his son Alexei, his daughters, Tatiana, Anastasia, Olga, and Xenia [sic], Doctor Botkin, and the servants, the cook, the waiter, and the maid. Each had several bullet wounds in various parts of their bodies. The faces of all of them were covered in blood, and the clothing of all of them was also bloody. The dead persons apparently were unaware of the danger threatening them until the very moment of the shooting. He himself, Medvedev, did not take part in the shooting. When he, Medvedev, came back to Yurovsky in the room, Yurovsky ordered him to bring several men from the guard to carry the corpses of the victims to a motorcar. He called up more than ten men from the guard, but does not recall exactly whom. Stretchers were made from the shafts of the two sledges standing in the courtyard under the shed; sheets were tied to them with cord, and thus all the corpses were carried to the automobile. They took from all the members of the imperial family, whoever had them, rings, bracelets, along with two gold watches. These were handed over at once to Commandant Yurovsky. He does not know how many rings and bracelets were taken from the dead persons. Then all eleven corpses were taken from the courtyard to the motorcar. The vehicle in which the corpses were placed was a special truck, which had been brought to the courtyard in the evening. The two members of the Cheka went off in the vehicle with the bodies, one of them being Yermakov, and the other the man described earlier, whom he did not know. The driver of this vehicle, it appears, was surnamed Lyukhanov, a man of average height, stocky, looked rather over 30, with a spotty face. The corpses of the victims were placed in the vehicle on a grey army cloth and covered up with the same cloth. The cloth was taken from the place in the house where it had been kept, in one piece. He,

Medvedev, does not know for sure where the bodies were taken and at that time asked nobody about it. After the corpses had been taken from the house, Commandant Yurovsky ordered the guard to be summoned to wash the floor in the room where the shooting had taken place, and also to wash the blood on the wall of the house, at the main entrance in the courtyard, and where the vehicle had stood. This order was then carried out by those who made up the guard. When all this had been done, Yurovsky left the courtyard and went to the office in the house. He, Medvedev, went off to the Popov House, where the guards' quarters were, and did not leave the quarters until morning.

Legally speaking Medvedev's story is *prima facie* evidence, the clear recollection of someone who was at the scene of the crime just after it had taken place, and saw the dead bodies.

The judicial enquiry also produced similar but weaker evidence. In October 1918, long before Sokolov took over, and well before the appearance of Medvedev, Judge Sergeyev had questioned another former guard called Mikhail Letemin. Letemin had an alibi for the night of 16 July, but said he had been told of the murders when he came on duty next morning. His informant was Andrei Strekotin, who claimed he had seen the family led into the basement and shot while he was on guard, between midnight and four o'clock in the morning. Letemin said he had queried the story, pointing out that there ought to be a large number of bullet holes in the room, which there were not. Strekotin replied: "Why so many? The tsarina's maid hid behind a pillow, and lots of the bullets went into the pillow." Letemin also suggested there should be a great deal of blood, but was told it had been cleaned up during the night.

We also have the testimony of two other guards, Philip Proskuryakov and Anatoly Yakimov, who turned up just after Medvedev in 1919. Proskuryakov said he got drunk with a friend on the night of 16 July and Medvedev had shut them up in a bathhouse across the road to sober up. Next thing he knew was being shaken awake at 3.00 am, and ordered to go across to the Ipatiev House. He found the basement room filled with the acrid smell of powder smoke, and covered in blood. There were also bullet holes. On Medvedev's orders, he and other guards cleaned up the mess. His information that all the family had been shot came from Medvedev and Strekotin.

The fourth account of the murder was provided by Anatoly Yakimov, who seems to have been the source of the very first account of the massacre, back in July 1918. Then he had told his sister, who had passed it on to an acquaintance, who in turn had told a man called Gorshkov. Gorshkov had then given it as testimony to White officials on 30 July 1918—within a fortnight of the Romanovs' disappearance. Judge Sergeyev had dismissed it as a "fabrication". Now, arrested seven months later, Yakimov told the story again, this time to Sokolov. He said that on the night of the murder he was woken at 4 am by two comrades, Kleshchov and Deryabin. After waking all the other exterior guards, they had told excitedly how they were able to watch all the Romanovs led to their deaths, by spying through the windows while on guard duty. Yakimov's tale was remarkable for the detail he provided, specifying exactly where each individual member of the imperial family had been placed in the murder room.

There are many discrepancies between the guards' testimonies, too detailed to go into here without giving their long statements in full.[6] They differ, for example, on the last words spoken before the shooting started; they disagree on the time of night everything took place, varying from midnight to dawn. Two accounts say chairs were brought for some members of the party, whilst another states specifically that everyone was shot standing up. Sometimes the testimony is so contradictory that one wonders whether the speakers were there at all, or whether they really said what is in their statements. One example is the description of the maid Demidova. She is described by Proskuryakov as "about forty, tall, thin and dark'. Yakimov, however, calls her a "tall and stout blonde, aged from 30 to 35 . . ." One does not expect the guards to have had photographic memories, but there was, after all, only one maid, and the witnesses are supposed to have seen her daily over a period of many weeks. At other times, the testimony is suspect for the opposite reason, when the witnesses display total recall of implausibly minute detail. Yakimov's reconstruction of the murder scene is just too precise for credibility, coming from a man who is supposed to have heard the story many months before, while half-awake in the early hours, from two excited guards who had spied on the scene from different angles.

The testimony and its flaws are themselves important, and would preoccupy a courtroom for weeks. But the one key factor is that not a single witness said he himself had seen the actual murders, and only one, Medvedev, claimed to have seen the bodies. In the light of the possibility that evidence was planted, as with the famous coded telegram, one must look carefully at the origin of these statements, and above all at that of Medvedev. If we examine the timing of the witnesses' appearance we see that they started turning up one after the other about the same time as the suspect telegram—when Sergeyev was being fired and Sokolov appointed. Until February 1919 there was only the fourth-hand testimony passed on by Gorshkov (who said all the members of the family were killed in the upstairs dining-room) and the weak version supplied by Letemin (who had not been there on the night and doubted the story when he was told next day). The really damning witness, Medvedev, suddenly appears on 11 February 1919, and then Proskuryakov and Yakimov surface in quick succession in March and April. All three were picked up by that diligent official, Alexeyev. Medvedev's testimony appeared in the dossier at the most crucial time of all—just after General Diterikhs interrupted the civilian enquiry and took over custody of the files and material evidence. New evidence, most of it unpublished, now reveals a suspect background to the whole Medvedev episode, and suggests his account was either tampered with by White officials, or perhaps completely invented.

First, how did Medvedev fall into White hands? It is an extraordinary story.

One might imagine that having been so deeply implicated in the murder of the Romanovs, Pavel Medvedev would have had the sense to stay well away from the avenging Whites. In fact the Whites claimed he did the exact opposite.

In December 1918, while fighting for the Bolsheviks near Perm, Medvedev was allegedly posted to a river bridge in the path of the advancing Whites. We hear what supposedly followed from a previously unpublished account by the arresting officer, Alexeyev:

They [*the Bolsheviks*] took him to the Kama Bridge over the River Kama near Perm. They showed him the equipment installed for blowing up the bridge . . . He stayed there till the occupation of Perm by government troops, that is until 24 December . . . at about 4 pm the commissar arrived with four packages and ordered him to blow the bridge . . . government troops were already approaching the bridge from the right bank and had already started firing . . . he, Medvedev, was sitting in his hut, and had done nothing, having decided not to dynamite the bridge and to go across to the side of the government forces. He stayed sitting in his hut for around twenty minutes, then came out of the hut, with the detonator in his hand, along with a Nagant revolver. It was now already dark. He was spotted from the bridge by the government troops on watch and they called to him, asking who he was. He replied that he was a Red Army soldier. They ordered him to come closer . . . and together with a number of Red Army men who had voluntarily given themselves up, sent him to the barracks near Perm . . . then to the dressing station at evacuation post 139 . . . At the evacuation post he told one of the nurses working in the dressing station about the shooting of the former Emperor Nicholas II and his family; he did not know her name, she was redhaired—the only redhead at the post.

So there it is. Medvedev, surely one of the most wanted men in Russia, almost certain to be executed for his role in the Romanov murders if caught, decided to give himself up to his mortal enemies; and having done that, he cheerfully blabbed all he knew. Yet that is what happened, according to the White dossier.

The detective, Alexeyev, took his long statement the day after picking him up, and then went to find the nurse Medvedev said he had talked to at the dressing station. Sure enough there was a redhead, called Lydia Guseva, and when confronted with Medvedev she agreed that the conversation had taken place. Alexeyev now sent telegrams to Judge Sergeyev at Ekaterinburg, asking him to prepare a special isolation cell for Medvedev. He added, in a slight understatement: "I have important information." And so Medvedev, now to be referred to in official correspondence as "the murderer of the tsar", returned once more to Ekaterinburg, this time in chains.

Judge Sergeyev, by now already dismissed and only waiting for Sokolov to replace him, is supposed to have conducted a second interrogation of the prisoner. Nikolai Ostroumov, an assistant prosecutor at Ekaterinburg, later wrote what purported to be a graphic description of the occasion:

> There were only three people present at the examination —myself, Sergeyev and Medvedev. It was an uncanny, fearful, and never-to-be-forgotten experience. Medvedev, white as a sheet, sitting on a chair by the desk facing Sergeyev. The realization that he was about to die showed on his face. He knew that nothing could save him from his punishment for the crime of regicide. Medvedev, in a low excited voice, told of how the emperor had been killed, the empress, the sick Tsarevich Alexei, the grand duchesses, and their servants . . .

This sounds convincing on first reading, but we must emphasize that Ostroumov's account, written a decade later, was part of a letter designed to persuade a supporter of the famous Anastasia claimant that the real grand duchess had died in the Ipatiev House. As we shall show, "Anastasia's" opponents in that affair were not always noted for their integrity.

The letter hints heavily at Medvedev's impending fate, and the star witness was indeed about to die. His death, like his defection, is wrapped in suspicion. The death certificate in the dossier gives the date as 25 March 1919, just after Sergeyev is supposed to have interviewed him; it names typhus as the cause of death. Now that is, on the face of it, quite plausible —there was a typhus epidemic in the area at the time. But General Diterikhs, who as the man in overall charge of the enquiry ought to have known what had robbed him of his best witness, said in 1920 that Medvedev died "of a heart attack" within three days of being interviewed. Heart attack at the age of 31? It might seem a small detail, but other witnesses tell us that Medvedev's illnesses were euphemisms for a grimmer end. Sir Thomas Preston told us in 1971 that Medvedev admitted his role in the crime "under torture". Staff Captain Nikolai Belotserkovsky, former head of Ekaterinburg Military Control, told a friend in exile that Medvedev died after "I hit him once too often". Both sides in the civil war used torture, but Medvedev's death by violence makes little sense if he really did testify, and if his testimony was true and uncoerced. Commandant Lasies, the French parliamentary deputy travelling with the French Military Mission, was in Ekaterinburg a few weeks after Medvedev's death, and was highly suspicious. He was given the typhus story, and later wrote wryly: "Don't you agree, it is disconcerting that this damned typhus should have come along and just happened to deprive historians, now and in the future, of the only witness to a momentous event which has up to now been insoluble?"

The Frenchman was not alone in his doubts. More evidence on Medvedev's demise comes from the "black bag" documents we found at the Hoover Institution, in a letter from Prosecutor Jordansky to his chief Nikander Mirolyubov, the Kazan public prosecutor. Outraged by the military takeover of the enquiry, Mirolyubov was keeping a close watching brief on behalf of the civilian judiciary and just three days after Medvedev's death Jordansky reported:

. . . I am hurrying to let you know of the most deplorable news I have just received. A short while ago Medvedev, the prisoner connected with the imperial case, fell ill with typhus, and on 25 March when he was already in the typhus block, he died. Before he was placed in the prison, a cell had been prepared according to my special instructions; despite the fact that there had been no illness in it, it was specially scrubbed down, because there had been a lot of illness in the same prison . . . Medvedev died on 25 March, but his death was only communicated to me by the head of the prison on 29 March. I was not informed at all of his illness . . . *one cannot help wondering whether there was some sort of corruption in this matter,* and whether he disappeared or escaped with somebody's collaboration. This is only

speculation, but with that in mind I gave the militia instructions to carry out a detailed inquest, giving personal
orders to this end and demanding a death certificate . . . in
the light of the incorrect handling of the affair by the prison
governor, I demanded through the prison inspector to know
why neither I nor Investigator Sokolov were informed of
Medvedev's illness, and why we were told so late of his
death . . . this is also unsatisfactory because, although he was
questioned thoroughly according to what facts were known
at the time, he should have been questioned a second
time . . .

But surely there was a second questioning? The dossier contains Medvedev's dramatic testimony, as given to Judge
Sergeyev, and there is Ostroumov's letter saying he was
actually present. Ironically, it is Sokolov himself who helps
demolish that testimony. In a rash moment at Ekaterinburg
he told Commandant Lasies something he must later have
regretted: "Alas, the witness died of typhus *without giving anything away*".[7] What then is Medvedev's full confession, allegedly
given at a second questioning, doing in the White dossier?

One even wonders whether the prisoner really was Medvedev. According to General Diterikhs Medvedev was known
as Bobykov when arrested. No photographs were taken of him,
nor indeed of any of the other guards questioned—a strange
omission in an enquiry which meticulously took pictures of
all the evidence, and had a contract photographer attached to
the team. In the end we have only the report of Alexeyev, the
shadowy figure who produced Medvedev, to authenticate the
confession. If it was Medvedev, what did he really tell his
interrogators? The senior American intelligence officer in
Siberia, Major Slaughter, said the witness at first "played
insane".

In March 1919 Sokolov knew of Medvedev's existence and
was eager to see him as quickly as possible. But it was then
that he died, and he may well have been killed. The Whites on
the spot had no reason to kill the man before Sokolov's arrival if
he was actually saying, unique amongst all other witnesses, that
he had personally seen the bleeding corpses of the entire
Romanov family. If they killed him on purpose there is only

20 Autumn 1918—
White Russian search
parties uncover and
rebury victims of
Bolshevik execution
squads near Ekaterinburg.
Hundreds of such bodies
were found, but none
belonged to the missing
Romanov family.

21 The "murder room",
showing the wall against
which the Romanovs are
supposed to have been
shot. But the extensive
damage shown in this
much-published
photograph was caused
only when investigators
dug out bullets for
examination.

THE WHITE INVESTIGATORS

22

22 Nikolai Sokolov, the investigator who produced history's version of the Romanov massacre "I do not pretend to know the whole truth."

23 Admiral Alexander Kolchak, White Supreme Ruler—"elucidation of the circumstances of the assassination was absolutely unwelcome to him".

24 General Mikhail Diterikhs, the military eminence grise behind Sokolov—investigation of alternative evidence "an absolutely useless waste of time".

23

24

26

25

26 Captain Pavel Bulygin, Sokolov's assistant—"I have spoken the truth without fear or favour."

25 Robert Wilton, correspondent for *The Times*—"Even if the imperial family is alive, it is necessary to say that they are dead."

one logical reason. His evidence was not what a certain faction wanted heard and he had to be liquidated before Sokolov arrived. If the military would go that far it would have been a small further step to tinker with the evidence, leaving the investigator with an uncheckable deposition—produced when Sergeyev was well out of the way.[8]

Prosecutor Jordansky's suspicions of the Medvedev affair throw doubts on the enquiry Sokolov hailed as satisfying the "demands of the search for the truth". Coupled with that fortuitous defection to the Whites, the manner of his death makes Medvedev's testimony unacceptable as key evidence.

Another pillar of Sokolov's case is dislodged.

II

OTHER GUARDS, OTHER STORIES

"A series of prisoners testify that the family was not shot, but was transferred from Ekaterinburg . . ."
(Starynkevich, White Minister of Justice, late 1918)

"You will have to be able to say they have really shot Nicholas II and not someone else in his place." On the moonless night of 16 July 1918, that was the reported reaction of senior Ipatiev House guards Ivan Starkov and Konstantin Dobrynin when Medvedev told them that all the Romanovs had been shot. They had heard shooting from inside the mansion, but reacted to the news with instant scepticism, with the feeling that something was being covered up. Starkov should have been expecting it because he had been warned hours in advance not to worry if he heard shooting. Yet he was doubtful, and more than doubtful, for he later told both his fellowguard, Proskuryakov, and Medvedev's wife, who was also interrogated, that the imperial family had been "taken away". Shortly after the Romanovs' disappearance Starkov was seen in the commandant's room with Commissar Goloshchokin and Chairman Beloborodov—both of whom obviously knew the truth. Perhaps he overheard something, or learned from them what had happened, but if so he never told the tale. He joins the casualty list—as "killed at the front". But another guard did give a dramatically different account of events at the Ipatiev House—and Sokolov suppressed it. It was ignored until we found it in the dossier.

Alexander Varakushev, a former mechanic from St Petersburg, was not only an Ipatiev House guard but also worked in the central staff headquarters of the Red Army at Ekaterinburg. He told a full story of the Romanovs' removal from Ekaterinburg, alive. We have it from his friend, Alexander Samoilov, who testified in September 1918:

I work as a conductor on the Omsk railway. In June and July of this year I lived in Flat 2 at 85 Vostochnaya Street, Ekaterinburg, in a wing together with a Red Army man, Alexander Semyenovich Varakushev . . . Varakushev served in a unit of the guard of the former Tsar Nicholas II . . . After the Bolshevik announcement that they had shot the former tsar, having read about it in the newspaper, I asked Varakushev if it was true. He replied that the dog, Goloshchokin, was putting out these stories, but in reality the former tsar was alive. Then Varakushev told me that Nicholas and his wife were put in manacles and taken in a Red Cross motor-car to Ekaterinburg station, where they were put in a railway carriage, and sent off to Perm. As for the former tsar's family, Varakushev stated that they were still in the Ipatiev House, but said nothing was said about where they were going to be sent . . . During this conversation Varakushev suggested to me that if I wanted to see Nicholas at the station I could, but on that day I did not go to the station. However, a couple of days before the surrender of the city I was at Ekaterinburg station to pick up wages and I met Varakushev there. He showed me a train of several first and second-class carriages standing on track 5 or 6, to which, at the front, was attached an engine with steam up. Beyond this train on the next track stood one first-class carriage, the windows of which had been painted black or covered with black curtains. According to Varakushev *the former tsar and his wife were in this carriage.* The carriage was surrounded by heavily armed Red Army personnel. Varakushev told me that the carriage with the former tsar was to go on the mining line. When and where this carriage was sent I do not know, and I did not see Varakushev any more. When the Czechs attacked, they [*the Bolsheviks*] sent us, several units, first to Bogdanovich station and then to Yegoshino where, meeting Commissar Mrachkovsky, I asked him where Varakushev had gone, and in general where all the former guards of Nicholas had gone. He replied that they had gone to Perm. From Yegoshino I went with other units by a roundabout route to the Alapayevsk factory, where there was talk about the former tsar amongst my comrades. The Bolsheviks asserted that he had been killed, and I asserted that he was alive, referring to Varakushev. For this I was reported to Mrachkovsky. He summoned me and *ordered me to say nothing about it, or I would be severely punished* . . .

This story, although second-hand, was told in private to a friend. Varakushev's *bona fides* as an Ipatiev House guard are good—his name appears on the staff list in the dossier. If, as we learn from testimony given by his girl friend, he also did duty in the central staff of the Red Army, then he may have picked up information that was not available at the Ipatiev House.

When the British high commissioner, Sir Charles Eliot, wrote of the mysterious train standing at Ekaterinburg station "with its blinds down", he was almost certainly referring to the Varakushev account. Sir Charles trusted the source enough to include it in his report to the Foreign Office.

Another Ipatiev House guard lived on outside Russia for 50 years, unknown to the Whites or to anyone else until 1964. Then he was traced by a lawyer working on the famous "Anastasia" case, who had followed up an intriguing clue. On a wall in the Ipatiev House someone had scrawled his name and the legend "1.T.K. Jäger, Trient". This identified an Austrian regiment, the 1st Tyrolean Imperial Rifles, and a check of unit records led to Rudolf Lacher, an Austrian prisoner-of-war who had acted as orderly to Commandant Yurovsky. On the whole Lacher was a disappointment to the lawyer. He was extremely reticent, and seemed to encourage his questioners to believe that all the Romanovs had been shot. In 1966, called to give formal evidence at the "Anastasia" hearings, Lacher managed to give the confusing impression both that he was hiding something and that perhaps he did not know the full story anyway.

He testified that on the night of the massacre Yurovsky had locked him into his room, but that he had been able to see the family coming downstairs by peeping through the keyhole. Lacher recalled the grand duchesses sobbing openly as they passed, and then that, half an hour later, he had heard a volley of shots. Some time after that, he said, he watched through his window as eleven "bundles"—one for each member of the imperial family and retinue—were loaded on to a truck in the gateway to the yard of the Ipatiev House. Early next morning he was released, told by Yurovsky that the prisoners had been "disposed of", and was ordered to clean up the scene of the night's shooting.

The judge, on the basis of two full days' interrogation, was not convinced that Lacher's evidence was always reliable. He found it implausible, for instance, that in the excitement of the moment, a man's first reaction would have been to start counting the precise number of bodies being loaded on to the truck. Apart from that, a glance at the layout of the Ipatiev House shows that from Lacher's window it would have been quite impossible to see the point where the lorry was being loaded. There is an oddity, too, in Lacher's statement about his part in the clean-up operation: "I found only a thin layer of sawdust in the murder room. The sawdust *was not bloody*." Whatever one makes of Lacher's court account, it is significant that—like the drunken guard Proskuryakov and his friend—he was locked up in his room on the night the Romanovs disappeared. This is particularly interesting because Lacher was not just another peasant conscript but the commandant's personal and trusted orderly. Whatever really happened in the early hours of 17 July, it was secret enough to be hidden from all but a privileged few. Since all the guards, including Lacher, were afterwards told openly that the Romanovs had been killed, the facts were almost certainly quite different.

Lacher died in 1973 before we knew of his existence, leaving behind him two tantalizing comments. The first, made off-the-record to the lawyer who found him, was: "I can almost believe someone did escape". The second, made in court: "I served the Russians well. I kept quiet."

Sokolov never found Lacher, but he did know about the testimony of a senior Ekaterinburg Communist who threw doubt on the massacre, and he suppressed it. This was Dr Sakovich, who had attended meetings of the local Soviet in his capacity as Commissar of Public Health. Captured by the Whites, he spoke of warnings from Moscow that the Romanovs must not be harmed, and added: "I do not believe in the shooting of the former emperor . . ." The doctor died in White hands, like so many other key witnesses. According to the dossier the cause of death was typhus.

Yurovsky, the man who achieved most notoriety for his part in the alleged massacre, made no recorded statement about the fate of the imperial family. He is said to have been captured and shot by the Whites elsewhere on the front, before it occurred to them that he was the Yurovsky who had been commandant at the Ipatiev House. According to one British journalist, however, Yurovsky survived and returned to Ekaterinburg as, of all things, an inspector of life insurance!

But perhaps the most important witness of all, Commissar Goloshchokin, is credited with a comment on the fate of the Romanovs. According to Sokolov he was pursued but never captured. This does not square with the account of a senior Czech officer, Jan Sipek, who was at Ekaterinburg in July 1918 as a prisoner of the Bolsheviks. He was released when the town fell, and later represented his country in the United States as secretary of the Czech Commission. In a *New York Times* article headlined "Is The ex-Tsar Still Living?", Major Sipek dismissed the mineshaft evidence, and said the Romanovs had been removed from the Ipatiev House alive, by motor-car. He asserted that Commissar Goloshchokin had been captured by the Czechs shortly afterwards, and said: "The tsar is not dead, he is well hidden, but I refuse to say where." Sipek thought Goloshchokin had told the truth, that the tsar was —at that stage anyway—alive. He believed the Bolsheviks were holding him as a valuable political pawn.

The major's statement is unique, and deserves attention. He was at Ekaterinburg, had no axe to grind, and was reliable enough to be made envoy to the United States a few months later. Goloshchokin may indeed have been captured by the Czechs and later released, possibly in exchange for senior Czechs in Bolshevik hands. The Czechs would not necessarily have executed him out of hand, or handed him over to the Whites; they were not monarchists but even more democratized than the Red Army was at the time, more interested in getting out of Russia than in defeating Bolshevism. Goloshchokin would not have needed to lie about the tsar to save his own skin.[9]

So in 1918 several important Communist prisoners were

insisting that members of the imperial family were still alive. Varakushev's statement that they had been transferred by train, and the notion that they were being held as political bargaining counters, was probably near to the truth. That impression emerges strongly from the new evidence we have turned up.

But none of it fitted Sokolov's fixed hypothesis—he suppressed it all.

12

BLOOD, BULLETS, FIRE AND ACID

"There are no miracles in our investigative trade."
(Nikolai Sokolov, 1924)

ON THE HARD evidence collected at the Ipatiev House and at the mine, Sokolov should have been on firmer ground. There is no doubt at all that blood and bullets were found in the notorious downstairs room, sinister clues which should be strong circumstantial evidence for the prosecution. Sokolov's treatment of them began reasonably enough, with a methodical inventory of how much was found and where, drawing mostly on the early inspections by Judge Sergeyev. Sokolov claimed that his predecessor had missed some details, noting for example four more holes three inches up the wall most damaged by bullets. These, he said, matched exactly the shape of the Russian infantry bayonet. He had the bullets themselves examined by an expert, who declared that most of them came from Russian Nagant revolvers. There were also several bullets from foreign guns—three probably from Browning revolvers, and at least one from an American Colt ·45 mm. automatic. There is nothing especially odd about that, for the tsarist government had bought large supplies of Brownings and Colts from the United States during World War I. Sokolov was to publish a picture of eleven bullets said to have been removed from the downstairs room; almost all appear unmarked by impact with the wall or floor, but this is not unusual with low velocity bullets. In 1975 a Scotland Yard ballistics expert did tests for us, firing Nagant 7·62 and Colt ·45 bullets into pine planking similar to that in the Ipatiev House, and found they did indeed emerge virtually undented. As for the evidence of the blood, Sokolov repeated the tests done by Sergeyev on stained pieces of wood from the murder room; positive results on at least four pieces confirmed the stains were human blood. But Sokolov made some remarkable claims about the blood. In a report prepared at the request of the British Foreign Office in 1920, the investigator made these specific assertions: "This wall was spattered with the blood of one of the grand duchesses", and "Near the damaged wall the blood of the empress is to be seen." Sokolov was just as positive about bullets, publishing a photograph of two bullet marks in the floor and identifying them categorically as being made by bullets which killed the tsarevich.

Once he had dealt with bullets and blood, Sokolov did not waste time considering alternative explanations for their presence. Not for him the doubts and suspicion that plagued Sergeyev and Sir Charles Eliot. Sokolov draws the firm conclusion:

It is thus proved that between the 17th and 22nd July 1918 (the day Ipatiev took up possession of the house again) an assassination took place in the Ipatiev House. This assassination was committed in one of the downstairs rooms. Alone, the choice of that room is enough to establish that the crime was premeditated. Once the victims were in that room, with the murderers covering the door leading out into the hallway, there was no hope, because the other door opened on to a storeroom with no exit. The only window was double-glazed, and shut off on the outside with a strong iron grating; and behind the window was a high fence concealing the house completely. The room was a basement; it was a trap from which the victims could not escape. I say the victims, because there were several of them. In fact, it is not possible that one person could have moved about the room so much, and have taken so many bullets . . . If the imperial family and the people living with them were murdered here, there is no doubt they were lured here from their living quarters by some false pretext. Our ancient law calls such murders "foul".

This tendentious account shows Sokolov at his worst, making the evidence fit his theories—the classic way not to do a murder investigation; in the absence of hard facts, the evidence must speak for itself, however little it tells. Sokolov always had useful circumstantial evidence of an imperial massacre. He would have served his own case better had he acknowledged its weaknesses.

It is clear from his work that Sokolov regarded the Ipatiev House of secondary importance in solving the case. He had predicted before even setting foot in Ekaterinburg that the key would be found at the Four Brothers mine, and it was there that he concentrated most of his time and effort. At first he found little more than his predecessors, and Sokolov had to report a lack of progress to General Diterikhs. He then quickly got impressive backing for a sophisticated operation. Diterikhs himself came from military headquarters at Omsk, specifically to oversee the work; and when he was not personally present he made sure General Domontovich, the White military governor of Ekaterinburg, was on hand.

With this support, Sokolov transformed the clearing between late spring 1919 and mid-summer. A special work commando laboured for weeks on end, using digging equipment, ropes and pulleys for exploration of the mineshafts, and even sieves for a meticulous search of the clay topsoil (*see plate 32*). But this search was the second time around, and almost all the important finds had already been made; the ground had been searched, and the various shafts around pumped out, by the very first investigators in the late summer of 1918. Even so Sokolov did find a variety of new objects, badly damaged and trampled into the earth, but all recognizable as items that had belonged to the imperial household. Taken together the investigators ended up with a remarkable haul —65 exhibits to be examined by jewellers, tailors, shoemakers, and surviving members of the imperial suite. We summarize them here, and list them in fuller detail at the end of the book.

First there was the jewellery, fragments of priceless pearls, splinters of emerald, sapphires, topazes, and safety chains from gold bracelets. All could be tentatively identified, and many were definitely part of the tsarina's jewel collection. At the top of the ominous list was a cross of emeralds, brilliants and pearls, set in platinum. This had certainly belonged to Alexandra, as had a pearl earring with a gold fastening.

Then there were the corset remnants, clasps, hooks and eyelets, and six pairs of front stays. Experts said they had been rather grand corsets, probably of French origin. Two former attendants said they were very like those worn by the grand duchesses, and some of the little secrets of the imperial bedroom now became significant evidence. The former nursemaid Tegleva testified: ". . . the empress and the grand duchesses and Demidova, always wore corsets. Only the tsarina sometimes took off her corsets when she put on a dressing-gown. Usually she insisted on this with the grand duchesses and would say that to go without a corset was indecent." In the Ipatiev House, with her daughters surrounded by rough peasant guards, the tsarina was probably not only concerned with fashionable niceties. But for Sokolov the most significant thing about this find was that the stays accounted for *six* corsets, exactly the right number to account for the six missing women of the imperial household—the empress, her four daughters, and the maid.

And the men were accounted for too, in Sokolov's list. There was a buckle, which four witnesses accepted as being very like one on a military belt worn by the tsar. Alexei was accounted for by another buckle, and pieces of cloth from his overcoat and his knapsack; pieces of lead foil, coins, and a used revolver bullet were identified as his playthings.

The macabre list had now dealt with all except Dr Botkin and the two male servants, Trupp and Kharitonov. But for the doctor, Sokolov already had the most personal evidence of all, the false teeth found many months before. It was a plate of rubber compound and gold, with fourteen upper teeth. The denture was encrusted with earth, and Sokolov believed it had been torn from the doctor's mouth as his corpse was dragged across the clearing (*see plates 34 and 35*).

There were other masculine items—a collar stud, military buttons, and parts of male suspenders. And there was also religious debris—four miniatures identified as belonging to the imperial family. One was of St Nicholas the Miracle-Worker.

It seemed an overwhelming pile of evidence, suggesting that there had been no miracles for the Romanovs. It established beyond reasonable doubt that some of the clothes, jewellery and personal effects of the imperial family had been torn, smashed and burned.[10] If the owners had been wearing the clothes and the jewellery at the time, it seemed certain that all had died.

But where were the bodies?

Sokolov still had only the finger and two small pieces of skin found the previous year. Although Dr Derevenko had been sure the finger belonged to his colleague, Dr Botkin, Sokolov and his experts considered it had been that of a middle-aged woman with long, slender fingers; they thought it had been removed with some cutting instrument, rather than blown off in an explosion. From now on it was called the "tsarina's finger".

There was also a small but inconclusive number of bones which Sokolov described in his book as: "debris of mammal bones". There were 42 bone fragments in all, showing signs of smashing and burning (*see plate 36*). The doctor consulted by Sokolov stated: "I do not exclude the possibility that these bones are all human. The appearance of these bones indicates that they were chopped and submitted to some destructive agent." Yet the fact remained that for those trying to establish that all eleven members of the imperial household had been hacked and burned to death at the mine, there were simply nothing like enough bones. General Diterikhs in his book mentions a "completely burned rib" found by the Officers' Commission, but said it had "crumbled to fine ash" in their hands. But Sokolov, the man who documented every last object and had access to all the records, does not mention the rib. He did list "debris of greasy matter, mixed with earth" and declared it was fatty matter from the corpses which, on burning, had melted and run into the ground. The investigator himself was so perplexed by the lack of human remains that he is reported as musing aloud: "Where are the cinders? That is the question; we have found too few . . ."

As the investigators combed the Four Brothers area in vain for more human remains, there was a curious little incident involving a witness to whom Sokolov should perhaps have paid more attention. Much earlier detectives had noticed a name carved in the bark of a birch tree nearby—"I. A. Fesenko". It led straight to its owner, a young mining engineer. He claimed he had been in the woods prospecting just a few days before the alleged murders, and had met Commissar Yurovsky by chance. Yurovsky had asked advice about the state of the track to the Four Brothers, and Fesenko had obliged. In mid-1919, he was brought back to the mine, and sat dourly watching as the Whites picked over the ground.

One day he suddenly exclaimed: "You will have to look very hard!" Pressed for an explanation, Fesenko then added: ". . . the story of the bonfires and the burning of the bodies was all a myth. See for yourself! How could they have destroyed all those bodies and left so few cinders?"

When Wilton mentioned this to Sokolov, the investigator dismissed Fesenko as:

> . . . just a young fool of a Bolshevik . . . the fact is, we hope he will give himself or some of the murderers away. We arrested him and let him go. He haunts this place, and is forever trying to prove that nothing could have happened here . . . He has probably been put up to it by the murderers or their spies. That is why we let him wander about.

Was Sokolov right to ignore Fesenko? Certainly he must have thought so a few weeks later, when the mine operation produced a piece of physical evidence which seemed conclusive to those who believed in the massacre. On 25 June 1919 the searchers found the corpse of a small dog at the bottom of the mineshaft. It was almost perfectly preserved, and was identified at once as Jemmy, the lap dog which had belonged to Grand Duchess Tatiana. Sokolov regarded this as the clincher. As he put it: "The mine gave up the secret of the Ipatiev House." The investigator was firmly on course towards his final conclusions. Now nothing would make him deviate.

The very last pieces of the assassination jigsaw now dropped neatly into place. Two brothers who had worked at the Soviet military garage under the Bolsheviks revealed that the Cheka, the Communist secret police, had ordered a motor-truck on the night of 16 July and had despatched it to the Ipatiev House. With a vehicle identified and a probable trail, Sokolov followed up energetically and personally walked the thirteen miles from the Ipatiev House to the Four Brothers. His marathon paid off at level crossing 184, where the old mining railway crossed the road to Koptyaki (*see map over page*). The crossing-keeper recalled that last summer a lorry had gone past filled with armed soldiers; it had woken him up in the middle of the night, and it struck him as remarkable because no motor vehicle had ever passed his remote house at that hour before. He could not remember the date, but did know that the morning after, villagers from Koptyaki had told him of roadblocks set up in their area.

It fitted perfectly—Sokolov of course knew all about the cordoning off of the mine area just after the disappearance of the Romanovs. Everything else now came into sharp focus. Where the road turned off to the mine it became a rough track, and there, in a deep rut, Sokolov found broken boards and oily rope, as though a truck had got stuck and been extracted with difficulty. A forester remembered that there had been the mark of a heavy vehicle all the way along the track, crushed branches and undergrowth, and wheel-marks going right up to the mine itself. Even the return journey was accounted for. A witness had seen the truck at crossing 184 again on the night of 18 July, and the garage mechanics confirmed that it had arrived back on the morning of the nineteenth. When it did return, the platform was heavily bloodstained. By a diligent piece of detective work, Sokolov had linked the Ipatiev House to the mine, but he still had to explain what had happened to more than half a ton of flesh and bone.

The answer, for him, was to emerge from that treasure trove of clues—the mine itself. Two peasants said that the previous July they had seen fragments of a box or packing-case near the mine, and the rope which had been used to fasten it. For Sokolov the box or boxes had contained the answer to the riddle of the vanishing bodies. He discovered that on 17 July a worker at the Commissary of Supply, Zimin, called at the Russian Company in Ekaterinburg with an order for a large quantity of sulphuric acid, signed by the regional commissar for supply, Pyotr Viokov. Later the same day Zimin had come back again with an order for more acid. Sokolov concluded that it was this acid which had been taken to the mine in wooden boxes, and also learned that large quantities of petrol had been ferried out to the Four Brothers. One witness had seen a metal petrol drum on the back of a lorry parked at crossing 184, and the crossing-keeper's son had even managed to cadge a bottle of petrol from the soldiers in charge. All in all, Sokolov estimated that at least 131 gallons of petrol had reached the mine.

In the acid and the petrol Sokolov had the solution he so

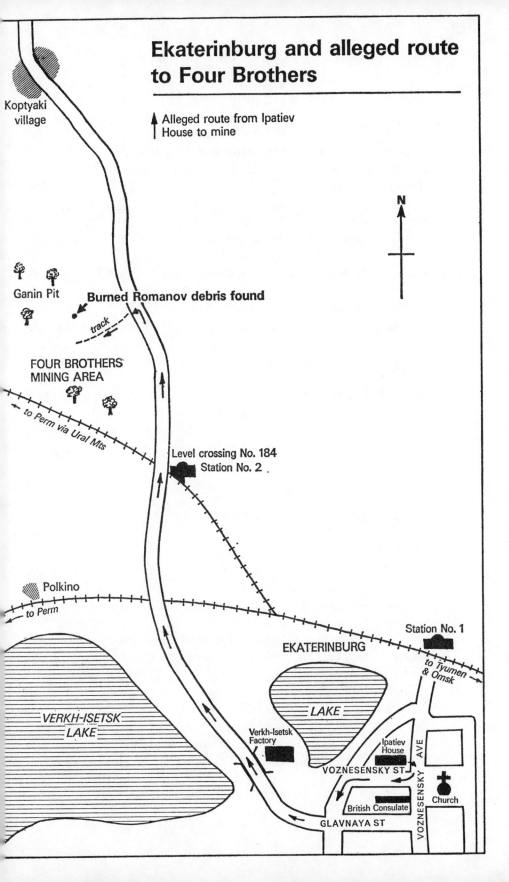

Ekaterinburg and alleged route to Four Brothers

▲ Alleged route from Ipatiev
  House to mine

Koptyaki village

Ganin Pit

Burned Romanov debris found

track

FOUR BROTHERS
MINING AREA

to Perm via Ural Mts

Level crossing No. 184
Station No. 2

N

Polkino

to Perm

Station No. 1

EKATERINBURG

to Tyumen
& Omsk

LAKE

VERKH-ISETSK
LAKE

Verkh-Isetsk
Factory

Ipatiev
House

VOZNESENSKY ST.

VOZNESENSKY AVE

Church

British Consulate

GLAVNAYA ST.

badly needed to account for the missing bodies—a chemical
solution. The bodies of the imperial family had been utterly
destroyed with fire and acid. It remained only to implicate
those who had organized the grisly operation.

Sokolov found a witness who had seen Pyotr Yermakov, the
military commissar of Verkh-Isetsk, near the Four Brothers on
the morning of 17 July. He was identified as one of the Bolsheviks who had been busy shooing local villagers away from
the area. Sokolov concluded: "On the night of 16 July he rode
to the mine in a motor-lorry, in streams of blood. He returned
to Verkh-Isetsk in the same vehicle, with empty petrol drums".
Because Yermakov was a local man who knew the area well,
the investigator decided that his role had been to organize the
transport of the Romanov corpses.

The part of starring villain was reserved for Yurovsky, the
commandant of the Ipatiev House. He had been seen near the
mine a day or two before the imperial family disappeared,
asking whether the road was passable for a lorry. It would, he
said, be heavily laden—with "grain". Sokolov decided that
Yurovsky had not only been in charge of advance planning,
but that he had presided over the whole business of destroying
the bodies. He noticed a tree stump in the clearing near the
mine, one that made an ideal seat for observing what was
going on around the shaft. Near the tree stump Sokolov found
an egg shell, lying beneath the previous year's grass and leaves.
He recalled how Yurovsky had ordered the nuns who delivered milk during the Romanovs' imprisonment to bring
also a basket of eggs on 16 July. For Sokolov that order now
made sense—Yurovsky was making sure his men would have
something to eat during their ghoulish labours in the forest.
In case the lone egg shell was not enough to link Yurovsky
with the mine, Sokolov triumphantly produced one more clue
from the clearing, pages from a medical manual soiled with
human excreta. Yurovsky had medical training, so the investigator decided it was he who had used the paper after
relieving himself at the Four Brothers mine.

It was again improvized lavatory paper which implicated
the other Bolshevik official, Commissar Goloshchokin, the man
who went to Moscow for a briefing shortly before the disappearance of the Romanovs. Sokolov said he also found soiled

27 The coded telegram, allegedly sent to Moscow by Commissar Beloborodov, Chairman of the Ural Soviet, on 17 July 1918. As interpreted by Sokolov, it informed Moscow that all the Romanovs had "suffered the same fate" as the tsar. But experts now doubt the authenticity of the document—partly on account of the signature. See (*inset*) another specimen signature, also attributed to Beloborodov.

28 Sir Charles Eliot, British High Commissioner in Siberia— he investigated three months after the Romanovs vanished. This paragraph in his report may be close to the truth of how the tsar's family left Ekaterinburg.

27

28

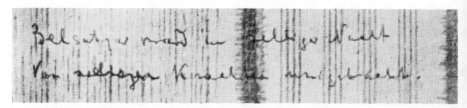

29 The inscription in German on the south wall of the basement room, reading:
"On the same night, Belsatzar was killed by his slaves."

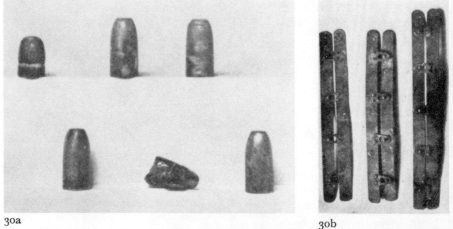

30a

30b

31

32

30a Bullets said to have been retrieved from the "murder room". How many were there really, and when did they appear?

30b Imperial corset stays— the right number were found for six females, but why no bullet damage?

31 Soiled newspaper found near the mine— Sokolov thought Commissar Goloshchokin had used it as lavatory paper.

32 The pit-head of the Ganin Shaft, better known as the Four Brothers mine. During investigations the shaft was twice pumped out in the search for clues.

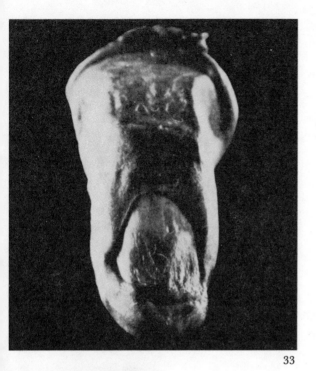

33

33 The finger—Sokolov implied it was the tsarina's, identifying it as that of a middle-aged woman with long tapering fingers that had been well manicured. Professor Camps, Home Office pathologist, in 1972 disagreed totally, accusing Sokolov of "practising the gentle art of self-deception to an incredible degree".

34 & 35 Upper denture containing fourteen teeth, found at the mine— assumed to have belonged to the family doctor, Yevgeny Botkin (*left*).

36 The disappearing bones—Sokolov identified them as human, but modern opinion suggests they came from animals. They were brought to Europe, but later vanished, along with other key evidence.

35

34

36

38

37

37 & 38 Home Office
pathologists Professor
Francis Camps (*below left*),
and Professor Keith
Simpson (*left*) studied
the forensic data in the
Romanov case for
the authors.

39

40

39 & 40 The corpse of
Tatiana's dog, Jemmy—
miraculously well-
preserved after the eleven
months it supposedly lay
dead in the mine. (*Above*)
General Domontovich,
in charge of search
operations when the dog
was produced, was
accused in an official
report at the same
period of being "involved
in corruption on a vast
scale".

scraps of paper torn from the German edition of a Communist newspaper, dated 26 June 1918 and printed in Moscow (*see plate 31*). Since Goloshchokin had been in Moscow about that time, Sokolov concluded that he too had been caught short in the woods.

It was time to draw all the loose ends together, and Sokolov did so with this grim conclusion:

On 17 July, under cover of darkness, a lorry carried their [*the Romanovs'*] corpses to the mine. The bodies were undressed, their clothes torn off and ripped up with knives. And that is how the hidden jewels were discovered. Some of them rolled on to the ground and were trodden in by the murderers, who didn't even notice them—there were so many. The bodies were chopped in pieces with cutting instruments; some of the jewels lay unnoticed on the ground, and were smashed by the blows. The bodies were destroyed with sulphuric acid, and by burning on the bonfires with the aid of petrol . . . The fatty matter in the corpses melted and spread over the ground where it became mixed with the earth. They also burned everything they had found on the bodies. And by breaking the ice which covered the bottom of the shaft, the murderers threw there objects which had resisted the fire, or which, in their haste, they had forgotten to destroy. Near the mine, as in the Ipatiev House, they tried to hide their infamous deed from the Russian people.

In his foreword, Sokolov said:

In our past there is a terrible, evil deed: the murder of the tsar and his family. I have tried to serve my people with a truthful account. So, bearing in mind the words of the great Russian historian, no matter how blindingly clear my own personal memories may be, I have tried to set out facts based exclusively on the results of a strict judicial investigation.

Sokolov, who if nothing else had an uncanny ability for prediction, also made this forecast: "I know the enquiring mind of man will find many questions unanswered by this investigation."

He was certainly right about that.

13

PROFESSOR CAMPS REPORTS

"Though circumstances cannot lie, they can mislead. They may even have been brought about for the very purpose of misleading . . . as when Lady Macbeth smeared the sleeping grooms with blood."

(Professor Kenny)

"History has been ill-served by Investigator Sokolov."

(Professor Francis Camps, 1972)

MODERN FORENSIC SCIENCE has kept pace with technology—police use blood-grouping, computerized fingerprint banks, infra-red sub-soil photography, and electronic microscopes that turn a speck of dust into a mole-hill. Sokolov had none of this. His was a rough-and-ready investigation conducted under the constant handicap of imminent battle, political intrigue and lack of trained staff. There is much in his work to admire—persistence, dogged interviewing and documentation. But because his work is virtually all history has to draw on for its conclusions on the fate of the Romanovs, it should be able to take some probing. To re-examine Sokolov's third pillar of evidence, the forensic data, we were able to call upon a man who in his own lifetime was called the greatest pathologist of the century.

Professor Francis Camps was pathologist at Britain's Home Office for nearly 30 years, a career that spanned the revolution in forensic science. Working at our invitation, he spent a month studying all the available data on the Romanov case, including the original photographs of the material evidence. Fortunately a large number of the original Sokolov negatives have survived, both at the London Public Record Office, and in Paris. We had some enlarged, for closer study of items like the blood-stained wood and bullets. The professor then recorded a television interview. Later, when asked whether it was fair to apply the technology of the seventies to a 1919 investigation, he pointed out: "After all, we have succeeded in investigating the stain on King Charles I's shirt and vest, which he wore when his head was cut off, and also of studying the material available on Jack the Ripper, and even the Sydney Street siege." In this case, Camps did not have the actual evidence, but the photographs were of good quality and the next best thing. We have taken his comments *verbatim* from the recording. First, his conclusions on the tests made on the blood at the Ipatiev House:

Mangold: "Would you accept those tests?"

Camps: "Oh, entirely, yes. The only conclusion they came to was that it was human blood, and I think there's no argument that it was human blood."

Mangold: "Now he says that one of the stains on the floor of the cellar was the blood from the body of the empress. How can he claim that?"

Camps: "He can't. This is pure imagination. I mean had it been grouped, which it wasn't, and had you known the empress's blood group, you might have said it was similar, but you can't say it was the same person."

[In 1918 the technique of blood grouping was not yet developed. Professor Camps's argument applies equally to the Sokolov claim that the blood on the wall was that of one of the grand duchesses.]

Mangold: "And again, he draws a conclusion that the amount of blood found shows that more than one person must have died in the cellar because one wounded person couldn't have distributed so much blood over so wide an area. Would you go along with that hypothesis?"

Camps: "No. A little blood goes a long way, and you've got to remember that according to his report attempts had been made to wash the blood away. Now this spreads it out. I would have thought it would have fitted just as easily into the hypothesis of somebody who was injured, or who had a very

severe nosebleed or something. Because that
again would have distributed it in different
places if he was moving about."

Quite apart from the professor's reservations, there is much
to suggest that the evidence of the blood and bullets was
tampered with, *after* the start of White investigations, in an
attempt to make the scene of the crime look more convincing.
The record suggests that more of both "appeared" over the
months. Sir Charles Eliot, the British high commissioner, who
inspected the house in early October 1918, was told that
some of the bullet holes had been stained with blood, but he
noted: "Otherwise, no traces of blood were visible . . ." This
picture is confirmed by another neutral observer, *New York
Times* correspondent Carl Ackerman. He arrived in late
November, shortly before the changeover from Sergeyev to
Sokolov, and reported that there had been ". . . no pools of
blood, and it seemed doubtful to me that seven persons should
die such a horrible death and leave only small 'blood-clots' in
the bullet holes and small blood-stains on the floor".

Significantly, the blood evidence changes after the Ackerman
visit. Sokolov, who visited the same room in spring 1919,
wrote: "Sergeyev *did not notice* the splotches of blood which I
discovered on the south and east walls." Yet Judge Sergeyev
had been pedantically thorough in his descriptions. Would he
really have left out such key details as blood splashes? If both
Sergeyev and Sokolov got their facts right, then the extra blood
"arrived" between the two investigations.

Again significantly, those around Sokolov really went to
town in their descriptions of the blood. Captain Bulygin wrote
of: ". . . so much blood that it had even soaked through the
floor and stained the ground beneath it. There was blood on
the floor in every room through which the bodies were carried,
blood on the gate, blood on the front steps, and blood outside,
where the lorry stood waiting." Robert Wilton said of his visit
in 1919: "So much blood had flowed that the marks of the red-
stained swab were distinctly visible a year later . . ." Strange,
for this was many months after the sections of stained wood
had been removed by Judge Sergeyev. General Diterikhs
writes of the investigators finding table linen, towels and

napkins with "large thick bloodstains" on which someone had wiped his hands without washing. Key evidence, surely, in a crime which desperately lacked evidence; yet the official investigators made no mention of it.

Even more striking discrepancies arise from a look at the evidence on the bullets. Pierre Gilliard returned to Ekaterinburg only a month after the disappearance of the Romanovs. At that stage, he testified about his visit to the lower floor: "At the time I left the house I could not believe that the imperial family had really perished. *There were such a small number of bullet holes* in the room which I had inspected, that I thought it impossible for everybody to have been executed." In a book two years later, the same Gilliard was to describe the same scene again, but quite differently:

I went down to the ground floor, the greater part of which was below the level of the ground. It was with intense emotion that I entered the room . . . Its appearance was sinister beyond all expression. The only daylight filtered in through a barred window at the height of a man's head. The walls and floors *showed numerous traces of bullets and blows with bayonets*. A first glance showed that an odious crime had been perpetrated there, and that several people had been killed . . .

There are two immediate explanations for the contradiction between these two accounts. Either Gilliard was forgetful, or he was deliberately falsifying one of the accounts. There is also a third possibility. After Gilliard's first visit to the Ipatiev House in late summer 1918, he stayed on to help both Sergeyev and Sokolov with their investigations. If new and more convincing evidence was planted at the Ipatiev House, and if some of these additions did happen during the Sergeyev–Sokolov handover, then a second Gilliard visit to the murder room could have produced a substantially different reaction to the first. Again, just as with the blood, the record shows the number of bullet holes growing as the weeks went by. Sir Charles Eliot recorded that when he visited the Ipatiev House in October 1918, Sergeyev told him there had been seventeen bullet holes. Captain McCullagh, a British intelligence officer, wrote of his visit to the Ipatiev House in late summer 1918: "There were sixteen bullet holes in the wall, and sixteen bullets were extracted from them by the Whites after they arrived."

But come Sokolov's account, the number of bullet holes leaps to 30—almost twice as many as the earlier versions. It is true that Sergeyev, as recorded by Sokolov, is supposed to have counted 27 bullet holes—close enough to the Sokolov version. But how then did the precise Sir Charles Eliot get the figure of seventeen? If, as one must consider, the evidence was tampered with, then perhaps Sergeyev's record was altered about the time of the handover to Sokolov.

In even starker contradiction is the evidence of a man who should have been qualified to describe the room immediately after the alleged massacre. Mikhail Letemin, the 36-year-old guard caught and interrogated after the fall of Ekaterinburg, gave Sergeyev this account of the way the downstairs room looked less than two days after the Romanovs vanished:

All that I heard about the murder of the tsar and his family interested me very much, and I decided, as far as I could, to check myself the information I had received. On 18 July, with this aim in mind, I went into the room where the shooting had taken place, and noticed that the floor was clean; on the walls also I found there were no stains. On the far wall, on the left hand side of the doorway, *I noticed three holes, each about a centimetre deep; I saw no other traces of shooting.* It was evening when I made the examination, and I was in a hurry, afraid lest one of the authorities should see I was interested in the affair. I noticed no bullet traces or bayonet holes on the floor which I examined, although I repeat, I was in a hurry. I did not see any traces of blood anywhere.

The rest of Letemin's testimony is a careful, intelligent account of his experiences at the Ipatiev House. And although he admits he was in a hurry, his specific remarks about the lack of blood, and the three lone bullet holes, have the ring of truth. How could he have missed the *27 other* bullet holes which Sokolov listed, or even the total of seventeen mentioned by Sir Charles Eliot? Sokolov, incidentally, uses Letemin's testimony in other areas, but typically omits this inconvenient statement.

Whatever the explanation for the discrepancies, the fact

remains that nothing at the Ipatiev House can be called conclusive evidence that eleven people died, let alone eleven
members of the imperial family and their suite. As if he too
sensed that, Sokolov relied most on the evidence at the mine
—all those mute objects he called "the very best, the most
valuable witnesses".

We suggested to Professor Camps that these were indeed
prima facie evidence of the death of the family—the numerous
family effects, the jewels, clothing, 40 fragments of footwear,
and those tell-tale corset stays. Before he began to deal with
the individual items, the professor produced this legal parable:

If all my clothes, and my pipe and my watch and shoes,
were to be found in a pile on top of Beachy Head, and if I
were never to be seen again, there might be considerable
speculation that I had died. Any historian or journalist could
easily build a case for my having committed suicide. However, suppose I turn up a few years later running a bistro in
Paris, that would have been just as feasible. The point I am
making—and it is an important legal principle—is that
circumstantial evidence of death, even good motive for death,
cannot, indeed must never, on its own, be proof of death.

Many a man has indeed faked his own suicide to escape
pressing problems. Most recently the runaway Labour MP,
John Stonehouse, was believed to have died after he disappeared
from a Florida beach leaving his clothing behind; he was later
found hiding in Australia. It is less common to simulate murder,
but, as we shall see later, there were motives for doing so in the
Romanov case.

Professor Camps was very dubious about Sokolov's mineshaft evidence. He was particularly sceptical over the corset
stays, which he was able to examine in detail from a blown-up
photograph (*see plate 30b*): "The stiffeners in the corsets should
have been subjected to firearm injuries; you see, I doubt
whether if you fire a lot of bullets into a person you won't
damage something in their chests."

In his work as a modern forensic investigator, the professor
had had little opportunity to observe firearm damage to
corsetry; hardly anyone wears it these days. But his point was

borne out in a shooting incident which took place in Eire in 1974. An elderly postmistress held up by an armed gang was shot in the chest, but saved from death because the bullets struck her corset stays. The corset was a write-off, but the lady survived. Professor Camps was making a vital point: if six women were caught in a hail of bullets, it stands to reason that some would have been hit above the waist; if, as Sokolov maintained, all were wearing corsets, it would be a miracle if every bullet missed every piece of stiffening in all six corsets. Yet that is what we are asked to believe, for none of Sokolov's exhibits shows any sign of damage.

In fact, there is doubt whether the six sets of corset stays were really found at the mine at all. They are not mentioned in earlier lists of discoveries at the mine drawn up by Sokolov's predecessors, even though those lists do include items like the jewellery and the false teeth. And the explanation is not simply that the stays only turned up later on, in 1919, during Sokolov's work at the mine. The *New York Times* correspondent on the spot in early December 1918, well before Sokolov's arrival, did mention that the corset stays had been found, but nowhere near the Four Brothers. Significantly, he recorded the discovery as being made *in the stoves at the Ipatiev House*, along with other burned effects.[11] Dozens of imperial possessions had been burned there in what appeared to be the Bolshevik clearing-up operation once the Romanovs were gone. At the house, the corset debris would have had none of the grim significance it took on when linked to the mine. But for anyone involved in faking evidence, they made perfect material for a scenario at the Four Brothers.

Professor Camps was bemused at the assassins' supposed efficiency in totally destroying all the bodies in their efforts to conceal the crime, and yet at the same time leaving easily destructible items such as clothing, a handbag, and bits of shoe leather lying around.

The professor did not feel sufficiently qualified on the subject of jewellery to deal with this aspect of the evidence himself. Our budget did not stretch to a practical demonstration of the effects of battering, fire and acid, on priceless jewels, but Camps consulted the expert he used in his own police work—Robert Webster, a consultant gemmologist.

Webster did his own research, and he too found fault with the Sokolov account, suggesting that the damage to the imperial jewellery did not correspond with the apparent heat of the fire. He was puzzled by the evidence about the brilliant belonging to the empress. Sokolov records that the platinum setting was damaged by fire, but the diamonds survived unharmed. Webster reported that the reverse should have happened. Platinum is extremely heat resistant, and should only have suffered *after* the diamond had been severely marked. Webster calculated that the fire must have burned at over 1,000 degrees centigrade to affect the platinum, and if that were the case, then it cast doubt on a further piece of evidence concerning the "jewelled cross". According to Sokolov, the cross had "undoubtedly been exposed to fire. This is indicated by the appearance of the platinum and by the fact that the bead on one of the sharp projections is a burned pearl." But Webster pointed out that pearls start to turn brown and become brittle at only 200 degrees centigrade. If the fire was five times as hot, hot enough to damage the platinum, then the pearl should have been completely destroyed. Yet Sokolov clearly refers to a "burned pearl" surviving.

Webster's criticisms are highly technical and may show only that Sokolov's "commission of experts" was not quite as expert as he claimed, or possibly that he misunderstood their comments. But with the jewels, as with so much of the evidence, there are other non-forensic discrepancies. Sokolov reports finding safety chains for bracelets at the mine, and suggested that these were broken off when the killers wrenched bracelets off the wrists of the dead tsarina and her daughters. That would be plausible save for the testimony of the most celebrated "eye-witness" to the "massacre", Medvedev. His statement said jewellery had been taken from the family before their death, and also that after the murders, but while the corpses were still in the downstairs room: ". . . they took from *all* the members of the imperial family, whoever had them, rings, bracelets, along with two gold watches . . ." The witness also described a very careful clean-up operation of all valuables. Next morning, under the eyes of the assistant commandant, "the objects of value were put in trunks brought from the coach-house".

If the Bolsheviks were so meticulous, and if bracelets and watches had been removed from all the bodies *at the Ipatiev House*, then what on earth were the bracelet chains doing abandoned at the Four Brothers mine?

Just as for Professor Camps and the cynical crowd which listened to the Communist announcement of the tsar's execution at Ekaterinburg, the crucial question remains—where were the bodies? Sokolov produced none, but accepted that the human finger, the handful of unidentified bones, and the "greasy matter, mixed with earth", were all that remained of the Romanov corpses. We asked Professor Camps what he thought of these meagre human remains, which he had been able to examine from photographic blow-ups. First the finger, which Sokolov assumed was the tsarina's, although Dr Derevenko said earlier it was that of his colleague, Dr Botkin (*see plate 33*).

Mangold: "Sokolov describes it officially as the index finger of a woman of middle age with long thin fingers and nails that had once been well manicured. Would you pass the same judgement on that finger?"

Camps: "Emphatically, no. I think, as I understand it, this was some time afterwards. One of the troubles about the finger is that first of all it would be decomposed; secondly, even if it had been preserved, it should have wrinkled. Now that finger does not look like the finger of someone who had looked after their hands very well."

At this point we showed the professor a close-up of the tsarina's actual hands, taken from a contemporary photograph. We then asked him what conclusions he drew from comparing the fingers with the one produced by Sokolov:

Camps: "Well, only that these are long slim fingers, with well-cared-for, long nails. On the other one, the nails are broken down almost to the quick."

Mangold: "You wouldn't then make the same judgement
as Sokolov on that finger? I mean, you wouldn't
make any except that it's a well-preserved
finger?"

Camps: "I don't think it's that old actually. I think if I
were Sokolov I might, because I think he's
practising the gentle art of self-deception to an
incredible degree."

The professor went even further, and suggested that the
finger might be a plant, in the light of his feelings about the
rest of Sokolov's work. In any case, he emphasized that nobody
could normally identify a person simply by their finger, even
if they had known them well for years—unless there was some
definite distinguishing mark.

We pressed on to the 42 bone fragments found at the mine,
and presented by Sokolov in a small photograph (*see plate 36*).
Professor Camps examined this under a microscope, and we
asked him whether the bones could possibly be all that was
left of eleven corpses after burning. He replied: "It's fantastic.
I think one must give the investigators one point—it looks as
though they've been cut or sawn. But you should be able to
say definitely that they're human, by proper examination. But
that doesn't represent eleven bodies, it doesn't even represent
one, I think."

An ordinary doctor at Ekaterinburg, consulted by Sokolov,
had said only that he could not "exclude the possibility" that
the bones were human. Professor Camps said that although it
was hard to tell from a mere photograph, some of them looked
very much like animal bones; he may have been near the
mark, for the dossier records the discovery of "bones of a bird"
and another observer refers to rabbit bones being found.
Faced with the paucity of bones, Sokolov fell back on the smear
technique by making the extraordinary accusation that previous investigators had found more bones, but threw them
away! The record indicates the reverse, showing that early
searchers handed in all evidence as it accumulated to the judiciary. One entry, as far back as 20 August 1918, lists the
objects handed over on that day to Judge Sergeyev, itemizing
them down to individual boot studs and buttons. Would even

the most amateur investigator bother to log and preserve
small items like this, but throw away burned and broken bones
which anyone could tell were vital finds?

The key point made by Professor Camps is that proper
forensic examination, even in 1918, could have determined at
once whether the bones Sokolov did have were human. The
investigator complains lamely that "the fall of the Kolchak
government prevented me from having a scientific examination
done on these bones". Yet the bones did reach Europe safely,
and were returned to Sokolov's care when he reached Paris.
He signed a formal receipt for them, and the other remains,
and they were stored in a bedroom of his hotel in the Latin
Quarter. Sokolov was to continue working on the case for four
years after this, so in fact he had ample time and opportunity
to have the bones examined. There were qualified specialists in
Paris. But Sokolov seems not to have bothered—an extraordinary omission in a man so quick to criticize the work of his
predecessors.

The story of what happened subsequently to the bones, the
finger, and the capsules of blood from the Ipatiev House is a
separate and labyrinthine tale, which we deal with more fully
elsewhere.[12] But the fact is that they subsequently vanished.
Veneration of heroes and martyrs is traditional in Russia, and
one would expect the Romanov bones to be enshrined somewhere, sacred relics for adoration by the exiled faithful. Their
disappearance was an improbable fate indeed for the only
known remains of a great ruling family. Sokolov's picture of
the dubious bones was published in the French edition of his
book, but strangely omitted in the Russian version which came
out a few months later. In the light of what we now know,
perhaps there were men who knew the relics were not authentic, or at least suspect, and found it safer and more expedient
that they should quietly vanish.

The total lack of Romanov bodies remains the yawning gap
in the evidence for the prosecution, but it did not appear to
bother Sokolov. He accepted that in two days and nights with
a ready supply of petrol and acid, the Bolsheviks had been able
to destroy the eleven bodies, and destroy them utterly. Professor Camps rejected this, and said it would be quite impossible.
He explained that in his ample experience it was extremely

difficult to burn the human body. To illustrate his point he showed photographs from his private black museum, the first of them a woman whose corpse was doused with paraffin and set alight. The result, although horrific, still showed the clear outline of a female body. The professor explained that what happens is that the corpse first chars, and the charring itself prevents the rest of the body being destroyed. He produced more pictures, one of a woman who had been repeatedly drenched in petrol and then burned over a long period, and another of a body which had been subjected to intense heat in a burning car. Both corpses remained quite recognizable as human bodies. But surely, in cremations, the body is reduced within minutes to a handful of ashes? Professor Camps explained that this is quite different. Modern cremations are performed in specially controlled clinical conditions, one at a time, in closed, gas-fired ovens fired by intense heat. As for Hindu funeral pyres, the professor destroyed our illusions about ashes on the surface of the Ganges, by revealing that it is common for large portions of charred bodies to be thrown into the holy river, creating a serious health problem for the Indian authorities.

Professor Camps also rejected Sokolov's theory that sulphuric acid would have been effective in getting rid of the charred Romanov remains after burning. His opinion was endorsed by Dr Edward Rich, of the US Military Academy at West Point, who said:

In three days [*the Bolsheviks had only two full days*] it's impossible to destroy eleven fully-grown or partly-grown bodies. The fire would destroy part of the musculature, and the epidermis, the hair and the outer structure. Merely pouring acid on them would not do too much damage other than disfigure the surface . . . At Indiana University we tried to dissolve various bones. There were lamb bones and beef bones, and we even supplied a cat for the purpose. And although there was a disagreeable mess at the bottom of the beaker, it took more than three days for them to reach that state—they never completely dissolved.

Mangold: "At the end of it was there enough bone structure left to identify it as bone structure?"

Dr Rich: "Yes."

Mangold: "I mean, would it crumble to the touch, or what?"

Dr Rich: "It was sort of unpleasant to feel . . . some parts remained hard and others of course crumbled."

Mangold: "Are you saying then that one could really get rid of the principle structure of the bone by using acid on it?"

Dr Rich: "If there was enough acid, and a large enough vat to contain them, similar to a cannibal's pot, perhaps they could dissolve them. But you can't do it in three days."

Dr Rich stressed that his experiment was carried out in a modern laboratory, and the bones tested were completely immersed in acid; it was, he thought, out of the question that these conditions could have been simulated in a forest clearing. Even so, we asked the experts to consider two accounts of the alleged destruction technique, supposedly provided years later by Commissars Yermakov and Voikov. Both, as we shall see, turn out to be apocryphal, but it is revealing to see how the accounts describe the petrol and acid routine. Voikov is quoted as saying: "When a giant and bloody heap of human bits and pieces—chopped arms, legs and heads—was ready beside the mine shaft, it was drenched in petrol and sulphuric acid and set on fire. The burning lasted 48 hours." The account attributed to Yermakov says:". . . we built a funeral pyre of cut logs big enough to hold the bodies, two layers deep. We poured five buckets of gasoline over the corpses, and two buckets of sulphuric acid, and set the logs afire. The gasoline made everything burn rapidly. But I stood by to see that not one fingernail or fragment of bone remained unconsumed."

None of this is credible. Both Professor Camps and Dr Rich said mixing petrol and acid is perilous and counter-productive. When ignited, sulphuric acid flares up and gives off highly dangerous fumes. In the mineshaft situation it would simply have burned momentarily and then run off into the ground beneath.

The last and most glaring forensic discrepancy of all is the fact that not a single human tooth was recovered. Teeth are the only components of the human body which are virtually indestructible, and they also happen to be *prima facie* evidence of identity. If the eleven members of the Romanov household were really taken to the mine, there are about 350 missing teeth to account for. Sokolov blithely ignores the point altogether, and only produces Dr Botkin's false teeth—with a flourish, as though they dealt with the whole problem. General Diterikhs, his mentor, suggests that all eleven heads were severed from the corpses and taken away. He writes of three iron drums brought back to Ekaterinburg from the woods, and speculates that the heads of the victims were inside. *The Times* man, Robert Wilton, who had the wit to see a potential trap in the vital question of the missing skulls and teeth, says, on no authority at all, that Commissar Yurovsky took the heads with him when he left for Moscow three days later.[13] But it is the accounts ascribed to Voikov and Yermakov that fall into the clumsiest trap of all.

Both stories say specifically that the heads of the victims were put on the fire with the rest of the corpses. Yermakov adds: "We had to keep the fire burning for a long time to burn up the skulls. But I wasn't satisfied till our pyre and everything upon it was reduced to powder." That statement is a scientific absurdity. In Professor Camps's words: "If those heads were in the fire, you were bound to get teeth left over. Teeth are the most difficult things to destroy." Dr Rich, in another of his experiments, proved the point. He tried to dissolve a few teeth in a beaker full of sulphuric acid, leaving them immersed not for two days, but for three whole weeks. They emerged from the beaker completely recognizable as teeth.

By their very absence the Romanov skulls and teeth have as much significance as all the rest of the forensic evidence. Nicholas, for example, could have been identified by the "Otsu" mark, the skull damage which was a legacy of an attempt on his life years before he became tsar. Even more important, the imperial dentist was still available, and could have identified the teeth of the family he had treated only months previously, at Tobolsk. If they had been found, the teeth would have been incontrovertible evidence that the Romanovs had all been killed. They were not found because, as we shall show, most of the family was probably still alive in late 1918.

Professor Camps' final forensic verdict on the Sokolov report was curt:

I utterly reject it. It is a classic example of a report wholly prejudiced in favour of a set of required conclusions. Those conclusions, based as they are on a series of assumptions, are inaccurate. This document would not be accepted in any British court of law today as evidence leading to a formal verdict of death. In the purely paper sense alone, the Russian imperial family did not die. History has been ill-served by Investigator Sokolov.

14

THE CORPSE OF A FEMALE DOG

"Outside, in the gloom of the twilight grey,
The little dog died when he'd had his day."
(Rupert Brooke)

THERE WAS ONE tangible, identifiable corpse, one which in Sokolov's opinion compensated adequately for the lack of human remains. This was the body of Tatiana's dog Jemmy, dredged up from the bottom of the mine on 25 June 1919, and triumphantly produced by the Whites as *prima facie* evidence. The murder of this one imperial pet implied that its masters had been murdered too. Sokolov published a photograph taken the day of the discovery, showing the dog bedraggled but clearly recognizable by members of the imperial staff (*see plate 39*). For the investigators the dog was the key which settled the mystery once and for all. But did it?

It has usually been assumed Jemmy died with her masters on the lower floor of the Ipatiev House, but a check of the guards' testimony shows there is not a single reference to the presence of a dog in the murder room. Yet, as we have seen, the descriptions are extremely detailed, and one would have expected a frightened, yapping dog to have attracted attention. We became curious to know why it was not mentioned, how the dog's corpse escaped detection in the earlier searches at the mine and how it had remained so perfectly preserved for almost a year after the alleged massacre. Sokolov avoided the first question altogether, whilst his colleague Robert Wilton dealt with the second by claiming that the cunning Bolsheviks had fixed a false floor at the bottom of the shaft, and that the dog was only revealed when "all the core of the shaft" was brought to the surface. As for the animal's miraculous state of preservation, Sokolov said it was "thanks to the low temperature of the shaft", while Wilton mentioned in a throw-away fashion that "ice remained in deep shafts like this one" even through the summer months. Both men infer that Jemmy had been preserved in a natural refrigerator for eleven months and eight days. But like his assumption about the Romanov heads being taken to Moscow, Wilton had no authority for his claim about the false floor, and both men were wrong about the crucial matter of the ice. The enquiry records tell a very different story.

When we located the long-lost dossier we checked all reports of the earlier search operations at the mine in August and September 1918, within a few weeks of the family's disappearance. They are detailed and thorough, and provide a unique technical description of the mine and the extent of the work done. A report by Alexander Sheremetevsky, who organized the early work, makes it clear that he succeeded in extracting all the water from the narrow pump-shaft of the mine, which is where Jemmy was allegedly found a year later. It was not a "deep" shaft—only 30 feet. Professional miners reached the very bottom—and there was no dog. What is more, the records state categorically that there was no ice at all in the shaft, only liquid water.

To double-check, we contacted the Department of Overseas Surface Climatology at London's Meteorological Office which, happily, still has temperature records for the Ekaterinburg area in 1918/19. There is no permafrost, or permanent freezing of the earth in that area. The average daily temperature in July 1918 was 70°F, and stayed above freezing until mid-October, when it dropped sharply to an average of 31°F. That is just below the freezing point of water, 32°F. The temperature then stayed below freezing all the winter months, until April 1919, when it moved above freezing and became warmer as the summer approached again. To know what conditions would have been in the mine during the same period, we consulted Dr Tony Batchelor, senior lecturer at the Camborne School of Mines in Cornwall. Armed with the data we had, and with his own knowledge of mines at a similar latitude in Canada, Dr Batchelor was able to set an accurate scene for the luckless Jemmy.

If we accept for a moment that the dog was in the mine in 1918, then it lay in water for almost three months from the time of its immersion in July 1918 until the freeze came in October. It would then have been frozen in ice through the winter, but would have been in water again for a further two months in the spring of 1919, *before* its discovery at the end of June. In other words, the dog was encased in ice for six months, but free in water for a total of five months. Dr Batchelor added that since the shaft was an iron mine, there would have been a high degree of acidity in the water.

In those conditions, would the body have decomposed as little as it did, going by the photograph supplied by Sokolov, and the autopsy report on the corpse which we found in the dossier? We put that question to Professor Keith Simpson, another distinguished Home Office pathologist. He replied:

> The photograph, when looked at with a lens, shows very little loss of fur. Only the hind legs and the near-bone remnants of the fore-legs seem to have been bared of fur. If this is so then the dead body cannot possibly have been floating in that water for the first two to three months. The winter freezing would preserve such conditions as were developed at the end of this first period—but by this time the hair should have loosened and come away. In man, these changes require only ten days to a fortnight in spring or autumn, less in summer. The head of a man or woman whose dead body has been immersed looks more like that of Yul Brynner or Kojak at the end of two or three weeks. No dog could retain such hair as this photo shows at the end of two to three months in cold water. Then, after freezing, to add another two months in water is in my view quite inconsistent with this picture.

The autopsy report, provided by an Ekaterinburg vet, said "the lungs, which survived intact, are a green colour". Professor Simpson said this would fit the description of the chest contents after only a week or two. He added that the description of the heart—"of normal size and density . . . ventricles empty"—was quite inconsistent with a heart dead for a year. It would become soft and slimy within a week. The professor wholly rejected the information that stomach, intestines, liver and spleen were all in normal condition. They are the first to soften and disintegrate, usually within a few days. Finally, he pointed out that the natural acidity in the water would actually have accelerated decomposition.

In other words, it would have been impossible for Jemmy's body to have survived so well in its watery grave for a year. What are we to make of this? If, as the forensic evidence implies, the dog was found when it had only been dead for a matter of days, then it must have been planted—almost a year after the disappearance of the Romanovs. But how, and by whom?

It is quite plausible that Jemmy should have been on hand in 1919, still alive and available for the deception. Another Romanov pet, Alexei's spaniel, Joy, was taken from the Ipatiev House alive and was recognized many months later, running around in the street. It was retrieved by an officer serving with the British Military Mission and taken back to England where it lived for several years on a farm near Windsor. If one dog was spared by the Bolsheviks, there is no reason why the same should not have happened to the other dog, Jemmy. We can even hazard a guess as to who might have been behind the planting.

In June 1919, when the dog was found, General Domontovich, the White military governor of Ekaterinburg, was in charge of the mine operation during the temporary absence of General Diterikhs (*see plate 40*). We are told so by Robert Wilton, who wrote: "When good Domontovich made this discovery he immediately telegraphed to us." Little else is known about Domontovich's role in the Romanov enquiry, but he emerges tarnished from a report on other matters. Prosecutor Jordansky, whose letters we found with the "black bag" documents in California, was not only concerned with sharp practice in the Romanov case. In one of his long reports he tells how the Czech general Rudolf Gaida commissioned him to mount an enquiry into bribery and corruption amongst high White officials: ". . . material came to light bearing witness to the huge malpractices of the . . . Commander-in-Chief General Domontovich." When Jordansky reported his findings to Gaida, it came as no surprise. The general, as a foreigner attached to the White forces, had to play a delicate diplomatic game, and he had wanted a White official to confirm what he already knew from his own men. Now, as he sat talking with Prosecutor Jordansky, Gaida "pulled from his desk an intelligence report by Czech Intelligence about corruption on a vast scale involving Regional Controller Postnikov, and Domontovich . . . handing me this report, he begged me to look after the enquiry into this corruption, being very careful to keep it a secret." It is not the best character reference for "good Domontovich", the man who produced Jemmy's corpse. He was close to General Diterikhs, in charge of the Four Brothers search operation, and thus in a position to fake evidence. What is more, June 1919 was the very moment the investigators needed some kind of clincher. After a year's work they were still plagued with a total absence of Romanov bodies. Time was running out—the Whites were now retreating in the Urals; because of the Bolshevik advance, Sokolov left Ekaterinburg within a fortnight of the dog being "discovered". The planting of the dog would have been a well-timed inspiration.

But what were the motives for such devious behaviour, and who benefited—the Bolsheviks or the Whites? The answer may be that both sides, at different times, stood to gain from consolidating the massacre myth. We now present a hypothesis to account for it—complex, but plausible in the light of the evidence.

The Bolsheviks removed almost all the Romanovs from Ekaterinburg alive, for pressing political reasons which will become clear later. Like Judge Sergeyev and Sir Charles Eliot we think only the imperial servants were killed at the Ipatiev House, and it was their bodies that were disposed of at the mine. The fact that Dr Botkin's dentures were found there suggests that he was a victim—it is unlikely that anything but violence would separate a man from his false teeth in the way suggested by the evidence. And other instances show that the Bolsheviks had no compunction in killing members of the imperial suite; it was in line with their policy of eliminating all supporters of the old regime. But once the imperial family had been transferred alive, there were cogent reasons for leaving the strong impression that they had actually been executed. In July 1918 Communist forces in the Urals were in serious trouble, and the anti-Bolshevik armies—combined

Czech and White forces—were advancing rapidly. When they took Ekaterinburg they first swept straight on through the town, in hot pursuit of the retreating Bolsheviks. Then they faltered, and paused to regroup. If the Whites had known that members of the imperial family were alive, and almost within their grasp, they might have pressed home the attack even more vigorously in an effort to rescue them. So the Ekaterinburg commissars had good strategic reasons to mount a murder scenario. It was after all not difficult. There was the empty Ipatiev House, with its sinister lower floor; and it was easy enough to suggest that the imperial corpses had been butchered and burned at the Four Brothers.

At first the Bolsheviks may have hoped to deceive the Whites by making the bodies of the four servants unrecognizable, and surrounding the remains with charred Romanov possessions. But a snag cropped up when the operation was already under way. More bodies were needed—four were not enough grave fodder to suggest the death of eleven people. There was of course no shortage of dead bodies in Ekaterinburg in summer 1918—"counter-revolutionaries" were being shot in droves every night.

It has always been assumed that no human corpses at all were found in the Four Brothers area, but that is untrue. Assistant Prosecutor Magnitsky, the officer who led the very first searches in the forest, says clearly in his report: ". . . information was checked as far as our means and manpower allowed . . . we found five corpses in the old mines, but all belonged to Austrians." Five human bodies discovered in the woods—a fact unforgivably omitted by Sokolov but saved from oblivion by the report made at the time. One is entitled to ask why he made no mention of these bodies. We know there were Austrians and Hungarians serving in the Ipatiev House inner guard, former prisoners-of-war co-opted into the Bolshevik secret police. Could it be that the five dead men were members of Yurovsky's guard detachment? It would have made a brutal kind of sense, providing extra bodies and at the same time silencing for ever some of those who knew what had really happened the night the family disappeared.

But whilst stand-ins for the Romanov corpses were available, a second weakness may have quickly become apparent as the operation progressed. Even when the bodies of the servants were butchered and burned, it must have become uncomfortably obvious that they were still recognizable to any competent detective. Or rather, they were certainly not going to pass muster as the corpses of the imperial family. The commissars in charge, Yurovsky and Goloshchokin, were just the men to appreciate this drawback. The first had medical training and the second was a dentist, and both must have realized that skulls and teeth are a primary guide to identification, especially when the alleged victims are the most medically pampered and monitored family in the land. The answer was to take away the heads of the real victims so that the deception would not be immediately obvious. After all, what possible reason could there be for wasting time on the messy business of butchering, burning and making unrecognizable the imperial servants, whose bodies had no political or religious value at all?

In the event, hardly any human remains were left behind. It may be that almost everything was removed, and the bodies of the five Austrians were jettisoned still intact. In the knowledge that a finger and false teeth do not make a massacre, the Bolsheviks now boosted the scenario as much as possible. Romanov clothes were available, because the family had been transferred in other clothing that would make them less conspicuous. So imperial clothes were ripped up and burned, and the jewellery inside them left lying around to advertise the identity of the owners even more blatantly. They had been brought from the Ipatiev House, along with other items from the large imperial wardrobe. That, incidentally, explains for the first time the presence at the mine of items which never matched the guards' testimony that on the murder night the Romanovs were dressed in indoor clothes, and not expecting to travel. For pieces of *outdoor* gear—overcoats, knapsacks and so on—were amongst the debris found. All these things were left in a highly recognizable mass of imperial litter, announcing to all the world exactly who had been "killed".

One must dismiss once and for all the notion that the Communists tried to hide what they had done. They made their operation as obvious as possible, creating a rumpus in the neighbourhood and ensuring that the locals would come and take a look as soon as the Bolsheviks had left. And so they did

—the first peasants who arrived saw the priceless debris, with the empress's emerald-studded cross headlining what had happened, and they hurried off to tell the Whites in Ekaterinburg.

For the Bolsheviks, according to our theory, it was only a holding device until the dust settled on the military situation. The scenario did not even satisfy some of the first investigators, like Captain Malinovsky with his deduction: ". . . I became convinced that the imperial family was alive. It appeared to me that the Bolsheviks had shot someone in the room in order to simulate the murder of the imperial family, taken them away during the night along the road to Koptyaki, also with the purpose of simulating a murder . . ." And months later, even after hearing "confessions", Judge Sergeyev thought the same.

But at Christmas 1918 the business of deception took a turn which must have amused the Bolsheviks. The White government at Omsk assumed, with some reason, that the Romanovs were dead—because they had not been heard of for almost half a year. General Diterikhs and his monarchist colleagues now decided to use the situation to their own advantage in the only way possible, as propaganda against the Communists. They therefore started pouring out gory stories of how the defenceless imperial family had been massacred. But they had no hard evidence to back up the melodramatic details, and the current investigator, Judge Sergeyev, remained inconveniently doubtful. So in January 1919 the White leaders replaced him with Sokolov, a man who could be steered into producing the required conclusions. Although Sokolov himself may have been only an enthusiastic dupe, the facts were now twisted to satisfy the premise; where good evidence was lacking, clues were planted.

A judicial enquiry became a political charade, and truth utterly irrelevant.

15

THE END OF SOKOLOV

"The knights are dust, and their good swords rust,
Their souls are with the saints, we trust."
(Russian poem quoted by Captain Bulygin, 1919)

IN LATE SUMMER 1919, the military situation forced Sokolov to close down his investigation at Ekaterinburg; his departure was a sorry affair. There had been embarrassing
interruptions to his labours, and one military man noted: "At
the slightest rumour that the Bolsheviks were marching towards
Ekaterinburg, Sokolov packed his valise and dashed off to
Omsk. Then we had to catch him and send him back to
Ekaterinburg. I can't tell you how much time was wasted in
this manner." There had been unseemly squabbling between
the investigator and General Diterikhs, suggesting that even
Sokolov was not tame enough for the general. Some documents imply that Sokolov, like his predecessors, was even dismissed at one stage. Certainly the regional prosecutor wrote to
Admiral Kolchak, the head of the White regime, asking him
to use his authority to reinstate the investigator.

Sokolov finally left Ekaterinburg in the second week of July
1919. He went first to White headquarters at Omsk and stayed
there about a month. Then he called it a day, and set off by
train, with his evidence packed into a private railway carriage,
for the Far East. His faithful shadow, Captain Bulygin, describes the scene:

We drank tea and discussed literature, particularly poetry.
I myself contributed the verse which stands as an epitaph to
this chapter:
        The knights are dust,
        And their good swords rust,
        Their souls are with the saints, we trust . . .

Sokolov, who was sitting on the sofa, in semi-darkness, raised his head, dishevelled as usual from his habit of running his fingers through the dark, thinning hair.

"What is it, Pavel Petrovich?" he said. "By whom? Read it out again, please."

I did so. For a few moments there was silence.

"How beautiful . . ." said Sokolov.

On his way to the Far East, Sokolov stopped at Chita, headquarters of Ataman Semyonov, a White warlord who was a law unto himself in the territory he controlled. Here he ran into accusations that he was purposely concealing information that the tsar was still alive; he met such great hostility that he thought his life was in danger, and Sokolov eventually left in a panic, helped by a British officer, Captain Bainsmith, whom we traced in 1975 in Cornwall. Captain Bainsmith recalls arranging a special train to remove the investigator, who was by then "in a very nervous and apprehensive state of mind".

About this time, Sokolov's dossier and his precious relics—the tiny collection of human debris, the jewellery, and the tattered imperial clothing—also began their precarious journey out of Russia. General Diterikhs forcibly took them away from Sokolov at Chita, an act resulting in an open breach between the two men. Bulygin wrote later:

> Sokolov flared up. His nerves by this time were in a terrible state, and he seemed to think it was a plot to isolate him from the records. I rushed back to General Diterikhs and he gave me a letter for Sokolov, inviting him to go. My chief, however, was too angry to listen to reason; he tore up the letter without reading it and said he was sorry to see me made an instrument of the general's wrongful actions . . . but the safety of the records had to come before all else.

Sokolov was perhaps right to fear a plot concerning the records. British diplomatic records show that Diterikhs held the volumes of evidence "ready bound and prepared but neither signed nor sealed". It was an ideal time for interference with the dossier. Diterikhs also had a small despatch box covered in mauve leather, which had once belonged to the tsarina. With great emotion he informed visitors that the box contained the "Great National Sacred Relics"—the charred remains found at the Four Brothers. This box was eventually handed over for safe-keeping to the British chargé d'affaires in the area, Miles Lampson, who in turn passed it to the American consul-general in Siberia. The American carried it across the far east in his railway compartment—"a wooden box tied up hastily with rope like an immigrant's luggage". He kept it under the dining-table, and refused to tell other passengers what it contained. At Harbin, Sokolov caught up with his boxes and for a while there was talk of him travelling with his evidence to England. When the Foreign Office took a long time deciding whether to grant him a visa, Lampson cabled: "Sokolov is getting restive at the absence of any reply and states that he is in danger from German agents . . . Sokolov's letter seems to me somewhat hysterical . . . I am tempted to think he has German machinations on the brain." In the event Britain refused, and Foreign Office correspondence shows a callous eagerness on the part of King George V to dissociate himself even from the last remains of his friend and cousin. An official notes: "It would be a source of great embarrassment to have that despatch box in England, and the King spoke to me about it the other day. If it is handed over to a suitable Russian we shall be well quit of it."

As we shall see in a later chapter, this is in line with the king's extraordinary attitude to the fate of the Romanovs, one which has never been satisfactorily explained. As for the relics, strong clues suggest they were delivered to the British royal family after all. Sir Thomas Preston has said that he learned direct from the king that at one stage they were sent from Paris to England. Sir Thomas was received in audience in February 1921, and quotes the king as saying: "The relics were in such a state that they had to be fumigated before they could be touched." The strangest information of all about the Romanov remains and the British royal family came to us from a former diplomat who was a close friend of the late Miles Lampson. He says that, according to Lampson, King George seemed totally ungrateful when the remains were brought to him, and begged Lampson to "get rid of them somehow". At his own request we are not naming Lampson's friend, but he is a life peer and a much respected academic. The explanation may lie in a comment Lampson made to his son-in-law, Lord Eliot. He says Lampson spoke of bringing home "the *alleged* remains of the tsarist family (including dog). *He had doubts.*" Lampson talked of the possibility that the box contained only the remains of the imperial servants—not of the Romanovs. That is in line with our own theory, and might explain the king's lack of interest.

By 1921, some three years after the disappearance of the Romanovs, Sokolov was in exile, installed at the Hotel du Bon Lafontaine in the Latin Quarter of Paris. With him in the same hotel were the trusty Captain Bulygin, and Pierre Gilliard. Robert Wilton, who had accompanied Sokolov out of Russia, also moved to Paris. This foursome now co-operated on the last stages of the enquiry—it is no coincidence that, along with General Diterikhs, all of them were to produce books retailing the orthodox version of the murder of the imperial family.

Even in Paris Sokolov continued to encounter doubt and disbelief. People continued to frustrate him by still believing stories that the imperial family had been rescued. Bulygin records: ". . . they began to imagine that we had all been sent to Europe by the tsar's rescuers to stage an elaborate pretence, to distract Moscow's attention, and enable the captives to escape . . ."

Nevertheless, Sokolov pushed on indefatigably with what had now become his life's work. He interviewed anyone in Europe who might be able to fill in the gaps in the picture —monarchists, military leaders, and Russian politicians in exile. Some of those Sokolov wished to talk to did not want to talk to him, notably the lady-in-waiting Baroness Buxhoeveden. Together with the two Romanov tutors, and Dr Derevenko, the baroness had had frequent contacts with foreign diplomats in Ekaterinburg in the summer of 1918, discussing ways of helping the imprisoned Romanovs. Others frustrated Sokolov with inadequate answers, or answers that did not meet with his approval. He had trouble with former members of the Russian Provisional Government, and claimed that "Kerensky and the senators" were trying to muddle him up.

By 1923 Sokolov was still in Paris, his report still unpublished.

However, he had found a patron in the shape of Prince Nikolai Orlov, another Russian monarchist in exile, related by marriage to the imperial family. Orlov encouraged the investigator with hard cash and goodwill, and provided him with an apartment on his estate at Fontainebleau.

October that year marked the start of the final bizarre chapter in Sokolov's life. In an American naval intelligence file, of all places, we found the ignoble story of how Sokolov met Henry Ford, the American automobile tycoon. In the United States Henry Ford was defending a lawsuit for antisemitism brought against him by a Zionist group including, coincidentally, Herman Bernstein, the journalist who had reported from Ekaterinburg in 1918. Ford was first approached by Boris Brasol, chairman of the Russian National Society, and advised that Sokolov and his researches could be useful. According to the American intelligence files, only declassified in 1972, the Sokolov enquiry

. . . showed conclusively that the murder of the imperial family was instigated by Jews and the actual killing was done by a group of men composed, with the exception of three, entirely of Jews . . . it appears that Brasol knew of the existence of this file and knowing Henry Ford's attitude towards the Jews and his unlimited means, he apparently conceived the idea of telling Ford about it, knowing that Ford would use it as anti-Jewish propaganda, and at the same time, the monarchist factions would get a tremendous amount of publicity throughout the world, including Russia.

This chicanery appealed to Ford, and one of his executives was sent on a special assignment in Europe to recruit Sokolov and check out his documents. There was a meeting in a Paris flat between Sokolov's patron, Prince Orlov, an American colonel called Lydig, and a former *Times* correspondent called Fullerton. Lydig told the Ford man that they shared a mutual attitude towards the Jews, and hoped Ford would see to it that Sokolov's work was published in America. The party went off to see Sokolov at Fontainebleau, and he agreed to become involved. Ford invited the investigator to America, all expenses paid, and Sokolov and his patron set sail for the United States.

On arrival in Boston, both Sokolov and Orlov talked to the press. The prince claimed he had "come to the United States with the idea of forming a possible connection with some automobile concern". That connection was made shortly afterwards at Ford headquarters in Dearborn, Michigan, when the Russian party met Henry Ford himself. According to the US intelligence report there was a dramatic interruption at a crucial moment in the negotiations:

> At the very moment at Dearborn when Henry Ford was interviewing Judge [sic] Sokolov and the Orlovs, he received a letter addressed to him from the Grand Duke Nikolai, who stated that the bearer had information of the utmost importance. Henry Ford stepped out into the anteroom, where he met one named Borodigan, who was instructed by the grand duke to inform Henry Ford that he had heard the secret documents referred to were to be turned over to Ford, and he wished to inform him that they were *entirely spurious*. Ford thanked him for his information and nothing more was said about having received them, or that he was in conference with Sokolov and the Orlovs.

This odd incident is later explained by Boris Brasol, in the American report, as a result of Grand Duke Nikolai's wish to avoid offending French Jews in the Paris banking community, from whom he was receiving funds. However, it's worth noting that the grand duke had, some time earlier, himself refused to accept Sokolov's evidence and records. Furthermore, French Deuxième Bureau records show that well into the twenties, the grand duke stated that his cousin the tsar could not be regarded as dead. Although the grand duke might have had his own political reasons for publicly persisting in this belief, his statements must be taken seriously. He had been commander-in-chief of the Russian armies at the start of the first world war, and again briefly after the tsar's abdication. He remained, until his death in 1929, a respected leader in exile, and a key Romanov likely to be considered as a candidate for tsar in the event of a restoration.

But at Ford headquarters in 1924, the grand duke's warning went unheeded. A Ford executive noted:

"The Sokolov documents have all the appearance of being genuine, but it is, of course, impossible to establish this fact without a thorough investigation of their contents . . ." Such an enquiry was hardly necessary for Ford, whose attitude to history was already enshrined in his famous remark: "History is . . . bunk." Ford's interest in Sokolov and the papers did not extend beyond their usefulness in producing anti-semitic "evidence". He made a deal with Sokolov by which the investigator would produce a memorandum "establishing the fact that the assassination had been planned and carried out by the Jews". Sokolov also handed over a copy of his dossier, which lies in the Ford archives to this day. And so the work that began in Ekaterinburg, fanfared as an unbiased judicial investigation into the fate of the most powerful monarch on earth, ended with a tawdry racist transaction in a Michigan office block.

The end was now approaching for Sokolov. A Ford executive described what happened next:

While Sokolov was here he was a very, very nervous and highly-strung man. I sent him to the Ford hospital to have him examined and see what was wrong with him. They called me up and wanted to know if the man was of any importance to us. I said: "Well, he is only a visitor here temporarily." They said: "We'd advise you to have him leave here and get away just as quick as possible because the fellow has a very, very bad heart. He is liable to die almost any time." I didn't want him dying on our hands, so I hustled Sokolov off. We hastened the thing through and got Sokolov back. I think he died a week after he got back to Paris.

About the time of this callous treatment, the French edition of Sokolov's book was being printed, but it is not clear whether he lived to see it published. Not only had Grand Duke Nikolai refused to accept Sokolov's work, but even the tsar's mother, the Empress Marie, cold-shouldered him. Although she had made a financial contribution towards Sokolov's work in Siberia, she never wanted to see him or his famous dossier. When news reached the dowager empress in Denmark that

Sokolov and Bulygin intended visiting her a telegram was sent saying: "Entreat Sokolov and Bulygin not to come."

Sokolov's last letters are pathetic. He wrote to Mirolyubov, the former civilian prosecutor who had theoretically been in charge of the Ekaterinburg area, and was also in exile: "I have been abroad nearly two years now . . . Everything is completely disintegrating here and I cannot get funds . . . I really beg you to write to me and not refuse to let me know where Shamarin, Ostroumov, Kutuzov, Jordansky, Sergeyev, and all the Ekaterinburg judiciary are." Several of these men were by now long dead—allegedly killed by the Bolsheviks for their part in the investigation. And Sokolov knew he too was dying; he wrote to Bulygin: "The old engine is worn out... must finish up the work and that will be the end... Why are you so far away, dear friend? I am lonely. The end is near. I fear we shall not see each other again... I send you from afar my parting embrace..."

So Sokolov died, a broken man, in November 1924. Not even his death was clear-cut. Some suggested he had been poisoned, others that he died as a mental patient. Robert Wilton had been sacked by his newspaper, and died in France within eight weeks of Sokolov. Captain Bulygin was shot in Argentina sometime in the thirties—motive unknown. Gilliard survived until 1962, and remained one of the most vociferous supporters of the massacre story. While testifying during the "Anastasia" case in 1958, he startled the judge by admitting that he had deliberately destroyed relevant documents.

We found the grave of Sokolov in a country churchyard at Salbris, south of Paris. An inaccurate inscription promotes the investigator to the "Presiding Judge", who "took on the enquiry into the murder of the imperial family of Russia". The epitaph on his tombstone reads: "Your Truth Is Truth Eternal".

16

A COMPENDIUM OF LIES

"The spheres are veined, with a dark crimson flush above, where the light falls upon them, and in a certain aspect you can make out upon them the three letters LIE."

(Oliver Wendell Holmes on "Truth")

THERE ARE A number of official ways of deceiving the public. There is the total silence, or the total lie, or the sort of double-speak evasiveness on which truth founders just the same. The United States, with its proud claim to be the world's most open society, has just lived through a decade of lies and official obfuscation. The covert bombing of Cambodia was successfully hidden from the public for a long time, in spite of the watchful eye of television and international news agencies. When difficult questions were asked, government spokesmen side-stepped the truth, just as they did over the clandestine war in Laos. The Watergate scandal remained hidden only briefly, yet its complexities took two full years to unravel. They were two years of official falsehoods and "inoperative statements", in which the full power of the executive was employed, very nearly successfully, against battalions of investigators. President Nixon managed to dodge appearing in court, and his exact role in Watergate may never be revealed. Watergate came just ten years after the American assassination of the century—the shooting in 1963 of President Kennedy—and controversy still swirls around that. One of the main reasons the public is still suspicious is, again, official obfuscation. Vital X-rays that would show the detailed bullet damage are withheld on the grounds they are too macabre—yet far gorier pictures of Kennedy's blood-stained clothing were readily released. In 1975 it emerged that the director of the Federal Bureau of Investigation, J. Edgar Hoover, ordered his men to destroy a threatening letter written by Oswald just before the killing; within days of the crime, solely to conceal the fact that his agents had had prior warning of danger, one of the senior officials in the land was deliberately hiding evidence.

Of course, official deception is nothing new. Recently the world learned of the "Last Secret", the cynical deal between Churchill, Roosevelt and Stalin at the end of the second world war by which two million Russian exiles were "repatriated" to the Soviet Union. Faced with the inevitability of death or incarceration under Stalin, many of them cut their throats or hanged themselves in the sealed trains in which the Allies sent them "home".

Communist Russia was a pioneer in the art of the official lie. Its flagrant rewriting of history and its total control of the media have made the world rightly sceptical of all Soviet news and government statements. In July 1918 there was a certain symbolism in the choice of the Ekaterinburg theatre for the official announcement of the tsar's execution. From that moment on, Soviet statements on the fate of the Romanovs were consistent only in their air of make-believe.

On 22 September 1918 *Izvestiya* published a news story saying that the body of the tsar had been exhumed from a grave in the woods, placed in a zinc coffin covered with Siberian cedar, and "exposed in the cathedral at Ekaterinburg under a guard of honour composed of the chief commanders of the army". It was of course a fable, for the excellent reason that Nicholas's body was never found. That piece of disinformation was capped a year later by a "court report" which appeared to deal with the fate of the rest of the family. *Pravda* reported that 28 people had recently stood trial at Perm for murdering the whole Romanov household. The defendants included three "members of the Ekaterinburg Soviet", one of whom allegedly admitted he had organized the crime so as to compromise the Soviet regime in the interests of the Left Social Revolutionaries—a rival extremist faction opposed to Lenin's policies. Fourteen of the accused were supposedly found guilty and executed.

This story, complete with names of the principal accused, was again rubbish. The identities of the leading Cheka and Soviet members at Ekaterinburg are known, and not a single name coincides with those published in *Pravda*. But the account served a useful double purpose. It was the first public admission of the murder of all the Romanovs, and it shifted the blame neatly away from Moscow and on to the Left Social Revolutionaries, with whom the Bolsheviks had been in conflict in July 1918. It also coincided with desperate efforts by the Bolsheviks to normalize relations with the outside world. In Britain, revulsion over the alleged massacre of the imperial family was still a cause of anti-Soviet feeling, and Moscow knew it. Within two months of this report, and after protracted negotiations, Soviet Russia successfully concluded an important agreement with Britain—the first with a major Allied power. Almost certainly the "Perm trial" report was part of the softening-up process for foreign consumption.

One semi-official Communist account appeared, in 1926, when the man who succeeded Beloborodov as chairman of the Ural Soviet, Pavel Bykov, published a volume called *The Last Days of Tsardom*. This is often held up as Red corroboration of the White version of the massacre, and seemed to account for the absence of human remains at the mine. Bykov wrote: ". . . what remained of the bodies after burning was taken a considerable distance from the pits and buried in a swamp, in an area where the volunteers and investigators made no excavations. There the bodies remained and by now have rotted away." The writer implied that this was done to prevent the Whites recovering anything they could revere as precious relics, and to hide what had happened. Yet the Communists did leave blatant evidence of what had occurred, and plenty of relics for the Whites to revere. A sharper look into its origins reveals that there is more to the Bykov account than meets the eye.

The trail leads back to an incident in 1921, in Germany. That year Investigator Sokolov visited Berlin, where he stayed at the house of a Colonel Freiberg. One night his flat was raided by an armed band of Russian and German Communists, a raid so well mounted that one of the thieves was left at the front door, posing as a policeman, while the robbery was taking place. When the raiders left they took a set of Sokolov's papers with them. A subsequent German police enquiry concluded that the files had been taken, via Prague, to Moscow. It was later that same year, 1921, that Bykov first

published a version of the murder story, as a short contribution
to a revolutionary pamphlet. He gave scant details for someone
who should have been in a unique position to provide names,
dates and first-hand interviews with those involved. Significantly, he drew heavily on information gathered by the
Whites, even going so far as to quote them.

This 1921 account did not deal with the question of the
missing bodies at all. But the next five years saw continuing
doubt about the massacre, focused largely on the fact that no
corpses had ever been found. In 1926 the Soviet authorities
seem to have felt it was time to deal with the issue at last.
Bykov told his story once more, again drawing almost entirely
on Sokolov and Diterikhs but this time slipping in his reference
to the bodies being taken to a swamp. He did it, moreover,
specifically to dismiss rumours that at least part of the family
were transferred from Ekaterinburg alive. It was expedient
but unconvincing.

Neither Bykov, nor any other Soviet source, ever again
mentioned those stories about the tsar's body being exhumed,
or the murder trial at Perm. As late as 1966 the youth newspaper *Komsomolskaya Pravda* simply retold the Bykov version.
The modern Soviet history book for secondary school children
omits the fate of the Romanovs altogether. The tsar disappears
from the record, becomes an un-person, with his abdication in
1917. In 1971 we asked the Soviet Foreign Ministry for an
up-to-date statement. After much correspondence through the
Soviet embassy in London, we were sent this quotation from
the Soviet Historical Encyclopaedia: "In July 1918, in Ekaterinburg, when the White guards began their offensive, the provincial council *took a decision* to execute Tsar Nicholas II, his
family and retinue."

In 1974 the Soviet journal *Zvezda* elevated the Ekaterinburg Soviet to the status of heroes, saying that they "resolved
the problem of removing the Romanovs from Russia's path
to a better future, bravely and audaciously acting inside a ring
of fire and facing a legion of enemies". As for the bodies, they
"threw their ashes to the winds". That sounds like a direct
quote from a fantastical story which appeared in the west in
1935, when an American called Richard Halliburton returned
from Russia with what purported to be an exclusive interview

with Pyotr Yermakov, the commissar who is supposed to have
played a leading part in the destruction operation at the Four
Brothers. Halliburton claimed he had travelled to Ekaterinburg and found Yermakov critically ill with cancer: "Yermakov
lay on a crude Russian bed . . . His mouth hung open, and from
one corner there was a trickle of blood . . . Two bloodshot and
delirious eyes gleamed at me." In a three-hour talk, Yermakov
is supposed to have come out with confessions like this: "I
fired my Mauser at the tsarina—only six feet away—couldn't
miss. Got her in the mouth. In two seconds she was dead . . ."
Of the destruction at the mine the assassin boasted:

> We didn't leave the smallest pinch of ash on the ground
> . . . I put the tins of ashes in the wagon again, and ordered the
> driver to take me back towards the highroad . . . I pitched
> the ashes into the air—and the wind caught them like dust
> and carried them out across the woods and fields . . . so if
> anyone says he's seen a Romanov or a piece of a dead one
> —tell him about the ashes and the wind and the rain.

Yet again, this is nonsense. There were of course *piles* of
cinders left behind at the Four Brothers, and this version is
packed with mistakes and contradictions. The story, like so
many others, collapses once its origins are investigated.

Richard Halliburton said he was tipped off about Yermakov
by the Moscow correspondent of the *Chicago Daily News*,
William Stoneman. We found Stoneman, at 71, still with the
paper's Paris bureau. What was his considered opinion of
Halliburton and his scoop? "In my view," said the veteran
reporter, "he was the worst kind of phoney." Stoneman explained that Halliburton's escort on his Russian travels had
been an official Soviet interpreter, and they are invariably
primed to feed visitors with Moscow's pre-packaged "facts".[14]

From the ragbag of legend about the massacre of the
Romanovs, we offer one more cautionary tale. Twelve years
after Ekaterinburg, a Russian exile called Grigory Bessedovsky
published his memoirs, including an account of the Ipatiev
House massacre attributed to Pyotr Voikov, the man Sokolov
linked to the murders through his purchases of sulphuric acid.
After the war Voikov rose to become Soviet ambassador to

Poland, and Bessedovsky was an official in his embassy. Bessedovsky later defected, and claimed in his book that Voikov had got drunk at a party in 1925 and poured out his memories of the massacre to an astonished Bessedovsky in the early hours of the morning.[15] The story was simply a rehash of the traditional version except that Voikov claimed he was himself in the murder room—a fact never mentioned in any of the descriptions collected by Sokolov. Although there is none of the inside information or new detail one might expect from one of the ringleaders, the Voikov account is often quoted as authoritative; those who do so should take a closer look at Mr Bessedovsky.

After the second world war he was unmasked as a highly successful faker, an industrious writer of fictitious history. Just one of the duds in his treasure-trove of exclusive memoirs was *My Uncle Joseph Stalin*, which Bessedovsky said he had ghosted for Stalin's nephew, Budu Svanidze. Stalin had no such nephew. Taxed with his unashamed ability to create phoney biographies, Bessedovsky is reported as answering: "I write books for idiots. Do you imagine that anyone in the West would read my books if I tried to reproduce the sense and shape of my subjects' statements?" Today, scholars agree that most of his "revelations" were fraudulent, and some identify him as having been an agent abroad of the Soviet secret police.

Sokolov records that the real-life Commissar Voikov was prone to making theatrical gestures, and had an eye for the ladies. When asked in female company about the fate of the Romanovs at Ekaterinburg he is quoted as replying: "The world will never know what we did with them." Perhaps, but only perhaps, he was right.

In 1971 Lord Mountbatten, the man to whom the tsar was "Uncle Nicky" summed up his family's reasons for accepting the Ekaterinburg massacre as fact: "We were told it had taken place, at least we were expecting it to take place, we had no reason to doubt it; and there may not have been any proof, but they in those days were not requiring proof. What else could we believe but the worst, as history appears to have shown was right? What was the alternative?"

Lord Mountbatten, who read the French edition of Soko-lov's book, agrees that although it may not have been perfect, it was that which finally convinced him. We have shown that it was much worse than imperfect: that damning telegram in code, the statement by the man who "saw the bodies", the sinister evidence at Ekaterinburg and the mine—all now ring false. The Romanov case is redolent of conspiracy and cover-up. But what indeed is the alternative? A key factor in convincing reasonable people that the imperial family did die at Ekaterinburg has been that, since then, none of them has been proved to be alive.

In fact the years have provided a host of alternatives, yet they make the real trail even harder to follow.

PART FOUR

Pretenders

17

THE CLAIMANTS

"To hell with the truth. As the history of the world proves, the truth has no bearing on anything."
(Eugene O'Neill)

"That story is a lot of crap."
(Henry Kissinger, 1975)

"WHERE AND WHEN did you last see the imperial family?" asked the general. "Well," said the colonel, "it was last year, at Rostov. I was walking along the Sadovaya when suddenly I saw the tsar, in ordinary clothes. I scarcely recognized him. He greeted me, and later I called on him several times and saw him, the tsarina, and their children."

The general was Baron Wrangel, commander-in-chief of the White forces in the Crimea, and the colonel a retired officer from the former Imperial War College. The date—spring 1920—just two years *after* the supposed death of the entire Romanov family.

The colonel went on to explain to General Wrangel that the family were all well, and remarked how tall the tsarevich had grown. General Wrangel rightly concluded that his companion was mad.

But the colonel's story was a symptom not of an individual madness, but of a collective lunacy born from the moment the world learned of the tsar's execution. The absence of a body, or bodies, gave rise to a durable mythology, an exasperating pot-pourri of mysticism, rumour, legend and lies.

The motives behind the Romanov "sightings" are complex. Some are mischievous, some are created for political ends or commercial gain, some through madness and some through genuine lingering hope. People need to see bodies, or photographs of bodies. No survival myths were created around Benito

Mussolini once the world had seen pictures of him strung by the heels from a lamp-post. But Hitler did not die visibly enough, and his deputy, Martin Bormann, remained elusively "alive" for 28 years, until a German workman accidentally uncovered his skeleton—just where historians had always claimed he had been killed in 1945.

The disappearance of not one, but of every member of the Russian imperial family, set an inevitable match to the flame of fantasy. The survival stories soon split into two distinct streams. One had the family surviving in some remote and inaccessible part of Russia, the other had them spirited out of the country, beginning new lives under assumed identities elsewhere. The first legend is the more traditional, conceived early on, perhaps before the loyalists grasped the fact that the Bolsheviks would never allow the Romanovs to live on in peace inside the country. Amidst the emotional chaos of the civil war, such legends flourished as travellers' tales. Some cropped up within weeks of the family's disappearance. One had them in the Crimea. Foreign newspapers printed this eye-witness account of someone who had seen the tsarina and all her children there:

> She looked listless, dull and defeated. The daughters are all beautiful and full of life, while the son looked plain and walked very badly . . . Many times my friends and I have in curiosity, passed the house where they live. The house is owned by a Russian-born count, whose grandfather was a German minister in Russia . . .

This Romanov fairytale came from an itinerant Swedish bandleader just back from south Russia.

Sometimes the source was a little more plausible; like Prince Obolensky, an officer in the imperial guard who confided in the daughter of a Hungarian general, during a train journey:

> "The tsar and his children, who are supposed to have died, are all alive."
> "But what about the newspaper stories of their assassination?" asked his startled companion, "And where are they?"
> "I cannot say more," replied the prince.

"To the north or the south?" persisted the girl.

"In the north, maybe ... don't ask me any more ... I shall not reply."

That piece of lady-killing gossip was to be inflated into front-page news. The theme of it persisted for years—all or some of the Romanovs were still alive, either in a monastery or convent inside Russia. A French secret service report dated December 1919 included, almost casually, this information:

It appears undeniable that Nicholas II and his family are alive. According to the latest information they are in good health. Nevertheless, written communications in the tsar's own handwriting and also those emanating from his immediate entourage are most laconic and leave unanswered the question of whether the tsarevich is still alive or not. According to this information and to information coming from people who have seen the imperial family, it would appear that the tsar has undergone a great moral change ... he seems to have been rejuvenated through suffering. He appears today as a strong-willed man, very determined, transformed by an immense mystical faith which makes him an apostle of a new era. The tsarina, on the other hand, undermined by sorrow and by a nervous disease, is today a being devoid of will-power and in a state of total collapse ... The fact that Nicholas II and his family were [sic] alive is being kept very secret, as above all is his hiding place; it is said to be in a convent in Russia.

The French Deuxième Bureau prefaced the entire report with the reminder that the source was "an agent usually well-informed, but sometimes tendentious". His information came from Berlin, from sources close to General Gurko, chief of the Russian Imperial General Staff until the tsar's abdication, and then working energetically to raise funds and troops for a military campaign against the Bolsheviks. Whoever inspired or encouraged that survival story knew the concept of a live Tsar Nicholas was still, in 1919, potent propaganda for a recruiting campaign. Nor was the deception much of a strain on monarchist creative powers, because there was a precedent.

Russians had long believed that a hundred years earlier
Nicholas's ancestor, Tsar Alexander I, faked his own death in
order to become a holy man. Farfetched as it sounds, that story
still enjoys some currency, even among modern Soviet writers.
Now the new "Nicholas" version of the story flourished, even
inside Bolshevik Russia, where it found willing exploiters. In
1922 the *New York Times* ran this story from Moscow:

> An extraordinary romance involving the alleged survival of
> the Russian imperial family comes from Penza, where three
> persons reported to be the former empress, her son and her
> youngest daughter had been hidden in various nunneries for
> the last three years. The story begins at the big Uspensky
> convent early in 1919 of a woman pilgrim . . . Her dignified
> appearance, her noble manner and, above all, her extra-
> ordinary resemblance to the empress, soon caused it to be
> bruited about the neighbourhood that it was indeed she and
> that she had escaped remarkably from death.

The "tsarina" was soon joined by her "son and daughter", but
these impostors did not enjoy their imperial role for long;
when the Bolsheviks hunted them down the "tsarina" turned
out to be a schoolmaster's daughter, the "tsarevich" the son
of a village priest, and his "sister" a peasant's daughter. The
three, who were not even related, were sentenced to seven years
in prison. In the course of our own research, more than 50
years later, we came across enduring stories of survival in con-
vents. Countess de Zarnekau, an expatriate living in Brussels,
told how in about 1923 a nun arrived at their home in Moscow
and announced mysteriously that the tsar and all the family
were alive "somewhere close to the border". She asked for, and
was given, woolly socks to warm the imperial feet. Those who
had been able to deal with the little matter of the tsar's rescue
were now apparently having trouble getting him the right size
in socks. The original yarn-spinner.

For any who found the recluse version unsatisfactory the
Romanov industry produced a more sophisticated model.
1920 saw a detailed account of how the Romanovs had been
spirited away from Ekaterinburg by a monarchist infiltrator in
the Ipatiev House guard. They had travelled by train to
Vladivostok, where a certain princess actually saw the tsarina

and her daughters boarding a ship for Japan. The family was now said to be hidden—some thought in China, under British protection, or "in a little Japanese town". 1920 was also a year that had the Romanov women living quietly somewhere in England.

But the Baron Munchausen Prize for 1920 must go to the author of the drama aboard an American freighter, the *Governor John Lind*. After the *Lind* arrived in New York one fine day in June, the ship was stormed by Manhattan reporters intent on discovering whether the ex-Tsar Nicholas II was amongst "a very distinguished group of Russian oilers, stokers, a bosun, and a mess boy". According to the *New York Times*: ". . . some of the crew pointed out a grimy figure who looked like the late head of the Romanov family—'There is the tsar,' said one of the crew with due impressiveness. 'Are you a member of the Romanov family?' asked the reporter. The distinguished oiler, in soiled denims, stroked his beard with a work-hardened hand. 'I really wish you would not ask me that,' he said in a quiet voice." Perhaps the long sea voyage, and a liberal rum ration, had made the "tsar" too weary to talk to the press.

In 1926, the Transalpine News Agency reported: "Information absolutely serious in character permits us to affirm that Tsar Nicholas is alive and hidden in a little corner of the Riviera between France and Italy. Nicholas II was only wounded during the massacre . . . and was saved by one of the soldiers who participated in the killing of other members of the household." In the light of all these survival stories, it is not too surprising to learn that by March 1927, nearly a decade after Ekaterinburg, the Russian Orthodox prelate in Berlin celebrated mass "for the health of His Majesty Tsar Nicholas II". Nine years later, and ageing accordingly, the imperial family was out and about again. A Pole, now living in England, told us how in 1936 the Romanovs had visited his home near the Russian border. He remembers "five ladies and one gentleman carrying a picture of St Nicholas. Father bowed down in front of them. The tsarevich was there too, now aged about 30. They stayed for two days before travelling on to Germany. The tsar left a royal badge as thanks for our hospitality."

In the league of who was to be faked most after 1918, the tsar and tsarina, with their well-known faces, were near the bottom.

The imperial children were a better bet: Olga, Tatiana, and Maria rate low, Alexei does quite well and the youngest daughter, Anastasia, remains the most popular. Not all the claimants are totally transparent. A woman calling herself Grand Duchess Olga, the tsar's eldest daughter, has been living since the twenties in various parts of Europe, and since 1939 has settled in northern Italy under the name of Marga Boodts. She says she was rescued by a loyal officer and then taken east to Vladivostok, across China, and on by sea to Hamburg, Germany. She was then recognized, she claims, by the exiled Kaiser Wilhelm II, who assured her financial independence during his lifetime. Since then her fortunes have foundered, but she has had an enduring supporter in the shape of Prince Sigismund of Prussia, the Kaiser's nephew and first cousin to the real Grand Duchess Olga. In an interview at his home in Costa Rica Prince Sigismund in 1974 confirmed that he was still convinced of "Olga's" authenticity. He has met her, and says: "We spoke about so many familiar matters that an outsider could not have known about, because they were things that had happened between us two." When we visited Mrs Boodts at her Italian home in 1975, she declined to speak about herself, or past events. Nothing at all emerged from the meeting to support the notion that she was either the Grand Duchess Olga, or even a Romanov.[16]

The tsar's only son Alexei was the youngest of the family, almost fifteen years old when he disappeared. Any would-be impostor must take on the major stumbling block that the real Alexei suffered from haemophilia. In the case of young Alexei the illness had brought him close to death several times, not least during the captivity of 1917 and 1918. But the problem of faking illness did not deter impostors. Pierre Gilliard told how a senior White general summoned him in June 1919, to examine the first "Alexei" of all:

He informed me that he wished me to see a young boy who was claiming to be the tsarevich. I knew in fact that for some time the rumour of the survival of the heir had been spreading at Omsk. He was said to be in a village of the Altai. I had been told that the population had demonstrated in front of him with enthusiasm . . . the schoolchildren had made collections in aid of him . . . and the postmaster had, on his knees, offered him bread and salt . . . General D had asked me to come, reckoning that my evidence would be conclusive. The door of a neighbouring room was opened and I could look, without him spotting me, at a young man, larger and stronger than the tsarevich, who seemed to be about fifteen or sixteen years old. By his sailor's outfit, the colour of his hair, and the way he wore it, he did look a bit, very vaguely, from a distance, like Alexei Nikolayevich, but that was as far as any resemblance went. Chance had put in my way the first of the innumerable claimants, who for many years, no doubt, were to be an element of trouble and agitation in the breasts of the ignorant, credulous mass of the Russian peasantry.

In the end, this first "Alexei" owned up to being a fake, but there were to be more down the years. Two at least seemed at first to have some of the right qualifications. We heard an intriguing tale about the first of them from Cecil Edmonds, CBE, a former political officer with the old Colonial Office. He bumped into an "Alexei" while serving in northern Iraq in 1926. Intense cross-questioning by the British director of the CID failed to shake the boy's story, and medical examination showed that he was a haemophiliac. Edmonds recalls that the case was eventually referred to King George V himself but that "His Majesty . . . rejected all possibility that the young man could be the tsarevich."

There have been several other Alexeis, but the most famous and persistent of them all is still alive and well and living on Long Island, New York. Unlike most claimants he is at least surrounded by genuine drama and mystery. The New York Alexei came in from the cold on Christmas Day 1960 when he crossed from East to West Berlin and introduced himself to American intelligence officers as Lieutenant Colonel Michal Goleniewski, a top operator in Polish intelligence. He has since been authoritatively described as an important defector who brought with him valuable information. After a senior CIA official described him as being "one hundred per cent accurate", Congress passed a special bill to give him American citizenship. But sometime after arriving in America Goleniewski embarrassed the CIA and amazed everyone by claiming to be, in his own words: "Aleksei Nicholaevich, Heir to the All-Russian Imperial Throne, Tsarevich and Grand Duke of Russia, Head of the Russian Imperial House, Etc., and August Ataman Etc., Etc." Typically, New York City has taken Goleniewski to its heart as only New York can. For years now he has attracted a steady flow of genial interest, has been interviewed on television and written articles for the *New York Daily Mirror*, by-lined as the heir to the Russian throne. In 1971 we talked to him at length on the telephone and encountered him briefly—a thick-set man with a strangely translucent complexion, sporting a large walrus moustache. He wrote rejecting our request for a television interview, saying that copies of his letter were also going to the President of the General Assembly of the United Nations, the FBI, and lawyers. Goleniewski has produced not a shred of evidence to show he is anything but a Polish defector. In 1974 a CIA official gave us a confidential briefing on the man, and said that, "as is the case with a number of defector types, he seems to have flipped his lid".[17]

But Goleniewski's appearance marked the start of a remarkable campaign in the United States to prove that all the Romanovs survived. Unlike anything previous, it has succeeded in attracting worldwide attention from researchers, the media and politicians—culminating in the early seventies with a claim that secret documents in America and Britain proved once and for all that the whole imperial family had been rescued.

In February 1963, shortly after Goleniewski's arrival on the scene, a Mrs Eugenia Smith of Chicago walked into the offices of New York publishers Robert Speller and Sons. According to Speller, she was none other than the Grand Duchess Anastasia, and nine months later he published her memoirs. At the same time *Life* magazine published a major cover story investigating the claim. Handwriting and anthropological experts reached the firm conclusion that she was not the tsar's youngest daughter. In London, we have since run our own check, giving pictures of the real Anastasia and Mrs Smith to photo-fit experts at Scotland Yard. The comparison went categorically against Mrs Smith's claim.

But Mr Speller continued to believe that she was genuine, and that Goleniewski was really the tsarevich. On New Year's

Eve 1963 he arranged for the two to meet, and says there was a moving recognition scene. When we met Speller in 1971, he also told us that Grand Duchess Maria was alive in Poland, and gave us her address. When our researcher in Warsaw found her, she indeed admitted to being Goleniewski's sister and claimed to be Maria. She produced a photograph of her father—"Nicholas II"—which she said had been cut from his passport after his death in 1952. The picture showed an old man with a beard in working clothes, and had allegedly been taken while the ex-tsar was working as a tram-driver in Poland. We showed it to Scotland Yard experts, who compared it with pictures of the real Nicholas. It came as no surprise that they said it could not be the tsar, but could very well be a Polish tram-driver.

The New York Romanov industry was to prosper during the sixties. A journalist, Guy Richards, wrote a book on Goleniewski called *Imperial Agent*, in which he went a long way to supporting the Polish colonel's claim. Richards, the Speller family, and other New Yorkers now formed a coterie of Romanov buffs dedicated to investigating the fate of the last imperial family. By 1970 their work led to another book by Richards, *The Hunt for the Czar*.[18] It suggested the whole family had been rescued, and the blurb on the dust-jacket asked: "Should history be re-written?" One serious reviewer in Britain, the late Peter Fleming, answered: "This book can be recommended to connoisseurs of the preposterous . . . it is easy to see what he [*Richards*] thinks a fact is: it is something that he wants to believe." One thing Richards wanted his readers to believe was that there was a secret "Romanoff File", now kept at the CIA and the National Security Agency after being transferred from the State Department. He based this mainly on one 1927 embassy despatch which bore the legend "Romanoff File". We have investigated that document, and find no mystery, only a mundane bureaucratic explanation which is totally plausible.[19]

But others were to share Richards's desire to believe, and carried the Romanov myth into loftier spheres. Two months after publication of Richards's book, in May 1970, a British MP asked Prime Minister Harold Wilson for a formal statement as to why the government was suppressing documents about the Romanovs, contrary to the 30-year release policy.[20] The Prime Minister replied that all documents relating to the Romanov massacre had been open to the public since 1966. The MP was Peter Bessell, Liberal member for Bodmin, and for him it was only the opening broadside in a strange campaign to prove the Romanovs escaped. For the New York buffs he was a new recruit and a distinguished acquisition. According to his own biographical notes he was "an historian who has made an extensive study of European history . . ." Bessell is a slim man with a dark handsome face and a resolute confident voice; his style is neither London conservative nor dapper New York, more a neat mid-Atlantic compromise. His close friend, the then Liberal Party leader Jeremy Thorpe, has described him to us as a "man of industry, loyalty and honesty". A month after asking his Romanov question in parliament, Bessell retired from active politics to devote himself to the family investment and finance broking business, which had offices in London and New York. In the United States he had become close to Guy Richards, and now devoted a lot of time to research into the events at Ekaterinburg. At Christmas 1970, Bessell contributed to a six-page article in the London *Observer*, in which he claimed there had been a secret codicil in the 1918 Treaty of Brest-Litovsk, by which the Bolsheviks promised Germany they would free the Romanovs. He did not explain how he had come by this startling information, but the *Observer* reporter recalls Bessell creating "an atmosphere of nose-tapping mystery".

On 27 April 1971, from New York, Bessell issued a long press statement declaring flatly that he was sure the Romanovs had escaped because: "I know that classified papers belonging to one of the former Allied powers, and which prove that the family did not perish, were recently made available to and read by a researcher of undoubted integrity". Shortly afterwards Bessell revealed to us that he was himself that researcher, and that he had been allowed access to classified US State documents on the rescue, with the help and approval of his friend Henry Kissinger. He had seen documents at the Executive Office Building of the White House and at the American Mission to the United Nations in New York.[21] In the next two years Bessell was to say he had been given further privileged sightings of the papers, and produced many pages of "notes" of their contents—never photostats or originals. He repeatedly claimed that the documents were shortly to be released under President Nixon's declassification programme. Nothing happened.

In May 1973, pressure from Bessell brought Jeremy Thorpe into the affair. Thorpe tabled a parliamentary question asking the then foreign secretary, Sir Alec Douglas-Home, to "place in the Library of the House of Commons the letter from Lord Hardinge of Penshurst to his late Majesty King George V, dated 3 June or 5 June 1919, containing details of the escape route of the former Tsar Nicholas II and other members of the tsar's family". The question was refused by the table office because it did not relate to contemporary events, but Thorpe pursued the matter in a letter to the foreign secretary, who replied that there was no such document in the archives. Our research on the "Hardinge letter" shows it to be a clumsy forgery.[22] It had been supplied to Jeremy Thorpe by Bessell. In January 1974, Peter Bessell vanished. When we located him two years later in California he had begun a new life after the collapse of his businesses. He offered an affidavit covering the curious affair of the Chivers papers and the Hardinge letter, but was still unable to prove that the papers are authentic—or indeed that they exist at all. In 1975 Guy Richards incorporated Bessell's notes on the alleged documents in yet another book, this one flatly entitled *The Rescue of the Romanovs*. Our research, and the verdict of historians we consulted, suggests that, at best, the documents are part of some disinformation scheme mounted at the end of World War I.[23]

And what is the opinion of Dr Kissinger, the man who is supposed to have let Bessell see the papers? We arranged for a colleague to raise the matter during one of his Middle East shuttles in 1975. Sitting in the special mission plane somewhere over north Africa, Kissinger admitted an acquaintance with Bessell but said he had not seen him since 1969, before the former MP started talking about the Romanovs. What about the Romanov rescue then, and those sensational documents?

"That story," said the American Secretary of State, "is a lot of crap."[24]

18

ANNA ANDERSON

"Yesterday evening at 9 pm a girl of about twenty jumped . . . into the Landwehr Canal with the intention of taking her own life."

> (Berlin police bulletin, 18 February 1920)

"The water streamed out of her hair and her clothes, but she said she was a real princess . . . now this is a true story."

> (Hans Christian Andersen,
> "The Princess and the Pea")

SHE LIVES TODAY in a tree-lined crescent of imposing white townhouses in the university town of Charlottesville, Virginia. The street is the epitome of American suburban affluence, but one house stands out. It is the home of "Anastasia". The garden is wild and untended, high grass spreads across the path and creeper bars the way to the front door, in a way that suggests visitors are few, and rarely welcome.

The door is answered by Dr John Manahan, a retired history professor from the University of Virginia. He is the man who married "Anastasia" at her presumed age of 67, to ensure her legal right to live in America. Manahan is in his fifties, crewcut, paunchy—a conventional American male who has let the conventions slip a little. The suit is baggy, the tie egg-stained. Once inside the house, and the professor immediately launches into a stream of historical small-talk, punctuated with apologies for the state of the house. He says he has spent the day clearing up for our arrival, but the living room is still an extraordinary muddle. In the centre, incongruously, is a huge tree stump; on the walls old pictures recalling the glories of imperial Russia contend in cramped space with bric-a-brac and childish daubings; over everything hangs the pervasive smell of cats. The balcony, which should be a pleasant place to contemplate the view, is piled high with a mountain of potatoes which have overwhelmed their container—a large plastic bath.

All this, says Manahan, is how "Anastasia" chooses to live. Although he is rich, and although this is America, the potatoes remain because his wife feared a hungry winter. The tree stump recalls her time in the Black Forest, and the cats—well, the cats are there simply because "Anastasia's" life is centred on her cats. Two hours pass, and still there is no sign of the woman we have come to see. Manahan continues to talk about her, about the Romanovs, and of his own sincere belief that his wife really is the Grand Duchess Anastasia, the youngest daughter of Tsar Nicholas II.

It is said even when people come vast distances to see her, "Anastasia" often refuses to appear. If that is so, we are lucky. In the middle of a conducted tour of the house, as we pick a tortuous path through grubby corridors and staircases groaning under the weight of books, the most famous Romanov claimant of all suddenly joins us.

She is frail, a tiny figure with dyed auburn-blonde hair, dressed in a red and white print blouse, bright red cotton trousers, and gold brocaded slippers. Everything she wears is a little too big for her (*see plate 44*). Later, at dinner in an eminently respectable country club, "Anastasia" wears a synthetic raincoat—and keeps it on throughout the meal. She clutches a rainhat filled with silver foil, ready to wrap left-over meat from the dinner, which she scoops up and saves for those feline friends of hers. Back at her home, we stay with "Anastasia" until the early hours, when she delays our departure by offering copious dollops of ice cream. But journalistically it has not been a rewarding evening. In seven hours, it is doubtful if we have managed to spend seven minutes talking to her about her claim to be the real Anastasia, or the events at Ekaterinburg in the summer of 1918, when, if she is really a Romanov daughter, she took part in one of the great dramas of the century. Far from revealing what may have happened, "Anastasia" has shied away from direct conversation, hiding a toothless mouth behind her hand, just as she has done in public for five decades. But in the rare flashes of lucidity she has been quite clear about her identity, without making any attempt to convince us of the fact. Indeed one enduring characteristic of "Anastasia" is that she herself has never insisted on persuading the world to believe in her. It has always been others who adopted her cause, others who took her claim to court, and others who ghosted her memoirs.

All we could say on leaving was that we had met a kind, amiable and highly eccentric old lady. And yet this is the woman who captured and held the public imagination for 50 years with her claim to be the sole survivor of Ekaterinburg. She is the tragic princess portrayed by Ingrid Bergman in the famous film named after her, the subject of a small library of books, and the woman whose claim has made legal history as the longest running case of the century. Litigation began in 1938, and continued intermittently until 1970. It may yet go to the World Court at the Hague.

Hers has not been a frivolous journey through the courts. Such a lengthy dispute would not have been possible if there had been no case to argue. She has caused senior members of the British and German aristocracy to spend fortunes in legal fees trying to prove she is not Her Imperial Highness the Grand Duchess Anastasia Nikolayevna. They have not succeeded, nor has she. In 1967 the president of the Hamburg Court of Appeal ruled that the onus of proving she was Anastasia lay with her, as plaintiff, and she had not brought sufficient evidence to do so. On the other hand, in a judgement 700 pages long, the three-member tribunal stated that: ". . . the death of Anastasia in Ekaterinburg cannot with absolute certainty be shown to be conclusively proved".

In 1970 the case went to the Federal Supreme Court in Karlsruhe. Like his predecessor, the president of the panel of five judges referred to the possibility that the claimant could be Anastasia, although she had failed in her action. He upheld the Appeal Court verdict, but described it as a *"non liquet"*—unsatisfactory to both parties: the claimant's identity with Anastasia had neither been established nor refuted.

The old lady in Virginia is in a class of her own when it comes to Romanov "survivors". She is the one whose claim deserves careful consideration and whose story is worth examination.

It is a story which began with a Berlin police bulletin dated

18 February 1920, some eighteen months after the Russian imperial family vanished from Ekaterinburg.

> Yesterday evening at 9 pm a girl of about twenty jumped off the Bendler Bridge into the Landwehr Canal with the intention of taking her own life. She was saved by a police sergeant and admitted to the Elisabeth Hospital in Lützow-strasse. No papers or valuables of any kind were found in her possession, and she refused to make any statements about herself or her motives for attempting suicide.

This was the woman later to be known as "Anastasia", but during the six weeks that she lay in the hospital she stubbornly said nothing at all about her identity.

On 30 March doctors and police gave up trying to get her to speak, and the nameless girl was taken for observation to the Dalldorf Insane Asylum. She was to spend two years there, sharing an open ward with a dozen mental patients. During most of that time she stayed in bed, refusing almost all conversation and showing no interest in what went on around her. Her health deteriorated, and her weight, which had been only 121 pounds on admission, dropped a further 21 pounds. The endless questioning continued throughout her stay, and although there is evidence that she took some of the nurses into her confidence, she remained adamant in her refusal to respond to bureaucratic examination. If she was Russian, as the authorities believed, and if she had entered Germany illegally, fear of repatriation was some justification for her silence.

One Sunday in March 1922 the first moves were made to break into the invalid's private world. Clara Peuthert, a fellow patient who had just been discharged, went to the Russian embassy church in Berlin. There she told a former tsarist officer, Captain Nikolai von Schwabe, that she had seen members of the imperial family when she lived in Moscow. And she was convinced that she had recognized the Grand Duchess *Tatiana* among the patients at Dalldorf.

Captain von Schwabe spread the word in White emigré circles, and visitors began to flock to the asylum—unaware that to some of the staff their patient was "Anastasia". Baroness Buxhoeveden was summoned. She came reluctantly to Berlin, and then found that the patient was not prepared to speak to her, or even show her face properly. Understandably the baroness's reaction was negative. In the wake of this fiasco many people lost interest in the false "Tatiana", but others were still determined to solve the riddle of the patient's identity.

Baron Arthur von Kleist, a former provincial police official in Russian Poland, spent two months gaining the patient's confidence, and offered to take her into his home. With the agreement of the hospital authorities the woman was discharged, still silent, and heavily veiled.

When the baron's family doctor examined the new arrival, his report was not encouraging. She was suffering from acute anaemia, slight lung haemorrhage, and the left lung showed signs of pleurisy. The doctor also noted that she had at some time suffered a severe injury to the head.

In June 1922, according to Baron Kleist, his protégée asked to speak to him and his wife in private. He said she told them both, quite categorically, that she was in fact the Grand Duchess Anastasia; that she had been present at the "massacre" of the imperial family and that she had been the sole survivor. She said she had hidden behind one of her sisters, had herself been hit by gunfire, and had then lost consciousness. When she came to she found herself with the family of a soldier who had realized she was still alive, and rescued her at the last minute from Bolshevik clutches. According to Baron Kleist, the grand duchess then travelled with the soldier's family by road to Roumania, and then made her own way on to Berlin. In another conversation, said the baron, the mystery girl added to the story. She named the soldier as Alexander Tschaikowsky, and said she had had a child by him, a son, conceived during the trek out of Russia. Tschaikowsky had been killed in a street fight in Bucharest, and her child had been placed in an orphanage.[25]

Once Baron Kleist broke the news that his ward claimed to be the Grand Duchess Anastasia, notoriety was assured. Her initial gratitude to the baron soon turned to resentment when he allowed innumerable visitors to pester her with questions and stare at her like an animal in a cage. Life continued to be a nightmare of insecurity and sickness. In July 1922 she collapsed choking and with pains in the lung, and was treated with digitalis three times daily, as well as morphia. The doctor's report noted: ". . . In her sleep she talks Russian with good pronunciation: mostly unessential things."

But the mystery patient made an astonishing recovery, and then ran away. Between 1922 and 1927 she was restless, moved around many times, and was admitted to one hospital after another. As the frustration of her life multiplied, her difficult character became even more intractable. Her health declined again, and she began to suffer from severe tuberculosis of the bones—a disease which almost killed her. But during these five years the royal families of Europe began to take an active interest. She was visited by Princess Heinrich of Prussia, the tsarina's sister, and by Crown Princess Cecile, daughter-in-law of Kaiser Wilhelm.

By 1925 the case was causing concern at the court in Copenhagen, where the tsar's mother, Dowager Empress Marie, now lived in exile with her younger daughter Olga. Marie's brother, Prince Valdemar of Denmark, asked Herluf Zahle, the Danish minister in Berlin, to look into the whole affair. The claimant was visited in hospital by Alexei Volkov, the tsarina's former servant. Grand Duchess Olga also asked Pierre Gilliard and his wife Shura, who had been the young Anastasia's nursemaid, to go and see her (*see plate 41*). If the Gilliards thought there was any possibility that the invalid was really Anastasia, they were to let the grand duchess know, and she would come herself.

When the Gilliards arrived from Switzerland, the patient was so ill that it was considered pointless to try to question her; but the visitors were distressed by what they saw, and were instrumental in having her transferred to another hospital, where she could have an operation. Some months later the Gilliards came again, and this time Grand Duchess Olga came with them. Precisely what happened during these dramatic confrontations, what the visitors' true reactions were, have long since been blurred by the indecorous bickering that followed. We shall deal with the opinions of the visitors later—but their coming marked the start of a vicious and prolonged family feud over the identity of the mystery woman. The years to come were packed with confusion and contradiction, and heavy with political implications.

In 1926, "Anastasia" was to go to Switzerland on medical advice, a journey which required *bona fide* travel documents. This was a problem for a mystery woman who, bureaucratically speaking, did not exist. By this time, Grand Duchess Olga had publicly stated, on the advice of Pierre Gilliard, that the patient was not her niece. But that did not deter the German Foreign Ministry from asking the Berlin Aliens Office to issue an identity card, alluding to "special reasons" for doing so. Dr Rathenau, a senior counsellor at the Prussian Home Office, noted that ". . . on the basis of police enquiries so far, the unknown woman is in all probability one and the same as the tsar's daughter Anastasia". It is worth noting that the invalid was also generally accepted as being authentic by her nurses and doctors—the people who spent most time with her. In June 1926, after her stay in Switzerland she was moved back to Germany, to a sanatorium in the Bavarian Alps, and was visited there by Tatiana Botkin, daughter of the tsar's doctor.

Madame Botkin had been with the imperial family in exile at Tobolsk, and had been one of the last to see Anastasia. She now arrived expecting to find a pathetic impostor, and intended to end the controversy once and for all. To her utter surprise, she felt at once that she was face to face with the real Anastasia. Soon she had not the slightest doubt, and remains loyal to the claimant to this day. It was the most important event for the invalid since she had appeared in Berlin, but she was by now under heavy attack from other quarters.

The Danish minister Zahle, who was still compiling his dossier for the Danish court, had himself come to believe the claimant was genuine. But even with his prestige as President of the League of Nations, he found it increasingly difficult to cope with the opposition now being mounted by some of the most powerful members of the families she claimed as relatives. At this point the president of the White Russian Association in Berlin asked a senior Romanov, Grand Duke Andrei, to undertake a thorough investigation. As the tsar's cousin, and as a jurist trained at the Military Law Academy, the grand duke was an ideal choice; he accepted, and set to work with the approval of the tsar's mother. But as soon as he started trying to gather hard facts, he too found himself obstructed and harassed by the claimant's opponents. Foremost among them was the tsarina's German brother, Grand Duke Ernst Ludwig of Hesse, and he made it clear to Grand Duke Andrei that helping the invalid could, in his own words, be "perilous". In one of his letters, Andrei came to sinister conclusions: ". . . it is plain to see that 'they' fear something and are very disturbed, as if the investigation could uncover something embarrassing and even dangerous for them . . ."

The fanaticism of some of "Anastasia's" enemies led to fears for her life, and it was a relief to her supporters when in 1927 Duke George of Leuchtenberg invited her to Castle Seeon, in Upper Bavaria. There the claimant's health improved, but outside the castle walls the ferocious attack continued. The Grand Duke of Hesse gave his powerful backing to a private detective, Martin Knopf, who claimed to achieve in a matter of days what the Berlin police had failed to accomplish in seven years. Knopf said he had identified the claimant as Franziska Schanzkowska, a Polish factory worker who had been reported missing in Berlin in March 1920 (see plate 45). His prime witness was a daughter of Franziska's former landlady, who came forward to say she recognized the claimant as the missing girl. The best way to show that the invalid was not Anastasia was indeed to prove that she was actually someone else—but the attempt miscarried.

At Castle Seeon, the claimant was confronted by Franziska's brother. At first he gave the impression that he recognized the claimant as his sister, but he refused to sign an affidavit to this effect. On the contrary, he suddenly admitted that any resemblance was purely superficial. His sister's teeth had been different; her feet had been larger and quite unlike those of the invalid, which had an obvious peculiarity of shape. Nor did the language and dialect tally with that of his family. The effort to fabricate an identity for the claimant had failed—but it was to prove a lasting slur.[26]

Life at Castle Seeon had become something of a circus, as the curious visitors came and went. It had the effect on "Anastasia" of making her impossibly irritable and difficult to live with. Her host was not sorry when, in 1928, she was invited to visit the United States as the guest of Princess Xenia Georgievna of Russia, the real Anastasia's second cousin. When she arrived, the princess was out of New York, but arranged for the claimant to be welcomed by a friend, Annie B. Jennings.

"Anastasia" was now presumed to be 27 years old and, perhaps predictably, the enigmatic, battered refugee became the toast of Long Island. She was briefly the darling of Amercan high society, and also a target for the Barnum and Bailey commercialism of her host country. She was talked of everywhere, the press pursued her, and a Hollywood-style legend grew apace (*see plate 42*). The image bore little relationship to the real-life woman, who remained uninterested in publicity and incapable of forming meaningful relationships. But for a while the ballyhoo continued. There was talk of plots against her by mysterious assassins, and in a piece of true Americana, private eyes with sub-machine guns were hired to protect her.

A less hectic six months with Princess Xenia and her husband ended with a quarrel. The princess had rashly promised to arrange a visit to see Dowager Empress Marie, the tsar's mother, in Copenhagen; when the visit failed to materialize "Anastasia" accused Xenia of breaking her word. Another friend was estranged, and the claimant now fell into the irresponsible hands of Gleb Botkin, the son of the tsar's doctor. He believed in her identity, but his help was never wise, and increasingly compromised her.

It was Gleb who took her from the protection of Princess Xenia, but thanks to the generosity of the famous Russian pianist Rachmaninov, she was able to stay for four months in the Garden City Hotel, Long Island. On 10 August 1928, to mislead pursuing journalists, she signed the register as "Anna Anderson"—the name which was to stick for 40 years.

Gleb retained a lawyer, Edward Fallows, and with his arrival on the scene the Anastasia saga became inextricably involved with complex manœuvres to obtain the legendary fortune the tsar had supposedly left in American, British and German bank accounts. Although Anna Anderson had no awareness or understanding of legal procedures or international finance, her name was now pinned to a business venture registered as the "Grandanor Corporation"—an acronym of Grand Duchess Anastasia Nikolayevna of Russia. The purpose of the whole dubious concern was to sue for the

alleged fortune and reward those involved by the issue of
shares. Fallows was to receive a quarter of any sum under
$400,000 which might be prised out of the banks, plus 10 per
cent of all further monies. Gleb was a director of the company.
Whether the Romanov fortune existed then, or does now,
"Grandanor" came as a propaganda gift to Anna Anderson's
enemies, and did nothing to help her case.

While her personal affairs got increasingly out of control, so
did Anna Anderson herself. She had always had a disarmingly
self-assured manner of treating anyone except relations of the
Romanovs as her personal servants. But now, during another
stay with the wealthy Annie Jennings, she behaved positively
despotically. At first nobody realized that she was becoming
mentally disturbed. In the spring of 1930 she was frequently
visited by a young Englishwoman called Jill Cossley-Batt, who
let it be thought she was really the Dowager Countess of
Huntingdon, currently on a special assignment for *The Times*.
The Jennings family were impressed, unaware that she was
mischievously encouraging the claimant to turn against them.
They very nearly surrendered their guest to the mercy of this
woman, but in July the "countess" was unmasked as a complete
fraud, and the shock drove Anna Anderson into a frenzy.
Some time before, she had been given a pair of parakeets,
which seemed to mean more to her than human companion-
ship, as animals have done all her life. Now, in a fit of anger,
she trod on one of the birds by mistake, and killed it. The
result was hysteria which lasted all night. Her hosts finally
lost patience and decided—quite ruthlessly—to get "Anastasia" out of the way. Three doctors were called in to sign a
document that made it possible to send her to a mental institution, a service for which the medical men were paid no less
than $1,250. After a humilating scene in which a crowd of
men burst into her room with an axe, Anna Anderson was
bundled into a car and driven through the night to the
"Four Winds" rest home—the rich man's euphemism for an
asylum.

The stay at "Four Winds" marked the end of "Anastasia's"
romantic image as the fairytale princess. In August 1931,
Anna Anderson was hustled off on another surreptitious
journey—this time to New York harbour, and cabin No. 90 on

board the liner *Deutschland*. The destination, arranged in advance by her erstwhile American friends, was Germany, and yet another mental hospital—at Ilten, near Hanover. One might have expected the return to Europe to be the end of the road, the final incarceration of an unstable woman, left alone with her delusions. In fact, although Anna Anderson still told her new German doctors that she was Anastasia, they did not think she was crazy. On the contrary, the director of the sanatorium wrote to Danish Minister Zahle: "from our observations so far, there can be no question of insanity . . ."

She was free to leave Ilten, but for want of anywhere to go, and because her fees had been paid in advance from America, she stayed on for some time. The period that now began was marked by more recognitions and fresh controversy. One of the doctors at Ilten was so favourably impressed that he reported his opinion to the exiled Kaiser Wilhelm, during a holiday in Holland. The result was a visit to Anna Anderson by Empress Hermine, the Kaiser's second wife, who showed sympathy and took her seriously. Another visitor was Prince Frederick of Saxe Altenburg, who had lost several of his Romanov cousins in the Revolution. He was to advise and protect Anna Anderson consistently for nearly 40 years. When she left Ilten in June 1932 she began a quieter, more dignified phase of her life—thirteen years of comparative peace living as the guest of European aristocracy.

But with her return to Europe the opponents got busy again. One example of their tactics was the publication of a news report that Anna Anderson had confessed to being a Roumanian actress. This said she had been caught out after a team had gone secretly to Ekaterinburg and succeeded in exhuming the bodies of the imperial family. The skeleton of Anastasia, the story implied, was now literally out of the cupboard. Anna Anderson's attorney extracted apologies from newspapers that had used the story, and rather more from the paper which had originated it in September 1932, *The News of the World*. The source of the report, said the newspaper, was the legal representative of a Romanov living in Paris.

The thirties also saw the real start, despite Anna Anderson's own apathy, of a prolonged legal battle for recognition. In 1933 a Berlin court granted certificates of inheritance to a

41

42

41 Anna Anderson, the claimant, at the Mommsen Clinic, Berlin, 1925.

42 The claimant, shortly after arrival in the United States, 1928.

43 The real Anastasia—an unpublished family snapshot.

44 Anna Anderson, now Mrs John Manahan, at home in
Charlottesville, Virginia, 1974.

45

46

45 Franziska
Schanzkowska, Polish
factory girl—the
claimant's opponents
alleged she and
Franziska were one and
same.

46 Anna Anderson after
World War II, outside
her hut in the Black
Forest. Note the bone
protruding at her left
elbow, the result of an
operation for a tubercular
abcess.

47

48

47 & 48 The claimant
(*left*), as an elderly
woman, in 1967. (*Right*)
Grand Duchess Xenia,
the tsar's sister and
therefore aunt to the real
Anastasia, photographed
at a similar age.

number of near relatives of the tsar. The beneficiaries were to include the tsar's two sisters Xenia and Olga, and his sister-in-law Countess Brassova. In Germany there was the tsarina's brother, Grand Duke Ernst Ludwig of Hesse, and her sister Irene, Princess Heinrich of Prussia. In England her other sister, Victoria, Marchioness of Milford Haven, was to benefit. The court in 1937 gave these relatives the right to divide amongst themselves what remained of the tsar's assets in Germany. They amounted to a trivial 300,000 Reichsmarks (worth just £6,000 in post-war values) held by the Mendelssohn Bank. But one of the certificates of inheritance specifically named Grand Duchess Anastasia as deceased, and being aware of Anna Anderson's claims, the bank wrote to warn her.

Assistance now came from an unexpected quarter—two top German diplomats. Count Albrecht Bernstorff and Dr Kurt Riezler, who had been senior counsellor at the German embassy in Moscow at the time of the Romanovs disappearance, came forward to recommend Dr Paul Leverkuehn, one of the best legal brains in Germany. With his help a petition was lodged in 1938 for the withdrawal of the certificate of inheritance which had presumed the death of Anastasia. Given the tiny amount of cash involved, this was clearly an attempt to establish identity rather than to get rich. In 1941 the action failed in the Central Berlin District Court, and was taken to the High Court. There were inevitable delays because of wartime conditions, and the allied bombing of Dr Leverkuehn's offices; then with the collapse of the Third Reich Anna Anderson found herself stranded in the Russian zone, and in real fear of the Soviet occupation forces. She was rescued by her friend Prince Frederick, with the help of the Red Cross, and after passing through a refugee camp on the border she was brought safely to Bad Liebenzell, in the Black Forest, in December 1946. But the era of hospitality in stately homes was almost over. Prince Frederick, her main protector, had lost his property in what was now to become East Germany, and was himself a refugee. Out of his own dwindling capital he bought Anna Anderson an old army hut at Unterlengenhardt (*see plate 46*). It was now a quarter of a century since "Anastasia" had been pulled from a Berlin canal. She still had no established identity—and the time had come to begin yet another new life. But at the presumed age of 46, the woman who could not find an identity could not even achieve obscurity for long.

A play about the Anastasia story was turned into the famous Hollywood film. Through the benevolence of the scriptwriter, Anna Anderson received a sizeable sum of money, some of which went to her lawyers, who had not been paid in twenty years. But the show business razzamatazz and her eccentricities combined to bring unwelcome attention from the international press. Journalists peered into the hut, snatched photographs, and pestered her for interviews; charabanc loads of tourists travelled from Stuttgart to gawp. The pre-war toast of Long Island was now presented as the post-war hermit of the Black Forest. Anna Anderson tried to avoid all contact, and shut herself away with one elderly female companion. She used the remains of the money from the film to build herself a small "dacha" next to her old hut. It was completed in 1960—a pleasant chalet equipped with modern facilities. Furniture, donated by German aristocrats who had never completely abandoned her, included a bed which had belonged to the mother-in-law of Queen Victoria, the real Anastasia's great-grandmother. Typically perverse, Anna Anderson continued to sleep on a couch while her myriad cats took over the royal bedstead. Guarded by four vicious wolf hounds, she barricaded herself into what was left of her private world. Her kingdom was a tiny patch of land that had come with the old hut, and she spent time and energy making it look attractive. But still Anna Anderson could not leave the world behind.

The legal machinery she had long ago blithely imagined would swiftly prove her identity was grinding inexorably on. The petition for withdrawal of the certificate of inheritance had continued in the courts until 1957, even though all but a paltry £1,000 of the tsar's money in Germany had long since been distributed among the relatives.[27] This petition, as such, was a failure, but one of the judges of the Berlin Court of Appeal had recommended a fresh approach. He said that in his opinion there was sufficient evidence for Anna Anderson to sue for recognition as the Grand Duchess Anastasia. It was a judicial turning point.

The logical course now was to bring a formal suit against

someone who had assumed the death of the claimant. The
passing of time had brought deaths in the scattered family, and
younger relatives were now technically responsible. The list of
potential defendants included the children of the tsarina's
sister, Victoria—the present Lord Mountbatten and his sisters
Princess Andrew of Greece (Prince Philip's mother) and Queen
Louise of Sweden. But Anna Anderson's lawyers decided to
keep the lawsuit within national frontiers by bringing the
action against the granddaughter of the tsarina's other sister,
Irene. This was a lady with the complex name and title of
"Barbara, Duchess Christian Ludwig of Mecklenburg, Princess
of Hesse and by Rhine, Princess of Prussia". She was not even
born until two years after the disappearance of the Romanovs
from Ekaterinburg, but she now became the formal standard
bearer for the opposition to Anna Anderson. The male heir
to the tsarina's brother, Prince Ludwig of Hesse and by Rhine,
volunteered his services as co-defendant. On 15 October 1957,
battle was joined in the High Court at Hamburg.

Legal costs alone had by now far exceeded any financial
benefit which could ever have been gained, but Anna Anderson's opponents still defended the suit vigorously, and their
interest was certainly not money. From the beginning, the
opposition had used all means at their disposal to discredit her,
and on more than one occasion this had involved accepting
the help of shady figures whose tactics were underhand and
plain dishonest.

A key opposition witness, who caused great damage to Anna
Anderson, was Hans Johann Mayer, an Austrian who in 1918
had been a prisoner-of-war in Russia. Mayer's connection with
the Romanov story had begun in December 1955 when—ironically—he had made contact with Anna Anderson's counsel,
through a friend. Mayer had volunteered the information that
he had been in the Ipatiev House on the night of 16 July 1918;
it was suggested that—for a consideration—he could testify
in favour of the claimant, and would state that Anastasia had
escaped the slaughter. The reward for his services was to be a
monthly payment of £250 for life, beginning from the date of
Mayer's appearance in court. If Anna Anderson should win
her case, this arrangement was to be superseded by a lump
sum of £200,000. Anna Anderson's lawyer rejected the offer

out of hand, and Mayer's representative was shown the door.

That could have been the end of the matter. But in May 1956, Mayer approached the editor of the news magazine *7-Tage*, which proceeded to publish a series of articles drawing on "exclusive" material provided by Mayer—and stating that he had seen the entire imperial family lying dead in the famous basement. All mention of Anastasia's survival had now disappeared, and Mayer supplied "documentary proof" of the massacre including a paper purporting to be an unused Bolshevik draft of the tsar's execution announcement. This bore the "signatures" of Beloborodov, chairman of the Regional Soviet, and of Commissar Goloshchokin. It showed the words "and his family" scored out by hand, as if the Regional Soviet had altered the proclamation at the last moment to announce the execution of the tsar alone. Mayer was paid more than £400 by the magazine. Because of the articles, the opponents of Anna Anderson introduced Mayer as a witness in the Anastasia dispute. He confirmed his statements on oath, and the Court accepted his evidence. In their judgement against Anna Anderson in early 1957, the judges made it clear they absolutely believed his testimony. At the time it was a crushing blow for the claimant; but gradually Mayer was exposed. First another former prisoner-of-war, Otto Stephan, came forward to state from personal knowledge that Mayer was a forger. He said that as long ago as 1938, Mayer, who was a cook with little literary talent, had asked him to help compile his memoirs. Stephan recalled the day when the aspiring author arrived with a handful of forged Russian papers relating to the Romanov murders; Mayer admitted having had them printed in Berlin, which was why they seemed so new, but after they had been scuffed on the floor they began to look less spurious. The next time Stephan saw them was in the 1956 magazine articles.

A second person was to come forward to expose Mayer. Robert von Lerche, a Russian exile, wrote to tell Anna Anderson's representative that the Mayer papers were full of errors. One flaw was the reference in Russian to the "Chief of the Revolutionary Staff", using the word *"Chef"* instead of the Russian *"Nachalnik"*. The name of Goloshchokin was wrongly spelt both in the text and in the signature. The spelling did not conform to that on Ekaterinburg documents long accepted as authentic. Mayer had also invented a list of Ipatiev guards who never existed—including, incidentally, himself. Mayer died in 1957, but his influence persisted. It was not until 1964, when the Anastasia case reached the Hamburg Court of Appeal, that Mayer's perjury was conceded. Anticipating exposure, the opposition lawyer quietly admitted that his witness had lied. The Mayer affair remains to this day a pitfall for Romanov specialists. Copies of his forgeries still circulate, and were even produced as proof of the Ipatiev House massacre in a learned book, *Letters of the Tsar's Family from Captivity*, published in 1974.

Given that there is supposedly no Romanov fortune at stake, the tsar's relatives in exile went to extraordinary lengths to smother the Anastasia affair. One example came from Britain from Lord Mountbatten. In 1971 he told us that he had personally contributed thousands of pounds to legal fees towards the battle against Anna Anderson's claim; and there is other evidence of the extreme sensitivity with which Lord Mountbatten regards the whole matter. In the autumn of 1958, shortly after the case reached the High Court in Hamburg, Lord Mountbatten read in the newspapers that a BBC film team was shortly to go to Germany to interview Anna Anderson. He immediately wrote to the then director-general of the BBC, Sir Ian Jacob, expressing shock that the corporation was considering such a film, and pointing out the expense and trouble the series of law-suits had given his relatives. He assured Sir Ian that there was not the remotest chance that "Frau Anderson" could be his cousin, and appealed to the BBC not to allow its facilities to be used by the "impostor's" backers. Within two days, Lord Mountbatten received assurances that the "Anastasia" project had been cancelled. The director-general was later to write to Lord Mountbatten thanking him for pointing out that the lady was an impostor, and reiterating the promise that the BBC would have nothing to do with her. In fact, Lord Mountbatten's letter had produced no new facts about the case—indeed it contained several inaccuracies; but the incident demonstrated how the Anastasia affair, after 40 years, could still touch a raw nerve at the highest levels.

This is not the place to deal with the minutiae of all the Anastasia legal actions. The court dossier itself has now accumulated over 8,000 pages—mute testimony, if nothing else, to the passion which has surrounded Anna Anderson's claims. But it is unlikely that the case will now go much further. The principal protagonists, including "Anastasia" herself, are nearing the end of their lives. But now that the dust has begun to settle on those voluminous legal files, and now that time has drawn some of the sting from the battle over her claim, it is a moment to take stock of the main evidence for and against "Anastasia".

Firstly, a look at the final line-up of senior Russian exiles and foreign relatives on the matter of recognition. The opponents make an impressive enough list. In October 1928, twelve surviving members of the Romanov family and three of the tsarina's relatives, signed a joint declaration stating their ". . . firm conviction that the woman now living in the United States . . . is not Grand Duchess Anastasia Nikolayevna". That list of signatories included both the tsar's sisters, Xenia and Olga; Grand Duke Alexander; the tsar's brother-in-law, Grand Duke Ernst Ludwig of Hesse; and the tsarina's two sisters, Victoria, Marchioness of Milford Haven, and Princess Heinrich of Prussia. The statement leaned heavily on the fact that the tsar's sister, Olga, had visited Anna Anderson, and that as a result she "states categorically that this person has nothing in common with the Grand Duchess Anastasia". The joint statement pointed out that Baroness Buxhoeveden and Pierre Gilliard also categorically rejected Anna Anderson's claim. These witnesses had all known the real Anastasia, so their rejection should have dealt the final blow to Anna Anderson. But on a little closer examination their statement loses much of its conviction.

It is not true, as is often alleged, that the declaration showed that the entire Romanov family disowned Anna Anderson. When it was drawn up, only two of the signatories had even seen the claimant. Grand Duke Andrei and Princess Xenia Georgievna, who recognized her, were not consulted. The statement was published in Copenhagen only three days after Dowager Empress Marie had died there. It was said that her approval had been given, but it is curious that, although the signatories were in Denmark for the funeral, the text was released two days earlier in Darmstadt, Germany, the capital of the Grand Duke of Hesse.

Grand Duchess Olga was the real Anastasia's godmother and favourite aunt, making her evidence most significant. In 1925 she visited Anna Anderson several times over a four-day period. In her memoirs, published after her death in 1960, she is quoted:

My beloved Anastasia was fifteen when I saw her for the last time in the summer of 1916. She would have been 24 in 1925. I thought Mrs Anderson looked much older than that. Of course one had to make allowances for a very long illness, and the general poor condition of her health. All the same, my niece's features could not possibly have altered out of all recognition. The nose, the mouth, the eyes were all different ... I had the impression she was getting tired of playing a part. She *nearly* admitted to me that some people always told her what to say on certain occasions ...

This total rejection came as a shock to the claimant's supporters, who always maintained that Olga had left Berlin unsure whether the mysterious patient was her niece or not, and certainly not repudiating her out of hand. Support for this view comes from Herluf Zahle, the Danish minister in Berlin, who accompanied Olga on the visit to Anna Anderson. He quoted Olga as saying: "I can't say that it's she, but I can't say that it isn't." We have now obtained two documents which show quite conclusively that this last version is the correct one, and that the "Anastasia" supporters were right all the time. The first is a letter written to Zahle by Grand Duchess Olga herself immediately after her visit to Berlin. In a "thank you" note, on 31 October 1925, she said:

I have had very long conversations with my mother and U. Valdemar all about our poor little friend; I can't tell you how fond I got of her—whoever she is. My feeling is that she is not the one she believes—but one can't *say she* is *not* as a fact [*Olga's italics*]—as there are still many strange and inexplicable facts not cleared up. How is she after our departure? I have sent her a post card and shall write from time to time so that she may feel we are near her . . .

We found further confirmation of Olga's lingering doubts during our research in American State archives. It is in a report sent in November 1925 to the State Department from the American Legation in Copenhagen. Olga had just returned from her visit to see "Anastasia" and had given a long briefing to the American envoy, John Prince. Prince, reporting on her reaction and that of her companions, said:

None of these people could establish an identification, but it is interesting to notice that the Grand Duchess Olga did not absolutely deny this woman's identity . . . she is convinced that [*the claimant*] is not consciously simulating, as she was given many opportunities to give false answers which she did not avail herself of, but neither could she give correct ones. The Grand Duchess Olga left Berlin without being able to give any definite answer as to the identity of [*the claimant*], although the grand duchess is almost sure that the claimant cannot be Anastasia . . . In view of the slight doubt still existing as to [*the claimant's*] identity, Prince George of Greece may continue to extend financial aid to the patient. The empress here and her immediate entourage are anxious not to have anything appear in the press regarding the investigation.

In spite of her uncertainty, Olga never bothered to visit Anna Anderson again. Perhaps this was a mistake, for she might have learned why her "god-daughter's" features could have altered so dramatically. Professor Rudneff, the surgeon treating "Anastasia" at the time of Olga's visit, wrote: "There was not a trace of fat on her body; her temperature fluctuated around 38°, and the pains in her arms were so bad that we had to give her eight normal injections of morphia every 24 hours. In these circumstances, her features may well have changed beyond recognition." It is known from the last description of the real

Anastasia as she left Tobolsk for Ekaterinburg in 1918, that she was "stout" and "pretty".

There are also problems with the evidence of Pierre Gilliard. He visited Anna Anderson in 1925, and later published a book discrediting her, called *The False Anastasia*. He asserted that she spoke only German, a language the real Anastasia allegedly did not know at all, and that she failed to recognize photographs of the old days at the imperial court. He scoffed at a reference by the claimant to a room in one of the palaces, decorated with green malachite. This Gilliard dismissed as "pure fantasy". But it was Gilliard who was fantasizing. Two years after his death in 1962, the school exercise books of the Romanov grand duchesses were recovered and produced in court. They revealed that all the girls had been learning German. Another document found amongst Gilliard's own papers was a time-table from the days of exile in Tobolsk showing that Anastasia was still receiving two German lessons each week. As for the "malachite room", the former head of the Court Chancery devoted a whole chapter to it in his memoirs, published years after the claimant had mentioned its existence. The room was used by the imperial family as a private assembly point before receptions, so perhaps Gilliard never saw it.

Grand Duke Andrei wrote of the Romanov tutor in 1927: "Gilliard has at last exposed himself as a petty man capable of lying, but incapable of understanding that it is his own lies which betray him." On another occasion the grand duke noted that Gilliard was spending much time at the home of the tsarina's brother and making many of his denunciations from there. He concluded that Gilliard was part of "a well organized intrigue". The Grand Duke of Hesse, always hostile, was consistently behind the opposition to Anastasia. In his role may lie the key to far more than the Anastasia riddle.

He never saw the claimant himself, but his sister, Irene, wrote after visiting her in 1922: "I saw at once that she couldn't be one of my nieces. Although I had not seen them for nine years, the fundamental traits couldn't have changed so much, particularly the position of the ears, the eyes etc." Princess Heinrich had of course met the claimant when she was physically at her lowest ebb, emaciated and toothless.

But how convinced was she really that the sick woman bore no similarity to her niece? In 1950 Prince Frederick of Saxe Altenburg had a tense conversation with the old lady, who became extremely agitated. She paced up and down the room, clasping and unclasping her hands, muttering: ". . . she *is* similar, she *is* similar, but what does that mean if it is not she?"

Why was the House of Hesse so hostile to the possibility that the claimant might be Anastasia? There is one clue which suggests why recognition could have been deeply embarrassing to the grand duke. In 1925, while in hospital and at death's door, "Anastasia" talked to a visitor, Amy Smith, granddaughter of a mayor of Hamburg, and implored her to bring the grand duke, her "Uncle Ernie", to her bedside. As Fräulein Smith was leaving the sickroom, she paused in the doorway to ask when the patient had last seen her uncle. Anna Anderson replied clearly: "In the war, with us at home." Everyone who heard her was taken aback and said she must surely be mistaken—for the simple reason that Germany and Russia had been enemies, and the Grand Duke of Hesse was a German general. But "Anastasia" stuck to her story and was annoyed at being contradicted. She was the first person known to have spoken of such a visit, and a first-hand.

Amy Smith did go to the grand-ducal court, armed with a mass of information about the claimant. At first she was courteously received by a senior aide, who indicated that his master was very interested. But when the grand duke learned of the specific remark about a wartime visit to Russia he at once let it be known that he could not become involved. Later, the court formally denounced the claimant as an impostor.

Despite universal scepticism "Anastasia" insisted that she was right about the visit, and later she elaborated on it in a talk with Herluf Zahle, the Danish minister in Berlin; she declared that "Uncle Ernie" had been on a secret mission in 1916, aimed at arranging a separate peace between imperial Russia and Germany. It was still the word of a grand duke against the allegations of an unidentified woman lying in a Berlin hospital, and the claimant's story was scorned. But time has brought considerable vindication for "Anastasia's" anecdote.

In 1953 Crown Princess Cecile made this formal deposition:

If the view is still held today that such a visit never took place, I can assert from personal knowledge—the source is my late father-in-law [*the Kaiser*]—that this visit was already known in our circles at the time. In my opinion [*the claimant*] showed by her statement, which I only heard about much later, strong evidence at least of her intimate knowledge of the high politics and of the most secret dealings of the imperial family.

Further support for the story was to come from a number of other witnesses. In 1966 the Kaiser's stepson, Prince Ferdinand of Schoenaich Carolath, also testified that the Kaiser had told him about the visit, and had said that he himself authorized the grand duke's attempt to establish a separate peace with Russia. Corroboration also came from the Russian side, from Prince Dmitry Galitzin. He testified on oath in 1965 that he had actually seen the Grand Duke of Hesse at Tsarskoe Selo palace in 1916; the German visitor had been wearing civilian clothes, a detail which was in marked contrast to the usual sea of Russian military uniforms. The tsar had refused to consider his brother-in-law's proposals, and the fact that he had been received at all was kept secret. Another witness, the Princess of Thurn and Taxis, Infanta of Portugal, recalled her uncle, the Archduke Joseph of Austria, talking about the mission; as a field-marshal in the Austrian High Command he had been informed about it at the time.

With hindsight, Anna Anderson's allegation is quite plausible. By 1916 both the German High Command and the German Foreign Office favoured knocking Russia out of the war by fostering internal revolution. The Kaiser opposed this policy, and it would have been in character for him to sponsor a secret peace mission in defiance of his own government, hoping to neutralize Russia with the imperial regime intact. It would have been in line with his early, albeit clumsy, "monarch-to-monarch" diplomacy with Tsar Nicholas. That Wilhelm did favour a separate peace with Russia is confirmed by an entry in the diary of General Hoffmann, the German chief-of-staff on the Eastern Front, as early as 27 August 1916: "HM still has a strange hope of coming to a separate understanding with Russia, so that it is thought wise not to offend the tsar over Poland . . ." On 12 December 1916 the German chancellor made a formal peace offer to all the Allied powers —one which was rejected. But during the discussions that preceded the offer, Wilhelm remained convinced that Germany's best hope lay in an approach to Russia alone. The timing fits with Anna Anderson's recollection of "Uncle Ernie's" visit, which she recalled as occurring in winter.

More evidence about the secret mission has surfaced over the years. Some of it is eye-witness testimony which actually traces the route taken by the grand duke—from north Germany to Norway, then overland to northern Sweden, and into Finland, which was still part of the Russian empire. In 1957 Baroness Marie Pilar von Pilchau gave evidence that her late brother, a diplomat, helped arrange the journey:

> My brother was well-known to the late Grand Duke of Hesse-Darmstadt. In the year 1916 my brother was working as counsellor at the Imperial Russian Legation in Oslo. During that period the Grand Duke Ernst Ludwig of Hesse sent an aide to Oslo, to my brother, to ask for his assistance in a journey to Russia by way of Haparanda [*border town on Swedish/Finnish frontier*]. With my brother's help the trip to Russia did take place . . .

Other witnesses who filled in the details of the mission included a Russian colonel who spotted the grand duke during his journey across Finland,[28] and a member of the grand duke's own staff, Fritz von Unruh, who had been tutor in the Hesse household. He stated that in 1916 the aide who had travelled with the grand duke to Russia, aware of Unruh's pacifist sympathies, told him about the peace mission while at the front.

One can understand why Grand Duke Ernst Ludwig might have wished to keep all this secret in the years after World War I. There was a strong monarchist movement in Germany and the grand duke, however unrealistically, still hoped for a restoration. To admit that he had been on enemy territory during the war, and probably without the approval of the German High Command, would have left Ernst Ludwig in a highly compromising position. It would have smacked of treason and would have been of enormous propaganda value to the German left-wing. Even so, it is hard to believe that the grand duke would wilfully have abandoned his sister's only surviving child, Anastasia. The claimant's supporters argue that he made a conscious decision to sacrifice his "niece" partly for the political reasons, and partly because she was considered unlikely to live much longer. It seems more reasonable to suppose that the grand duke did not believe the sick girl was Anastasia, but decided not even to investigate the case, in order to avoid further exposure of the Russian mission. His entourage, in deference to his wishes, then systematically contrived "proof" of imposture. It is more difficult to see why the Hesse family continued as late as the 1960's to deny the peace mission. The Grand Duke was long dead, and the matter had ceased to be of current political relevance.

We have given considerable space to the subject of the alleged Hesse peace mission, partly because it is of historical importance in its own right, but also because of its special significance in the context of the Anastasia affair. Today the weight of evidence suggests that Anna Anderson's casual remark in 1925 was perfectly accurate; whatever her identity, she apparently had early, exclusive access to a tightly kept state secret, and became the first to mention it in public. But there were a number of witnesses who were satisfied, without such compelling evidence, that the mystery woman really was Anastasia.

Anna Anderson was recognized by such an impressive list of relations and acquaintances of Anastasia that it is hard to understand how a complete phoney, a total impostor, could have attracted this amount of distinguished attention and support. There is no historical precedent.

First let us consider the man who investigated the case both as a relative and jurist, and devoted more serious study to it than any other Romanov. Grand Duke Andrei had been an active aide-de-camp to Tsar Nicholas throughout the war. As a result he had seen the imperial children regularly, unlike the tsar's sister, Olga, who saw Anastasia only twice during the war, and the tsarina's sister, Irene, who did not see Anastasia after 1913. In January 1928 Andrei spent two days with Anna Anderson, and wrote a few days later to Olga, who had seen the claimant three years earlier, when she was critically ill.

The Grand Duke's reaction now was as positive as Olga's had been doubtful:

On 30 January [she] was brought to Paris, and I went there personally to see her at last and to find out who she really is, about whom so heated a controversy has arisen, so many fables have circulated, and whose name has caused so much discord and family dissension. I have spent two days with her, have observed her carefully at close quarters, and to the best of my conscience I must acknowledge that Anastasia Tschaikowsky is none other than my niece, the Grand Duchess Anastasia Nikolayevna. I recognized her at once, and further observation only confirmed my first impression. For me there is definitely no doubt; it is Anastasia. I can only regret that you have not decided to see her again: you would certainly have recognized her now, just as I recognized her.

You do not know, Olga, what I have been through these days as I sat beside her and looked at dear Anastasia—but so ill and careworn. If you had seen her lovely, still so childish smile, those eyes full of pain and suffering, it would have broken your heart, like mine. Now she is already far away, in America, and we shall not soon see her again—if we ever see her again. What will she experience there in that distant foreign land? God alone knows. Certainly grave thoughts will trouble her and an agonizing question will obsess her, which nobody can now answer for her. Whether Anastasia will outlive these new ordeals—who knows? But I pray to God that she may survive and recover, and return to us from strange lands, not as a hunted and persecuted creature, but with her head held high, and that she may find in herself the grace to forgive those who bring her so much misfortune.

After the meeting in Paris, Grand Duke Andrei's conclusion was leaked to the press against his wishes. He always disliked bringing family dissension into the open, and did nothing to confirm the report. So with time, his recognition of the claimant came to be regarded as a mere rumour. But in 1960 the letter to Olga was made public, as a result of a blunder by the Grand

Duke's son, Vladimir. He had always tried to maintain a neutral position to avoid upsetting other Romanovs who were hostile to Anna Anderson. Vladimir therefore tried to make good the damage done by the publication of his father's letter. He released the text of another one, said to have been written by Andrei to the same Grand Duchess Olga, in 1950. In this document the grand duke appears to want to heal past differences and asserts that he had never been entirely convinced of the claimant's identity. But this second letter has only been seen in the form of an unsigned transcript; the first one, on the other hand, has been firmly authenticated, and there is more evidence that Andrei really was convinced. In 1928 he wrote to the president of the White Russian Association in Berlin: "I am still unable to understand how she had not been recognized sooner. That is absolutely incomprehensible." Even after 1950, when he is supposed to have expressed uncertainty, he had in fact not lost faith. When asked in court what the grand duke's attitude had been shortly before his death in 1956, his niece replied: "He tried to convince me."

The complex family differences over the Anastasia affair are best demonstrated by the curious dialogue which took place when Grand Duke Andrei's widow, Mathilde Kschessinska, gave a television interview in 1967. This was the internationally famous ballerina who had been the tsar's mistress before either were married. When interviewed about "Anastasia" for French television she was 95 years old, but still remarkably alert and coherent. Her son Vladimir was present at the interview, and had supervised all the arrangements for it. He had even prepared a written statement for his mother to deliver, not very spontaneously, in the course of the interview. This had been handed in advance to the French interviewer, Gilbert Proteau, and said that she and her husband, Grand Duke Andrei, had merely been struck by the resemblance between the eyes of the claimant and those of Tsar Nicholas, her lover of so long ago. But Mathilde Kschessinska decided not to stick to the script, and when the key question was asked, a very different answer emerged:

Proteau: "Princess, in 1928, in Paris, you met the woman who in those days was called the 'Mystery Woman of Berlin'."

Kschessinska: "I did see her—once."
Proteau: "And what did you think of her?"
Kschessinska: "That it was she."

Witnesses agree that this reply was given quietly and firmly; it was followed by a moment of stunned silence, and then there was an angry interruption from her son: "Niet, niet, cut! You must cut!" The cameras stopped turning, but two tape machines continued to record what followed. Vladimir, speaking in Russian, told his mother: "You must answer only what has been written." But his warning came too late, and was unheeded. The old lady remained unabashed, and continued to talk for another half hour, expressing full confidence that the claimant really was Anastasia.

There were many other important supporters of Anna Anderson's claim. Princess Xenia Georgievna wrote:

Her voice, manner, vocabulary and knowledge of languages were such as to accord with the claim made on her behalf. One of the most convincing elements of her personality was a completely unconscious acceptance of her identity. She was herself at all times and never gave the slightest impression of acting a part. In this connection I observed many tastes, interests, and idiosyncrasies reminiscent of our family, and our childhood together . . . I am firmly convinced that the claimant is in fact the Grand Duchess Anastasia of Russia.

Then there was Prince Sigismund of Prussia, son of the tsarina's sister Irene and Prince Heinrich, the Kaiser's brother. The real Anastasia was his first cousin, and they had known each other well as children. Here again there was a family division: his mother rejected the claimant but Sigismund has repeatedly recognized her. In 1932, when he first received information that suggested she should be taken seriously, he was already living in Central America. The prince therefore decided to send a list of questions to Europe to be put to Anna Anderson by a third party. We have obtained some of them, questions which Sigismund felt were the acid test of her acceptability.

He asked the claimant to say when and where they had last met. Her answer was that it had been in 1912 at Spala, the imperial hunting lodge in what was then Russian Poland. This was correct. Secondly, the prince asked where he, Sigismund, had been accommodated. Anna Anderson replied that it had been in the quarters of Baron [later Count] Fredericks, the minister of the court. Not only was this also correct, but Sigismund was impressed because it was a trivial fact which had been published nowhere; indeed there was no reason for anybody outside the tsar's intimate circle to remember it. Prince Sigismund eventually testified that these answers and the answers to a further fourteen questions had satisfied him totally: "The replies were perfectly correct and could only have been given by the grand duchess herself. This has convinced me . . . that [she] is without doubt Anastasia of Russia."

Recently the prince confirmed to us that he had since visited Europe, in 1957, and met Anna Anderson. The face-to-face meetings had strengthened his conviction that she was genuine. We must note, however, that Prince Sigismund has also met, and believes in, the "Grand Duchess Olga" of Lake Como. It is a belief in which he is almost entirely alone.

Crown Princess Cecile was a second cousin to the tsar and the daughter of a godmother to the real Anastasia. She had met her as a child on several occasions, without being on close personal terms. Cecile first met Anna Anderson in 1925 when the claimant was very ill, and wrote:

I was certainly struck at first glance by the young person's resemblance to the tsar's mother, and to the tsar himself, but I did not see anything of the tsarina in her. There was no opportunity, however, of establishing her identity, because it was virtually impossible to communicate with the young woman. She remained completely silent, either from obstinacy or because she was utterly bewildered. I could not decide which.

In 1952, after Princess Cecile had revisited Anna Anderson three more times, and seen her in better health, her attitude became much more positive: "Today I am convinced she is the tsar's youngest daughter, now that she is an ageing woman.

Not only can I detect her mother's features in her; but most of all I can sense the kinship in her manner of behaviour and hospitality, in all the bonds of intimate knowledge and association which link people of the same origins together." From then on, the German Crown Princess acknowledged Anna Anderson absolutely. Thanking her by postcard for a gift of chocolates sent on her birthday, she ended with the words: "God bless you, a tender kiss from your loving Aunt Cecile."

For a woman branded by so many as an impostor, Anna Anderson certainly received remarkable attention from members of German sovereign families. Apart from those who formally recognized her, there were others who took the trouble to meet her after her ignominious return from America in 1931. There was the benevolence of the Kaiser's second wife, Hermine, which we have noted; Feodora, Princess Reuss, provided her with an outstanding lawyer; and Marianne, Princess of Hesse Philippsthal, invited her to stay and later went out of her way to help the claimant's legal counsel. Not surprisingly, Anna Anderson today refers to the Kaiser and his relations with respect. Her detractors would answer that this alone proves she is no Romanov, because Tsar Nicholas broke with the Kaiser after Germany declared war in 1914. But the relationship with Wilhelm, and German involvement in the fate of the Romanovs, cannot be summarized in such simplistic terms. It is a complex and vital subject which we shall be dealing with separately—but it is worth noting here the acceptance of Anna Anderson by one highly-placed German who may have had special knowledge of what really happened in July 1918.

In 1927, at the height of controversy over her identity, the former chief-of-staff of the Eastern Command, General Max Hoffmann, declared his conviction that this was indeed Anastasia. One of the people Hoffmann spoke to about the affair was Baron Magnus von Braun, father of the famous space scientist, Wernher von Braun. The baron testified that General Hoffmann died in July 1927, shortly after making his curious assertion, and just before he was due to visit Anna Anderson. He had been reported as saying: "I don't have to see her, I know", as though he had inside information which had come his way years before. As one of Germany's top commanders who had been in charge of the 1918 peace negotiations with the Bolsheviks, he may have had access to privileged intelligence about German efforts to help the Romanovs, and what became of them. But here we are left speculating—in the general's published papers and diaries the fate of the Russian imperial family is notable only by its complete omission.

Some of the most striking recognitions of Anna Anderson came from witnesses who were not relatives, but had known the real Anastasia well. One was Felix Dassel, an officer who had been wounded in 1916 and treated for several months at the Tsarskoe Selo hospital, near the imperial palace. The hospital was then under the patronage of Anastasia and her sister Maria, and both were regular visitors to the war wounded. Dassel got to know them well, and after his discharge the tsarina appointed him their escort. When he learned about Anna Anderson's claims, in Germany in 1927, Dassel devised a way to test her on that specific period in the real Anastasia's life. Before meeting her he wrote down a series of minute details about those hospital days, details which only the real Anastasia and Maria could have known. He sealed the notes in an envelope and had them put in a safe by the Duke of Leuchtenberg, who was at that time Anna Anderson's host. He then met and questioned the claimant, making deliberate mistakes to discover whether or not she would correct them. The claimant passed the test with flying colours. She correctly identified "Mandrifolie" as her sister Maria's nickname. She put right Dassel's deliberate error of placing the billiard table at Tsarskoe Selo upstairs—it had been downstairs. When Dassel mentioned that she and Maria had come to the hospital every day, often with their brother the Grand Duke Alexei, she accurately pointed out that they had only been able to visit the hospital two or three times a week, and they had never brought Alexei along. The clincher for Dassel came when the Duke of Leuchtenberg referred to an old Russian colonel, whom Dassel remembered well. In Dassel's words:

. . . she was seized suddenly by a little laugh, a little laugh which rang in my ears, a trifle muffled, a little uneven, but exactly, exactly as of old . . . I could not remain seated, I jumped up and grabbed the back of my chair. "The man

with the pockets!" she said. "The man with the pockets?"
Yes, yes. He had been given that name—and naturally I had
forgotten it a long time ago. It was Anastasia who had given
it to him, because the warrior from the front, impulsive and
blunt, always natural, had often forgotten etiquette and
spoken to the grand duchesses with his hands in his pockets
. . . Abruptly I recognized her, I was convinced.

Lili von Dehn was one of the tsarina's closest friends, had
spent long periods at Tsarskoe Selo from 1907 to 1917, and knew
the real Anastasia well. Because she later went to live in
Venezuela she did not meet Anna Anderson until 1957; but in
spite of the 40-year gap she formally recognized her as Anastasia—after visiting her for several hours each day for a week.
Her deposition contains the following remarks:

> . . . I had a real shock when first I saw her, a poor, pale and
> wrinkled little face! The first impression was of a terrible
> sadness, but the moment I heard her voice . . . it was so
> familiar to me, so real—the voice of the Grand Duchess
> Anastasia . . . No-one can imitate the voice and the way of
> talking of a person he has never seen before . . . We spoke of
> Anja [*Anna Virubova*], and she knew many details concern-
> ing her and her friendship with the empress. She spoke of an
> occasion when the empress was very displeased, even angry
> with Anja. That was only known to the empress, Anja,
> myself and the little grand duchess who was present, but too
> young to understand the meaning and only remembered
> the fact. We spoke of the officers we mutually knew, and she
> never made a mistake . . . She did not like or want to speak
> Russian, but the few words which escaped her were abso-
> lutely correct; the family names, real Russian ones, were
> pronounced in exactly the right way. Her hands reminded
> me very much [*of*] the hands of her mother . . . What can I
> say after having known her? I certainly cannot be mistaken
> in her identity.

By 1957 Anna Anderson could of course have learned scores
of little details about court life—from the growing library of
memoirs, or directly from people who had been there. Yet if

Anna Anderson was deliberately cheating, she found some unlikely dupes.

We have noted that Tatiana Botkin, the daughter of the tsar's doctor, is a confirmed believer in Anna Anderson as the Grand Duchess Anastasia. She first played with the real Anastasia as a child on board the imperial yacht in 1910, later frequently met her at Tsarskoe Selo, and was one of the few who travelled with the family to Siberia and imprisonment. Madame Botkin today lives in genteel poverty in Paris, wholly convinced that the claimant is Anastasia. She met her in Germany in 1926, and said of the meeting: "When I saw her face at close quarters, particularly her eyes, so blue and full of light, I at once recognized the Grand Duchess Anastasia Nikolayevna. The height, figure, and colour of hair are exactly those of the girl Anastasia . . . The eyes, the eyebrows and ears are completely similar." Madame Botkin recalls how "Anastasia" was tired after their meeting, and late in the evening she decided to put her to bed. She remembers saying to the claimant in 1926:

"I'll undress you as my father used to undress you when you were ill . . ." "Yes, measles," she answered, and I realized that she had become completely aware of who I was. For it was when the tsar's children had measles, and only once then, that my father stayed up with the princesses by himself and looked after them like a nursing sister. This fact has never been published, and apart from my father, I was the only person to know of it.

Since that first meeting, Tatiana Botkin has seen the claimant many times, and is one of the very few who have never given up in despair, or deserted her. She is also one witness whose integrity has never been questioned.

There are no easy explanations of the totally opposite attitudes of those who knew Anastasia, and differed over the claimant. If the disbelievers can fairly be accused of simply following their leaders, of closing their minds too quickly because the existence of a surviving Romanov daughter was both incredible and inconvenient, then it can also be said that Anna Anderson's supporters have included some opportunists and some wishful thinkers. Most witnesses are no longer alive, and it is unlikely now that human testimony will ever reveal the truth. But there remains the physical evidence, which should, theoretically, lead to dispassionate, unbiased conclusions.

When "Anastasia" first appeared, forensic science was in its infancy, and the expert evidence on her covers a period of vast strides in identification technology. Over the years the claimant has submitted reluctantly to endless medical examinations, finger-printing, and handwriting tests—the results were all destined for the German lawcourts. For the subject it was a humiliating experience, being poked and prodded, asked to show her scars, and photographed from every conceivable angle. This is how the physical evidence has shaken down after the years of litigation.

Fingerprints could of course have ended the controversy long ago, but no prints of the historical Anastasia were ever available to compare with those of the claimant. Next to fingerprints, the best identifying feature should have been the teeth, but as we have pointed out, not a single human tooth was found in the forest near Ekaterinburg—from a supposed total of eleven corpses. Nevertheless there have been efforts to draw some conclusions from the teeth of the claimant.

One of the 38 medical practitioners at the imperial court was a dental surgeon, Dr Serge Kostritsky. He had travelled to Siberia and treated the imperial family at Tobolsk as late as 1918. In 1927, when he was an exile in Paris, Kostritsky declined an invitation to visit Anna Anderson in Germany, but was sent two plaster casts of the claimant's jaws. According to her current dentist in Germany there were obvious characteristics which should have provoked comment from an expert, but Kostritsky spoke only in general terms, and gave the impression that he did not want to get involved. Pierre Gilliard, whose word we must treat with caution, quoted him as saying: "These two plaster casts, by the placing of the teeth, and the shape of the jaws, do not bear any resemblance to the teeth or the placing of the teeth and the shape of the jaws of the Grand Duchess Anastasia." Apart from the fact that it was produced by Pierre Gilliard, this statement cannot be regarded as damning. In fleeing from Russia Kostritsky had not brought with him either dental records or plaster casts of the imperial teeth. He had to rely on his memory, not having seen the real Anastasia's teeth for nearly a decade. The judges of the Hamburg Court of Appeal rejected Kostritsky's statement as too vague to have any judicial value. They also pointed out that since the claimant had lost many teeth in the years since 1918, it was possible that her remaining ones had altered position accordingly. "Anastasia" did have sixteen teeth extracted while in Germany. Her supporters said they were loose as a result of a battering with rifle butts at Ekaterinburg. Her opponents say it was a side-effect of tuberculosis, and some even said she had several teeth pulled unnecessarily, with intent to defraud. In 1965 evidence submitted by three dental experts testifying in the Hamburg Court of Appeal agreed that it was impossible to determine after so many years what had caused the loss of teeth, but that violence could not be ruled out. In short, the dental evidence remains inconclusive.

Anna Anderson's supporters have always asserted that while their claimant had not been killed in the Ipatiev House, she had been severely wounded by bayonet thrusts. Anna Anderson does have a triangular scar on the top and bottom of one foot. The marks suggest that a sharp instrument was driven right through the foot, and are not unlike those that could have been made by the triangular blade of a 1918 Russian army bayonet. There is also a groove, one inch above her right ear, which experts agree could be a bullet scar. There is little doubt the claimant did suffer violent injury at some time—but that is far from making her Anastasia. There are, however, physical characteristics which do correspond with what is known about the real grand duchess.

Both of Anna Anderson's feet have a malformation of the joint at the root of the big toe. The visual impression is as if the knuckle, greatly enlarged, protrudes towards the side. This is a condition known medically as *Hallux valgus*, which is usually formed in adulthood by people who spend too much time on their feet, or wear unsuitable shoes. It is not rare, but is much less common as a genetically inherited defect. Grand Duchess Anastasia did suffer as a child from *Hallux valgus* and, as with the claimant, the deformity was more pronounced in the right foot. Grand Duchess Olga, questioned in 1959 about her visit to the claimant in Berlin, testified: "In my presence, Shura [*the former nursemaid*] looked at the feet of the invalid, noticed a prominence at the root of the big toe, and said it reminded her of Anastasia's feet, which also had such a malformation."

The coincidences, if that is what they are, continue. Anastasia was reliably reported to have had an unsightly mole on her shoulder, which was cauterized as she grew up so that it would not show when she wore a ball-gown. This left a small scar, and Anna Anderson does have such a mark. Anastasia's fingers were unusually regular in length, the middle finger being not noticeably longer than the index and ring fingers, especially on the right hand. The claimant's fingers have the same feature.

Ever since Anna Anderson's case began to cause controversy, both believers and opponents have tried to prove that her handwriting offers conclusive evidence for their case. One early test on these lines was made in 1927 on the initiative of Anna Anderson's enemies at the court of Hesse—and the results were not at all what they expected. The Cornelius Institute, then based at Prien, in Bavaria, concluded that the claimant and the grand duchess were identical. This report was suppressed until 1958, when the expert who had made it wrote to Anna Anderson's lawyers.

The science of graphology has, over the last 30 years, become sufficiently exact for it to play a crucial part in a trial. In cases where there might be a lack of good prosecution evidence, the opinions of the trained and qualified handwriting expert can be decisive. In 1970 the trial of the two West Indians accused of the first ever kidnapping for ransom in Britain was a case in point. The prosecution evidence on handwriting was accepted and was an important factor in the final verdict of guilty. In 1964, in the Anastasia case, the Hamburg Appeal Court appointed their own independent handwriting expert, Frau Minna Becker, an eminent German specialist. She was asked to compare the writing of the Grand Duchess Anastasia with that of both the claimant and Franziska Schanzkowska, the Polish peasant with whom her opponents tried to identify her. Becker found that there was no similarity between the handwriting of the claimant and that of Schanzkowska. However, in the comparison between the handwriting of the claimant and that of Anastasia, she found no less than 137 identical characteristics. She said that her experience as a sworn expert for the courts had convinced her that no two people could write with such consistent similarity. In her opinion that could not even occur in the case of identical twins. Becker had no hesitation in concluding that the claimant was indeed the Grand Duchess Anastasia.

Although Anna Anderson was sent to a series of mental institutions in the twenties and thirties, responsible medical opinion supported neither the suggestion that she was clinically insane, nor that she was deliberately lying about her identity. Dr Lothar Nobel, a specialist at the Mommsen Hospital in Berlin, had the opportunity to study the claimant for eight months, and reported:

> I should like to state that in my opinion no mental de-rangement of any kind is present. I, at least, during a long period of observation, have never noticed any trace of insanity in the patient, nor any kind of auto-suggestion by persons unknown. Although her memory has suffered, per-haps owing to the evident head injury, and although she is subject to moods of melancholia, these have in my opinion nothing pathological about them . . . moreover it is psycho-logically scarcely conceivable that anybody who for some reason was playing the part of another should behave as the patient does and show so little initiative towards furthering whatever plans she might have.

The doctors formed the impression that their patient's strange behaviour might be the manifestation of some kind of amnesia. Dr Karl Bonhoeffer, a specialist in psychopathology at the same hospital, said in his report in 1926: "Combined with other facts about her memory, there seems to be a strong probability of an auto-suggestive amnesia originating in the wish to suppress unpleasant experiences. The question of hypnotic influence over the patient by a third party must be ruled out; the same applies to conscious pretence."

One of the most perplexing factors in the Anastasia case has always been the claimant's consistent refusal to speak Russian. It has seemed a glaring defect, out of which her detractors have made considerable capital. But once again the picture is not so simple. The imperial children were in fact brought up speaking mainly English within the family. They of course knew Russian, and often spoke it with their father, but it was to a great extent a secondary language used for addressing outsiders and the palace staff. This was because the tsarina, being German, spoke it badly and found it less embarrassing to express herself in English. She spoke that language perfectly, having been brought up largely in England under the care of her grandmother, Queen Victoria. After the revolution, however, the family were often compelled to speak Russian so that their guards could understand their conversation—and this has been used to explain the claimant's reluctance to speak the language, on the grounds that it had painful associations with the time in prison. But several witnesses have in fact affirmed that she did talk Russian in the first years after her appearance in Berlin. One of them was Erna Buchholz, a Russian-speaking Balt who nursed the claimant from 1920 to 1922. She even referred to a "polished" manner of speech, "as only happens in highly-placed families". Felix Dassel, the former escort, stated that whilst she would not speak Russian, she clearly understood it: "Once when we were walking through the wood, she suddenly exclaimed 'Ryshik' [a Russian word for a red-topped toadstool] when she saw a mushroom of a certain type. No non-Russian can pronounce this word correctly. Not even a Pole." Even Pierre Gilliard wrote: "During the course of our visits we tried first to interrogate her in Russian. We were able to convince ourselves that she understood it, although with a certain difficulty . . ." Anna Anderson's staunch friend, Tatiana Botkin, has accounted for "Anastasia's" refusal to speak Russian as follows:

Her attitude to life is childlike, and altogether she cannot be reckoned with as an adult, responsible person, but must be led and directed like a child. She has not only forgotten languages, but she has in general lost the power of accurate narration, although not of thought. Even the simplest stories about her pet cat she tells incoherently and incorrectly; they are really only words strung together in impossibly ungrammatical German. She lays out games of patience, and although she says that during the last period in Siberia she laid out many games of patience, she can nevertheless not succeed in distinguishing between the eights and the tens. Her defect is obviously in the region of the memory and in eye trouble. She says that, after her illness, she forgot how to tell time and had laboriously to learn it again, and even now practices it often. She adds that without constant practice she forgets everything. Every time she has to force herself to dress, to wash, to sew, so that she does not forget how. Recently, she has not been practising writing, so that she can hardly write any longer.

Quite apart from the possible side-effects of violence, there is an uncanny echo here of something the English tutor Gibbes said about his pupil in 1918, long before the mystery woman turned up in Berlin. Describing the real Anastasia, he commented that she had been a slow learner and: "It seemed as if her mental development had been suddenly arrested . . ."[29]

Perhaps the most important of the scientific evidence is that of the anthropologists, based on a detailed comparison of minute anatomical characteristics. The first study of this kind was commissioned in 1927 by Pierre Gilliard, who chose a friend and colleague at Lausanne University, Professor Marc-Alexis Bischoff. His report seemed devastating: "It is impossible that [the claimant] and the Grand Duchess Anastasia Nikolayevna could be identical." Bischoff's unequivocal conclusion was grasped with delight by those members of the family who signed the 1928 declaration against the claimant. But time and developments in forensic science have demolished his verdict.

A prime factor in the Bischoff report was comparison between photographs of the ears of the claimant and the real Anastasia. In 1958 Professor Baron von Eickstedt, of Mainz University, established that his predecessors, including Bischoff, had fallen into the trap of comparing photographs taken from different angles, or with different lighting; this resulted in distortion of the subject under study. He personally visited Anna Anderson, took measurements, and photographed her from the same distance and angle, and with the same lighting, as in pictures of the historical Anastasia. As far as the ear was concerned, Baron von Eickstedt concluded that "this ear does not count clearly against, but altogether *for* the identity". He came out strongly in favour of the claimant's identity as the authentic Anastasia. It was dampening news for Anna Anderson's enemies—and more was to come.

The Hamburg Court decided not to rely on any of the earlier studies, but to appoint its own independent expert. With the approval of both sides in the dispute, the man chosen was Professor Otto Reche, president of the German Anthropological Society, and professor at the University of Vienna. He enjoyed an international reputation, and was a man at the very top of his profession. He spent months examining hundreds of photographs of the claimant, of the real grand duchess, and of her paternal and maternal relatives. He also visited Anna Anderson, and she was once more measured and photographed. In December 1959 he too dismissed all earlier reports, except that of Baron von Eickstedt, as incompetent. His long analysis ended with the words: "The general conclusion is therefore: proof that Frau Anderson is the Grand Duchess Anastasia."

Very recently that opinion has been corroborated by an eminent modern expert in the same field. In 1971, Moritz Furtmayr, a leading identification expert with the West German police, came up with the same result. He used a new system based on the principle that the cardinal points of the skull, once formed, retain the same relationship with each other till death. In his opinion, this system is as reliable as finger-printing, and no two persons produce the same "head-print". It is already used in German police work, and has been introduced as evidence in the courts. In studying the Anastasia case, Furtmayr also applied the Mathews identification test, which has long been internationally recognized, and he cross-checked the results with yet a third system employed by the police in Germany. Furtmayr's conclusion was: ". . . it can be considered as proven and verified that Mrs Anderson now living in the United States is without doubt one and the same as the Grand Duchess Anastasia". When we interviewed Furtmayr in 1975 he repeated that the claimant had not failed to satisfy a single test applied by him, and repeated his total conviction that she really is Anastasia.

As the German court case moved slowly towards a conclusion, in the sixties, Anna Anderson herself stayed well out of the limelight, displaying no interest whatsoever in the legal proceedings. She declined to co-operate with her lawyers, and was prone to snap at her supporters: "I know perfectly well who I am, I don't need to prove it in any court of law." At all events, she has so far failed to do so. But the court verdicts of 1967 and 1970 have left the case tantalizingly unresolved. On the one hand, said the judges, the claimant had failed to prove beyond question that she was the Grand Duchess Anastasia —on the other hand, they refused to accept the death of Anastasia at Ekaterinburg as a firm historical fact. Indeed, the five judges of the Federal Supreme Court emphasized that Anna Anderson could indeed be Anastasia. They delivered their judgement on 17 February 1970—50 years to the day after the claimant was dragged from the Landwehr Canal in Berlin. By then Anna Anderson had settled in the United States, and had married her American professor, John Manahan. As a result of that union she at last acquired a real name, and the security she had always lacked. In her late sixties, she slipped quietly out of the interminable humiliation, frustration and controversy, into the most peaceful years of her adult life.

Yet the riddle remains a riddle. The greatest weakness to her claim, from the very start of her story in Berlin, has been that she failed to explain convincingly how she alone survived the massacre of her family in Ekaterinburg. The story of her miraculous survival, and the melodramatic cross-country flight to Roumania, lacks credibility and corroboration.[30] There have been witnesses who testified that one grand duchess was rescued from the Ipatiev House, and that a house-to-house search took place in the neighbourhood the night the imperial family vanished in 1918. But the testimony about the escape did not convince the German judges, and nor does it convince us. Those who know Anna Anderson well say that she is characteristically discreet about family matters, and always tightlipped about the events of 1918. It is possible that the implausible escape story, whoever first conceived it, has served the claimant as a strategic alibi. Perhaps Anastasia, who was known to be the impulsive hot-headed daughter, broke away from the rest of her family, and thus imperilled their position. Anna Anderson did once confess to Tatiana Botkin that she had a heavy burden on her conscience. She never explained what that burden was, but if it was connected with the fate of the other imperial prisoners, it may have been a secret she could not, or dared not, disclose. Whatever the reason, the "escape" story has not served her well in the efforts to prove her identity.

Yet it would take a computer to work out the odds against a total impostor achieving so many coincidences as exist between Anna Anderson and the real Grand Duchess Anastasia. The identification work, the handwriting evidence, the recognition by so many witnesses—all these factors leave the case wide open. If others hoped to use the claimant in a conspiracy to defraud, the woman from the Berlin canal seems an unlikely choice. With a Romanov fortune supposedly at stake, would the conspirators really have selected such an eccentric and sick young girl? How many impersonators could have behaved for so long as this strange woman has done, and still not be exposed as a fraud? This same woman was chosen by a senior German aristocrat, the Hereditary Grand Duke of Saxe-Weimar Eisenach, to be godmother to his son and heir. It is an honour she shares with Queen Juliana of the Netherlands. Before his death Duke George of Leuchtenberg reserved a place for Anna Anderson in the family vault—an improbable resting place for one whom many dismissed as a Polish peasant with delusions. After years of research for the royal family of Denmark, Herluf Zahle said of the Anastasia case: "I have done my utmost that my royal house may be blameless in the eyes of history. If the Russian imperial family wishes one of its members to die in the gutter, there is nothing I can do."

In 1964, a German diplomat provided information on the case from the rarest source of all—the Soviet Union itself. Dr. Günther Bock told the Hamburg tribunal what he had learned in 1926, when he was German vice-consul in Leningrad. The Anastasia controversy was then beginning to attract international attention, and Bock asked the opinion of a member of the Bolshevik hierarchy with whom he was on friendly terms. This official replied that all the Romanov family were dead, with the exception of one of the women, who was known to have gone missing. Dr Bock wanted to know if the survivor had been the Grand Duchess Anastasia, but the Russian merely shrugged and turned away.

The Bolshevik official was Commissar S. L. Weinstein, head

of the Leningrad office of the Soviet Foreign Commissariat. During his career he had been an associate of Georgy Chicherin, and of Grigory Zinoviev, both of whom had been members of the Central Executive Committee in 1918. Zinoviev, as we shall show later, was personally linked to the fate of the Romanovs after Ekaterinburg.

This chapter is intended as a factual account, not as a new investigation into Anna Anderson's claim. We have tried to strip away some of the misconceptions, and have included many unpublished details, without attempting any conclusions. But we note, finally, that the claimant herself has twice declared that the written and courtroom account of her survival is inaccurate. Anna Anderson's affidavits had been pieced together in good faith by her supporters, who assumed, like everyone else, that the Sokolov version was basically correct.

True to form, her own comments on the fate of the family remain an enigma. During the sixties she told Prince Frederick of Saxe Altenburg: "Events in Ekaterinburg were quite different from what they say. But if *I* say that, they think I'm mad".

In 1974, when we were with her in Virginia, she suddenly exclaimed: "There was no massacre there . . . but I cannot tell the rest."

PART FIVE

Cousins

19

KING GEORGE SLAMS THE DOOR

"I shall always remain your true and devoted
friend . . ."
(King George V to Tsar Nicholas, March 1917)

"IT IS UNDENIABLE to me that undisclosed events occurred
at Ekaterinburg, and the probability that one of the emperor's
daughters escaped remains credible . . . 'They' fear something
and are very disturbed, as if the investigation could uncover
something embarrassing and even dangerous for them . . ."
Those words of the jurist, Grand Duke Andrei, pondering on
the murky politics behind the Anastasia case, hold the key to
the real fate of the Romanovs. By "They" the grand duke
meant those powerful factions throughout Europe which
joined forces to discredit Anna Anderson. What had they done
in connection with the Romanovs that needed covering up?
As he delved into the mystery, the grand duke also said: "I am
absolutely convinced that this investigation will lead us
steadily back to Ekaterinburg, Tobolsk, the events of 1917 and
even further." He was quite right—the truth does have its
roots in the blundering behaviour of two great relatives long
before the grim events of Ekaterinburg.

When the tsar abdicated in spring 1917 only two foreign
powers were strong enough to influence his fate—Britain and
Germany. Of these two, Germany had been an enemy for
three bitter years. In principle the one country from which the
Romanovs could expect open ungrudging help was Britain.
This was the ally the tsar had steadfastly supported throughout
the war, the nation which owed him the greatest debt. The
Romanovs probably never learned how England responded in
their hour of need, and perhaps it is just as well. For it was an
episode without honour, which began with King George V
behaving churlishly and his government vacillating. Only
when the imperial family's life hung by a thread may Britain

have made belated, covert efforts to save them—efforts which remain secret to this day.

King George and the tsar were first cousins because their mothers—both Danish princesses—were sisters. The tsarina was also cousin to George, because her mother and his father were both children of Queen Victoria. The king and the emperor were not only cousins, but close personal friends, as close as two royal heads could be in the days before air travel shrunk the world (*see plates 48a and 48b*). Twenty-three years before the tsar's abdication George had visited Russia to attend Nicholas's wedding to Alexandra, and wrote home: "I do think that Nicky is a very lucky man to have got such a lovely and charming wife . . . Nicky has been kindness itself to me, he is the same dear boy he has always been . . ." The two monarchs maintained close contact as the years went by. In 1909, when the Russian imperial family made their last visit to England, there had been a hint of things to come. Because of the danger of assassination by exiled revolutionaries, the Home Office advised against an imperial trip to London. The tsar never left the Isle of Wight, which remained sealed off by British police in a security operation unprecedented for its time. Once war broke out there could be no more friendly visits aboard luxury yachts, but the two monarchs kept in close touch by letter as their peoples joined in the struggle with Germany. When news of Nicholas's abdication reached King George in the spring of 1917 his reaction was swift and predictable. Within four days, on 19 March, he cabled his condolences: "Events of last week have deeply distressed me. My thoughts are constantly with you, and I shall always remain your true and devoted friend as you know I have been in the past." It is a symbol of what was to come that Nicholas never received this affectionate message. The Russian Provisional Government was reluctant to forward the telegram because "it might be misinterpreted and used as an argument in favour of detention". In London, the king was respectfully invited to reveal its contents to the prime minister, David Lloyd George; it was agreed that the message was indeed too politically sensitive, and the British embassy in St Petersburg was ordered to make sure it was never delivered.

Things had changed since the Russian visit to the Isle of

Wight. The fuse of socialism was already sputtering audibly in the England of 1917. London had long been a haven for Russian revolutionaries and anarchists, and many remained to foster discontent abroad even when their comrades went home to Russia. Quite apart from that, the British people were feeling their own strength, an unrest expressed at republican rallies in the Albert Hall and demonstrations in industrial centres like Glasgow and Liverpool. Even before the war ended there was trouble in the armed services, a malaise that within two years was to explode into an army mutiny, with 3,000 soldiers marching on Whitehall, and the possibility of a coup d'état. It is against this simmering background that Buckingham Palace and Whitehall were to consider the plight of the Romanovs in 1917.

For many years after the disappearance of the Romanovs it was believed that King George had done his very best to get them out, but that the British government, fearful of appearing sympathetic to the leader of a cruel autocracy, abandoned the tsar. George has usually been cast as the impotent constitutional monarch who had to do as he was advised. In 1971, that is how Lord Mountbatten, the tsar's closest surviving relative in Britain, summed up George's role: "Oh yes, in the early days he discussed it with my mother, he was very anxious to offer them asylum over here, but the government, the prime minister, Lloyd George, was understandably opposed on political grounds at that time of the war, and I think it would have been very difficult therefore to go against him . . ."

Lord Mountbatten was of course speaking in good faith, but the record shows a very different picture. It was the "true and devoted friend", King George, not his ministers, who strongly objected to giving the former tsar asylum in Britain. Pieced together from state documents and personal memoirs comes the account of what really happened—actions which can fairly be said to have sealed the fate of Nicholas II and all his family. In London the actors in the drama were King George V, the Liberal prime minister Lloyd George, and his foreign secretary Arthur Balfour. In St Petersburg there was Alexander Kerensky, minister of justice and later prime minister of the new Provisional Government, and Pavel Milyukov, the foreign minister. The British ambassador, who acted as go-between, was Sir George Buchanan.

In the first days after the tsar's abdication Britain seems to have given serious thought to rescue plans. The War Office sought the advice of General Wallscourt Waters, a personal friend of the tsar and King George; Waters had for years been British military attaché in St Petersburg, and in 1917 he forecast correctly that Kerensky's moderate regime would soon be replaced by extremists. He suggested there would still be a good chance of rescue "if a fast torpedo boat and a few bags of British sovereigns should be promptly dispatched to the Gulf of Finland", where there were embarkation points not far from the palace where the Romanovs were being held. On the diplomatic front, London did put a warning shot across the Russian bows. On 19 March the Foreign Office cabled Sir George Buchanan, authorizing him to say: "Any violence done to the emperor or his family would have a most deplorable effect and would deeply shock public opinion in this country." But the Provisional Government had no thought of harming the Romanovs. That same day Sir George Buchanan was able to report an encouraging conversation with Foreign Minister Milyukov:

> . . . the emperor . . . had requested the government to allow him to go to Tsarskoe Selo and to remain there till his children had recovered from measles and subsequently to proceed to Port Romanov. His Excellency gave me to understand that this permission would be granted and asked me whether I knew if arrangements were being made for HM to go to England.

Next day, even before London had had time to reply to that note, Sir George reported that the Russian foreign minister was now positively pressing for the tsar's departure, and was taking it for granted that Britain would send a ship to pick him up.

On 21 March the Foreign Office made a cautious reply, pointing out that no invitation had yet been made, and suggesting it might be better for the tsar to consider going to Denmark or Switzerland, rather than England. When this news reached him, Milyukov became "most anxious", and now asked formally if ". . . the king and His Majesty's government would at once offer emperor asylum in England". Faced with a formal request, the British now had to make up their minds. There was a cabinet meeting, and a meeting at Downing Street on 22 March between the prime minister, the chancellor of the exchequer, Bonar Law, Lord Stamfordham, the King's private secretary, and Lord Hardinge, permanent under-secretary at the Foreign Office. A firm decision was made —England would offer the tsar asylum. The good news went at once to Sir George in Petersburg:

"In order to meet the request made by the Russian government, the king and His Majesty's government readily offer asylum to the emperor and empress in England, which it is hoped they will take advantage of during the war." The cabinet felt that in England there would be less risk of the tsar becoming a pawn in the hands of disaffected Russian generals, who might want to place him at the head of a counter-revolution, a move London felt would play straight into German hands. So the ex-tsar could come to England, but Buchanan was ordered to make one condition clear: "In order to avoid any possible doubt in the future as to the reason for asylum being given . . . you should emphasize the fact that the offer made has been entirely due to the initiative of the Russian government." In other words, a slightly qualified "invitation" —but an invitation. There was even a touch of meanness, which rather ignored the vast wealth of the British royal family: "Can you possibly ascertain what are the private resources of the Emperor? It is very desirable that His Majesty and his family should have sufficient means to live in a manner befitting their rank as members of an imperial family." But while London worried about the cash, the Provisional Government in Russia was increasingly concerned to expedite the Romanovs' removal in the face of growing hostility towards them from the extreme Left. When the Foreign Office heard about this, it sent a chaser to Sir George (23 March): "You should immediately and urgently press Russian government to give absolute safe conduct to whole imperial family to Port Romanov as soon as possible . . . we rely on Russian government ensuring the personal safety of His Majesty and the imperial family." There was now a week's delay, in which the Russian foreign minister spoke of increasing pressure from extremists to prevent the tsar leaving. There was also a problem with illness. The imperial children had measles, and the family could not travel until they were better. The delay turned out to be fatal.

In the end it was neither measles nor extremism which sealed the fate of the Romanovs, but a volte-face by the tsar's own cousin, King George. The British monarch abruptly changed his mind about the offer of asylum in England, and did it in such a way as to enfeeble any future discussions on the subject between London and St Petersburg. On 30 March, just one week after the firm British offer of asylum, the king sent a message to the foreign secretary by the usual channel, a letter from his private secretary, Lord Stamfordham:

The king has been thinking much about the government's proposal that the Emperor Nicholas and his family should come to England. As you are doubtless aware, the king has a strong personal friendship for the emperor, and therefore would be glad to do anything to help him in this crisis. But His Majesty cannot help doubting, not only on account of the dangers of the voyage, but on general grounds of expediency, whether it is advisable that the imperial family should take up residence in this country. The king would be glad if you could consult the prime minister, as His Majesty understands no definite decision has yet been come to on the subject by the Russian Government.

The British government was taken aback by this message from the king, and Balfour replied on 2 April:

His Majesty's ministers quite realize the difficulties to which you refer in your letter, but they do not think, unless the position changes, that it is now possible to withdraw the invitation which has been sent, and they therefore trust that the king will consent to adhere to the original invitation, which was sent on the advice of His Majesty's ministers.

King George accepted this argument, but only grudgingly.

On 3 April his secretary replied that if this was the government's wish, then "he must regard the matter as settled". But George did not stick to his word. During that first week of April, the King received two letters, one from Lord Carnock, and one from Lord Beresford, both drawing attention to mounting public opinion against the Romanovs coming to Britain. On 6 April the king took the extraordinary step of having his secretary fire off two letters to the foreign secretary on the same subject in a single day. The first said:

> Every day, the king is becoming more concerned about the question of the emperor and the empress coming to this country. His Majesty receives letters from people in all classes of life, known or unknown to him, saying how much the matter is being discussed, not only in clubs, but by working men, and the Labour Members in the House of Commons are expressing adverse opinions to the proposal. As you know, from the first the king has thought the presence of the imperial family (especially of the empress) in this country would raise all sorts of difficulties, and I feel sure that you appreciate how awkward it will be for our royal family who are closely connected both with the emperor and the empress.
>
> You probably also are aware that the subject has become more or less public property, and that people are either assuming that it has been initiated by the king, or deprecating the very unfair position in which His Majesty will be placed if the arrangement is carried out.
>
> The king desires me to ask you whether after consulting the Prime Minister, Sir George Buchanan should not be communicated with, with a view to approaching the Russian government to make some other plan for the future residence of their imperial majesties.
>
> Yours very truly,
Stamfordham

There is a postscript: "Most people appear to think the invitation was initiated by the king, whereas it was his *government* who did so."

Before the day was out the king had clearly become even

more agitated. The secretary was called in yet again, and the second letter of the day went off to Balfour:

> The king wishes me to write again on the subject of my letter of this morning. He must beg you to represent to the Prime Minister that from all he hears and reads in the press, the residence in this country of the ex-emperor and empress would be strongly resented by the public, and would undoubtedly compromise the position of the king and queen . . . Buchanan ought to be instructed to tell Milyukov that the opposition to the emperor and empress coming here is so strong that we must be allowed to withdraw from the consent previously given to the Russian government's proposal.

The king was now going as far as a constitutional monarch dare to interfere with his ministers' decision. Buckingham Palace had made its point crystal clear and this time the message went home. Within twenty-four hours the foreign secretary forwarded the king's letters to the cabinet secretary, adding a minute: "We may have to suggest Spain or the south of France as a more suitable residence than England for the tsar." Mr Balfour even exhorted the cabinet secretary to "try to keep an eye on anything that may be put into the war cabinet minutes likely to hurt the king's feelings. He feels sure that the prime minister has not the slightest wish to 'froisser' [offend] the king, and if he sins, he does so inadvertently, so it is up to you . . ." Had Tsar Nicholas known what was going on in London, it would have been he who was offended.

In Russia, the moment King George changed his mind was just the moment a little British pressure could have helped the tsar. The Provisional Government was talking of a delay until the emperor's correspondence had been examined, and hoped there would be no immediate attempt to hasten his departure. Now, nothing could have suited the British better.

By 13 April the asylum offer had quietly evaporated. Lloyd George repeated the king's arguments to the cabinet, almost word for word, but without mentioning their source. The king's direct involvement in the withdrawal was not to be publicized. Buchanan, in St Petersburg, was sent a message marked "personal and most confidential", asking him to avoid the subject with the Russian government from now on, and suggesting it would be preferable if the tsar went to France. Four days later Lord Hardinge wrote privately to Lord Bertie, British ambassador in Paris, asking whether the French would take the tsar. He added, in a rare flash of bureaucratic honesty: "It is a situation of grave embarrassment here, for naturally the king, who is devoted to the emperor, would not like to show him the cold shoulder." The king's secretary also wrote a private letter to Lord Bertie, asking the same question, making it quite clear that King George had been against the idea of British asylum from the outset: "It is very hard on the king, who never wished it: but the government agreed to Milyukov's suggestion that they should come—and already people think it was His Majesty's idea." There is no record of any concern for the Romanovs' feelings, and by now, of course, Nicholas was getting the cold shoulder from everyone. Lord Bertie replied from Paris on 22 April:

My Dear Charlie,
    I do not think that the ex-emperor and his family would be welcome in France. The empress is not only a Boche by birth but in sentiment. She did all she could to bring about an understanding with Germany. She is regarded as a criminal or a criminal lunatic and the ex-emperor as a criminal from his weakness and submission to her promptings.

But even before Lord Bertie's letter was written England had effectively abandoned the tsar. In early May Sir George Buchanan told the Russian Foreign Minister confidentially: ". . . we should probably refuse permission to any members of the imperial family to reside in England during the war." Because of internal pressure the Russian Provisional Government found this temporarily convenient, but they still intended to send the Romanovs abroad, and the British ambassador's heavy hint was not taken seriously. Some weeks later, when the uproar from the left-wing extremists eased slightly, the Russians decided to revive the British asylum offer. In Kerensky's words, they again asked London "at what date a cruiser could be sent to fetch the former tsar and his family." Kerensky was taken aback by the British reply, and Sir George Buchanan, who delivered it, was also shocked. Kerensky recalled:

> I do not remember exactly whether it was late in June or early in July when the British ambassador called, greatly distressed . . . He brought with him a letter from a high official of the Foreign Office, who was also intimately connected with the court. With tears in his eyes, scarcely able to control his emotions, Sir George informed the Russian minister of foreign affairs of the British government's final refusal to give refuge to the former emperor of Russia . . . I can say definitely that this refusal was due exclusively to considerations of internal British politics.

Years later when this account appeared in Kerensky's memoirs, there was a storm of denials in England. The former prime minister, Lloyd George, and the former British ambassador, Sir George Buchanan, both contradicted Kerensky, suggesting that the British asylum offer always remained open. In 1927 General Sir Alfred Knox MP asked the Foreign Office for the documented facts, so that the heresy could be squashed once and for all. The Foreign Office began by calling Kerensky's allegation a lie, and offered as "complete refutation" the early cables offering asylum—but omitting any later "refusal" messages. When a former first secretary at the British embassy in St Petersburg came forward to say he remembered the "refusal" message arriving in Russia, the Foreign Office stuck to its lies, suggesting the diplomat's memory was at fault. In 1932 the ambassador's daughter, Meriel Buchanan, finally nailed the official version. She said her father had gallantly falsified his memoirs to cover up what had occurred. He had little choice, said his daughter—the Foreign Office had threatened to stop his pension.

The disinterment of this shabby affair did result in one terse minute being entered in the Foreign Office papers: "I understand . . . that Mr Lloyd George was not responsible for the decision, but that it is not expedient to say who was . . ."—a dry historical footnote to a tale of royal expediency. The British government may have locked the door on the Romanovs, but it was King George who closed it.

20

THE JONAS LIED AFFAIR

"There were plans, while the imperial family were at
Tobolsk, and they involved George V and others . . ."
(Grand Duke Vladimir,
Romanov Heir Assumptive, 1974)

THERE IS NO obvious explanation of the king's behaviour,
except perhaps that in spring 1917 he did not understand how
serious the situation was for the Romanovs. But as the months
went by and the Bolsheviks took power, it became obvious to
everyone that the plight of the imperial family had become a
matter of life or death. One would expect this to be reflected
in further correspondence between the palace and the Foreign
Office, perhaps showing a change of heart. But there is an
extraordinary, and highly improbable, gap in the files.

For the three months after the withdrawal of the offer of
asylum in April 1917 the subject of the tsar disappears from
official correspondence altogether. In 1932 Major Hardinge, a
new royal secretary, went through the papers, and was so
puzzled he wrote to the Foreign Office referring to "gaps in
the record". The Foreign Office was unable to help and
Hardinge could only conclude: "It seems extraordinary that
the correspondence comes to a dead end towards the end of
April and is not resumed until the end of July when the *fait
accompli* of the emperor's removal to Tobolsk is reported." This
was confirmed to us in 1974, by the royal archivist, Robert
Mackworth-Young, who wrote: ". . . I am afraid we can offer
no explanation for it."

In August 1917 there is one lone exchange of correspondence, when the king asks the Foreign Office whether it is true
that the Romanovs have been moved from Tsarskoe Selo to
Tobolsk, in Siberia. The transfer is confirmed, but then the
void in the files continues for a further nine months until
May 1918, when the king expresses concern about the family's

treatment. After that there is again total silence until July, the month the Romanovs vanished. We can draw two conclusions from this paper silence. Either the king lost all interest in the fate of his cousin Nicholas, which is improbable, or there was more correspondence which has been excised from the record. From bitter experience, in this investigation alone, we incline towards the more sinister theory.

Few people in Britain have ever heard of the "weeders", the officials who decide what material is fit for the public eye, and what should be suppressed. Yet such men exist—tried and trusted civil service officers spend their days sifting the tons of documents which qualify each year for declassification, in principle, under the 30-year rule. Ironically, they do so by specific provisions in the Public Record Acts of 1958 and 1967, laws which were made to ensure that the people do eventually find out what its past governments have been up to. Before papers get anywhere near the Public Record Office the weeders, for that is what they are called in government circles, have first bite; beavering away in Whitehall basements, they plough through the documents accumulated by all government ministries, deciding what should be suppressed. It is left to them, in collusion with inspectors from the Public Record Office, to remove papers which might compromise or embarrass individuals or departments—even if the papers in question are half a century old and the writers long dead. Files considered unsuitable for release are submitted to the Lord Chancellor's office, which decides whether to keep them secret, or destroy them irrevocably. Anything controversial that does spill out onto the public record has either received clearance because it is considered harmless, or—occasionally—because the weeder has been too lenient. Secret service records, of course, never see the light of day. The papers of the royal family are easily controlled internally by the royal archivist, with the monarch holding the ultimate power of veto.

It would perhaps be utopian to expect the masters of our semi-secretive society to leave paper skeletons lying around for future generations to pull out of the cupboard, and some documents never even reach the weeders. It is not really surprising to find huge holes in the Royal and Foreign Office records of a matter which was once highly sensitive—the British involvement in the fate of the Russian imperial family. But the system works against historians, and is ideal for the cover-up of anything from treachery to plain incompetence; in the soil which the weeders have worked, rumour—the seed of historical inaccuracy—is sure to flourish. In the Romanov case we must assume that full disclosure of events in 1917 and 1918 would have compromised either the royal family, or the government, or both.

We do know of a specific document which may have been removed from the royal files. In December 1917 the Romanovs sent a secret plea for help from Tobolsk to the British royal family in London. Realizing that a direct message would be intercepted, the tsarina asked the English tutor, Gibbes, to ghost a letter for her to Miss Margaret Jackson, a retired governess living in London who had been one of her childhood teachers. The letter was designed to help a potential rescuer, describing the lay-out of the Tobolsk house in detail and even enclosing a rough groundplan (*see plate 51*). It contained coded hints that the letter was to be passed on to the British royal family, and Gibbes later confirmed that it was a carefully planned appeal for British assistance. However, we know of the letter only because Gibbes preserved his drafts; the original was forwarded to London through Petrograd in the diplomatic bag, and there is no reason why it should not have reached Buckingham Palace. It is missing, however, from the royal archives.[31]

The reason may simply be archival inefficiency, or royal shame that nothing effective was done in response to the tsarina's plea. But it is likely that help was considered late in the day—plans for rescue that left no tell-tale trail in the archives. We have found traces of secret plans to rescue the tsar in papers left by a prominent Norwegian, mysteriously summoned to London in spring 1918 for talks with intelligence chiefs. The story involves senior British politicians and King George V himself. It came to nothing, but does suggest for the first time the extent to which the British establishment was prepared to consider serious rescue plans.

The Norwegian was a remarkable figure called Jonas Lied. In 1918 he was 36, and already had a distinguished career behind him. Much of his working life had been spent in imperial

Russia and Siberia in particular, where Lied had made a great deal of money from timber and mineral concessions. His business operations had taken him close to politics too, and Nicholas II personally granted Lied honorary Russian citizenship. He had Norwegian diplomatic status as consul for Siberia—the biggest consular territory in the world—and during World War I he shrewdly built up contacts amongst those who were to seize power in the revolution. Later he was to become an aluminium magnate and as such a founder of the Soviet aircraft industry. He finds his place in the Romanov story because of a great achievement early in his life: the pioneering in 1913 of a new trade route from Siberia to western Europe and America (see plate 52). With a British partner, Lied had formed the Siberian Steamship and Manufacturing Company, opening up a transportation service along river and sea passages so often frozen that they had previously been considered impractical. Lied had personally travelled and charted every mile of them, and his river steamers plied from a northern exit point on the Kara Sea, south by various river systems to Tobolsk, in Siberia. Tobolsk was where the Romanovs were being held in early 1918, and it was while they were there that Lied got his summons to London. He kept a diary, much of it in English, throughout his life, and it is from that diary that we piece together the strange episode that followed.

26 February 1918: "Wire from Armistead to Kria [*Oslo*] asking if he gets us visa, I would come to London to discuss expedition from England to Siberia. I wired consent . . ." Four days later Lied was bucketing across the North Sea on the steamer to Aberdeen, and by 3 March he was noting: "Arr. London. Colonel Browning arranged a suite of rooms at the Savoy. Met Armistead and discussed expedition. Saw Sole Gov. of Hudson Bay."

Colonel Browning, who arranged the suite at the Savoy, was Frederick Browning, a senior British intelligence officer working as personal assistant to Mansfield Cumming—head of MI1C, the foreign operations branch of the British Secret Service, better known now as MI6.

Two days after his arrival in London Lied's diary reads: "5 March. Saw Mitchell-Thompson, who was not very helpful.

48a

48b

49
50

48a & 48b The physical
likeness between King
George V (*left*), and his
"Cousin Nicky" (*right*),
was so great as to cause
wild rumours after World
War I that the tsar had
survived. But in 1917,
when his relative was in
danger, George pressed
the British cabinet to
withdraw its asylum offer.

49 Alexander Kerensky—
"I will not be the Marat
of the Russian
Revolution."

50 Sir George Buchanan,
British ambassador to
Moscow—threatened
with the loss of his
Foreign Office pension if
he told the truth.

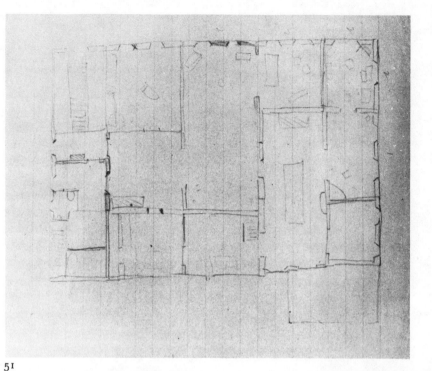

51

52

53

51 Groundplan of the Governor's House at Tobolsk, where the Romanovs were held through the winter of 1917. It was prepared for sending with a coded plea for help from the tsarina to the British royal family.

The message was sent, but today the Royal Archives deny any knowledge of it. This original draft is held today by the family of Sydney Gibbes, the English tutor who was with the Romanovs at Tobolsk.

52 Jonas Lied (*ringed*) aboard ship on the Kara Sea route out of Russia—the way he planned to rescue the Romanovs in 1918. On the right is the famous Norwegian explorer, Nansen.

53 Vassily Yakovlev—British agent, German agent, or Moscow's fall-guy? (*Soviet artist's impression*)

Had interview with Arthur Balfour foreign minister at Foreign Office. Seeing Lord Robert Cecil tomorrow."

Important doors were now opening for the Norwegian guest. Balfour was indeed foreign secretary, and Lord Robert Cecil was the senior official who had been dealing personally with the Romanov affair. It was he who answered enquiries on their behalf from royalty, including persistent pleas for British help from the tsarina's sister Victoria.

Three days later, Lied saw the head of naval intelligence: "8 March. . . Had dinner at Sir Reginald Hall's house with his wife and daughter and Armistead. What is all this about?"

From foreign secretary to top spy-masters, Jonas Lied was being vetted. Sir Reginald Hall was chief of the department most likely to be running any Romanov rescue operation. He was already a wartime legend as Director of Naval Intelligence, working closely with MI1C. Hall's empire was the cornerstone for the formidable reputation acquired by British intelligence during the first world war, and lasting long after his death. His personal reputation stood so high that he was spoken of as a future foreign secretary, and he had extensive influence in high places. Hall had met the tsar in 1914 when he visited Russia as captain of HMS *Queen Mary*, part of an official visit by a Royal Navy squadron to St Petersburg. In the tsarist capital two ships had been lashed together to make a huge dancing floor and supper room for a banquet attended by the imperial family. At Tsarskoe Selo palace it was Hall who had introduced brother officers to the tsar and tsarina. Politically he was well to the right; it would be no surprise to find him involved in a plan to rescue the Romanovs, and there was no more ruthless or well-connected operator.

Lied's swing through the power centre of London continued to bring meetings with influential people: "13 March. Had lunch with E. Shackleton at his Marlborough Club during which Prince of Wales came up to our table and we had a few words about Siberia."

One week later Lied tied Romanov rescue plans into his diary for the first and last time:

20 March. Saw Sir Francis Barker and Grand Duke Michael at Vickers House about saving Nicholas II from Tobolsk by

fast motor boat through Kara Sea. Hagen would give £500. Sir F. listened very interested, then asked me to keep his name out of it. Introduced me to Michael in next office (he was director at £800). He understood he said, why I came, but would I keep his name out!"

"Michael" was the Grand Duke Mikhail Mikhailovich, a cousin to the tsar. As a Romanov fortunate enough to be safe in England already, having been banished from Russia by the tsar for contracting a morganatic marriage, he seems to have had no loyal impulse to help his relatives. Vickers, in 1918, was one of the arms and shipbuilding firms which had made millions out of the war, supplying both England and imperial Russia. Until the revolution, its agent in St Petersburg had been none other than Sidney Reilly—the "Ace of Spies"—one of Britain's best known agents in revolutionary Russia.

This entry, the last clue in the diary to the rescue plan, shows Lied canvassing support rather as though the scheme was his private inspiration.[32] The rescue operation may indeed have been planned by him, in terms of logistics, but there is no doubt Lied was called in for consultations by the British, and that his suggestions were seriously considered. Many years later he made that crystal clear to a close English friend, in a series of conversations. Ralph Hewins, author and former diplomat, is a specialist on Scandinavia and has been a British newspaper correspondent there since 1939. He knew Lied for sixteen years, and this is how he remembers the Norwegian's story:

> He told me he was asked by Metropolitan-Vickers (or anyway a Vickers outfit) to berth a British boat at his sawmill depot at the mouth of the Yenisey and to transport the imperial family from Tobolsk downriver in one of his cargoboats. The plan was feasible. The torpedo boat was to take a course far north into the Arctic, through Novaya Zemlya, so as to avoid wartime minefields and possible Bolshevik pursuit.

Clearly, this plan was born of desperation and fraught with problems, political, military, and logistic. But March, two months before the full thaw, was the right time to be planning it—and that is when Lied was in London. With his knowledge of the route, his influence, and his existing staff network in Russia, he was uniquely equipped to give advice. But, says Hewins, the plan fell through: "King George backed the plan. But the prime minister, Lloyd George, had no use for the tsar. Whatever the reason for the change of plan, Lloyd George virtually murdered the tsar. Lied had it on his conscience for the rest of his life that the plan failed to materialize."

This suggests a startling reversal of roles. In the spring of 1917 it had been Lloyd George who believed Britain must honour its asylum offer to the Romanovs, and King George who pressed for the offer to be withdrawn. Now, realizing at last the deadly peril his cousin faced, King George may have argued for a rescue attempt—however slim the chances of success. But by spring 1918 the British government was flirting with the Bolsheviks and it looked for a while as though some compromise could be reached, and relations normalized. Allied intervention against the Bolsheviks did not come until the summer. So Lloyd George may now have felt that intervention on behalf of the tsar could rock the diplomatic boat, and should be avoided. The king, as a constitutional monarch, must have had to bow reluctantly to his prime minister's decision. But next time a royal relative was engulfed by revolution George was to behave differently, as Lord Mountbatten explained to us:

He did learn his lesson because when his other first cousin, my brother-in-law Prince Andrew of Greece [*Prince Philip's father*], was arrested and very nearly shot by General Pangalos and the revolutionary people in Greece—in 1922—he, on his own, sent out Captain Talbot and rang up the Admiralty to send the cruiser *Calypso* to go to Athens to see if they could get him away. This time he went ahead of the government and the government didn't object.

We asked Lord Mountbatten whether it was at all possible that the king could have mounted his own operation, with secret service help, to rescue the Romanovs. He replied: "I don't say it would have been inconceivable. But in the light of the government's attitude, and the fact that King George V was a constitutional monarch, it would have been virtually impossible."

In 1974 we asked the heir assumptive to the Romanov throne, Grand Duke Vladimir, about 1918 plans by the allies to rescue the tsar. Vladimir hedged, but admitted knowing Lied, and added: "There were plans, distinct from monarchist plots, while the imperial family were at Tobolsk, and they involved George V and others . . ."

Whatever the precise nature of that involvement, Jonas Lied's plan became of academic interest before it could ever have got off the ground. Four weeks after the Norwegian's talks with British intelligence, the tsar was spirited away from Tobolsk.

This was the one serious attempt to get the Romanovs away, and it is still shrouded in mystery.

21

THE YAKOVLEV MISSION

"How narrow is the line that separates an adventure from an ordeal, and escape from exile."
(Harold Nicolson, King George V's biographer)

In April 1918 Tsar Nicholas was beginning his second year as a prisoner. He still seemed imperturbable, and had settled into a firm routine during the bitterly cold winter at Tobolsk. He exercised as much as he could in the garden, and whiled away the evenings playing bezique with Alexandra, or ploughing through another Conan Doyle mystery. But beneath the composure Nicholas must have realized how alone he was. Communications with the outside world were poor, but the tsar did know his country was spiralling into civil war. Apart from making him rue his abdication, the rise of left-wing extremism meant that his own family was threatened as never before.

Nicholas was aware that there had been a series of harebrained monarchist rescue plots, but he must also have understood how hopeless they were. Since January a new, ambiguous figure had joined the bevy of Romanov watchers in Tobolsk. This was a young man with a toothbrush moustache called Boris Solovyov, the son of a churchman who had studied in Berlin, dabbled in hypnotism, and spent some time in the army. When the imperial family moved to Siberia he cultivated the tsarina's gullible friend, Anna Vyrubova, and married Rasputin's daughter Maria who lived near Tobolsk. Geographically and socially, Solovyov seemed perfectly qualified for the role of imperial watchdog. He made contact with the Romanovs through the woman who delivered the bread, and raised the hopes of the imperial family whenever he could. He arranged for an officer to whisper: "Put your faith in us, your majesty!" as the tsar knelt in prayer at a church service. It certainly took in the tsarina, who assured her companions that

"300 faithful Russians" were in the area, and only waiting for the moment to act.

History has branded Solovyov as a dangerous triple agent, paid by the Germans to supply information, in league with the Bolsheviks, while posing all the time as a monarchist hero. Loyal officers travelling to Tobolsk were briefed to contact Solovyov en route, and walked straight into a trap. At least three were captured and shot by the Bolshevik secret police —just after they had met Solovyov and voiced suspicion of his motives. Until now efforts to help the imperial family had been bogged down in indecision and bungling, and now they were being obstructed by a traitor.

But in the second week of April 1918 Solovyov's activities were abruptly interrupted. A man called Bronard turned up—ostensibly for consultations. In fact he pulled a neat doublecross, turned the local Bolsheviks against Solovyov, and had him thrown into jail on suspicion of being a counter-revolutionary. Bronard was later identified as a French agent, and his dramatic intervention did more than mark the end of the comic-opera phase in schemes to rescue the Romanovs. It was the first sign of allied involvement, and it coincided with the one definite attempt to get the tsar away from the extremists, and out of Siberia.

On 22 April, just after Solovyov had been neutralized, the quiet of snowbound Tobolsk was shattered by the arrival of a stranger at the head of 150 horsemen. This was Vassily Yakovlev. In his thirties, with jet-black hair, tall, lean and energetic, and dressed in naval uniform, he seemed well-educated and cosmopolitan. The first thing he did was to visit Colonel Kobylinsky, the officer in nominal charge of the Romanovs, and ask him to summon the guard. For some time now, the day-to-day fortunes of the family had been subject to the prevailing political loyalties of the guard detachment. They were heavily politicized, and by the spring of 1918 the soldiers had polarized under two separate leaderships, each vying for control. Both Omsk, in western Siberia, and Ekaterinburg, in the Urals, claimed jurisdiction over the imperial family, and both had sent their men in to achieve it. The Omsk delegation was relatively moderate, but Ekaterinburg had sent a force of Red Guards to try to force the transfer of the Romanovs to

"The Hill", the local jail. It was at this tense moment that Yakovlev arrived.

He introduced himself as a Special Commissar, and produced impressive credentials which he said came from the Bolshevik leadership in Moscow. Yakovlev flourished three documents, which said he was on a mission of great importance, and threatened anyone defying him with summary execution. The key signature on the papers was that of Yakov Sverdlov, chairman of the Soviet Central Executive Committee, and Head of State. This was not quite enough to convince the more militant members of the guard, who peered at the imposing seal on the papers with suspicion. Yakovlev did not force the issue, and left them to think it over. At a second meeting he deftly turned the men from Omsk against the hardliners from Ekaterinburg, and the moderates came out on top. The leader of the Ekaterinburg unit was booed and hissed for spreading false alarms about escape plots, and left the meeting. It was only then that Yakovlev summoned the guard committee to announce his mission—to take the Romanovs away from Tobolsk. After all his groundwork, the bombshell seems to have gone down quite well, and the commissar now arranged to meet the emperor.

Standing in the hall of the Governor's House, Yakovlev bowed, addressed Nicholas as "Your Majesty", and told him to be ready to leave during the night. The tsar said: "I refuse to go." Yakovlev warned him that he must either take him by force or resign his post: "In that case the committee would probably send a far less scrupulous man to replace me. Be calm. I am responsible with my life for your safety . . . Be ready, we are leaving tomorrow at 4 am." Yakovlev made it very clear that time was of the essence; although little Alexei was too ill to travel, he was determined to leave at once with the tsar, and make arrangements for the tsarevich later. He bowed and left.

The imperial family spent the next few hours in anguished discussion about who should travel and who should remain behind with Alexei, still confined to bed after his latest haemophiliac crisis. Their decision depended very much on guessing Yakovlev's true intentions, and where he was taking them. The imperial family played detective, trying to solve the riddle. Kobylinsky pointed out that Yakovlev had said he would be coming back to fetch Alexei, and had calculated that the round

trip would take about eleven days, including a stopover at
their destination. The schedule suggested Moscow, and Yakovlev claimed he had been sent by Moscow. The tsarina, afraid
that the tsar was being taken there for some political purpose,
decided to go with him, and leave her son behind in the care of
three of his sisters.

Meanwhile, the humiliated Ekaterinburg representative had
sent word to his home base of what was going on. Yakovlev
seemed to realize the Ekaterinburg Communists could still ruin
his mission, and made feverish preparations for departure. By
two o'clock in the morning the courtyard was filled with
stamping horses, sleighs, and men hurrying around with
baggage. At half past three the tsar, the tsarina, and their
daughter Maria came out, wrapped in furs, to take their places
in the sleighs. The tsarina wanted to share one vehicle with her
husband, but Yakovlev objected. He insisted on sitting with
Nicholas himself, and ordered Alexandra and her daughter to
another sleigh. By now, Yakovlev was openly behaving with
more respect towards the tsar than any of the commissars the
Romanovs had seen. One of the servants later said:

> He didn't just act well towards the emperor, he was full of
> attention and kindness. When he saw that the tsar was wear-
> ing only a topcoat against the bitter cold, he exclaimed
> "What! You're only wearing an overcoat." "That's all I
> ever wear," said the tsar. "But that's out of the question,"
> replied Yakovlev, and he ordered his men to bring another
> coat, and spread it on the bench of the sleigh.

When the tsar took his seat, Yakovlev saluted him.

Yakovlev headed first for Tyumen, the nearest accessible
railway station. It was a tough 24-hour journey, almost non-
stop and through melting snow. Relays of horses were waiting
along the way, and Yakovlev travelled as if he had the devil
behind him. As indeed he had, in the shape of the frustrated
unit from Ekaterinburg; they now shadowed Yakovlev all the
way, becoming increasingly suspicious of his motives. At
Tyumen a special train was waiting with steam up, and ready
to leave. But after putting the Romanovs on board, Yakovlev
went to the telegraph office. He made a point of going alone,

and used his personal operator to work the Hughes telegraph. We do not know who he called, although it has always been assumed he was reporting back to the Bolshevik leadership in Moscow, and asking advice about the threat from Ekaterinburg. Yakovlev was away several hours, and when he got back to the station he announced his intention of heading for Moscow, not by the direct route through Ekaterinburg, but via Omsk (*see map below*). This would involve going about 500 miles in the wrong direction, and then doubling back on a line which passed well south of Ekaterinburg.

The Yakovlev Mission

1 *Tobolsk to Tyumen by sledge*

2 *After feint towards Ekaterinburg train reverses eastwards*

3 *Bolsheviks stop train, forcing Yakovlev to return west to Ekaterinburg*

Yakovlev certainly did all he could to deceive the men from Ekaterinburg. When the train pulled out, at five o'clock in the morning, it actually started out in the direction of Ekaterinburg, only to reverse back through Tyumen again, with all lights extinguished, on the way to Omsk. But news of Yakovlev's plan had already reached Ekaterinburg by telegraph. As the train moved eastwards, the Ekaterinburg Soviet declared

Yakovlev an outlaw and traitor to the revolution, and asked the Omsk comrades to turn the train back to Tyumen.

It was a race against time, and telegrams go faster than steam engines. Before arriving at Omsk, Yakovlev learned from railway workers that a hostile reception committee was waiting for him. He stopped, uncoupled the engine, and left the Romanovs while he went into Omsk to reason with the local Bolsheviks, and use the telegraph again. But by this time Yakovlev had run out of tricks. He was faced with no alternative but to take the family to Ekaterinburg. Once there he found himself so suspected of treachery that he needed all his wits to save his own neck. Yakovlev used the time-worn defence that he had only been obeying orders, and even produced parts of his telegraph conversations, printed on tape, to show that his orders really had been to take the tsar to Moscow. Chairman Beloborodov and Commissar Goloshchokin remained sceptical, but they now had what they wanted. The tsar and tsarina were locked up in the Ipatiev House, so Yakovlev was allowed to go free. A few days later he sent a terse message to those members of his unit he had left as a rearguard at Tobolsk: "Gather the detachment. Come back. I have resigned. I take no responsibility for the consequences." A fortnight later, when Alexei was well enough to travel, he and his sisters were brought to join their parents at Ekaterinburg.

Yakovlev had failed, but it had been a sophisticated, bold operation. He had tried to get the tsar away from under the noses of his enemies, and had come within a few miles of doing it. But what was behind it all, and who was Yakovlev?

The only Soviet account tries to explain the whole thing by saying that Yakovlev indeed arrived as Moscow's trusted envoy, sent to transfer the tsar to Ekaterinburg. But he betrayed his orders in mid-operation and "knowing that execution awaited the Romanovs, decided to save them, and to alight with them on the way to Samara and to hide them for a time in the hills . . ." In other words Yakovlev turned traitor. That alone was embarrassing enough for the Communists and the Soviet explanation skates over a number of unanswered questions. Not least is how Moscow could possibly have risked putting Yakovlev in charge of such a vital mission, if he was not 100 per cent reliable. And if he was a traitor, what was his cause?

The most common way historians have dealt with the conundrum is the German scenario. This suggests that the Kaiser and his government were now thoroughly alarmed at the prospect of international revolution spreading out of Russia. So, having been instrumental in its downfall, Germany now prepared to support a restoration of the Russian imperial house. As a first step the German ambassador to Russia is said to have approached the Bolshevik leaders and pressured them to bring the tsar away from the dangers of Siberia and to the comparative safety of Moscow. According to this theory, Moscow gave the impression of agreement whilst actually arranging an elaborate doublecross. Yakovlev was indeed ordered to bring the tsar to Moscow, but at the same time the Ekaterinburg Communists were forewarned to ruin the plan, so that Nicholas ended up in their hands after all. Then Moscow would be able to tell the Germans, "We tried our best", and still have the tsar tucked away well out of Berlin's reach. Yakovlev would merely have been the stooge. This theory seems to us implausible. Above all, the deception would have been too finely balanced, and could so easily have misfired. Indeed, Yakovlev was so highpowered that he very nearly did succeed in getting the tsar out of Siberia, and that would have left the Bolsheviks acutely embarrassed.

Consider another possibility, that Yakovlev was a cog in an arrangement by which the Bolsheviks agreed to the tsar's departure abroad in return for vital concessions on the part of the Germans, or the British, and conceivably both. Suppose for a moment that a humanitarian arrangement had been made, at some stage, although it later fell through. Some of the evidence bears this out.

The best source on the episode at Tobolsk is the commandant, Colonel Kobylinsky, who was present when Yakovlev met the tsar. Afterwards he seemed optimistic and quickly scotched a rumour that the tsar was being taken to Moscow for a show trial. "Trial!" he exclaimed. "There will be no trial. From Moscow they are to be taken to Petrograd, then to Finland, Sweden and Norway."

The tsar's aide-de-camp, Prince Vassily Dolgorukov, who picked up his information on the journey to Ekaterinburg, told cellmates in the Ekaterinburg city prison that he believed

Yakovlev had been "taking the tsar to Riga". In April 1918 the town of Riga, on the Baltic, was controlled by the Germans, so Dolgorukov's comment has usually been taken to mean that Yakovlev was a German agent trying to get the tsar to German-held territory. But Riga is a port, and a quite reasonable point of departure if the tsar was to be taken to Scandinavia. It does not necessarily clash with the outline plan as Kobylinsky understood it. But there is yet more testimony on the role of Yakovlev, and this specifies the eventual destination—England.

After Yakovlev's meeting with Nicholas in the hall, the doctor, Yevgeny Botkin, hurried to tell his children the following news: "Yakovlev has finally announced that he has come to take us all to Moscow . . . It is actually true that the Soviets have promised Germany to release the imperial family. But the Germans have had the decency not to demand that the imperial family go to Germany. Accordingly it has been decided that we shall be sent to England . . ."

Dr Botkin's son, Gleb, recalled all this in detail, and England appears to have been on everyone's lips. He and his sister Tatiana spent the afternoon packing the sort of clothes they would need in England, and dreamed of an idyllic English summer, with tennis matches and long lazy afternoons. Tatiana confirms that after the meeting between the tsar and Yakovlev, everyone felt happier, certain they were to go abroad. That night Dr Botkin wrote his children a farewell letter, and Gleb recalled: "It sounded more cheerful than anything I had heard him say since the revolution. Evidently he was quite certain that we were all actually going to England, and it was to our forthcoming journey and our future stay in England that most of his letter was dedicated . . ." Dr Botkin was perhaps the most level-headed man in the whole imperial household, a good friend to the tsar and likely to have been well briefed on the emperor's talk with Yakovlev. But was it all a cruel deception? The real answer lay in the identity of Yakovlev, and that remains shadowy to this day.

Sokolov marked him down as a German agent, but produced no supporting evidence—only the curious fact that the Tobolsk traitor, Solovyov, had marked in advance in his diary the very date that Yakovlev's transfer operation began. Another Russian source identifies Yakovlev as being a former deserter from the

imperial navy, who had absconded to Canada in 1905. There
he had come under British influence, and only returned to
Russia in 1917, at the time of the tsar's abdication. He is then
said to have been an assistant on the commission appointed by
the Kerensky government to investigate the tsar's affairs; under
cover of revolutionary zeal against the old regime, he in fact
used his influence to protect the family from outright violence.[33]
Yakovlev would thus have been concerned with the Romanovs
from the start of the revolution, and an obvious choice to send
to Tobolsk to deal with the transfer. On the basis of this, it has
been suggested that he was all the time a British agent with an
excellent cover, a cover that was only blown when the Tobolsk
gamble failed.

All this is guesswork, but Yakovlev's activities after Tobolsk
at least provided firm clues to his personal loyalties, and to the
fact that he had powerful protectors. Later in 1918, after the
start of Allied intervention against the Bolsheviks, Yakovlev
defected from the Bolshevik side. He then gave a bland interview to a monarchist newspaper, throwing no real light on the
origins of his Romanov mission, but making it clear where his
sympathies lay:

I had the impression that he [*the tsar*] was a good man,
deeply religious, who genuinely loved his family . . . He talked
to me about the life of the people, of humble folk, for whom
he clearly had feelings of sympathy and interest. The tsar
and tsarina and the grand duchess put up with the journey
bravely . . . They never complained.

Clearly Yakovlev, whoever he was, would have been a key
witness for the investigation into the fate of the Romanovs. The
irony is that he was located, but mysteriously spirited away
before he could be questioned. From unpublished material in
the official dossier, it now emerges that White investigators
knew exactly where Yakovlev was with the White armies. Two
formal requests were made to Kolchak's minister of war to have
him made available for questioning. The requests went unheeded and only in June 1919, after a six-month delay, did
Military Counter-Intelligence admit that they had traced
Yakovlev—and lost him again. Their report stated lamely:

Yakovlev was arrested on the instructions of General Shenikh, and escorted to Western army headquarters and from there to the town of Omsk, in accordance with instructions from the 1st Quartermaster General of the Supreme Command Staff. But *because of a mistake by the escort* Yakovlev was transferred to the command of Colonel Zaicek on 2 January 1919, and all further trace of him was lost after this. According to the same report, Yakovlev offered 500,000 roubles in return for his freedom.

Faced with this nonsense even Sokolov must have wondered what was going on at Omsk, where his mentor, General Diterikhs, was taking all vital decisions about the Romanov enquiry. It was the last clue about Yakovlev. Some accounts say he was killed fighting for the Whites, another says he was "shot by mistake". The mistakes, the fatal accidents and illnesses, multiply. Yakovlev vanishes without trace, another silent witness.

Significantly, British and German Foreign Office files make no mention of Yakovlev until long after the disappearance of the Romanovs from Ekaterinburg—and then there are only passing references. Yet in England at any rate, this was the moment that King George V was at last beginning to bother the Foreign Office with enquiries about his cousin's plight, and asking what could be done about it.[34] There should now have been in-depth reports by diplomats and intelligence officers, analysing the puzzle of the single recorded attempt to whisk the Romanovs out of extremist hands. But there is nothing at all in the official files.

The French historian, Jean Jacoby, recognized the disappearance of "Yakovlev" as the work of "those powerful influences whose interest was to put the investigation off the track".[35] The silence in the files of Whitehall and the Wilhelmstrasse is also deafening, and heavy in its implications. Both seem to have had solid political reasons for burying the Yakovlev affair, and they succeeded.

Once the Romanovs were at Ekaterinburg, it seems unlikely the British could have done much to help the tsar. British approaches to the Bolsheviks now had little hope of success, for it was at this point that the British started troop landings in north Russia—the first stage of the prolonged Allied attempt to bring down the Bolsheviks. The chance of doing a deal over the Romanovs had been missed.

It was also unlikely that London could put a rescue operation together. The royal prisoners were in a Bolshevik stronghold which was itself in the middle of a war zone. The only option left was the sort of James Bond operation to which governments can give a nod of approval, while disassociating themselves if things go badly. We have no evidence that any such operation ever happened, although there were Allied agents in Ekaterinburg by July 1918, and they may have been planning help for the Romanovs. Carl Ackerman wrote of the way certain unnamed persons kept watch on the Ipatiev House right up to the moment the family vanished. He also suggests the watchers actually made contact with the tsar:

> . . . news travelled to and from the tsar through signals from the attic of the brick house across the street from the Ipatiev residence . . . A private telephone in this house was connected with the house of a certain prominent business man. The man in the attic and this merchant communicated with each other day and night, and I remember learning from one of them some of the secret phrases they used in talking, so that if any one should by chance overhear them the Bolsheviki could not understand. When the observer under the roof of the house across the street saw the tsar in the garden he would phone, "The baggage is at the station" and then messages would be communicated to the tsar.

Major Sergei Smirnov, a Siberian officer also in Ekaterinburg in July 1918, wrote an almost identical account of the foreigners watching the Ipatiev House. His source was an unnamed American he met at the time, and the major gathered from him that the watcher in the attic across the way was the British consul. Sir Thomas Preston has never confirmed this story, but it is possible his consulate was used to observe the house. By July at least one British officer was living secretly at the consulate, for Preston writes in his memoirs of "a British officer in plain clothes, who had come through the lines from General Poole's expeditionary force at Archangel". Preston identifies the officer as "Captain Jones", and says he had been sent to liaise with the advancing Czechs. Coincidentally, the name "Jones" appears scrawled in the margin of Sir Charles Eliot's October 1918 report on the disappearance of the imperial family; we have been unable to discover who he was, or his connection with the Romanovs.

If anything was planned, it all came to nothing. There is no doubt at all that London, and the king in particular, eventually believed in the death of all the family. When Thomas Preston returned to London and was received at Buckingham Palace, King George V wrote in his diary:

> 19 February 1921:
> Saw Mr Preston, our consul at Ekaterinburg, who was there when dear Nicky and Alicky and their family were murdered, he told me many interesting things.

King George had been convinced of the deaths of all the Romanovs since 1 September 1918, when he wrote to the Marchioness of Milford Haven that everyone had almost certainly been murdered. In that letter he had added, with some rancour: "The awful part is that they might all have been saved if W had only lifted a finger on their behalf."

"W" was the German Kaiser, Wilhelm. Ironically, he had been even quicker off the mark with recriminations than King George. On 21 July 1918, just after the Bolsheviks announced the tsar's execution, a German foreign ministry official noted:

> His Majesty was especially insistent today upon the necessity of taking advantage, for propaganda purposes, of the manner in which the Allied powers, particularly England, forsook the tsar, even though it would have been easy to obtain safety for the imperial family . . . For the dethroned tsar, for whom England had no further use, neither the British government nor the king, his cousin, did anything.[36]

Whatever King George did or did not do to help his cousin, the record shows that, in fact, Cousin Willy did lift a finger for the fallen Romanovs. He may also have tried to do a great deal more.

THE GERMAN CONNECTION

"The blood of the poor tsar is not at my door, not on my hands."
                    (Kaiser Wilhelm II, in exile, 1935)

THE GERMAN CONNECTION is the key to what really happened at Ekaterinburg. Time and again in our story there have been suggestions, sometimes tiny clues and sometimes heavy hints, that there was a teutonic involvement. There was the White officer at Ekaterinburg, convinced that what he saw was a simulation of massacre, who did not believe that the German Kaiser would have allowed such an outrage. There was the tsarina's brother, the Grand Duke of Hesse, over-eager to discredit the Anastasia claimant, potentially his own niece, probably to cover up some compromising political involvement. It was a senior German foreign ministry official who suggested a lawyer for Anna Anderson—the same diplomat who in July 1918 had played an important role at the German embassy in Moscow. General Hoffmann, the German general who negotiated peace with the Bolsheviks in 1918, acknowledged "Anastasia", saying enigmatically "I don't have to see her, I know". And there was Kaiser Wilhelm himself, taking a surprising interest when one of the claimant's doctors briefed him on "Anastasia", and allowing his wife, the German empress, to visit the invalid in hospital. These were not mere coincidences, and we must now unravel the German involvement in the fate of the Romanovs.

Kaiser Wilhelm scarcely seems a good candidate for the role of rescuer. Even before the outbreak of World War I his relationship with the Romanovs was shaky. Wilhelm was headstrong and impetuous, and the Allies' mistrust of him is well illustrated by a popular anecdote. It was said that his wish to divide Europe into spheres of influence was rebuffed by Nicholas's father, Tsar Alexander III, with the words:

"Don't be a whirling dervish, Willy. Look in the mirror!" The
glass would indeed have reflected an odd character, with the
vainglorious moustache, the withered arm, and the love of
bizarre uniforms. The Kaiser was distantly related to Tsar
Nicholas by blood, and more closely by marriage. But it was
Alexandra who represented the closest link with Germany. She,
like Wilhelm, was a grandchild of Queen Victoria, which
made them first cousins. Above all Alexandra herself was
German born, being a princess of Hesse. But even internal
German relations, between the House of Hesse and the Kaiser's
Prussian family, had been strained for more than a generation.
The tension had continued unabated since 1866, when the
political changes brought about by Prussian expansionist
policy had not only aroused feelings of bitter and lasting
resentment in Hanover and Denmark, but had also alienated
Hesse, and other states as well.

Nevertheless, Wilhelm supported Alexandra's marriage to
Nicholas and used it, in his own way, to forge a relationship with the new tsar. Nine years older than Nicholas (*see
plate 54*), he took it upon himself to bombard his relative with
advice on how to run Russia—advice that may have contributed to the collapse of the Romanovs, for Wilhelm was
very attached to the principle of absolute monarchy. In Germany the Kaiser was styled "the all-highest", and he advised
Nicholas that the devoted Russian people would, in the end,
always place their faith in their tsar, "and worship his hallowed
person".

The two emperors maintained personal contact by letter, the
famous "Willy-Nicky" correspondence. They last met in 1914
when Nicolas visited Berlin—and they were still good friends.
But whatever friendship had existed disintegrated when the
two great nations slid into war in 1914. As their governments'
official ultimatums came and went, the two emperors did their
own bargaining in a long series of telegrams. Until the last
moment both referred to their "long and tried friendship", as
even Nicholas called it, but the declaration of war tried it
beyond breaking point. Speaking of Wilhelm, Nicholas subsequently told the French ambassador: "He never was sincere,
not for a moment . . . in the end he was hopelessly enmeshed
in the net of his own perfidy and lying . . . I felt that all was over

forever between me and Wilhelm." As far as the tsar was concerned, then, 1914 certainly marked the end of the relationship, although his less sensitive German neighbour may never quite have appreciated it.

The supreme irony came in 1917, when the German government fostered Bolshevism to defeat Russia from within and remove her as a military threat on the Eastern front. So the German "All-Highest", who had for so long urged Nicholas to preserve the autocracy in Russia, eventually found himself presiding over its humiliating and bloody collapse. It was largely thanks to Germany that Tsar Nicholas was toppled and the balance of world power abruptly and savagely changed.

For many years after the war, public vilification of the defeated Kaiser remained obligatory in Britain, and he was accused of callously ignoring the plight of his relatives. But this may be far from the truth. If Wilhelm lit the flames that destroyed the House of Romanov, there is evidence that he later tried to put them out again. Wilhelm, with his own peculiar interpretation of personal honour and gallantry, may have attempted to make amends.

Years later, himself exiled at Doorn in Holland, he talked about the matter to the distinguished British soldier, General Wallscourt Waters. From his days as British military attaché in Berlin, Waters knew the Kaiser well. By visiting Wilhelm in exile after the war, the general brought upon himself the fury of King George V, but he obtained fascinating information about the Kaiser's readiness to help the tsar. Following a long conversation in 1935, the general considered the Kaiser's story sufficiently important to put into writing in a series of detailed notes. The Kaiser then personally approved Waters's notes, so one can take them as the authorized account.

Wilhelm declared that in 1917, while the moderate Provisional Government was trying to get the Romanovs out of the country, the Danish court approached Germany for assistance in rescuing the tsar. According to the Kaiser:

The German chancellor was approached from Copenhagen with the suggestion to attempt the rescue of the poor tsar and his family by Germany. I remarked to Herr von Bethmann [*the German chancellor*]: "How am I to do that? There are two fighting lines of German and Russian troops facing each other between him and me." Nevertheless I ordered my chancellor to try to get in touch with the Kerensky government by neutral channels, informing him that if a hair of the Russian imperial family's head should be injured, I would hold him personally responsible . . .

According to the Kaiser, that contact was made at the very time that Kerensky's Provisional Government was negotiating British asylum for the imperial family. Wilhelm gave that plan his blessing, and told General Waters how he issued secret instructions to his army and naval commanders not to hinder the tsar's departure, and to provide an honour escort if necessary. The Kaiser's claim is confirmed by Kerensky, who said Berlin promised that German submarines would not attack any British warship carrying the imperial exiles. But of course all that fell through—Britain spurned the Romanovs and sent no warship. In any case, a German offer of safe conduct in 1917, when the war seemed to be going their way, was a very different matter from going out of their way to negotiate a release, let alone mount a rescue operation, in 1918. Yet, however belatedly, that is what may have happened.

We know that in early 1918, as the Romanovs shivered through their winter at Tobolsk, a group of right-wing Russian politicians despaired of monarchist efforts to save the tsar, and decided to turn to the Germans. For eminent White Russians it was degrading even to consider such a thing while still at war with Germany, and the tsar himself would have been appalled. But the right-wingers, including a former minister and a senior general, decided there was no alternative. Germany was now the one foreign power in a position to exert real influence over the Bolsheviks, who were desperately suing for peace with Berlin. Lenin had allowed the arrival in Moscow of a German commissioner, Count Mirbach, and the Russian right-wingers decided to appeal to him. Early in the New Year of 1918 they trooped along to Mirbach's office in Denezhny Street, and asked for German pressure on Moscow to save the tsar. The count made no promises, but one monarchist quoted him as saying: "Be calm. We Germans have the situation well in hand, and the imperial family is under our protection. We know what we are doing, and when the time comes, the German imperial government will take the necessary measures." The monarchists thought the reply too vague, and wondered if the German was fobbing them off. Was the situation really in hand?

While they worried and wondered, German and Bolshevik representatives were meeting in a dirty, snowbound town on what is now the eastern border of Poland. In war-ravaged Brest-Litovsk, Germany and the new masters of Russia were moving slowly towards one of the most astonishing treaties in history.

Militarily, the Kaiser's armies had Russia at their mercy, and the Bolsheviks had few cards to play. To consolidate their still precarious hold on Russia they needed peace at any price, and the cost was to be astronomical. Under the terms eventually agreed on 3 March 1918, Russia lost vast western territories, including a third of her agricultural land, more than a third of her population, 90 per cent of her coal mines, and half her heavy industry. The Germans now hoped to transfer whole armies to the western front to smash the Allies, and at the same time plunder the newly-gained Russian territories for vitally needed supplies. The German press called Brest-Litovsk "a peace of understanding and conciliation"; a more objective observer has since called it "a peace that passed all understanding". For Russians it meant total and unprecedented humiliation at the hands of the enemy, but it gave Lenin the one thing he so desperately needed—the breathing space to establish and consolidate Bolshevism against the gathering forces of reaction.

Over the years it has repeatedly been claimed that there was a secret codicil in the Treaty of Brest-Litovsk providing for the release of the tsar and his family. This was suggested in reputable newspapers at the time of the negotiations, and the allegation has been produced ever since by those who say the imperial family was not murdered. Extensive research fails to confirm this, but there is an alternative possibility to a written clause. In a formal memorandum to the Foreign Office, on 27 December 1917, Robert Wilton of *The Times* referred to "overtures made on their [*the Romanovs'*] behalf by the Germans at Brest-Litovsk". Despite Wilton's later subjective reporting of the Romanovs' fate at Ekaterinburg, it was his business to have well-informed official sources on Brest-Litovsk—and the Romanovs may have been discussed. It would have been characteristic of the Kaiser to use Brest-Litovsk to raise the subject of the Romanovs' safety. It is equally likely that his political advisors would have disapproved of any written reference to these discussions. But the one certainty about Brest-Litovsk was its public display of the power and dominance of the Kaiser's Germany over Lenin's Russia.

It was with that in mind that as soon as the treaty was signed, King Christian of Denmark wrote to the Kaiser asking him to intervene urgently on behalf of the Romanovs. Wilhelm's reply was not very encouraging; he pointed out that angry noises from Berlin might be misinterpreted in Moscow as a desire to bring about a Romanov restoration, and that could endanger the imperial family even more. He suggested that the neutral governments of Scandinavia were better placed to make overtures. But he did hold out a ray of hope: "I cannot deny the imperial family my compassion from the human point of view, and when it lies in my power I will gladly do my part to ensure that the Russian imperial family has a safe and suitable situation."

But the pressure on the Kaiser's conscience was now building up, just as the danger to the Romanovs became more obvious. In April 1918 the right-wing group in Moscow made a new and desperate appeal not just to Germany, but direct to the Kaiser. Count Benckendorff, former grand marshal of the old imperial court, wrote a long personal letter to Count Mirbach, whom he had known well before the war. The letter placed responsibility for the safety of the Romanovs squarely on German shoulders, and Benckendorff insisted that the appeal should be delivered to the Kaiser himself. Count Mirbach, who had now formally become German ambassador in Moscow following the Brest-Litovsk treaty, is said to have received the latest approach coldly, commenting: "The fate of the tsar is a matter for the Russian people. We now have to concern ourselves with the safety of the German princesses on Russian territory." Those two sentences are probably the key to the vital role Germany was to play in the events of Ekaterinburg. Berlin did not want to be seen by the Bolsheviks to be openly favouring the monarchy, and to make a fuss about the tsar might be seen as foreign meddling. But Germany could intercede for the tsarina, because she was a German princess. The official record shows that this is exactly what now happened; messages between Moscow and Berlin in the early summer of 1918 express concern for the tsarina and her sister Elisabeth. On 10 May, within three days of receiving Benckendorff's letter, Mirbach reported to Berlin:

> I have . . . delivered to the People's Commissars a statement regarding our expectation that the German princesses will be treated with all possible consideration, and specifically that unnecessary petty annoyances, as well as threats against their lives, will not be permitted. My statement was received by Karakhan and Radek [senior Bolshevik officials dealing with foreign affairs] with an indication of understanding and a complete willingness to insist that such action be prevented.

Between May and June the concern was to broaden into demands for assurances about all the Romanovs, and they were to become "emphatic". But while the German ambassador was busy on the diplomatic front, other Germans were active behind the scenes, and playing a shabby game.

It has long been suggested that Berlin made a number of undercover approaches to the tsar himself—offers of help indeed, but with strings attached. The mandarins of the German Foreign Office, and the High Command, were by now seriously worried that the Marxist revolution in neighbouring Russia would prove contagious and spread to Germany. Having encouraged Bolshevism initially as a device to throw Russia into internal chaos, they now hoped, in the long term, for a Romanov restoration. Tsar Nicholas's own abdication was legally irrevocable, but Romanov endorsement of any successor would be desirable. In the coming weeks Berlin was to offer support as future tsar to any member of the Romanov family who would counter-sign the Treaty of Brest-Litovsk—and all were to refuse. It is conceivable that the Germans even toyed with the notion of making little Alexei into a puppet tsar; although Nicholas had also abdicated on behalf of his son, there was some doubt whether, strictly speaking, he had the right to do so. The last thing in the world the tsar wanted was to involve his pitiable, haemophiliac son in politics—that was precisely why he had altered his own abdication document to exclude Alexei from the throne. But whether that was part of the German proposals or not, any offer of help tied to political conditions was sheer blackmail, and the tsar stubbornly rejected it. Nicholas considered it dishonourable to deal with the Germans on any terms; he had been fiercely patriotic during the war, he disapproved totally of the Brest-Litovsk peace, and as far as he was concerned Russia was still at war with Germany. That much is clear from those who talked to him in the spring of 1918. Nevertheless, German envoys seem to have persisted in their suggestions, and it is here that the tsarina's brother, Grand Duke Ernst Ludwig of Hesse, comes into the picture. It may help to explain his later hostility to the Anastasia claimant.

Ernst Ludwig was very close to his sister, and desperate to help her. As a top German general he possessed the necessary qualifications to promote a scheme to extricate the Romanovs —and excellent contacts up to and including the Kaiser. In his concern for Alexandra he may have blinkered himself to the immorality of attaching conditions to help for the Romanovs, and decided that the end justified the means. This is not mere hypothesis—fragments of the grand duke's role leaked out years later in spite of tight security. In the late twenties, as the tsar's cousin Grand Duke Andrei struggled to understand the Hesse attitude to Anna Anderson, he stumbled across the trail of Berlin's covert approaches to the tsar—and found that Ernst Ludwig had been deeply involved. He learned that in the spring of 1918 a monarchist officer, Lieutenant Sergei Markov, had contacted the Grand Duke of Hesse through the German embassy in Russia, offering his services in any enterprise that might help the Romanovs. This was the response, as recorded by Andrei: "Markov apparently received a personal letter from the Grand Duke of Hesse to be given to the tsar, and the instruction to apply for assistance to two German agents in Russia who served German intelligence during the war. With their help he reached Tobolsk . . ." We know that Markov did indeed get to Tobolsk, and did make contact with the imperial family. As for the role of the tsarina's brother, Andrei added on an even more sinister note: ". . . the mention of his name as Regent prompts the assumption that he knew everything. That the conduct of the Germans was not disinterested requires no proofs . . ." This reference to the Grand Duke of Hesse as a possible "Regent" is an even more startling indication of Berlin's grandiose vision of the future. The Germans actually seem to have dreamed of a Romanov restoration with a puppet tsar, and a German proconsul holding the reins. The Germans did have a definite plan to create a chain of puppet monarchies in conquered states from the Baltic to the Black Sea.[37] If even part of Andrei's intelligence was accurate, the Grand Duke of Hesse had a great deal to hide.

Virtually nothing is on record concerning Wilhelm's personal role in the Romanov affair during the crucial months of spring and summer 1918. Significantly General Waters, after interviewing the Kaiser at Doorn, published only his notes on the German emperor's attitude immediately after the tsar's abdication in 1917. The key period in 1918 is omitted altogether. The full unedited Waters's notes were lodged with the British royal archives following the general's death, and are still held there. However, our request to see them in 1975 was refused on the pretext that there were "insuperable administrative difficulties" in arranging access. The possible reason for this may be contained in the letter written by General Waters's heir in 1945, on handing the documents over to Windsor: "The Kaiser series . . . seemed to me to be of historical interest and liable to cause trouble if they got into the wrong hands."

Similarly hardly anything was allowed to go on the official German record about the part Wilhelm played. But we do know that by June 1918 he was being informed and consulted daily about developments, and that his brother Prince Heinrich was deputed to deal personally with communications about the Russian imperial family. We have unearthed a further clue as to what was going on, and to the Kaiser's attitude, in a snippet of intelligence passed to London in a British diplomatic report from Switzerland on 19 June 1918. It noted remarks made by Queen Olga of Greece, who had just passed through Berne on her way home from a visit to Berlin. In Germany she had spoken with Crown Princess Cecile and, said the British report: "The crown princess informed her that the tsar says he will not be saved by Germany at any price. *His attitude much disturbs the*

German emperor, who spends sleepless nights in mourning over the Romanovs' fate."

This piece of royal gossip confirms that the Germans had been getting secret offers of help through to the captive Nicholas, who had bravely turned them down. But was the Kaiser really losing sleep over the Romanovs, as the family grapevine claimed? There is new evidence that the German emperor did suddenly initiate real action on their behalf in those last vital weeks of June and July.

On 17 July 1918, the very day the imperial family disappeared from Ekaterinburg, the British consul in Geneva, Middleton Edwards, was visited by two Russian monarchists in exile. They briefed him about a German plot to save the tsar, and handed him a letter on the subject addressed to the British foreign secretary. The consul listened, and wrote a memorandum for his chief in Berne. The key passage reads:

It appears that the Duke Leuchtenberg, a cousin of the ex-tsar, was in Berlin a month ago. He has now returned to Russia . . . Apparently the Germans have approached the ex-tsar and offered him assistance, which assistance, however, he has refused. Berlin is considering kidnapping the ex-tsar and his family and bringing them to Germany, and has asked the Swiss section of the League for the Restoration of the Russian Empire whether they agree to the plan that Berlin has hatched to kidnap the ex-tsar and bring him to Germany, whether he will or not.

This dramatic information went to the British Legation in Berne, and then as a cipher message to London. Late in the evening of 21 July, marked secret, it landed on the desk of the permanent under-secretary for foreign affairs, Lord Hardinge of Penshurst. Coming as it did three days after the official Bolshevik announcement of the tsar's execution, the document may have looked at first like a bad joke. Lord Hardinge merely penned his graceful initial "H" to the report, indicating that he had read it, and two other officials added laconic minutes: "Late in the day" and "I suppose there is no reasonable doubt of the tsar's murder?" But Whitehall's *sang-froid* may not have done the message justice. The same message had also reached

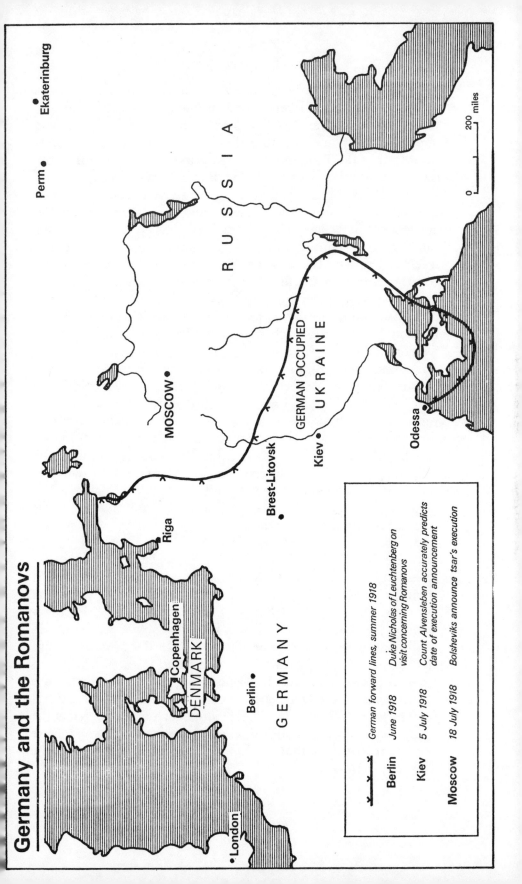

Germany and the Romanovs

⊁⊁⊁		German forward lines, summer 1918
Berlin	June 1918	Duke Nicholas of Leuchtenberg on visit concerning Romanovs
Kiev	5 July 1918	Count Alvensleben accurately predicts date of execution announcement
Moscow	18 July 1918	Bolsheviks announce tsar's execution

Ekaterinburg

Perm

R U S S I A

Moscow

GERMAN OCCUPIED

U K R A I N E

Kiev

Odessa

Brest-Litovsk

Riga

Copenhagen

DENMARK

Berlin

G E R M A N Y

London

0   200 miles

the French secret service in Switzerland, and their agent's report to the French foreign minister took the matter seriously. It said the plan was "well-defined", and involved freeing the imperial family and ensuring their departure for Denmark. It stressed that the Romanovs were in grave danger, and that the rescue would be above all for humanitarian reasons. The French agent suggested that the Romanovs should be moved through German-occupied Russia, and then across the Baltic aboard a neutral ship. He assures Paris that he can arrange for the French response to be sent "secretly without leaving any trace". As in the London files there is no follow-up material, but the silence in the files can hardly reflect the real reaction in Whitehall and the Quai d'Orsay.

The source of the intelligence was sound; it came from two leading Russian monarchists who had produced accurate information before. Maurice Poznanski had been commercial attaché at the Russian embassy in Berlin before the war, and had married into a German banking family. Swatowski had also been a diplomat in Vienna. British military intelligence reported that both were "under German influence, if not in German pay". With these connections both were well-placed to hear of German plots concerning the tsar. By the time the information reached Whitehall in July the Germans had had a full month, perhaps longer, to put their plan into effect. The evidence is that there was such a plan, and that a rescue operation actually got under way.

A first clue is the reference in the British report to "Duke Leuchtenberg", who had just come from Russia for consultations in Berlin. The Leuchtenbergs were of international significance, mainly through their relationship with the sovereigns of Sweden, Baden and Russia. The Leuchtenberg on the mission to Berlin was Duke Nicholas, second cousin to the tsar, who had promoted him to general for his services in the war, and he had been an aide-de-camp to the tsar at headquarters. Now, in 1918, he was fighting the Bolsheviks with a White army on the Don; and when he returned from his mysterious mission to Berlin his logical stopover point was Kiev, the capital of German-occupied Ukraine (*see map p. 283*). Sure enough it is at Kiev that we find the next fascinating link in the German connection.

Midway between western Europe and the Russian heart-
land, Kiev in 1918 was an ideal base for senior tsarist politicians and soldiers of the old regime. Two such men were a
White general, Prince Alexander Dolgorukov, and a member
of the Ukraine State Council, Fyodor Bezak. On 5 July Bezak's
phone rang. It was the start of a bewildering episode.

The man on the other end of the line was one of Berlin's top
diplomats in the Ukraine, Count Hans Bodo von Alvensleben.
At 35, he held the sensitive role of liaison man between the
German High Command and the puppet government at Kiev.
The count was popular with Russian monarchists because he
himself had Russian blood and he openly favoured a Romanov
restoration. Alvensleben was now telephoning to ask Bezak and
Dolgorukov to meet him at once for an urgent talk. He said he
had vital information. Bezak agreed and the three men met
within the hour. We know what took place at that extraordinary
meeting from General Dolgorukov, who told the story at length,
on oath, three years later.

Count Alvensleben went straight to the point—he announced that "Kaiser Wilhelm wished at all costs to rescue the
sovereign, Tsar Nicholas II . . ." He then made some puzzling
requests, saying that the precise present location of the Romanovs was not clear, and asking that Russian officers be sent to
get firm information. Army headquarters would, he said, supply
travel passes for the officers chosen to cross German-held
territory. None of this made much sense to General Dolgorukov,
who commented later:

> I felt there was something strange, something incompre-
> hensible in the logic of what Alvensleben was saying—why
> was it necessary to send Russian officers in search of the tsar
> in hostile territory when the Germans had their huge secret
> service there, their official representative in the person of
> Count Mirbach, and could easily, at any given moment,
> have exact information as to the whereabouts of the tsar?

Dolgorukov's confusion was justified. The Germans did have
an excellent intelligence network in the Urals, and there were
German personnel in strength in Ekaterinburg itself. During
May and June a German contingent had arrived openly in the

city, were welcomed by the local Bolsheviks, and lived in style on a luxurious train parked at the main railway station. The group included German generals and was—ostensibly—a Red Cross mission concerned with prisoners-of-war. But with the Russian Emperor locked up a few hundred yards away, the German officers had other things on their mind than the welfare of stranded soldiers. *The Times* correspondent reported flatly: ". . . a German mission came to Ekaterinburg at the end of May to ascertain all about the life of the residents of the Ipatiev House . . ." An intelligence report in American archives confirms that the Germans were still operating in the city as late as July, when the Romanovs disappeared.

So it does not make sense to find Alvensleben, a top German diplomat, asking White Russians to go and discover where the Romanovs were. Berlin's own people at Ekaterinburg could report back far quicker than Russian officers setting out from Kiev, 1,000 miles away. For some reason Germany wanted to distract the Kiev monarchists by sending them off on a wild goose chase—and, puzzled though they were, off they went. Two officers did reach Ekaterinburg, but only long after the disappearance of the imperial family.[38]

Alvensleben had something else to say at that puzzling meeting in Kiev, and it astounded his listeners. In General Dolgorukov's words:

> . . . [he] warned us that *between 16 July and the 20th rumours would be spread about news of the death of the tsar, and that this rumour or news should not alarm us; like the rumour of the murder of the tsar, which was current in June, it would be false, but it would be necessary for certain reasons, namely for the tsar's rescue.* I well recall that in our talk with him, which took place as I have said on 5 July or 6th, Count Alvensleben indicated as a precise period, that the news of the murder of the tsar would be falsely spread between 16 July and 20th. At the same time he begged us to keep our conversation with him secret, and to give the impression that we believed the news of the tsar's death.

It is easy to imagine Dolgorukov's utter astonishment when the prophesy came true:

. . . between the 16th and the 20th I read in the local papers that the tsar had been shot, and that the family had been taken away somewhere . . . I was amazed at the way Alvensleben had had such accurate information, and of course did not believe the newspaper reports. Immediately on reading the news bulletins I set off for the conference hall and met Bezak. We decided to hold the requiem mass in the cathedral all the same; it seemed to me that many, perhaps even the majority, did not fully believe the sad news was true. Many people came to me and Bezak with questions. Our position was difficult. We did not deny that the tsar could, possibly, have escaped. General Skoropadsky was not at the requiem service in the cathedral and held a service in his own home, with Alvensleben also present. Word spread quickly that Alvensleben had "wept" during the service. Bezak and I said to each other "How skilfully he is playing his role!"

A few days later, far to the north, another requiem service for Tsar Nicholas took place at the Russian church in Copenhagen. Amongst the mourners were King Christian of Denmark, the tsar's Danish uncle Prince Valdemar, and a host of foreign dignitaries. Afterwards a curious little incident occurred —one that might be insignificant if we did not know about events in Kiev. The tsarist ambassador, who was still accredited to Copenhagen, took the French envoy aside and told him that certain of his Russian colleagues believed the tsar was not really dead. The execution announcement, they declared, was only a cover to assure the tsar safe passage out of Russia.[39] It was a remarkable echo of Kiev, and we can hazard a guess at what lay behind it. The French intelligence report from Switzerland about the German rescue scheme had spoken of Denmark as the imperial family's ultimate destination. If there was substance to the plan and preparations had been made, then someone in Denmark would have had to be briefed in advance. Both at Kiev and Copenhagen, those in the know apparently believed everything was going according to plan.

Their expectations, of course, were to be disappointed. Tsar Nicholas and his family did not appear safe and sound, not in the coming weeks, nor ever. In Kiev, Count Alvensleben avoided Bezak and Dolgorukov after the requiem service, and then hurried off to Berlin. When he returned in August, Dolgorukov met him in the street and asked him about the tsar. Alvensleben said he was sorry, it had not been possible to do anything, and the emperor had apparently been killed.

The Germans, then, had been playing a very odd game indeed. Even though the tsar was apparently dead, Alvensleben had been absolutely right about the date Nicholas's fate would be resolved—one way or the other. Unless he was psychic, he must have had some very specific advance knowledge the day he made his remarkable prophecy. This poses several possibilities. The first is that the Germans, knowing the tsar was going to be executed, and exactly when, wished to deceive the monarchists into believing the news was false. Seen as part of Berlin's policy of courting both Bolsheviks and Whites simultaneously, the motive would presumably have been to avoid a collapse of monarchist morale following the execution announcement. But the assumption that Berlin knew well in advance of the tsar's execution leads to a sinister conclusion —that the Germans effectively collaborated with the Communists in the murder. Sokolov, the White investigator, was rabidly anti-German, and used a snippet of the Alvensleben story to support just such a hypothesis.

That theory may have satisfied contemporary political passions, but it is implausible. It does not square with the pattern of events and national motives in summer 1918. There is no hint anywhere that the Germans wanted Nicholas killed. Kaiser Wilhelm certainly did not, and the German High Command had no reason to encourage such a brutal act. Some have suggested that Germany was afraid that if the tsar fell into White hands alive he would become a rallying point for a renewed conflict with Germany. But Nicholas' abdication was irrevocable, and the Whites were in no condition militarily to hurt the Germans. They had quite enough on their hands fighting the Bolsheviks.

Nor is it logical to believe Berlin had advance intelligence of precise Bolshevik plans to kill the tsar, but simply looked the other way. That would fly in the face of all the diplomatic enquiries they had been making about the Romanovs' safety during June and July. If the Germans had advance knowledge

54

55

54 A smile on the face of
the Kaiser, receiving the
tsar in Berlin before
World War I started. In
1918, did he plan a
last-minute rescue?

55 Together before the
war, Nicholas and
Alexandra with the
tsarina's German
brother, Grand Duke
Ernst of Hesse (*centre*).
What role did he play in
the Berlin intrigues of
July 1918?

1918   Stockholm

TO   Marchioness Milford Haven

Ernie now telegraphs that has heard from two trustworthy sources that Alix and all the children are alive

Crown Princess Sweden

56

57

Hans Bodo Graf v. Alvensleben-Neugattersleben (1882–

58

56 The telegram to the tsarina's sister, the present Lord Mountbatten's mother, raising hope that Alexandra and her children had survived. "Ernie" refers to the Grand Duke of Hesse, who was communicating through neutral Sweden, because Germany was still at war with Britain. Note the date—all the Romanovs had supposedly been killed more than two months earlier.

57 Count Alvensleben, German diplomat in occupied Ukraine—"the news of the murder of the tsar will be falsely spread between July 16th and 20th".

58 Prince Max of Baden —declared the tsar died "at a military execution, not an assassination".

of an execution date, they would surely have redoubled their "emphatic" intercessions. Count Alvensleben's advance knowledge was far more probably of a German scheme to extricate the tsar alive. The British and French intelligence reports from Switzerland, with their origin back in mid-June, lend weight to this. Alvensleben could well have been in the know at Kiev, the German army's most easterly permanent headquarters, and a natural base for any scheme involving Ekaterinburg. It is harder to understand why the count broke security by leaking his knowledge so early to monarchist leaders. It was not careless talk, because Alvensleben deliberately arranged the meeting with Bezak and General Dolgorukov to give them "some important information". That meeting would have made sense after the Romanovs were safe in German-held territory, but to talk about the operation ten days *before* it was due to take place does not add up.

Yet the vital point is that Alvensleben and his masters knew when the tsar's death would be announced, ten days before it happened. The man who held the key to the riddle kept it to himself. Alvensleben lived till 1961 without telling what he knew. German archivists say the count's papers have been lost. In the memoirs of other senior German diplomats and soldiers, the fate of the Russian imperial family tends to be strangely neglected. But in 1975 the Alvensleben family archivist reminded us that in autumn 1918, when violent revolution broke out in Germany, it was the same Count Alvensleben who was personally entrusted by the Kaiser with ensuring the safety of the German empress and her children.

Whatever became of those last-minute plans to extricate the tsar, the Germans had early intelligence of what had allegedly occurred at the Ipatiev House on 16 July. Their information was in line with what our analysis of the Sokolov evidence implies—that the tsar may have died alone. The German account was picked up by British military intelligence in Switzerland, which reported to London on 22 July:

Prince Max of Baden has informed the former Russian diplomat here that the ex-Emperor of Russia was shot on 16 July. *The act was a military execution according to my informant, not an assassination.*

This dispatch was forwarded to King George V, filed in White-hall without comment, and was later to be submerged in the stories of mass killing at the Ipatiev House. But the source was not one to be ignored; Prince Max of Baden was a German general who became chancellor of Germany three months later. His information, depicting Nicholas facing a firing squad, in some form of "legitimate" military execution, lays a vital emphasis. The tsar died alone—and his family were not with him. But the German plans to rescue the Romanov family had clearly gone tragically wrong, leaving the tsar dead and his wife and five children still in Communist hands.

Early in the morning of 23 July Kaiser Wilhelm took break-fast in the imperial train, his mobile headquarters. He com-plained to his aides that he had not slept a wink, and one of them noted in his diary: "He spoke of a vision in which all his English and Russian relatives . . . filed before him, some of them taunting him."

Worry about those Russian relatives had been keeping Wilhelm awake at night one month earlier. Now, when he knew the outcome of schemes to help them, he was having night-mares.

23

MOSCOW BARTERS WITH BERLIN

"Crime is common. Logic is rare. Therefore it is upon
the logic rather than upon the crime that you should
dwell."

(Sir Arthur Conan Doyle)

IT WAS LENIN who decided what was to happen to the
Romanovs. While the Kaiser schemed and fretted, the political
genius who actually held the imperial aces was working freneti-
cally in the palace where 22 years earlier Tsar Nicholas had
walked down a crimson carpet to his coronation. The man
whose brother had been hanged for plotting to murder a tsar
now had the whole imperial family at his mercy. They had
become cards in a complex game of diplomatic poker, and
Lenin was a master of the art.

For a long time after coming to power, the Bolsheviks in
Moscow had not bothered much about the Romanovs. When
Lenin took the reins in November 1917 Nicholas had been off
the throne for months; he was a political anachronism, safely
under lock and key in distant Siberia. There were far more
pressing problems to be solved: the Bolsheviks had only a very
shaky hold on the country, and Russia had to be extricated from
the war with Germany. Of course the tsar was still "Bloody
Nicholas", as Lenin had called him so many times in speeches,
and one day he would be called to account. The matter had
come up at a meeting of the politburo in June 1918, when Lev
Trotsky had urged that there should be a public trial, relayed
daily across the nation by radio, a propaganda exercise to
catalogue all the sins of the old regime. But Lenin had felt it
was not feasible in the present chaotic situation, and the subject
had been dropped. But by mid-June Lenin knew that he would
soon be forced to take some action, if only because of the
deteriorating military situation around Ekaterinburg. Combined forces of Czechs and Whites were advancing steadily on
the town, and Communist troops were unlikely to hold it much
longer.

This could have been the moment to decide on the quick, savage solution, extermination of the whole family. But all the clues suggest Lenin's policy was anything but one of ruthless vengeance. During June there was a spate of press reports that the tsar had been executed, and on Midsummer's Day some newspapers carried a specific story saying that Nicholas had been shot in a train taking him away from Ekaterinburg. Another story had him killed by Communist soldiers near the town. Historians claimed later that these rumours were officially inspired by Moscow—kites flown to test what effect the death would have on public opinion. If that is true then few people of any importance can have shared in the plan. Just after the rumours Jan Berzin, commander-in-chief of the Red Army in the Urals, sent an urgent message to Moscow about the Romanovs. We know about it from a telegram found at the Ekaterinburg post office. It was typed on a piece of grey telegraph paper and glued to a blue telegraph blank. The despatch was sent on 27 June addressed to the Central Executive Committee, the Council of People's Commissars, the Commissar for War, and the Military Press Bureau. It read:

Military Telegram No. 487. To Moscow. From Ekaterinburg Headquarters No. 3190.

In many Moscow newspapers received is printed an announcement about the murder of Nicholas Romanov at some railroad crossing near Ekaterinburg by Red army men. I inform you officially that on 26 June with the assistance of the "V" military inspectors the military commissar of the Urals military region and a member of the All-Russian Investigatory Commission [secret police] I made an inspection of the quarters where Nicholas Romanov and his family are kept and a check on the guard and watch. All members of the family and Nicholas himself are alive and all reports of their death etc. are a provocation.

198. 27 June 1918. o hours 5 mins. Commander-in-chief northern Ural front Berzin.

Lenin himself apparently intervened personally to make quite sure the Romanovs came to no harm. Three telegraph operators at Ekaterinburg post office later testified to eavesdropping on a direct telegraph conversation between Lenin in Moscow and Berzin in Ekaterinburg, in which Lenin "ordered Berzin to take under his protection the entire imperial family and not to allow any violence towards them whatsoever; if there was any such violence, Berzin would answer for it with his own life". Whatever motivated Lenin's concern at the end of June, it would have made very little sense for him to allow the Romanov family to be wiped out two weeks later in a wanton act of butchery.

Presumably as a result of Berzin's assurances, Lenin specifically denied all rumours about the ex-tsar's death in a press interview published on 4 July. It can be no coincidence that on the same day, the chairman of the Ural Soviet sent the following message to Moscow:

Beloborodov to Sverdlov and Goloshchokin (Moscow).

Syromolotov has just gone to organize the matter in accordance with instructions of centre. No cause for apprehension. Avdeyev removed. His assistant Moshkin arrested. In place of Avdeyev, Yurovsky. Internal guard entirely replaced by others.

Now this key message about the changing of the guard at the Ipatiev House has always been interpreted as meaning that the drunken Avdeyev had been replaced by the trusted Yurovsky, the man who could be relied upon to carry out execution orders. Given the other information we have, it seems far more likely that on 4 July at any rate, Yurovsky was appointed primarily to reassure Moscow even further that the Romanovs were now in safe hands. There was no longer "cause for alarm" that discipline at the Ipatiev House would collapse, leading to anything from abuse of the women to uncontrolled murder. Moscow had asserted control—but with what end in mind? The Beloborodov message refers to Syromolotov, a member of the Regional Soviet, going "to organize the matter in accordance with instructions of centre"—but there is no way of knowing what that mission was.

To understand Moscow's real intentions it is important to explain Lenin's sudden concern for the Romanovs. Why did he need reassurance that the imperial family was safe? The

founding father of Soviet Russia was certainly not lying awake
at night worrying about the Romanovs for any humanitarian
reason. Lenin may have disliked violence for its own sake, but
he was single-minded about violence which furthered the
revolution. In January 1918 he had publicly declared: "We
can achieve nothing unless we use terror," and he consistently
endorsed mass terror and execution of the former middle and
upper classes. Lenin had even praised the doctrine of the extremist Nechayev, who advocated the destruction of the entire
Romanov dynasty.

On the strength of this alone one can be sure that Lenin
would have approved the execution of the tsar, and all the
grand dukes, in the name of the revolution. But Lenin also distinguished himself from the other revolutionary ideologists by
his pragmatism, his awareness that politics was the art of the
possible. The revolution itself was a matter of pursuing ideals,
but always with an eye to the harsh realities of a changing
situation. This was the Lenin who could say: "one step forward,
two steps back . . . it happens in the lives of individuals, and it
happens in the history of nations . . ."

All Lenin's common sense is summed up in one address to
his colleagues, seething with fury over a German ultimatum
at the time of the Brest-Litovsk negotiations: "It is time to put
an end to revolutionary phrases, and get down to real work
. . . To carry on a revolutionary war, an army is necessary, and
we do not have one. It is a question of signing the terms now,
or of signing the death sentence of the Soviet government three
weeks later." Lenin won his comrades over, and the treaty was
signed on 3 March. But the peace with Germany remained
fragile. Against furious internal opposition, Lenin had to con-
trive to keep Berlin at arm's length, fighting for time to consolidate Bolshevism in Russia.

A look at the timing of Lenin's sudden concern for the
Romanovs in late June, and the abrupt changes at the Ipatiev
House that followed, strongly suggests it was all linked to his
pragmatic German policy. At the end of June, in the wake of
the execution rumours, the German ambassador, Mirbach, had
asked after the welfare of the Romanovs. He did not ask for
their release, but merely that they be well treated. For Lenin
this was just a gentle prod from Berlin, and must have seemed

the least of his problems. The man who in March had signed away a third of Russia's population to appease the Germans, would surely not have found it hard to accede to a mild request about one redundant imperial family. So prison conditions at Ekaterinburg were improved, Yurovsky restored discipline, and doubtless the Germans would shortly have been assured that all was now well.

But even as the "no cause for alarm" message arrived from Ekaterinburg, momentous events were brewing in Moscow which were to upset the delicate relationship with Germany, and come very close to destroying all Lenin's peace efforts of the past year. That same day, 4 July, delegates from all over Russia gathered in the Bolshoi Theatre for the All-Russian Congress of Soviets. For the first time publicly, Lenin and the top Bolsheviks were faced with the full fury of opposition to the Treaty of Brest-Litovsk. Passionate feelings, until now bottled up, exploded in the most serious internal opposition Lenin had yet faced. The Left Social Revolutionaries led the protest, howling: "Down with Brest! Away with the German butchers!" Amongst the diplomatic corps in the audience sat the German ambassador, and much of the abuse was directed personally at him. Count Mirbach maintained his self-control and sat impassively as the assembly screamed, literally, for his blood.

Two days later they got it.

Early in the afternoon of 6 July, the phone rang in Lenin's office with horrifying news. Count Mirbach had been shot dead at his embassy by two Left Social Revolutionaries. Lenin was appalled, and foresaw immediately that the Germans might use the murder of their ambassador as the excuse for invading Russia. "There is ample opportunity for it," said Lenin after hearing the news; "now at any price we must influence the character of the German report to Berlin." Together with Yakov Sverdlov, the chairman of the Central Committee, and his top foreign affairs experts, Chicherin and Radek, he hurried personally to the German embassy to offer condolences, and salvage what he could from the wreckage of his German policy.

Later, in a message to the Ural Soviet, Sverdlov was to make it quite clear just how close the Bolsheviks had come to catastrophe: ". . . after the murder of Mirbach, the Germans demanded that they be allowed to send a battalion to Moscow. We categorically refused and were within a hair's breadth of war."

The expected German invasion was probably averted because Germany was not having its anticipated success on the Western front, and could ill afford the military muscle for a new Russian adventure. But on 6 July, and for some time afterwards, Lenin was not to know that. From the moment the telephone rang with the news of the Mirbach assassination, Lenin knew he had a double crisis. In the car on the way to the German embassy he turned to Sverdlov and remarked: "In future, we Bolsheviks must carry the burden of the Revolution alone." Lenin now had to cope with an imminent external threat from the Germans, and an internal confrontation with the extremist Social Revolutionaries of Left and Right. Although the German menace was to pass within a couple of weeks, the internal uproar continued and worsened. The Bolsheviks accused the Social Revolutionary Party of engineering uprisings across Russia, and the strife culminated in August with a near fatal attempt on the life of Lenin himself.

It appears highly likely that the true fate of the Romanovs was bound up within this greater crisis. Lenin may have felt he could gamble on Germany treating the execution of the tsar himself, however grudgingly, as an internal Russian affair. But it would have been totally irrational, at this critical moment in relations with Berlin, to offend the Germans unnecessarily—and nothing was less necessary than the killing of the tsarina and her daughters. It would have been foolhardy to compound the murder of the German ambassador by flouting Berlin's repeated concern for a German princess and her daughters ten days later. Instead, it made sense for Lenin to play his hand according to his character, preserving the tsarina and the girls alive as an ace in the hole against an uncertain future. This does not mean that he wanted to save the family for ever, or ever intended to hand them over to Berlin, or any other foreign power. We can compare his likely thought processes with his attitude over the Treaty of Brest-Litovsk a few months earlier. Having staked his career on signing the treaty, he then made his own attitude clear to his colleagues: "I don't mean to read it, and I don't mean to fulfil it, except in so far as I am forced." On the treaty Lenin's pragmatism paid off handsomely. Russia was saved in the short-term, and within eight months Germany was defeated, and the hated treaty annulled.

What remains of the diplomatic record suggests that the Romanov women were used as pawns in a similar strategy. Immediately after the announcement of the tsar's execution, the Germans protested about the "murder", and at once made new demands for assurances that the rest of the family were alive and being humanely treated. The subsequent cables between Berlin and Dr Riezler, the counsellor at the German embassy in Moscow who took over after Mirbach's assassination, show that Germany believed the Romanov women were still alive—and that, after some doubts, they continued to believe it for months. The grim evidence at the Four Brothers was not even mentioned.

The day after the announcement, 19 July, Dr Riezler asked Berlin for guidance as to whether he should again make firm representations on behalf of the tsarina. The response was positive, because the next day Riezler visited Karl Radek, the head of the European Department of the Bolshevik Foreign Commissariat; he condemned the shooting of the tsar and gave "urgent warning against further action of this nature". Radek's response came as a surprise, and is historically very important. In Riezler's words:

> Radek thinks personally that if we show a particular interest in the women of the imperial family who are of German extraction, they might be permitted to leave the country. In case Joffe [Soviet ambassador in Berlin] . . . should really offer to make an immediate, strong move against the allies, with support from us against contingencies, our acceptance might be conditional on their undertaking to grant freedom, on humanitarian grounds, to the tsarina and the tsarevich (the latter on the basis that he is inseparable from his mother) . . .

On further instructions from Berlin, Riezler was back at the Foreign Commissariat on two successive days, 23 and 24 July.

This time he saw the top man, Georgy Chicherin, and pressed the German demand, asking particularly for a firm assurance that the family was safe. The first time Chicherin listened in silence, and the second time he answered—rather vaguely— that, so far as he knew, "the tsarina *has been taken to Perm*". He evaded giving any solid assurance or making any promises. Dr Riezler began, quite reasonably, to suspect that he was being played along by the Bolsheviks to avoid further fury from Berlin. But there could be a simpler explanation for Chicherin's uncertainty; when he told the German envoy that he *thought* the tsarina had been taken to Perm, the Bolshevik foreign minister was not necessarily being devious. At the best of times, communications between the Urals and Moscow were not just a matter of lifting the phone. The means of contact was the Hughes telegraph; the telegraph line ran along the railway, and in July 1918 it was frequently cut by anti-Bolshevik forces. 24 July, the day Chicherin was unsure of his facts, we now know to have been the eve of Ekaterinburg's fall to the Whites. The Bolsheviks still in the town were encircled, and fighting a desperate rearguard action. If ever there was a day when contact would have been lost, this was it. On any day that week, even if Chicherin knew the Romanov women were supposed to be en route from Ekaterinburg to Perm, it is possible that—quite genuinely—he had not yet received confirmation of their safe arrival.

There are other reasons to believe Chicherin was telling the truth. First, he knew perfectly well the Germans had a highly efficient intelligence network in the Urals, which would rapidly be able to expose any Soviet lies. If the Bolsheviks were lying, they were setting out on a dangerous game; for during the weeks to come they were not only to confirm that the Romanovs were still alive, but were even to use them as bargaining counters.

It was Commissar Radek who again took the initiative in proposing that the Romanov family could be exchanged for prisoners held by the Germans. It was six weeks since the disappearance of the imperial family from Ekaterinburg, and Berlin had upped the pressure, demanding assurances again about their safety, and now actively pressing for their release. Radek's response firmly indicated that the Bolsheviks really did have a live Romanov card to play. On 29 August he specifically suggested "an exchange of the imperial family for the Polish Social Democratic leader, Leo Jogiches, a member of the Spartacus group, who is under arrest in Berlin". Radek said he would discuss the matter further with Lenin at once. On the same lines Moisei Uritsky, a member of the Central Executive, suggested that Karl Liebknecht, key German revolutionary, should also be released from prison in Germany. He too was to be part of the deal over the surviving Romanovs.

These proposals are the strongest possible diplomatic evidence that the imperial family was still alive. The Bolsheviks would not have treated lightly the release of their comrades in Germany, especially where it concerned Karl Liebknecht. He was a long-time disciple and friend of Lenin, and one of the most important revolutionary politicians in Europe. Lenin badly wanted him freed. Radek was the Kremlin's expert on German affairs and like Lenin was above all a realist. If the Romanov bargaining counters were already dead, it would have made no sense to barter with their lives for the freedom of such vital colleagues. If the deal had been accepted by the Germans it would have meant both sides making a delivery rather on the lines of modern spy exchanges across the Berlin wall. If the Romanovs had all died at the Ipatiev House, there would have been nobody to deliver, and the proof of trickery would have maddened the Germans. But if a deal was in the offing, fate intervened.

Just as the murder of Count Mirbach in early July may have influenced Bolshevik policy on the Romanovs, so new violence in Moscow now jeopardized negotiations for their release. On 30 August Uritsky was murdered by Right Social Revolutionaries, and Lenin himself was severely wounded. A woman called Dora Kaplan fired two bullets at him at point blank range, and for many days Lenin hovered on the brink of death. The immediate sequel was a series of ruthless and bloody reprisals. The attempt on Lenin was used as an excuse for the wholesale liquidation of people whose offences were in no way connected with the Social Revolutionary cause. Across Russia, thousands of people were summarily executed. With Lenin personally out of action, and the Moscow leadership in confusion, it is at the beginning of September rather than in mid-July that one could well imagine the surviving Romanovs might have been butchered. But Moscow was still bartering with them as late as 10 September, and the German consul sounded positively encouraged:

10 September (German Consulate Moscow to Berlin)
I talked with Radek again today about releasing the tsarina and children. Like Chicherin, he takes the position that there is no objection in principle, but that an equal exchange must be obtained. I referred to the necessity of removing the imperial family from its present situation, in which it is exposed to danger from which the government is powerless to protect it, to a place of security near here. Radek promised me that he would propose this at once. In view of the increasing authority which he has acquired, I have hopes that this move will be carried out.

This telegram indicates that not only were the Germans still bargaining for live Romanovs, but that they also knew where they were. But shortly after this message the news from Moscow became less hopeful, and as the days went by the Bolsheviks started avoiding the issue, and spoke more and more vaguely about where the tsarina and her children were. It has since been assumed that the Communists had been bluffing all along, and that the entire Romanov family had indeed been killed at Ekaterinburg back in July. But, as we have already pointed out, Germany had an excellent intelligence network in the Urals, and Moscow would have had a hard time convincing Berlin the family was alive if it were not true. Indeed, there is strong evidence that the Germans did receive their own, independent confirmation that the Romanov females had survived Ekaterinburg.

It comes in the form of a private telegram, carried up the drive of an English country home by the village delivery boy on 27 September 1918—two and a half months after the Romanovs' disappearance. The addressee was the tsarina's sister, Victoria, Marchioness of Milford Haven. Since the news of the tsar's execution she had been worrying desperately about Alexandra and the children, but, because of the war, it would not have been politic for her to communicate directly with their family in Germany, headed by her brother, Grand Duke Ernst Ludwig of Hesse. Now she received news from him, passed on by their mutual cousin, the crown princess of neutral Sweden (*see plate 56*). The telegram read: "Ernie [the Grand Duke] now telegraphs that he has heard from two trustworthy sources that Alix and all the children are alive." Only days earlier Victoria had been told exactly the opposite by her trustworthy British source, King George V. But in Germany her brother, deeply involved in his country's intrigues concerning the Romanovs, had information that the family was still alive. As a German federal sovereign he had access to excellent sources. He referred to two of them, and we can take it that this was more than a reflection of the diplomatic reports from the German embassy in Moscow. It was almost certainly information provided by German intelligence in the part of Russia where the family was being held.

We learn this from the statement of Sergei Markov, the monarchist officer who went to Tobolsk in spring 1918, allegedly as a secret courier carrying the German political proposals and offers of assistance to the tsar. By July 1918 Markov was back in St Petersburg when the news broke that the tsar, and only the tsar, had been executed. Assuming that the Bolsheviks were telling the truth when they announced that the rest of the family had been taken to a place of safety, Markov began a personal effort to help the survivors. He determined to make use of his German contacts, and with that in mind made his way to Kiev, in German-occupied Ukraine. There, in mid-October, well after the good news from the Grand Duke of Hesse reached England, he obtained an interview with a German agent called Adolf Magener. We know that Magener, with another spy called Cornel, had been seconded to the Romanov case for months, and was reporting directly to the Grand Duke of Hesse, who was paying his operating expenses. Markov's evidence in 1921 described the meeting in Kiev:

Herr Magener stated categorically that the imperial family was alive, that he knew nothing of the tsar, but that in any event the tsar was not with his family. He learned this from German intelligence in the province of Perm . . . At the end of 1918 I made the acquaintance of a German spy, whose last name I do not recall, but I do know that he worked for two and a half years during the war on the radio-telegraph in Moscow. He told me his nephew had recently been operating in Perm province, and had reported to him that the imperial family was unquestionably alive and constantly being moved about within Perm province . . .

The Germans knew the secret of where the Romanov survivors were, partly because they made it their business to know, and partly because Moscow had told them.[40] Lenin told the Germans because the threat from Berlin was the reason he had preserved the family in the first place; but it was a secret he kept from all but a necessary few of even his Bolshevik colleagues. Saving the life of the hated "German" tsarina and her children to humour the Germans, and then bargaining over their lives, would have been considered outrageous by those Communists aggressively against any further concessions to Berlin. Vladimir Milyutin, one of the earliest members of the Central Executive Committee suggests that most senior Bolsheviks were indeed not told what was afoot. Here is his account of how the news of the tsar's execution was broken to the Council of People's Commissars on the evening of 18 July 1918:

During the discussion of the draft Public Health Law, in the middle of Semashko's report, Sverdlov came in and sat down on a chair behind Ilyich [Lenin]. Semashko finished. Sverdlov came up, bent down over Ilyich, and said something. "Comrade Sverdlov wishes to make a statement."

"I have to say," Sverdlov began in his customary even tones, "that we have had a communication that at Ekaterinburg, by a decision of the Regional Soviet, Nicholas has been shot.[41] Nicholas wanted to escape. The Czechoslovaks were approaching. The Presidium of the All-Russian Central Executive Committee has resolved to approve." Silence from everyone.

"Let us now go on to read the draft clause by clause," suggested Ilyich. The reading clause by clause began.

No mention here of the tsarina and the children. Whatever had happened to them was clearly not judged suitable for the privileged ears of the people's commissars. Even Lev Trotsky, then commissar for war, was apparently not let into the picture; in two separate books, written years later in exile, he refers to the death of the entire Romanov family. In one he says Chairman Sverdlov told him all had been killed, and in the other—a book on Stalin—he says it was Stalin who was responsible. But Trotsky's source for the "Stalin" version is hopelessly compromised. It is none other than Bessedovsky, the former Soviet diplomat whose memoirs, as we have noted, have been exposed as bare-faced fiction. Trotsky himself puts his knowledge of the affair into perspective, by admitting that he was away at the front during the vital period, and writing: ". . . I was never interested about how the sentence was carried out, and frankly I do not understand such curiosity . . . my recollections about the case of the tsar's family are rather fragmentary."

No Moscow official ever came up with all the answers about the disappearance of the Romanovs, but those few who said anything at all hinted at the survival of the rest of the family. Chicherin, the commissar for foreign affairs, was quoted in the British press in early September 1918 as saying that the tsarina and her children were still alive. At that time of course he could hardly say anything else, given that he was still saying as much to the German diplomats. But four years later, in 1922, a foreign journalist put a direct question to Chicherin at the Genoa Conference. He asked whether the Soviet government had ordered the killing of the tsar's daughters and if not, had the murderers been punished? Chicherin replied: "The fate of the four young daughters of the tsar is at present unknown to me. I have read in the press that they are now in America . . . the circumstances of the case have not yet been cleared up." Chicherin's little joke, perhaps.

Three other leading Bolsheviks, two of them Central Committee members, are also credited with saying that some members of the family survived. Felix Dzerzhinsky, the founder of the Soviet secret police, was reliably quoted as saying in private that the Romanov women had not been killed at Ekaterinburg. Maxim Litvinov was quoted from Copenhagen as "admitting one part of the murders, but denying the other". This was in December 1918, long after the need to continue play-acting with the Germans. Grigory Zinoviev, then a top member of the Communist leadership, was reported in the American press as telling a foreigner shortly after the alleged murders that "only the tsar had been put to death and that his family were living in safety in a city in Siberia, the location of which he refused to disclose". As we shall see, Zinoviev was in all probability well qualified to know that the family was alive, and exactly where it was being kept. He had come closer than any other Bolshevik official to actually telling the truth about the Romanovs.

PART SIX

Perm

24

THE END OF NICHOLAS

"All our ancient history . . . is no more than accepted fiction."

(Voltaire)

PRESS FOR TIMES NEW YORK. OMSK FIRST. While tsar's fate remains mooted question in Ekaterinburg, city where he was executed, I have obtained manuscript describing tsar's last days and trial before Soviet, written by Parfen Alexseyvitch Domnin, who served tsar as majordomo 22 years and accompanied him into exile. This, the first detailed account of life of Romanovs in Ekaterinburg, states tsar was shot after trial before Ural District Soviet where he was charged with being party to counter-revolutionary plot to overthrow Bolsheviki, and with carrying on secret correspondence with Generals Denikin, Dutoff, Dogert, who were endeavouring to liberate him. Domnin was with Nikolas until night July sixteenth when he was tried and taken away for execution. He states that other members imperial family were taken away in motortruck which corroborates testimony of Sister Maria of famous old Ekaterinburg monastery who took eggs to tsarevitch. Domnin manuscript of tsar's last days in Ekaterinburg is most representative description I have seen and will remain an historic document . . .

THIS STARTLING ACCOUNT of the tsar's execution, and the removal of his family alive, was written by Carl Ackerman of the *New York Times*, reporting from Ekaterinburg in mid-December 1918, when most people had given up all hope for the Romanovs. His report was one in a series of major articles, all of which were to doubt the Ipatiev House massacre. We reproduce it—with basic punctuation added—from the original draft which Ackerman hammered out on his portable typewriter, sitting shivering in a compartment of an Allied military

train drawn up at Ekaterinburg station. We found it, a yellow-
ing sheet of foolscap in a tattered folder amongst the Ackerman
Papers at the Library of Congress in the United States.

Carl Ackerman was in no doubt that he had a scoop on his
hands. He spent three days and an astronomical, even by today's standards, $6,000 getting the text through to New York.
He wrote to his wife: "In Ekaterinburg, I obtained a 3,000-
word manuscript describing the tsar's last days and his trial
before the Bolsheviki. It is a splendid story and one of the best
stories I obtained." Everyone makes mistakes sometimes, but
here was a journalist with an international reputation, writing
a lead story for one of the world's most respected newspapers;
Ackerman was also rather more—he was a personal friend and
confidant of President Wilson's foreign affairs adviser, Colonel
House—a 1918 version of Henry Kissinger. House corresponded
with Ackerman frequently, and regarded him highly enough
to ask him to file political intelligence reports from Europe
—reports that were forwarded to the White House in code,
courtesy of the State Department. Ackerman had no need to
produce sensational stories to make a name for himself, and
with his reputation and contacts could not afford to make a
fool of himself. He remained sure enough of the Domnin document to use it again, without reservation, in a subsequent book
about his Siberian tour.

The first part of the full Domnin manuscript, preserved in
Ackerman's papers, deals with the final days in the Ipatiev
House, and tells how on 15 July, the day before his execution,
the tsar was taken away from the Ipatiev House to a kangaroo
court held by the Regional Soviet. There he was told that a
new rescue plot had been discovered, led by the White Cossack
General, Alexei Dutov; the tsar himself was accused of having
secretly corresponded with a General Dogert, and was told
that, in view of this, and the evacuation of Ekaterinburg, he
was to be executed. Here is the last section of the manuscript,
taken from the original crude English translation in Ackerman's personal files:

> Later it proved that nobody, except his wife and son, of all
> his beloved were allowed to bid farewell to the former czar.
> Nikolai Alexandrovitch, his wife and son remained together

till there appeared still other five soldiers of the Red army with the chairman of the Soviet and with two members of it—workmen. "Put on your top-coat!" resolutely commanded the chairman of the Soviet. Nikolai Alexandrovitch, who did not lose his self-possession, began to dress, kissed his wife, son, the lackey, once more made the sign of the cross over them, and then addressing the men who had come for him, said in a loud voice: "Now I am at your disposal . . ." Nikolai Alexandrovitch was taken away, nobody knows where, and has been shot in the night of the 16 July by a group of soldiers of the Red Army consisting of 20 men. Before the dawn of day the chairman of the Soviet again came to the room where Nikolai Alexandrovitch had been held, and with him some soldiers of the Red army, a doctor and the commissar of the guard. The doctor gave assistance to Alexandra Feodorovna and to Aleksei Nikolaievich. Then the chairman of the Soviet asked the doctor: "Is it possible to take them at once?" "Yes." "Citizen Alexandra Feodorovna Romanova and Aleksei Romanov—get ready, you shall be forwarded from here. You are allowed to take with you only the most necessary things, not over 30–40 pounds," said the chairman. Mastering themselves but tumbling from side to side mother and son got ready. The chairman did not permit them to bid farewell to their beloved ones, hurrying them all the time . . . Alexandra Feodorovna and Aleksei Nikolaievich were at once taken away in an automobile—it is not known where.

The document ends with "Domnin" being expelled from the house in an atmosphere of confusion as the Bolsheviks begin their withdrawal from Ekaterinburg.

The Domnin account did not become "an historic document", as Ackerman expected; it was forgotten, as the White enquiry into the Romanov case began to produce its massacre version. The document contains the gist of what we believe did happen at Ekaterinburg, but it has one awkward discrepancy. Parfen Domnin, its star witness, did not exist.

There was nobody of that name in the imperial household, and no servant is supposed to have survived the mayhem at the Ipatiev House. The only person Parfen Domnin could be is the imperial valet—Terenty Chemodurov. Although Chemodurov did come to Ekaterinburg with the Romanovs, he became sick in late May, and was taken from the Ipatiev House to the hospital wing of the local prison. There, according to the French tutor, Gilliard, "he was forgotten, and thus miraculously escaped death". If the valet was in the prison hospital he could not have witnessed events at the Ipatiev House on 15 and 16 July. And another, personal, detail does not match with Ackerman's "Domnin". The real valet was born in the Kursk province, while "Domnin" is described in the *New York Times* as being named after his native village—"Domnin" in the Kostroma district.

On the other hand, there are also striking similarities between the two valets. Both are said to be in their sixties, both say they have done long service in the tsar's household. And there is one tiny clue to suggest they are actually one and the same person. In the version eventually published in the *New York Times*, the name of the valet is dropped from the narrative altogether and replaced by the first person singular. But in the Domnin manuscript the valet is referred to on one occasion not by the patronymic mentioned earlier: "Alexseyevich", but as "Ivanovich", which was indeed the patronymic of the real valet— Chemodurov. It may well be that, in spite of the efforts to conceal the informant's identity, the writer has forgotten to change the name in one sentence. It is common practice in journalism to protect an interviewee with anonymity, and the use of pseudonyms was common 50 years ago. If "Domnin" was simply a cover-name for the real valet, then his remarkable story suddenly fits into place. For the real Chemodurov also stated categorically that the tsarina and her children had left Ekaterinburg alive.

Colonel Kobylinsky, the officer who had previously been in nominal charge of the imperial household at Tobolsk, met the tsar's servant after the fall of Ekaterinburg to the Whites and later testified: ". . . Chemodurov did not believe that the family had been killed. He said that Botkin, Demidova and Trupp were killed, and that the family had been taken away; he told me that by killing the people above-mentioned the soldiers simulated the murder of the family, and for the same reason possessions in the house were removed." Chemodurov told the same story to two other witnesses. Gibbes was baffled when the valet exclaimed: "Thank God the children are safe!" And more than a month later, after he had himself seen the basement room and the sinister evidence in the woods, Chemodurov was still sticking to his story. In Tyumen he met Gilliard, and his first words were: " 'Thank God, the emperor,[42] Her Majesty and the children are alive—but all the others were killed . . .' He told me that he had been to the room in the Ipatiev House where 'Botkin and the others' had been shot . . . He told me that all the others had been obliged to put on soldiers' uniforms and had been taken away."

Those who met Chemodurov at this time found him a nervous wreck, rambling in his conversation, and concluded that his story was the delusion of a broken-hearted old man. Sokolov omitted his statements altogether. But the man had a few weeks before been personal manservant to the emperor, hardly the sort of responsibility likely to be placed on someone mentally unstable. But even if his listeners misjudged him, how had Chemodurov/Domnin been able to witness the last hours of the imperial family at Ekaterinburg when he was supposedly shut up in the prison hospital? Perhaps he had been discharged, and returned to the Ipatiev House shortly before the end. But if so, why did the Communists not kill him when they murdered the other servants? The account is so totally different from the orthodox version of the fate of the Romanovs that we must treat it very warily. It would be reasonable to suspect that, however good a journalist, Ackerman had bought a pup. But approval for his story comes from a very different source—the senior military intelligence officer with the American Expeditionary Force in Russia.

Ackerman's correspondence reveals that en route to Ekaterinburg he shared a railway carriage with a "Major Slaughter, American military attaché with the Czechs, and with American Consul Palmer of Ekaterinburg". A check of military records in the United States shows that this was Major Homer Slaughter, who had gone to Vladivostok as military attaché in the spring of 1918. Later, he had become liaison and intelligence officer attached to the Czech army headquarters on the Ural front.

A further search of American Military Intelligence files

revealed a second copy of the Domnin account. This time it was a five-page document, typed up and annotated by Major Slaughter himself. On 12 December 1918 it had been sent from Ekaterinburg to General William Graves, commander of American Forces in Siberia, who forwarded it to the office of the chief of staff, military intelligence branch, in Washington D.C. Major Slaughter had added his own note at the end of the Domnin story:

> The above manuscript was secured by the American consul in Ekaterinburg from the monastery in Ekaterinburg where Parfen Ivanovich Domnin stayed for some days after he left the service of the tsar, and where he returned and remained for some weeks . . . *Actually this is the best piece of evidence that I have seen which at all bears any relation to the final end or disposition of the tsar and family. Everything else is rumour and hearsay.*

This report was sent five months after the disappearance of the Romanovs. So if pups were being sold they were being bought not only by Ackerman, but also by the American consul and the top American intelligence officer in Siberia. Consul Palmer is dead, and his family could not help, but we had more success with Major Slaughter. After the first world war he went on to be assistant chief of the G-2 [military intelligence] section at the Command and General Staff School, and was promoted to full colonel. Because of his expertise in Russian affairs, he was offered the delicate post of military attaché in Moscow when the United States resumed relations with the Soviet Union. In retirement he became professor of Military Science and Tactics at Iowa University. In 1974 we found his widow and his son John—a history professor. Professor Slaughter still has an old army trunk containing his father's papers but regrets that "people who had access to the State Department and other files or archives have abstracted some documents or reports and extracted some which may never be released for reasons of State". The trunk has also been raided since his father's death by amateur family researchers, and "the parts dealing with the death of the imperial family are missing".

But Colonel Slaughter's widow and son do remember some

details of what he said in private about the events at Ekaterinburg. They reveal that Slaughter had one important advantage
over most investigators—he was actually in Ekaterinburg before
the Bolsheviks left. A fluent Russian speaker, he slipped into
town with a Czech officer about 20 July—three days after the
alleged death of the imperial family, and before the town was
taken by the Whites. Although his family's memories are fragmentary, Slaughter's version of events in Ekaterinburg seems
to have been totally different from the "orthodox" story. Instead of being roused in the middle of the night, the tsar was,
apparently, eating a breakfast of scrambled eggs with his
family when he was led away for the last time. In later years,
when the White version of the massacre was generally accepted,
Major Slaughter gave lectures on his time in Siberia, in which
he clearly said that all the family had been killed. But he was
no disciple of Investigator Sokolov, who once wrote asking for
comments on his work. According to the major's son: "My
father never sent word or message to Sokolov, and his face
turned to stone when asked about him . . ." Meanwhile,
Slaughter's elderly widow recalls that at the time he returned
from Russia her husband told her that the tsar and his son
were killed separately from the tsarina and the girls.

Time and again, we are led back to this vital new concept of
the tsar meeting death apart from his wife and daughters; in
the end, the clues become just as numerous as any of those in
the old mass-murder story. In Sokolov's files we found the
testimony of Zinaida Mikulova, an Ekaterinburg citizen, who
learned about the death of the tsar from a Bolshevik in a good
position to know. She said she had been forced into an affair
with Cheka official Konstantin Kanevstev:

. . . I was repelled by him but surrendered myself physically.
Because I was not interested in their Bolshevik affairs, I never
asked him about their secrets. I remember that about two
days before the announcement of the murder of the former
tsar, Kanevstev came round to my apartment at about 4 pm
and told me that the Bolsheviks had killed the former
emperor; it seemed to me that as he said this Kanevstev had
tears in his eyes, and he sort of turned away. He told me,
when I asked, that they had buried him—out in the open

space—and that he had 52 bullets in him . . . he said the
tsarevich was dead. My talk with Kanevstev was on the
seventeenth.

Predictably, Sokolov suppressed this testimony.

Another, much stronger, source substantiates the lone execution theory. In summer 1918 a Dane called Poul Ree was his
country's vice-consul in the town of Perm—the town to which
the Bolsheviks retreated after losing Ekaterinburg. In 1967
Ree, retired and living in Copenhagen, answered a British
researcher's request for information on the Romanov case. He
wrote:

> My knowledge about where and how the tsar was shot is
> different from what the research committee at Ekaterinburg
> arrived at. I had my information from one of the men who
> condemned the tsar to death and who fled to Perm—whereas
> the committee started the research a long time after the deed
> and after all the guilty were fallen on the front or had
> disappeared from Ekaterinburg . . . I feel convinced that the
> news I got a few days after the deed is with all its details the
> right one . . . The tsar was shot in the woods near the pit
> [*the Four Brothers mine*], when he descended from the car of
> the Oblasnoje Kommissar . . . the whole story of the murder
> of the tsar is a fake.

Ree also indicated that he had separate information about the
fate of the tsar's family. But unfortunately his letter was never
followed up, and Ree died before we heard about him. The
Danish Foreign Ministry say they have no official reports from
him, and referred us to the Danish royal archives; that is a
dead end, because documents concerning the royal family or
its relatives are closed for 100 years.

The source Ree quoted could not have been better—"one
of the men who condemned the tsar to death". The top
Ekaterinburg commissars did move to Perm after the fall of
Ekaterinburg in July 1918, and Ree would have had to deal
with them there; they of all people did know what had happened
to the imperial family. Ree says the tsar was shot after leaving
the car of the "regional commissar", just as the Domnin

account mentions that Nicholas was summoned by the "chairman of the Soviet". This can only have been Beloborodov, chairman of the Ural Regional Soviet, and it seems probable that he or a senior colleague would indeed have accompanied the firing party.

In the light of these new leads, all from separate sources, we can give houseroom to an unknown Soviet account, the earliest one of all, which was picked up by a few European newspapers eight days after the Romanovs' disappearance, quoting *Pravda* as their source. This read:

> . . . on the morning of 16 July the ex-tsar, accompanied by two armed Red guards, was driven from his prison to a military exercise area outside the town where ten more Red Guards were waiting. The chairman of the Soviet read out the sentence of death, upon which the ex-tsar asked permission to see his wife before being executed, and to say a few words to his children. This was refused. The tsar, without a struggle, and perfectly composed, stood in front of the Red Guards, and the execution was carried out. The body of the ex-tsar was taken away by car.

This unique Communist account squares with the other stories of lone execution. The location is "a military exercise area outside the town", and we know that the Bolsheviks did use the Four Brothers area for army exercises. And once again, the chairman of the Soviet is present. The whole picture fits the general style of Communist executions at that time— prisoners were usually marched or driven out of town, and then executed in isolated woods or fields, often near a convenient ditch or mineshaft. For once this Soviet version may have been a flash of the truth, leaking out before the official propaganda machine started grinding out its stream of Romanov concoctions. This, and the other stories, fit exactly with the statement by the German general, Prince Max of Baden, that the tsar died alone at a military execution. He made it before anyone else, apparently drawing on exclusive German intelligence. Given what we now know of German involvement, the prince had good reason to be well informed.

The full version of the *Pravda* story contained more detail, including a summary of events shortly before Nicholas's execution, and now that too falls into place. The tsar, said the report, had been taken out of Ekaterinburg in mid-June and later taken back to the town. A while before his execution there was an attempt on his life, "in the course of which a bomb was thrown".

If historians had ever unearthed this early account of the death of the tsar, they would probably have dismissed it as another pack of Bolshevik lies, typical disinformation to make the killing sound more palatable. They could have claimed that nothing was corroborated by other sources, including for example, the reference to a bomb-throwing incident. Rubbish, the experts would say, there is not a single mention of this in all the copious literature about the last days at Ekaterinburg. They would be wrong.

By pure chance, we found it mentioned in a private letter written by Poul Ree, the Danish vice-consul, to his mother. He had just completed a short visit to Ekaterinburg from his base at Perm:

> While I was there, a bomb was thrown over the fences around the tsar's villa. Lots of noise—little damage. The man got away in the smoke and the dust. Next day there was nothing to see. They say though that the tsar's heir died of fright and was secretly buried at 6 am, some say in the prison yard . . . I think the government arranged the bomb at Ekaterinburg. I don't believe Alexei died of fright.

Whatever the result, and whatever the motive, there clearly was a bombing incident. Such a public event must surely have been the talk of Ekaterinburg for a day or so, yet it is reported nowhere. Even Thomas Preston failed to mention it. If interested observers missed a noisy bombing, could they not also have missed the removal of members of the imperial family by car, with a small escort, even in broad daylight? The bombing affair adds credence to the *Pravda* story, which in broad outline matches the Domnin account.

The reference to the tsar being removed from Ekaterinburg to an estate nearby a month before his execution is unique, but not necessarily untrue. *Pravda* made no attempt to explain why

Nicholas II had been temporarily transferred, but with hindsight one can postulate a sound reason for the move. The paper suggests it happened in mid-June—and that is the very time we know the German Kaiser was making last-ditch offers of German help for the tsar. Nicholas's temporary excursion is perhaps tied in with this in some way; it is conceivable that the Bolsheviks were persuaded to allow talks between the tsar and German envoys—although it would clearly have been under supervision and such discussions would not, openly at any rate, have referred to Berlin's restoration schemes. There may simply have been talks between a senior Bolshevik representative and Nicholas, perhaps to negotiate the terms under which he might be allowed exile. Whatever the reason for talks, it made sense to get the tsar away from prying eyes at the Ipatiev House, away from the influence of the tsarina, and naturally in conditions of total secrecy. It was certainly in the days just after this that the final decisions were made.

On the basis of all we have learned, we now make our final hypothesis, reconstructing that vital first fortnight of July 1918, sixteen days that sealed the fate of Tsar Nicholas.

In late June, while talks with the Germans were going on both at Moscow and perhaps at Ekaterinburg, we know that Commissar Goloshchokin was called from Ekaterinburg to Moscow for consultations. We know he had talks with Chairman Sverdlov of the Central Executive Committee, and he probably also saw Lenin. The matter of the Romanovs came up, and it was at this point that Ekaterinburg was ordered to change the guard at the Ipatiev House and ensure adequate protection for the imperial family. Then on 6 July, before Goloshchokin left for home, the German ambassador was murdered. The Bolshevik leadership feared a German invasion, and moved heaven and earth to avert it. When Goloshchokin boarded the train back to Ekaterinburg we can reckon that he carried confirmation of Lenin's existing orders—the Romanovs were not to be harmed, for the moment at any rate. The commissar was back in Ekaterinburg by 14 July, and we know that he, Chairman Beloborodov, and Commissar Yurovsky, held talks far into the night, huddled in Room 3 of their headquarters, the Hotel America. In those sessions Goloshchokin, the firm Lenin man, probably ran into opposition from his Ekaterinburg colleagues; they were under great pressure from local hardliners for the tsar to be executed, and probably the rest of the family too. Time was running out, the city was about to fall to the Czechs, and events forced a quick decision. Lenin may have already discussed such an eventuality with Goloshchokin in Moscow, and there was a possible compromise. Berlin was insisting specifically on the safety of the German princess, the tsarina, and her children, but it was a fair gamble that they would regard the death of the tsar as an internal Russian affair. So Goloshchokin caved in on the call to kill the tsar, but won his colleagues over on the matter of the females, persuading them that it would be folly to kill them in the face of the threat from Berlin. And so, on or about 16 July, it happened. Nicholas was shot, and probably his son Alexei too, because he was the male heir. But Alexandra and her four daughters were transferred from Ekaterinburg—alive.

But how was the transfer effected? It was obviously a secret at the time, so it is not surprising that the trail is at first hard to follow. Yet there are tell-tale clues, some of which we have come across already, and now fall into place. There were sound reasons for moving the family in some form of disguise, because it would have been inviting recognition to let the family travel in their stylish, tailored clothes. In any case, as we have seen, the Bolsheviks may have needed their usual clothing to set the decoy murder scene at the Four Brothers, where indeed most of their clothes were found. The valet, Chemodurov, said the family were "obliged to put on soldiers' uniforms and had been taken away". Then there are the different coloured hair-cuttings found in the house—identified positively as belonging to the grand duchesses: haircuts all round would have been one obvious step in disguising the girls. If the idea sounds far-fetched it is worth recalling that the British high commissioner, Sir Charles Eliot, accepted the principle of disguise when he wrote in his report: "It seems probable that the imperial family were disguised before their removal."

Two other clues suggest that, before the decision was taken to kill the tsar and perhaps his son, preparations were also made to remove them in disguise. There was the evidence of the visiting priest, who noticed on 14 July that the tsar seemed to "have cut around his beard". And there is the report by Colonel Rodzyanko, not mentioned by Sokolov, that part of the tsar's beard had been found hidden in a chimney at the Ipatiev House. Sokolov also suppressed a snippet of testimony which is inexplicable in terms of a massacre, but ideally suited to a disguise theory. The young guard, Philip Proskuryakov, told how Sednev, the teenaged kitchen-boy in the Ipatiev House, was transferred by Commissar Yurovsky to the guardhouse across the street on the day before the imperial family vanished: "He slept on my bed and I spoke to him . . . At the time he complained that Yurovsky had taken away his clothes". Now what possible reason could Yurovsky have had for a kitchen-boy's clothes—other than wishing to use them on another boy, and the only remaining teenage boy in the Ipatiev House was the tsarevich—Alexei. It is poignant to imagine Nicholas and his son getting ready, psychologically and practically, to leave Ekaterinburg with their family, only to learn at the last minute that their tickets to survival had been cancelled. They died, and the distraught mother and daughters were taken away, bewildered and with surely little real hope for their own futures.

The logical way to move the family was by rail—the principal and almost the only practical way to travel long distances in Russia at that time. For some months before the Romanovs vanished and then after they had, it was rumoured that this was the means of transport. Sir Charles Eliot, again, reported: "On 17 July, a train with the blinds down left Ekaterinburg for an unknown destination, and it is believed that the surviving members of the imperial family were in it." There was the Ipatiev House guard, Varakushev, who took his friend to the station, pointed out a train with the windows blacked out, and claimed the Romanovs were on board. The British consul's deputy, Arthur Thomas, was still repeating the train theory in official reports as late as Christmas 1918.

We have seen clues to the separate shooting of the tsar, and testimony suggesting removal of the rest of the family by train. But if it has any basis of truth, where did the Bolsheviks take the Romanovs, and what happened to them next?[43] Until now there has always been this one fatal flaw in the transfer hypothesis. It has remained untenable for the good reason that, after 16 July 1918, not one of the Romanovs was ever seen alive again. Not a single credible piece of evidence has yet been produced to show that anyone survived Ekaterinburg.

But witnesses were found, and evidence did exist. It was all suppressed.

25

TO PERM AND BEYOND

"History must not be written with bias, and both sides must be given, even if there is only one side."

(John Betjeman)

8 MARCH 1919—eight months after the disappearance of the imperial family from Ekaterinburg. The sworn testimony of Natalya Mutnykh, a nurse, of 15 2nd Zagorodnaya Street, in the town of Perm:

> I found out by chance that the family of the former Sovereign Nicholas II—his wife and four daughters—were transferred from the town of Ekaterinburg to Perm . . . the former imperial family were kept very secretly in Perm and were guarded only by Communists of the Regional Soviet and official party members, even to bringing them food at night. I was interested in the keeping of the former imperial family at Perm, and made use of the fact that my brother Vladimir Mutnykh had to go on duty at the place where the imperial family were being kept, and asked him to take me with him, and show me them; my brother agreed and we set off. This was in September. At Berezin's rooms we went down to the basement and I saw the room where in the poor candle-light I could make out the former Empress Alexandra Feodorovna and her four daughters, who were in a terrible state but I recognized them only too well.

This formal testimony, along with that of other witnesses, says categorically that all the Romanov women were held prisoner by the Bolsheviks in Perm, late in the summer of 1918 and on into the autumn. The testimony shows they were still there in early December—more than four months after their alleged deaths at Ekaterinburg.

Several of the statements are from eye-witnesses, giving first-hand evidence of identification and precise locations of where the Romanovs were held. Most of the new evidence comes from the original Sokolov dossier. Sokolov was fully aware of its contents and each document bears his signature, formally accepting the testimony as evidence. He never made use of it. Corroborative evidence of the imperial family's presence at Perm also appears in the "black bag" documents we found at the Hoover Institution in California—in letters between Professor Mirolyubov, Public Prosecutor of Kazan Assizes, and his colleague, Prosecutor Jordansky.

The town of Perm was held by the Bolsheviks until Christmas Eve 1918, when it fell to a surprise attack by the White "Siberian" army. Perm was then a town of 60,000 inhabitants, some 200 miles north-west of Ekaterinburg. It was a provincial capital, lying on the European side of the boundary between Europe and Asia (*see plate 70*). For the Whites it was one of the most important prizes in the Urals. Five months earlier it had been on the natural line of withdrawal for the Bolsheviks retreating from Ekaterinburg—it thus became the next important target for the White offensive in the Urals. The capture of Perm by anti-Bolshevik forces was a major strategic step towards the link-up with White forces in the north, and a potential springboard for an advance on St Petersburg itself. When Perm did fall, the Bolsheviks fled so quickly that the Whites were able to capture many important military objectives intact. One was the key railway bridge over the River Kama, not blown—we are told—because Medvedev, the former Ipatiev House guard, and Sokolov's key witness, failed to obey orders. Once in Perm the Whites captured hundreds of railway engines, thousands of trucks and fieldguns, and 30,000 prisoners.

It was a major victory, but a sobering moment for the foreign observers who followed the White army into Perm. The British consul, Preston, wrote: "The noise of the battle and the red glare in the sky caused by the burning of some of the houses, together with a complete absence of any life in the streets, appeared to us to be nearer a picture of an inferno than anything imaginable." A French intelligence officer reported: "The city is completely dead. The few inhabitants that one meets in the streets have yellow faces from which their bones protrude, green lips, haggard eyes which cannot fix on anything, in which stark horror remains clearly written . . . All the children under the age of one are dead."

One of the victorious generals who took the town was the Czech general fighting for the White cause, Rudolf Gaida. He had been commander of the forces which overwhelmed Ekaterinburg in the summer, and he now underlined his military reputation with the capture of Perm. Gaida already had his own interest in the fate of the imperial family, having actually installed himself in part of the Ipatiev House after the fall of Ekaterinburg in July.

Shortly after taking Perm, information reaching General Gaida prompted him to launch his own investigation into the fate of the Romanovs. This was just the period when the White leadership was starting to make its first outrageous statements about rape and mass murder in the Ipatiev House, and just before the replacement of Judge Sergeyev. Gaida apparently decided to keep the army investigation quite separate from the other enquiries. In a statement subsequently made by the Perm district prosecutor, Shamarin, we learn: ". . . on the orders of General Gaida, military control was carrying out a secret investigation into the murder of the imperial family . . . their findings would not be handed over to Judge Sergeyev."

The investigators who worked for General Gaida were members of the *Ugolovny Rozysk*—Criminal Investigating Division (CID). Of all the investigators, they were probably best placed to operate in a war situation. Many CID men were cı ilians, drawn from the network of agents who had operated for the old tsarist Ministry of the Interior. Nevertheless, this was technically a military organization, responsible to "Military Control". This gave the CID real clout and the freedom to operate across the country unhindered by provincial or judicial boundaries. The CID had its own style searches, mass arrests, and infiltration of agents behind Bolshevik lines. In the first few months of 1919, their investigation uncovered evidence and testimony that points inexorably to the fact that the surviving Romanov women were taken, alive, to Perm. For the sake of clarity we shall take the evidence according to the picture it eventually produced, rather than in the sequence in which it trickled in to the army investigators.

The CID linked Perm with that persistent story about the

train at Ekaterinburg station—the one seen on 17 July with its
blinds down, and believed to have been carrying members of
the imperial family. Here is the testimony of Vera Karnaukovaya, a resident of Perm:

> When I learned from newspapers and party sources of the
> shooting of the former sovereign in Ekaterinburg, I was very
> interested in the case, and in order to know for sure what did
> happen around 20 July in Ekaterinburg, I turned to my
> brother, Fyodor Nikolayevich Lukoyanov, former chairman
> of the Regional Committee of the Cheka. I turned to him
> because he held a high and responsible post in the Ural
> Region, and should know all about what had happened . . .
> My brother said it was not easy to talk about what happened
> in mid-July at the Ipatiev House in Ekaterinburg, and he
> could simply assure me that only the former sovereign was
> killed at Ekaterinburg, and the rest of his family, including
> the former tsarina, were transferred from Ekaterinburg on
> the train which carried all the treasure. There was a passen-
> ger carriage amongst the wagons that held the treasure, and
> it was in that carriage that the imperial family were held.
> The train was parked at Perm Station II, and strictly
> guarded, I did not see this train myself, and am going on
> what my brother told me. He never lied to me, and I there-
> fore had no reason to disbelieve him.

The witness's reference to a train carrying "treasure" fits in
with what we know of the Communist evacuation of Ekaterinburg. Because it was the commercial centre of the richest
mining area in Russia, the city's banks were packed with
precious bullion, and the Bolsheviks made a point of holding
on to Ekaterinburg until they removed as much of it as possible
—to Perm. The witness also refers to "treasure" on the train
that carried the Romanovs, and some of this may have been
part of their personal property; apart from the small items
carried about their persons, the Romanovs had arrived at
Ekaterinburg with a whole train-load of possessions—and
some of the valuable items seem to have reached Perm. The
first White commandant of Perm after its fall at Christmas
1918, Vitold Rimashevsky, later testified that White counter-

intelligence had seized "a variety of extremely valuable objects" and "used female clothing". He informed Colonel Nikiforov, the new head of Military Control, who discovered that members of counter-intelligence had quietly "liberated" some of these objects. The colonel traced and collected them again, and informed the commandant that:

> many valuable objects had been found during a search of [counter-intelligence] quarters, and amongst these valuables were some which by their origin one could tell had belonged to the former imperial family; Colonel Nikiforov was certain about a particular gold icon-lamp, studded with precious stones . . .

Colonel Nikiforov was an intelligence officer who had been close to the search for the imperial family back in Ekaterinburg. In January 1919, when he was transferred to Perm as head of Military Control, he was well-placed to make enquiries there. He got more leads from a woman called Alexandra Krivopdenova, whom he hired to infiltrate Bolshevik circles in the town. In 1920 she recalled:

> In mid-January [1919] I was at a house in Motovilovka [a suburb of Perm] where I heard a conversation about Nicholas II's underwear, with crowns and monograms. I asked where such underwear was to be found. They said to me: "Surely you know that the imperial family was in Perm, and lived in the Excise Administration House? The Yids, for certain, killed them and divided everything up." "But who saw the underwear?" They showed me the laundry-woman who used to wash this underwear for a Yiddish doctor. I found the laundrywoman who stated that indeed she used to wash underwear for a Jewish doctor, underwear with crowns and monograms—shirts and pants. She did not know the doctor's name, but she knew the house where he had lived, on Monastery Street—the house belonging to Kusarkin. I personally passed this on to Nikiforov, as we had agreed—that as far as the imperial family was concerned, I was to speak only to him. At the end of January, I went to see Nikiforov at the appointed time. He said to me: "Let's

go into the study," picked up a package, locked the door, and then unwrapped the package, and in it there were gold objects and diamonds . . . I was especially fascinated by the oval earrings with large sapphires in the middle, and other diamonds. I gazed at them for a long time, and asked if they were the tsarina's. "Yes," he said . . . Colonel Nikiforov said there were more than two million roubles' worth there. I asked him where he had obtained them. Nikiforov said he could not tell me for the moment, but asked me not to give up the case, and to keep working . . .

This witness also shows that at first evidence that the Romanovs had been in Perm came in painfully slowly; so much so that at one point Colonel Nikiforov gave up hope of making any further progress. She quoted him: "I have begun to despair. I hear many rumours, but nothing definite or positive." It was about this time that he decided to delegate most of the responsibility for the Romanov enquiry to the assistant head of Military Control, Alexander Kirsta. It was Kirsta who was to do the real spade-work, and made the key breakthrough.

On 8 March 1919, acting on a tip-off from Krivopdenova, who had been infiltrating former associates of the Bolsheviks, and an intercepted letter, Kirsta raided a house at 15 2nd Zagorodnaya Street. One of the occupants he questioned was the nurse, Natalya Mutnykh, whose dramatic testimony opened this chapter. Kirsta found her statement about having actually seen the imperial family at Perm vitally important, but also knew it needed checking over and over again. During the next six weeks he grilled her not once but three times. The following is taken from her final statement:

As I was often with my brother Vladimir, who held the position of secretary to the Ural Regional Soviet, I frequently listened to my brother's conversations with comrades Safarov and Beloborodov. They often mentioned the imperial family. From my brother's conversation I knew that Nicholas himself and the heir were shot and their bodies burned outside Ekaterinburg, but that the family, consisting of four daughters and Alexandra Feodorovna, were taken to the city of Perm. There was every possible kind of rumour about their presence, and nobody knew what to believe. But one day in September I went with my brother's fiancée, Anna Kostina (secretary to Comrade Zinoviev, temporarily commanding in Perm), to see my brother at the Regional Soviet. My brother was not there so we went to see him where he was on guard duty. I was very interested in the imperial family, and asked my brother to take me into their room and show them to me. They were staying at that time in Berezin's rooms on Obvinskaya Street in the basement. When I entered I saw the pale rather tired faces of young women. I do not remember exactly how many there were. But I saw that the conditions they were kept in were not luxurious. They slept on pallets, without sheets or bedding, right on the floor. The weak light of a tallow candle was the only illumination in their room. One of the grand duchesses was sitting and softly whistling. It seemed to me this was the Grand Duchess Olga, and I had heard before from my brother that Duchess Olga was one of the tsar's arrogant daughters. I was in the same room as them for several minutes. Then, saying goodbye to Vladimir, we left. Later, I learned that the family of the former tsar had been taken to a convent under more strict arrest because one of the grand duchesses had made an attempt to get away . . . Wishing to learn more details about the imperial family I began to make more enquiries. It appeared that the imperial family, on its arrival, first lived in the building of the Excise Office, at the corner of Obvinskaya and Pokrovskaya streets, where they were held in good conditions, and not under very secure arrest (*see town plan p. 328*). But when one of the duchesses (perhaps Tatiana) attempted to escape they moved them to the Berezin house, in the basement, where I saw them. In spite of the strict surveillance one of the grand duchesses nevertheless did escape, but was captured—and later died either from beatings or was killed on the orders of the Regional Soviet. I do not know for certain about this story . . .

Natalya Mutnykh's statements place all the female members of the imperial family in Perm months after their supposed death in July. At her final interrogation she did not refer specifically to the tsarina, but she had done so on both the

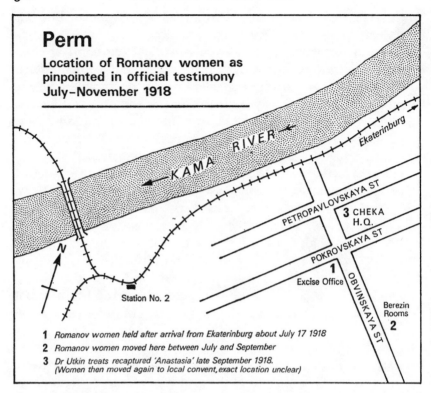

Perm

Location of Romanov women as
pinpointed in official testimony
July–November 1918

KAMA RIVER

Ekaterinburg

PETROPAVLOVSKAYA ST

3 CHEKA
H.Q.

POKROVSKAYA ST

1
Excise Office

OBVINSKAYA ST

Berezin
Rooms
2

N

Station No. 2

1 *Romanov women held after arrival from Ekaterinburg about July 17 1918*
2 *Romanov women moved here between July and September*
3 *Dr Utkin treats recaptured 'Anastasia' late September 1918.*
   (Women then moved again to local convent, exact location unclear)

other occasions she was questioned: 8 March, which we
quoted earlier and 2 April:

> . . . on the floor were four mattresses, on which were lying
> the former tsarina and three daughters, two of whom had
> cropped hair and were wearing scarves. One of the grand
> duchesses was sitting on the mattress. I saw how she looked
> at my brother with scorn; on the mattresses together with
> the pillows were soldiers' overcoats, and the tsarina had a
> small pillow on top of the military coat . . .

Mutnykh's testimony is vastly strengthened by the discovery that her brother, Vladimir Mutnykh, was indeed, as she
claimed, secretary to the Ural Soviet. From the writings of
others imprisoned in the area, we learn that he was more than
a mere secretary, he was personal aide to Beloborodov himself, chairman of the Ural Soviet, and one of the very few men
who knew exactly what had happened to the Romanovs.

Sources confirm that after the fall of Ekaterinburg he moved to Perm where he continued to be the liaison man with Moscow on matters involving important prisoners. Natalya Mutnykh could not have had a more authoritative original source for her information that the mysterious women prisoners were the Romanovs. Certainly, at Ekaterinburg, Sokolov was never able to produce any such witnesses, able to quote Beloborodov or Goloshchokin on the fate of the Romanovs.

The CID, working to Alexander Kirsta, found other witnesses who tended to corroborate the Mutnykh story. A German refugee, Ivan Girschfeld, said that at least two grand duchesses were being held by the Perm Cheka at the end of August, or in early September. A post-office clerk, Sibiryev, testified: "... after the fall of Ekaterinburg the Grand Duchesses Olga and Tatiana Nikolayevna, with a maid, were living at the Perm House of Invalids, and a lot of property belonging to the imperial family was kept in that building; it was marked thus on boxes . . ."

These two witnesses, referring to just two Romanov prisoners, seem to have picked up only part of the story. Their evidence is ill-defined and second-hand—Girschfeld's source was his lodging-house keeper, and Sibiryev heard it from a patient at the House of Invalids. But Kirsta located a further three witnesses whose statements were consistent with Mutnykh's, and had the tsarina and her four daughters all being held together.

First there was Yevgeniya Sokolova, a history teacher at Turgenev High School in Perm, who said: "I managed to find out that the former empress and her four daughters, who had been evacuated from Ekaterinburg, were living in rooms guarded by prominent Communists, who did not entrust this to Red Army soldiers, because the troops made great sport of the family." This was encouraging testimony, but still second-hand—the teacher had heard about the Romanovs being in town from various sources, including students from the families of local Communists. But on 30 March 1919, Kirsta found another eye-witness; this was Glafyra Malysheva, the wife of a Perm Communist, and when traced she was found to be in possession of napkins bearing the imperial insignia. This woman testified:

I don't recall the month, but it was at the time my husband
Rafael, who worked at the Meshkov factory, had not been
coming home. I sent to my mother-in-law and learned from
her that my husband was on duty at the Excise Office building on the corner of Pokrovskaya and Obvinskaya Streets,
across from the pawnshop—a red building. I went there, and
in the entrance of the ground floor found my husband, and
with him several other men in civilian clothes, all factory
workers. I asked my husband what he was doing, and
learned from him that he was on duty, guarding the daughters of the former tsar. I said I would like to see one of them,
and my husband told me to wait until one of them should
come down from upstairs, where their luggage was. And,
indeed, soon I saw a young girl come down the staircase
—not tall—probably average height with cut hair and
glasses in gold frames, fair hair with an auburn tinge. She
was thin, pale, worn out and ill-looking. She went past me
quickly. I was standing at a distance and only saw her
briefly. I did not talk to my husband any more about it.

Glafyra Malysheva, like Mutnykh, was questioned repeatedly, and she came up with two explanations of how she
had come by the Romanov napkins found in her possession.
First she said her husband had brought them home from the
Excise Office, worn and dirty, after they had been thrown out.
Later Malysheva admitted—presumably under pressure—that
the truth about the napkins was that she herself had removed
them: "I took them myself from the floor on the occasion I saw
the girl in the Excise Office who, my husband said, was this
grand duchess. The napkins were lying on the floor in the
corridor. I was told nobody needed them and they had been
thrown out."

The army investigators also interviewed Malysheva's mother-
in-law and she confirmed part of the story:

My son, Rafael Malyshev, is a Communist, married, and
lives apart from me, but often visits me; and I recall that
this son, Rafael, coming to see me, said he had just come off
duty from guarding the family of the former tsar. Rafael left
Perm about two weeks later, but where to and why I do not

know, as he did not say goodbye. When I asked Rafael where the imperial family was living, he said: "In rooms," but he did not say exactly where.

To sum up so far then, the evidence that the Romanovs were alive in Perm consists of an eye-witness, Natalya Mutnykh, who said she had seen and recognized the Romanov women; a second eye-witness, Glafyra Malysheva, who also said she had seen one of the grand duchesses, but only because her husband, one of the guards, assured her in advance that it was indeed the daughters of the tsar he was guarding. The description: "not tall—probably average height, with cut hair and glasses in gold frames, fair hair with an auburn tinge," could fit Olga's description. But the witness admits she only had a brief look at the "grand duchess" and we can build no more on her identification. Nevertheless, Mutnykh, old Malysheva, and Sokolova all say that the family were being kept in "rooms", and Mutnykh and Malysheva agree that at one stage this was the Excise Office building. Both Mutnykh and Sokolova agree that the prisoners were of sufficient importance to merit a guard of senior Bolsheviks rather than ordinary peasant conscripts. Mutnykh, in her 8 March statement, says that the family were: "guarded only by Communists of the Regional Soviet and official party members, even to bringing them food at night."

If the family were guarded only by senior Bolshevik officials, this must have made the task of procuring first-hand evidence of their presence in Perm all the more difficult for the CID. All Bolshevik officials naturally fled the town as the White armies approached in December 1918. Mutnykh's testimony remains the key evidence that the Romanov women were being held at Perm, and her deposition contains one more vital clue that her story was the truth. She mentions that she had gone to the Berezin rooms to see the Romanovs in the company of "Anna Kostina, secretary to Comrade Zinoviev". Grigory Zinoviev was a prominent member of Lenin's leadership team, was on the Central Executive Committee, and was also a specialist in German affairs. If Moscow needed a reliable person to supervise or keep a watching brief on the arrangements for the surviving Romanovs, then Zinoviev's secretary made an eminently sensible choice; she was a woman who could keep an eye on the special risks involving female prisoners, and above all her first loyalty was to Moscow.

We have established that Anna Kostina was in the Urals, and very probably therefore at headquarters in Perm, at just the time Natalya Mutnykh claimed she was. In Sokolov's photographic portfolio, discovered in Paris, is a copy of Bolshevik telegram 4852, sent from Ekaterinburg to Petrograd [changed name of St Petersburg], on 18 July 1918 (*see plate 71*): "Petrograd Smolny to Zinoviev. The Ural Regional Soviet and Party District Committee considering absolutely necessary the participation of Comrade Kostina in the special responsible work, is retaining her therefore in the Ural region . . . (Signed) Regional Soviet Committee." In other words the signatories, Chairman Beloborodov and his men—those responsible for the Romanovs—were asking for Anna Kostina's continued services on 18 July—a significant date. It was within a day of the disappearance of the Romanovs from the Ipatiev House. The nature of the work is described as "special responsible"—the same designation, in Bolshevik jargon, that had been applied to matters concerning the imperial family's captivity at Ekaterinburg. The address, "Petrograd Smolny to Zinoviev" indicates that the message was indeed meant for Grigory Zinoviev of the Central Executive Committee; during this period all other top Bolsheviks had left the Bolshevik headquarters at Smolny, in Petrograd, to take up duties in Moscow, the new capital —except Grigory Zinoviev, who stayed on in Petrograd for some time. Given the Perm testimony, it is more than likely that on 18 July, Comrade Kostina was busy escorting the Romanov women on their journey from Ekaterinburg to Perm; and that for weeks afterwards her "special responsible work" was supervision of those prisoners, while Moscow haggled with Germany over their fate. It is not surprising to find her boss, Zinoviev, saying to the press—as we have noted—that the tsar's family were alive in a city "the location of which he refused to disclose".

The city was Perm.

*

In the spring of 1919 Kirsta's investigators, puzzling over the accumulated testimony, found repeated references to a strange new element—the story of the escape of one of the Romanov daughters. The imperial fugitive seems to have been the Grand Duchess Anastasia.

It may be highly significant that this evidence was collected in early 1919, eleven months *before* the woman calling herself Anastasia turned up in Berlin.

At Perm, the witnesses Mutnykh and Sokolova both referred to the escape. Mutnykh spoke of two incidents—the first an abortive escape bid, apparently by the tsar's second daughter, Tatiana. Then, after the family had been moved for greater security to the Berezin house, one of the Romanov girls did allegedly succeed in getting away, however temporarily. In Mutnykh's words: "In spite of the strict surveillance one of the grand duchesses nevertheless escaped, but was captured . . ." This must have encouraged the detectives to believe the rest of Mutnykh's story, because it matched precisely a detailed and extraordinary account of the escape they had picked up weeks before. Eighteen witnesses in all, speaking of different events at different locations, provide the picture of "Anastasia's" escape from the Communists at Perm. We have used the sworn depositions of those witnesses to reconstruct events as they allegedly occurred.

There was a mass of consistent testimony about an incident at Siding 37 on the railway line north-west of Perm. First the evidence of a signalman, Maxim Grigoryev, whose usual routine was interrupted by an exciting episode one chilly day in autumn 1918. He did not remember the exact date, but other witnesses fix it as on or about 21 September. Grigoryev stated:

> I recall that at about 12 noon I was at Siding 37 when someone told me that Red Army men had caught a daughter of the tsar in the woods and had taken her to the sentry box near the siding. I ran over to see. A young girl, who looked about 18 to 19 years old, was sitting in the sentry box, near the stove, in a chair. She was not crying, but you could see she was utterly miserable. She was wearing a skirt—I do not recall the colour—and a white blouse with red bloodstains on the chest. She had no scarf on her head. Her hair was cropped, and of a dark colour. There was blood on her face

and bruises around her eyebrows. She was cut around the lip. She peered out fearfully, frowning but saying nothing. I noticed she had a lump on her nose . . . I was not at the sentry box long because the Red Army fellows sent me away. While I was there they said to the girl: "Get dressed!" They held her in the sentry box for about an hour and, after putting an army coat and hood on her, took her along the railway line in the direction of the Kama Bridge. There were five or six Red Army men in the sentry box. Two took her away, the others remained. The Red Army fellows mocked her, in particular one rather short chap, who said: "So here you are!" and continued to sneer as they took her away. He and another Red Army fellow went off with the girl.

The signalman's story was confirmed by another local witness, Tatiana Sitnikova:

. . . I tried to gain entry to the sentry box to have a look at the arrested woman, but the Red Army men would not let me right in; however I managed to catch a glimpse, and saw a lady sitting in the corner by the stove, with darkish hair, a swelling on her nose, and a huge bruise by her eye; there was blood all over the chest of her blouse; she was sitting forlornly and stared frightened at those watching her. The Red Army men were laughing at the lady, obviously teasing her. I offered her bread, but she turned it down saying she could not eat. They put a soldier's greatcoat on her, and took her away to Perm. According to what I heard, when the prisoner was sitting in the guard-room she admitted she was the daughter of Tsar Nicholas II. Not long after the arrested daughter of the former tsar was led away, a company of Red Army men arrived from the town and Red Army troops were everywhere, and the peasants were not allowed into the woods. The captured girl was dressed in a dark skirt and a white blouse, and was wearing shoes. When I offered her bread, she asked me: "What will they do to me?" . . . As far as I remember, there were two Red Army men who took the grand duchess to Perm. I did not know them.

Sitnikova's son, Fyodor, a soldier in the 5th Tomsk-Siberian

Regiment, had been staying with his parents at Siding 37 in September 1919. He gave evidence corroborating his mother's statement, and adding detail about exactly how "Anastasia" had been caught:

> I learned from some Red Army men who were there that they had just caught a daughter of the former tsar, Anastasia, at the fringe of the woods this side of the station towards the mountains. I asked how it had happened, and the Red Army men told me they had gone into the woods to do a little shooting, caught sight of a woman walking at the edge of the woods, shouted to her to stop, but she ran off. They fired, and she fell. Then they arrested her and brought her here . . .

Another three witnesses, all railway workers, corroborated all or part of the incident at Siding 37. Switchman Ivan Kuklin, Signalman Vassily Ryabov, and Signalwoman Ustinya Varankina. Matrena Kuklina, a middle-aged woman also living at the siding, had seen the girl at the sentrybox cleaning herself up with water given her by a guard. All the Siding 37 witnesses were interviewed in late March 1919. Most were simple peasants, and the simple humanity, the spontaneity of their detailed testimony, makes their evidence compelling. What they said about the "Anastasia" escape was corroborated by a witness far removed from them, an educated man, a Perm doctor. He had in fact given his end of the story two months *before* the Siding 37 witnesses were found.

On 10 February 1919 Dr Pavel Ivanovich Utkin, aged 44, made this remarkable deposition:

> In September 1918 I lived in Perm on the corner of Petropavlovskaya and Obvinskaya Streets, in the building of the Peasant Land Bank (*see town plan p. 328*). This is a large building with three floors. At the end of the first half of September the Cheka began to occupy the building. It first occupied the lower floor, where the bank itself was located, and then began to evict the apartment dwellers and occupy their premises. Finally they occupied my apartment too, leaving me with one room where I settled with my family: my wife Zoya Alexandrovna, and two small children. Whilst I was living in this room, shortly after 20 September, at

about 5–6 o'clock in the evening, an orderly came to me from the Cheka and said: "Doctor, go at once to Malkov." Malkov, as I knew, was chairman of the Cheka. I went at once with the orderly. He took me to the second floor of the building, to a rectangular room in which were Bolsheviks who worked for the Cheka: Malkov, Lobov, Vorobtsov, Shlenov and others. They took me to the adjoining room. This adjoining room looks semi-circular because one of its walls, and perhaps part of two others, were curved, forming a bow. In this room a woman was lying on a couch. I realized they had called me to a sick person.

The agents from the Cheka I have named came into this semi-circular room with me, along with several others. With the agents was another woman, not known to me, about 22 to 24 years old, blonde, of average height and build. I remember her general appearance and can describe separately some of the features of her face. Her nose was fine and straight, her mouth not large, lips thin, hair braided and swept back, forming—as it were—a Grecian hairstyle. I do not recall her eyes. I definitely do not remember what she was wearing.

When I entered this room one of the Bolsheviks who came in with me said to me: "See if you can help her." I started to examine the woman lying on the couch. I remember well that under one eye, the left one I think, she had a large bruise running from the corner of the eye along the cheek-bone. The corresponding corner of the left lip had been cut. This injury was of a superficial nature. The general impression was that the sick person had been beaten; she had, for a start, been struck with a fist along the cheek-bone, had been given a black eye, and the corner of her mouth had simultaneously been torn with a fingernail. Having examined the injury I have described, I started to examine her chest. On her chest there were no marks of violence. At this time, as was obvious, the sick woman was in an unconscious state. She was shaking violently. When I started my examination of the sick woman all the men left the room; one woman remained, of whom I have spoken. A little while after I began my examination the sick woman regained consciousness and looked at me. I asked her: "Who are you?"

59 Lenin—the Romanov regime hanged his brother. Now the imperial family was at his mercy.

60 **Yakov** Sverdlov, Communist head of state —he was Moscow's link with Ekaterinburg.

61 Commissar Karl Radek—proposed a deal with Berlin involving live Romanovs, *after* they are supposed to have been dead.

62 Major Homer Slaughter, of U.S. Military Intelligence in Siberia—he filed a report showing that the tsar died alone.

63 Poul Ree, Danish diplomat at Perm—he tried to tell what he knew, but nobody was listening.

64 Carl Ackerman, *New York Times* correspondent "circumstantial evidence that they may still be alive".

62
63

64

THE EMPRESS AND HER DAUGHTERS

According to official testimony they all survived Ekaterinburg

65 Olga

66 Tatiana

67 Tsarina Alexandra—in prison
her heart condition got worse.

68 Maria

69 Anastasia—eighteen witnesses
to her escape attempt.

70 The town of Perm, where according to the evidence uncovered by the authors, the tsarina and her four daughters were held for several months after their disappearance. Witnesses named precise locations where the family were housed, and stated that they were again transferred alive, in late November 1918.

71 Captured Bolshevik telegram 4852, dated 18 July 1918, requesting the continued services of "Comrade Kostina" for "special responsible work". Elsewhere, Kostina is firmly linked with the supervision of the imperial prisoners after they left Ekaterinburg (*for full translation of message see p.* 332).

72 General Rudolf Gaida—he launched the enquiries which uncovered the trail of the Romanovs through the autumn of 1918.

In a trembling voice, but quite distinctly, she answered me, word for word—as follows: "I am the emperor's daughter Anastasia." I wanted to continue the examination and made a movement to raise her clothing. But the woman agent, who had remained near me all this time, called out: "Comrades!" At once several men entered the room and I was told: "Doctor, that is not part of your examination." I was forced to interrupt further examination. Then I went into the adjoining room and asked for paper on which to write a prescription. They gave me a blank form of Doctor Ivanov's, on which I listed for the sick woman iodine, Goulard water, bromide salts, with valerian and bandage material. Shlenov wrote on the back of the prescription and somebody was sent for the medicine. I went to my apartment, and one of the Bolsheviks told me: "We will send for you shortly."

In fact I hadn't had the time to drink a cup of tea before somebody from the Cheka came for me again. Once more I went to the sick woman. The medicines and bandage material had already been brought. I washed the sick woman's injured place, painted the corner of her mouth with iodine, applied the Goulard water, and gave her the mixture. After that I remained at the patient's bed in order to give her more of the mixture myself. I recall that on this occasion I was beside her for about an hour, and gave her four spoonfuls of the mixture. You ask me why I did this. I did it as a doctor, from moral convictions. Having taken care of prisons and places of detention under the Bolsheviks, I have seen how they deal with the sick; a sick detainee is supposed to be waiting, you come, and he's not there. Wishing to be sure that the medicines prescribed would be given to her, I stayed with her—as I say—for about an hour. The sick woman was semi-conscious. She would open her eyes, and then would close them again. The woman who was with her, and obviously a "spy", never left her. I was therefore unable to converse with Anastasia Nikolayevna. When I left I told the "spy" that they should continue to give Anastasia Nikolayevna the mixture every hour.

At about nine or ten o'clock in the evening, I went again to Anastasia Nikolayevna on my own initiative. The Bolsheviks were once again in the rectangular room, but there

were fewer of them. I simply stated that I had come to see
the sick woman, and entered without hindrance. The same
woman—the "spy"—was still in the room with Anastasia
Nikolayevna; I asked her: "Well, how does the patient feel
now?" It seems Anastasia Nikolayevna awoke on hearing
my words. She opened her eyes and looked at me with gratitude. I felt that she wanted to express her gratitude to me
silently, with her eyes. I said to her: "Well, you may feel
rough now—but you'll get better". At these words Anastasia
Nikolayevna, in reply, extended her hand to me and said:
"I am very grateful to you, dear, dear doctor." In the
morning I again went to see Anastasia Nikolayevna. Shlenov
and some other Bolsheviks were in the rectangular room.
One of them said to me: "The sick woman is no longer in
need of your assistance." So I did not see Anastasia Nikolayevna again.

I can thus describe the external appearance of the girl
who told me she was Anastasia Nikolayevna. This girl was
somewhat above average height, very well educated, in
appearance about eighteen or nineteen years old; at least I
would say she was fully that age. She was brown-haired; her
nose was absolutely regular, straight with a small hump.
Her eyes were dark, elongated. I do not recall the shape of
her eyebrows; high forehead, not flat, slightly oval. I cannot describe her mouth—it was constantly twitching; the
lips were neither thick nor thin; rounded chin; I did not pay
attention to her ears. Her neck was round and short. Her
hair was cropped and did not reach her shoulders. Whether
she had previously had some sort of coiffure I cannot say—I
only recall that her hair was cut short. Her face created a
lovely impression, a charming face beautifully formed. I
want to say that not only did she not have any pathological
deficiency, medically speaking, but was in general magni-
ficently formed, so far as her figure was concerned. Her
plumpness was not excessive in proportion, for example, to
her height. She was remarkably well shaped. Her breasts
were fine but not greatly developed, and admirably suited
the rest of her appearance. She was wearing a beautiful
blouse of fine material. There was no lace on it. The collar
of her blouse was cut fairly low, so that part of her breast

was visible. Over her blouse she was covered only with a bedsheet. The bedsheet was also of fine material. I did not see any markings either on the blouse or on the bedsheet. When Anastasia Nikolayevna gave me her hand I looked it over: the hand was plumpish, pretty, and all parts of her hand were rounded; the fingers were beautiful, of average size; the nails cut, and absolutely clean. I did not notice if they were manicured.

When I was going home after prescribing medicine for Anastasia Nikolayevna, one of the Bolsheviks asked me: "What do you think is wrong with her? What do you diagnose?" I replied: "Insane. She has simply been possessed by megalomania. Send her to a psychiatric hospital." Nobody answered me. Only Shlenov looked at me in a sidelong sort of way, you know, to give me an idea what he was thinking. I said this to the Bolsheviks at the time, of course, deliberately; she would of course have been able to get away more easily from a psychiatric hospital. I did not have the slightest doubt that she was the daughter of the emperor, then or now. What would be the purpose, you see, of a person hastening their own end, calling themselves by their true name, when someone comes upon them by chance? At that time I based my opinion on the words of the patient, on her statement to me. Personally I had never in my life seen Anastasia Nikolayevna—I never had occasion to see her. Of the imperial family in general, I did see the emperor, the empress and Alexei Nikolayevich in 1913. Of the daughters, I saw at that time Tatiana Nikolayevna and Olga Nikolayevna. In my opinion, Anastasia Nikolayevna had a resemblance to Elisabeth Feodorovna, whom I saw in Moscow in 1913. It was in Moscow that I saw the imperial family.

At that time, I definitely told nobody except my wife that I had had occasion to help Anastasia Nikolayevna. I did tell her, and at the same time forbade her to talk to anyone about it. Perm was liberated from the Bolsheviks on 24 December. At the end of his testimony the doctor adds . . .

"I request you to alter my testimony in only one respect. Anastasia Nikolayevna did not say to me exactly what you have written: 'I am the daughter of the emperor (*imperatora*),

Anastasia,' but the following: 'I am the daughter of the ruler (*gosudarya*), Anastasia.' "

The Perm authorities considered Dr Utkin's statement so important that they sent him to see Sokolov in Ekaterinburg. Sokolov also took a statement from the doctor—and never used it. In his book, General Diterikhs mentions the doctor's testimony obliquely but dismisses him as being "nervous and confused". Typically, Diterikhs adds the ultimate stigma—that Utkin was a Jew.

But was Utkin's story true, as an event, and as an event involving the real Grand Duchess Anastasia? The story is confirmed as a real incident by an admirable piece of detective work. After Dr Utkin testified, he was asked to trace his original prescription at the chemist. The doctor assumed naturally that the medicines had been collected from the Soviet chemist, partly because it was a Soviet establishment, partly because it was the closest one to Cheka headquarters. In fact the prescription was found at the Rural Council chemist's, a shop less convenient to Cheka headquarters. Dr Utkin found this a little odd, and it moved him to record a detail he had forgotten in his original testimony. He remembered that he had written the prescription just after his patient had revealed her identity. Because of that, he had not been sure whose name to put on the prescription:

> I gave some thought as to how I should do it—for whom should I prescribe the medicine, in the name of Romanov, or not? I remember I even asked the Bolsheviks about it at the time, and was told to use a letter of the alphabet. I filled in the prescription with the letter "N". In the chemist's shop this attracted some attention at the time as being an odd thing to have done.

Anastasia's formal name was of course Anastasia Nikolayevna —"daughter of Nicholas". That would explain the "N". Whoever she was, the patient was clearly of sufficient importance for the Bolsheviks, and the Cheka in particular—an institution scarcely noted for its tender loving care of prisoners—to go to the trouble of calling a doctor. As far as the identity of the patient is concerned, one can only make guesses. Physical descriptions by witnesses, especially after a lengthy period of time has elapsed, can be notoriously unreliable; nevertheless everyone concerned agreed that the mystery girl was eighteen or nineteen years old. The real Anastasia had been seventeen years old the previous June.

The doctor described his patient's eyes as "dark"—the real Anastasia had grey-blue eyes. The mystery girl's hair is variously described as "brown" and "darkish", the real Anastasia had brown, and some sources refer to an auburn tinge. Any accurate report on colour of hair and eyes tends to depend on available light. The girl was seen inside a sentry box, and again in an internal location by Dr Utkin. It is interesting that the mystery girl's hair was cropped as was that of at least two of the girls seen independently by Natalya Mutnykh. The hair found at the Ipatiev House, belonging to the four grand duchesses, suggested their hair had been cut short before departure.

Dr Utkin described his patient as "somewhat above average height", whilst Anastasia was said to be shorter than her sisters. However it is difficult to see how the doctor could judge height, bearing in mind that his patient was horizontal and covered with bedclothes, and that examination below the breasts was expressly forbidden by the Bolsheviks.

Dr Utkin speaks of his patient's "plumpness", and this was indeed a feature of the real Anastasia. Her puppy fat was something of a family joke. Dr Utkin also notices the patient's "beautiful fingers". The Romanov women were noted for their elegant hands.

One group of witnesses did make positive identifications of the girl they had seen as being the Grand Duchess Anastasia, although the method used was imperfect by contemporary identification standards. Of the eight witnesses to the incident at Siding 37, four had only glimpsed the prisoner through the door of the sentry box, and had not seen her face clearly. But the investigator Kirsta asked each of the remaining four, who said they had seen the girl properly, to examine group pictures of the imperial family in editions of the magazine *Neva* published in 1913 and 1915. Switchman Kuklin testified: "You have shown me a photograph of these people, and I recognize this one." "This one" was Anastasia as shown in the 1915 group picture, and Kirsta noted that the witness "pointed to the Grand Duchess Anastasia". Signalman Grigoryev, Tatiana

Sitnikova, and her son Fyodor Sitnikov, all examined the photographs separately, and each picked out Anastasia as being like the girl they had seen in the sentry box.

But Fyodor Sitnikov did add a jarring note to the testimony. He said that a few days after the incident at Siding 37 a Red Army soldier had told him: "It was Anastasia Gracheva, who had stolen a fur coat, and that was why she was arrested." Yet one witness specifically stated that when the girl was arrested she had with her a "coat of simple country cloth"—so she was not arrested red-handed with a fur coat. Furthermore, the evidence variously describes the soldiers as happening upon the fugitive while they were doing "a little shooting" or "looking for mushrooms"; either way it was quite by chance. In the light of other evidence it may be that the Red soldier had confused two stories, or that the Bolsheviks deliberately spread word that the mystery prisoner was an impostor; for there is indeed more evidence that other women were arrested at this same period—none of them Anastasia—and there seems to have been confusion about just who had been seized by whom, and for what.

We know of one of these cases from the memoirs of Sergei Smirnov, an officer imprisoned in Perm in late summer 1918, along with Princess Helen of Serbia. He tells how as early as August, the Bolsheviks asked Princess Helen to come and identify a girl claiming to be Anastasia. When she eventually saw the girl she turned out to be "a prostitute". In September, nearer the date of the incident at Siding 37, a witness called Stefanida Podorova testified to Kirsta that she had heard, from a combination of two other people, that a girl *and a boy* had been arrested on board a train: "the girl who had been caught in the carriage was the daughter of the former sovereign . . . it was known that a search had been carried out in the train . . . she had been badly beaten up, her cheek was slashed, she had been beaten with a whip, and taken to some carriage which was standing in the road, together with the boy . . ." Out of this grew a rumour that the Grand Duchess Anastasia was on the run with her brother Alexei.

One thing does emerge without any doubt from this strange period at Perm in the early autumn of 1918. The Bolsheviks were certainly mounting searches and looking very hard for somebody, and it must have been a person of some importance. The Communists in this beleaguered town would scarcely have spent the time and energy looking for a nonentity, nor for a grand duchess who they knew had been killed weeks before at Ekaterinburg. For the Bolsheviks then in control in Perm were the same as those who had been in charge at Ekaterinburg.

The real rumpus near Siding 37 started, curiously enough, *after* the capture of the girl. All the witnesses agree on this, and Switchman Kuklin specifies that the girl was taken away to Perm at twelve noon, whilst "at about three o'clock" many soldiers came to search the woods. Matrena Kuklina makes it clear that headquarters were in earnest, whoever they were chasing: ". . . a company of Red Army men came from the city, Letts and Hungarians; they began to look for someone in the woods, and after that for a long time we were forbidden to go into the woods without permission, even for the cows. They searched the woods for three to four days."

Letts and Hungarians, as we have seen from their use at Ekaterinburg, were among the best troops available to the Bolsheviks, and to divert a body of crack soldiers for three days or more implies a hunt for something more important than a stolen fur coat. Furthermore, trains were being stopped in a serious attempt to catch the runaway. Witness Podorova reveals that at a railway station outside Perm: ". . . a search was carried out . . . by the Reds, who arrived in a steam train from Perm, and waited for the train to arrive."

The best confirmation that the Bolsheviks really were looking for Grand Duchess Anastasia comes from an impeccable, independent source. The Swedish Red Cross delegate in Russia, Count Carl Bonde, was travelling through the area at this time by train. Years later, he wrote a letter about an interruption on that journey:

In my capacity as the chief of the Swedish Red Cross mission in Siberia in 1918, I travelled in a private railway-car. At some place, the name of which has escaped my memory, the train was stopped and searched in order to find the Grand Duchess Anastasia, daughter of Tsar Nicholas II. The grand duchess was, however, not aboard the train. Nobody knew where she had gone.

Apart from hunting for Anastasia, the Perm Bolsheviks themselves talked about her. The history teacher, Yevgeniya Sokolova, quoted a Communist ·contact as saying not only that the Romanov females were being kept in Perm, but also that: "one of the daughters ran away from the quarters and then was captured in the lower Kurya, was beaten up there, and then escorted to the Perm Cheka, where she stayed for about three days under the guard of the Communist Baranova."

This phase of the escape attempt was also corroborated by Natalya Mutnykh, the witness who said she had actually seen the Romanov females when she went to Obvinskaya Street; her source was again her brother, who was secretary to Beloborodov and the officials of the Soviet: "The fugitive grand duchess was captured on the other side of the River Kama, badly beaten by Red Army men, and brought to the Cheka where she lay on a sofa behind a screen in the office of Malkov. Her bed was guarded by Iraida Yurganova-Baranova." This female Bolshevik, Yurganova, was almost certainly the "spy" who stayed in the room while Dr Utkin examined his mysterious patient. Kirsta traced one of her friends, a telegraph operator called Klavdiya Shilova, and her description of Yurganova tallies with that of the doctor: "blonde, a little more than average height, looks like a cop, staccato way of talking, peremptory. She lived in Perm . . ." Shilova also stated: "My friend Iraida Yurganova . . . stated that on the other side of the Kama they had captured a daughter of the former tsar who had been hiding there disguised as a nurse . . . Yurganova said she was caught by the Bolshevik militia." Although second-hand, this testimony is significant because it shows a *Communist* official corroborating the story of the escaping grand duchess.

The outstanding question today is of course—what became of "Anastasia" after she had been treated by Dr Utkin? We lose track of her as an individual from the moment the Communist official told Dr Utkin: "The sick woman is no longer in need of your assistance." Some may take that as sinister, suggesting the girl had been finished off—and there were very vague rumours in Perm that the mysterious prisoner was eventually killed. But these were nothing more than hearsay, and sound more like a deliberate Communist obfuscation.[44] If the presence of the Romanovs in Perm had been kept secret until September 1918, the Anastasia escape must have come close to blowing it. It quickly became the subject of much gossip, and the Bolsheviks may have tried to deter the inquisitive by letting it be known that whoever the mystery girl had been, she was now dead. But if the fugitive was really Anastasia, it seems most likely that in September 1918—with negotiations over the Romanovs' lives still going on between Berlin and Moscow—her life would have been spared. Whether or not she was reunited with her family, all would now have been kept under much tighter security than before.

Certainly both Natalya Mutnykh and Yevgeniya Sokolova refer to a change of prison and tightened guard arrangements. They also told Kirsta what he needed to know next—how and when the family left Perm, and where they were initially taken.

According to Mutnykh the family were moved "to a convent under more strict arrest" after the escape attempt. They were held there, still in Perm, until the end of November 1918:

When they [the Bolsheviks] began to evacuate the larger institutions from Perm, about three weeks before the occupation of Perm by the Siberian forces, the imperial family was taken to Perm II station, and from there to Glazov. They were all placed in a village near Red Army barracks, less than 10–13 miles from Glazov; they were accompanied and guarded there by Alexander Sivkov, Rafael Malyshev and Georgy Tolmachev, and soldiers. From the village near Glazov they were taken towards Kazan by these same three men.

Yevgeniya Sokolova, the teacher, quoting Bolshevik contacts, supplied the CID with almost exactly the same story:

Then when the family of the former sovereign was taken from Perm, one of the Communists whose family lives here in Perm accompanied them to the station. I know from the same sources that the family of the former sovereign, that is the tsarina and three daughters, were evacuated from Perm to Glazov to a remote village, and from there through Moscow to Kazan . . . The Communists guarded the family tightly in Glazov, because it feared attacks by Red army men who had more than once abused the family.

This witness refers to only *three* daughters, because, like Mutnykh, she was one of those who believed Anastasia had died after her escape attempt. Her route for the imperial family squares with Mutnykh's as far as the remote village near Glazov, but then—as it stands in the dossier—makes little sense. A glance at the map (*below*) shows that nobody would travel from Glazov to Kazan through Moscow, because Kazan sits between Glazov and the capital. It is reasonable to guess that this is a misprint by Kirsta's secretary, who should have

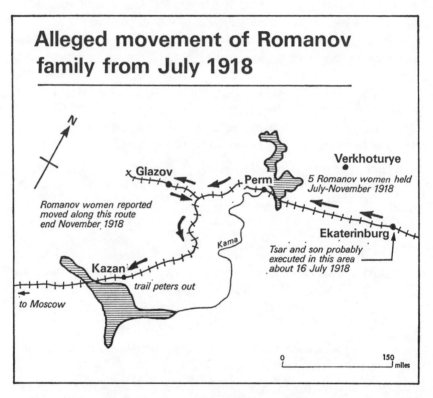

Alleged movement of Romanov family from July 1918

Verkhoturye
5 Romanov women held July-November 1918

x Glazov
Perm

Romanov women reported moved along this route end November 1918

Kama

Ekaterinburg

Tsar and son probably executed in this area about 16 July 1918

Kazan

trail peters out

to Moscow

0   150
              miles

written "through Kazan to Moscow". Moscow was, after all, a plausible destination for the tsarina and her children, if the Kremlin was still pulling the strings.

A third and important witness talked about the Romanovs' travels after Perm, and confirmed the first part of the route. This was Mikhail Solovyov, a Bolshevik prisoner-of-war who had been picked up doing undercover work behind White lines. He is important because he appeared quite independently of the other witnesses, and while on a mission for none other than Beloborodov, the chairman of the Ural Soviet who had been in charge of the Romanovs at Ekaterinburg. Solovyov testified at Perm:

> I offer my services to acquaint you with the work of the Communists, and their hiding-places. Separately from that I ask you to accept my services in the search for the family of the former tsar, since I as a Communist know very well that the former tsar was killed at Ekaterinburg. I cannot say what happened to the heir, the tsarevich. As for the tsarina and the four daughters, I know very well that they were taken through Alapayevsk to Perm, lived here, and then, before the evacuation of Perm, were taken from Perm towards Vyatka. I do not know where they are now, but will make an effort to find out and tell you. My testimony is the truth, and I am aware that if I am lying I will be punished. I want to help, and I will help you in this matter. I swear to fulfil the responsible and important work given to me.

Solovyov's testimony squares with Mutnykh and Sokolova about the departure from Perm. He said he knew the family had been taken "towards Vyatka" [since renamed Kirov], which was indeed on the same rail-route as Glazov, the first stop mentioned by the two female witnesses. Unlike them, however, Solovyov suggests that the tsarina and all four of her daughters left Perm alive. This would support our hypothesis that the Bolsheviks behaved logically, and kept Anastasia alive in spite of the escape bid. But the greatest value of Solovyov's testimony is that his knowledge, gleaned at a time he was in contact with Chairman Beloborodov, postdates the Romanovs' stay at Perm. The witness had been in Bolshevik-held territory well after the fall of Perm to the Whites, and his story, if true, confirms the continued survival of the imperial family into the early months of 1919.

Could all this new evidence reflect a complex attempt by the Bolsheviks to suggest the Romanov women were alive, when in fact they had all been killed at Ekaterinburg? The motive would presumably have been to hoodwink German intelligence in Perm, and thus bolster the diplomatic assurances they were giving in Moscow. But since witnesses actually saw a group they "recognized" as the imperial family, we would have to accept that the Bolsheviks went so far as to use actors as understudies for the missing Romanovs, and kept them locked up for many weeks just to create the necessary illusion. That seems most improbable and in any case the timing of the Perm episode, and the date the evidence came out, rules out any such deception theory. From October onwards, at the very latest, Germany ceased to be a military threat to the Bolsheviks or anyone else. The war ended altogether in November. Yet the evidence collected at Perm covers the Romanovs' travels up to and after the fall of Perm to the Whites as late as Christmas 1918; some of the testimony was still turning up in June *1919*, a year after the family vanished from Ekaterinburg.

In other words, the evidence of survival at and after Perm covers a period when the Bolsheviks no longer had a motive for deceiving anybody.

By 7 April 1919 Alexander Kirsta, who had done most of the vital detective work, was convinced he had effectively broken the case. He reported to General Gaida: "I have carried out Your Excellency's order concerning the enquiries into the case of the imperial family, according to the facts available in Perm; and now as far as Perm is concerned there remain some details and a few facts to check to complete the picture as reconstructed by me."

Kirsta was eager to follow through, but pointed out that until now he had been working with scant facilities and man-power, often in his own free time. He now requested more official support, and submitted proposals for the next stage of the search for the Romanovs. Knowing that the family's route was Vyatka-Kazan-Moscow, he suggested his investigators should move ahead as fast as possible, travelling with the advancing White forces. Two detectives would remain in each town captured in the advance, to do further undercover work under the umbrella of Military Control. They would report to Kirsta, who asked for the formation of a central investigation unit drawn from the Siberian Army general staff, and working under the supervision of Perm district prosecutor, Tikhomirov. Kirsta also hoped to gather fresh information, by sending agents in advance of the army, behind Communist lines. What Kirsta could not foresee was a development that meant the beginning of the end for White hopes in the civil war, and with it the last chance of a successful conclusion to the Romanov investigation.

It is doubtful whether Kirsta's boss, General Gaida, ever took any on-going decisions about the enquiry he had started at Perm. He probably received Kirsta's memorandum late, if at all, because in April, ironically enough, he was busy capturing Glazov, one of the towns Kirsta so badly wanted to investigate. But it was one of the last White victories in that part of Russia; from now on the military campaign in the Urals gradually lost impetus and then turned into defeat. Territory won during the past year was lost once again to the Bolsheviks, who had regrouped and been reinforced. In June 1919 the Whites lost Perm itself, an event which coincided with the climax of a long-simmering row over military tactics between Gaida and the White leader, Admiral Kolchak. Within a month of this Gaida was dismissed as White commander-in-chief in the Urals, and departed fuming for the Far East. By a perverse twist of fate, it was General Diterikhs who replaced Gaida as commander in the Urals. Diterikhs had already, for months, been doing all he could to put an end to any enquiries into the Romanov case except those of his appointee, Sokolov. He had banned CID enquiries and ordered Military Control to hand over their dossiers to Sokolov. In the face of all this, it is hardly surprising that the independent investigation now disintegrated; and in any case time was running out for any further work at all. In the chaos of defeat, Sokolov did not, conceivably could not, follow up the Perm leads himself.

But, in spite of Diterikhs's ban, we know Alexander Kirsta obstinately went on working, virtually alone, to the bitter end. In June 1919, just four days before the fall of Perm, he was still there recruiting undercover agents. We do not know what happened to him after that, nor do we know the fate of his colleague, Colonel Nikiforov. Kirsta, the man who made the breakthrough in the Romanov enquiry, vanishes, leaving behind the files that had to wait 57 years to see the light of day. On 14 July, as the White retreat became a shambles, even Ekaterinburg passed back into Communist hands, almost a year to the day since the disappearance of the imperial family.

It is a final irony that we only have the Perm evidence thanks to the veto put on CID work by General Diterikhs. Because the army had been ordered to hand over their files to Sokolov, at least some of their evidence ended up in the official dossier. We can only guess why Sokolov chose to ignore such crucial material—and none of the possible reasons is defensible. One was that it had all been collected by rival investigators, working apart from Sokolov and commanded by General Gaida, a foreigner who was on the worst possible terms with Sokolov's mentor, Diterikhs, and his ultimate boss, Admiral Kolchak. Once in exile, surrounded by people like Robert Wilton, harbouring their own sweeping prejudices, the investigator stuck rigidly to his original task, which had been all along to establish the martyrdom of the entire imperial family at Ekaterinburg. The Perm testimony did not fit that premise. So although it deserved as much thought, attention and space as anything else in the Romanov dossier, it was unceremoniously dumped.

Later, General Diterikhs poured blanket scorn on the CID in general, scoffing at them for following leads that suggested the tsar alone had been killed at Ekaterinburg. He also expressed disapproval of Kirsta, alleging that in 1918, at Ekaterinburg, the investigator had been briefly suspended from his work for unspecified reasons "unconnected with the imperial case". He acknowledges, though, that Kirsta prospered under General Gaida, and showed that he knew about the Perm evidence, while making no attempt to refute it. He simply implies that since it was the result of CID work, and not Sokolov's, it could not possibly be valid.

Kirsta also struck a raw nerve in a Communist, Pavel Bykov, the man who produced the Soviet account of the Ekaterinburg massacre by plagiarizing the Sokolov version. Bykov's reference to Kirsta was itself a comment on his own standards, for it was totally inaccurate: ". . . Particularly dear to monarchist hearts was the version supported by Kirsta, that the whole family had escaped from Ekaterinburg disguised as aviators, and that the Bolsheviks had executed other persons in their place . . ." There are four lies in that one sentence. Kirsta's investigation was not at all dear to monarchist hearts, he did not claim the family had escaped from Ekaterinburg, and nowhere in his reports does he speak of aviator disguises or substitute victims. In fact Kirsta earned a distinction few military men could claim during the Romanov enquiry, the formal approval and respect of the civilian judiciary in his area.

Tikhomirov, prosecutor of the Perm District Court, was present at the interrogation of many of Kirsta's witnesses. On 2 April 1919 he put this statement, a tribute to Kirsta, on record:

Having constantly observed the enquiries being carried out by Alexander Kirsta into the case of the imperial family, and being advised continually by him of all details of the research and testimony gathered in his own free time, I find that the method and means of the investigation used by A. F. Kirsta are absolutely correct, and have already—in spite of less than adequate means—yielded positive and incontestable results: the testimony, the material evidence such as the couch, the prescription and the napkins. I therefore suggest it is absolutely vital to allow A. F. Kirsta to carry out the plan worked out by him for the investigation, and to finish the research he has started; and for my part, I declare myself more than ready to continue working on this case with A. F. Kirsta—until completion and the arrest of all guilty parties.

That, of course, never happened, and one is now left with the great new mystery: what happened to the tsarina and her daughters after their trail petered out along the rail route to Moscow? All the signs are sinister.

In September 1918, after the weeks of negotiation with the Germans over the lives of the family, the Bolsheviks suddenly changed their tune. On the fifteenth, the German consulate in Moscow reported:

Yesterday and the day before yesterday I again brought up with Chicherin and Radek the matter of the imperial family, and was informed that, upon enquiry, a report was received from the front to the effect that those Red forces which had custody of the tsarina and all of the children following the Bolshevik evacuation from Ekaterinburg were cut off from the troops reporting, so that their whereabouts are unknown. Radek conjectures that the Red Guards and their captives were scattered to places as yet unknown . . .

Five days later, in Berlin, the Bolshevik ambassador, Joffe, repeated to the German Foreign Office the highly improbable story that Moscow had, quite literally, lost the imperial family; he added airily that they might have escaped.[45] In mid-October the Germans did release the imprisoned revolutionary leader, Karl Liebknecht, but there is no further evidence that this was linked to a deal over the Romanovs. There were, briefly, press reports that the tsarina and the children were on their way to exile in Spain, following a deal between Moscow and Berlin; such reports were never substantiated. Effectively, the imperial family now vanished, for ever, from the official record.

Moscow's story about having lost track of the family was of course sheer evasiveness—the Perm testimony, and independent German intelligence reports, show them alive in Bolshevik hands for months afterwards. But the date of Moscow's vagueness—mid-September—is significant. This was the time that it was becoming quite clear that Germany was losing the war. Lenin could afford to start obfuscating about his imperial pawns. As the Kaiser's armies stumbled to defeat, Germany was sliding into a revolution of its own. By November, Kaiser Wilhelm himself was forced into abdication and exile.

If in July 1918 the Romanov family were hostages to German fortune, then their hope of survival dwindled daily from the moment they arrived at Perm. All the odds were now against them. The Russian civil war was at its most savage, and the Red Terror had begun in earnest; nobody connected with the old regime was safe from the Cheka execution squads. At the end of January 1919 four Romanov grand dukes were taken from their cells in the fortress at St Petersburg and shot. The timing of this event is close to the date when the tsarina and her daughters are last reported to have been seen alive. We can guess that the Romanov pawns had become redundant, and that Lenin now washed his hands of them. Moscow either ordered their elimination, or simply left the imperial women to their fate.

Even without the slightest clue as to the circumstances of that fate, we are faced with nothing like the grim finality of the traditional massacre in the cellar. We cannot conclude that all definitely died, for we have no proof. The evidence suggests one daughter made her escape, however brief, during the Perm period. It is feasible that events repeated themselves during the journey to Moscow, and someone may have survived. If we allow for the possibility that, after her first escape, the injured Anastasia was moved separately from the rest of her family, it is conceivable that Anastasia was such a survivor.

Today, the official Soviet line is either to say nothing, or simply to acknowledge the Ekaterinburg massacre. Moscow has good reason to suppress information that most of the imperial family left Ekaterinburg alive. As far as the outside world is concerned, there is no point in revealing that the family did not die at Ekaterinburg if they were in fact slaughtered somewhere else later on. Internally it would never have been acceptable to admit that Lenin temporarily preserved the German-born tsarina and her daughters as part of a devious negotiation with the hated Germans. Even after a second world war, with Soviet paranoia about Germany now part of a fixed foreign policy, the motive to keep the secret remains.

In Germany after 1918 men like the Kaiser and the tsarina's brother, the Grand Duke of Hesse, stood only to lose by revealing their role in the events of Ekaterinburg. Both men dreamed, however unrealistically, of being restored to their former positions. There was nothing to gain by revealing the details of a plan to extricate the tsar not just for humanitarian reasons, but as part of a deal which included proposals that the tsar should collaborate in German political schemes. Nicholas, faithful to the Allied cause, had rejected their advances, and the plan had fallen through. Berlin had then humiliatingly failed to obtain the release of the tsarina and the children; in a heartless diplomatic game the Germans had been soundly trounced by Lenin. For the Whites, pathetic and dispossessed in exile, the "massacre" at Ekaterinburg seemed to provide one tangible inheritance of a disastrous reign—a Romanov martyrdom, of epic proportions, at the hands of the Reds. The orthodox version of the fate of the imperial family had become mutually acceptable to all sides. It remains today a symbol, a historical punctuation mark which nobody wishes to change.

Perhaps General Gaida, the man who ordered the Perm enquiry, came closest to summarizing the stalemate in which the Romanov case really ended. Years later he wrote of the Sokolov investigation: "I emphasize that . . . the results of the enquiry were, on the whole, superficial. Not one fact was cleared up with certainty, and all the published reports are based largely on speculation . . . The future may explain this tragedy better." We are now living in the future Gaida foresaw. It has indeed produced a few answers, but they in turn provoke fresh riddles and new questions.

Grand Duke Andrei, the tsar's jurist cousin who conducted his own searching enquiry into the Anastasia case, placed an intriguing restriction on his vast dossier. Before he died in 1956, he stipulated that his Romanov file be kept secret, "until the public release of documents of the German general staff, documents the Kaiser had, and documents in the Kremlin". Access to the Kremlin archives remains a researcher's dream. The answer must be in there somewhere—a few paragraphs perhaps, filed amongst the rewritings of Soviet history, unaltered by the army of weeders and cosmetic historians who have refurbished the darker corners of Soviet affairs since 1917. There may even be a handful of aged contemporaries, ancient revolutionaries still alive, who could yet tell sad stories of the death of kings.

If the remaining facts ever do emerge, they may reveal something less melodramatic than the death in the cellar, and less exotic than survival. Until then, the truth about the Romanovs remains a casualty of history.

And the file on the tsar stays open.

NOTES

BIBLIOGRAPHY

INDEX

SOURCES AND NOTES

For brevity main source books herein are referred to under the authors' names. Full details of these will be found in the bibliography.

Chapter 1

Page 31   Evening of murder—Papers of Arthur Thomas, McCullagh, p. 129, and BBC interview with Sir Thomas Preston 1971
Buivid testimony—Sokolov, Russian edition, chapter 23

Page 40   30 April 1918—This book refers throughout to dates by Gregorian reckoning. Until the Revolution, Russia still used the Julian calendar, which was 13 days behind the Gregorian.

Chapter 2

Page 41   Receipt for Romanovs—Sokolov, Russian edition, illustration no. 13

Page 43   Yakimov testimony—Sokolov papers, Houghton Library, Harvard University, Vol. IV, document 18 [by permission of Harvard College Library]
Alexei description—V. Alexandrov, p. 217

Page 44   Chemodurov testimony—Houghton Vol. I, document 23
Servants' account of life—Prince Lvov statement: Sokolov, French edition, chapter 13

Page 45   Doggerel—Houghton Vol. III, document 27

Page 46   Preston intervention—BBC interview 1971
Storozhev testimony—Houghton Vol. I document 42

Page 47   Telegram 4558—Houghton Vol. I, document 30
Yurovsky description—Houghton Vol. I document 81

Chapter 3

Page 52   Nuns' testimony—Sokolov, French edition, chapter 23
Guards' description—Yakimov testimony: Houghton, Vol. IV, document 18

Page 53   Sverdlov's statement—Sokolov, Russian edition, chapter 25

Page 54   Telegram 339—PRO document FO 371/3335
Moscow/Ekaterinburg conversation—Sokolov, Russian edition, chapter 25

Page 55   Fyodor Ivanov testimony—Houghton Vol. I, document 39

Page 56   Tsar's execution notice—*The Times*, 1920, special Romanov series (article 10)
            Women question soldiers at Ipatiev House—Mirolyubov report; enclosure in Foreign Office report 12/12/18; PRO/FO 371/3977

Chapter 4   No sources or notes

Chapter 5

Page 65   Peasants' testimony—Sokolov, Russian edition, chapter 20

Page 67   Gorshkov testimony—Houghton Vol. I, document I
            Nametkin inventory—Sokolov, French edition, chapter 16

Page 69   Malinovsky testimony—Houghton Vol. V, document 9

Page 70   Nametkin's death—Letter from Ostroumov, former Ekaterinburg assistant prosecutor, to Princess Xenia Georgievna of Russia, 1928

Page 71   Secret reports—Botkin, Gleb, *The Real Romanovs*, p. 224

Page 72   Mirolyubov report (as above—source to p. 56)

Page 77   Dr Derevenko's identification of finger—Magnitsky testimony: Houghton Vol. I, document 77

Page 78   Value of jewels carried—Trewin/Gibbes, p. 64

Page 79   Agafonova testimony (Yakimov's sister)—6 December 1918, Houghton Vol. I, document 73
            CID Reports—Houghton Vol. I, document 60; Vol. I document 39 *et alia*

Chapter 6

Page 80   Captain Voitkevich's information—Reports from Archangel to Foreign Office received 29 August 1918 PRO/FO 371/3325
            Military intelligence message—PRO/FO 800/205

Page 81   Summary of military intelligence message sent to Windsor Castle, 31 August 1918—Broadlands Archives
            Letter from George V to Marchioness of Milford Haven 1 September 1918—Broadlands Archives

Page 82   Report from Thomas Preston passed to Foreign Office via Vladivostok, 16 September 1918—Broadlands Archives

Page 84   Summary of Sir Charles Eliot's report—Telegram
             142, Vladivostok to Foreign Office received 10
             October 1918: PRO/FO 371/3335
             Full report from Sir Charles Eliot to Balfour,
             reached London January 1919—PRO/FO 371/3977
Page 86   *Murder of other Romanovs referred to by Eliot:*
  Note 1   At Alapayevsk, a hundred miles to the north,
             Sergeyev found the bodies of several Romanov
             relatives including Grand Duchess Elisabeth, Grand
             Duke Sergei Mikhailovich, three sons of Grand
             Duke Konstantin, and a son of Grand Duke Pavel.
             Their bodies were intact at the bottom of a mine-
             shaft and forensic evidence showed that most of
             them had been thrown in alive. These murders are
             known to have happened the night after the dis-
             appearance of the Romanovs from Ekaterinburg,
             so it is often suggested that because they happened
             at the same time, the Alapayevsk murders are
             further indication of what happened in the Ipatiev
             House. The crucial difference was that while
             Alapayevsk produced *prima facie* evidence—actual
             bodies—at Ekaterinburg there were no corpses, and
             only an assumption of death.
Page 87   Rodzyanko account—Report of Director of Intelli-
             gence, Scotland House, London, 11 June 1920:
             PRO/FO 371/3977
Page 88   Sokolov on Sergeyev's attitude—Sokolov, French
             edition, chapter 16
Page 89   Bernstein article—*New York Times Book Review and
             Magazine* 5 September 1920

Chapter 7

Page 90   Ostroumov complaint—Letter from Ostroumov to
             Princess Xenia Georgievna of Russia 1928
             Starynkevich complaint to General Diterikhs—
             document dated 31 January 1919, in Sokolov papers,
             traced in Paris
Page 91   Tatishchev substitution story—*New York Times* 28
             December 1918. Also British Wireless Service—
             New York Times 9 January 1919
Page 92   Boyle—*New York Times* 4 February 1919, and docu-
             ments provided by Boyle's daughter

Page 92 Dowager Empress's belief in son's survival, Crimea—Report British C-in-C Mediterranean to Admiralty, 23 November 1918 PRO/ADM 137/953
Malta—recollections by Captain R. Ingham; BBC interview 1971 and *What Happened to the Empress* by Robert Ingham (booklet)

Note 2 *Dowager Empress's Attitude to Disappearance of Imperial Family:*
Empress Marie persisted in her refusal to accept the death of the Romanovs right up to her death in 1928. Historians have usually interpreted this as the pathetic faith of a deranged old lady. Yet it is wrong to suggest Marie was unbalanced. The present Romanov Pretender, Grand Duke Vladimir, told the BBC in 1971 that Marie had died perfectly sane. Other sources confirm this, and there is one, unpublished, anecdote which puts her attitude in perspective. Prince Frederick of Saxe Altenburg told us how in 1924 he asked Empress Marie's brother, Prince Valdemar of Denmark, about it, and Valdemar replied: "Because of her position in the family, it is safe to say that all reports reach her sooner or later; and until two reports tally, she refuses to accept any as final." This seems a reasonable judgement, even today.
Page report to Washington—4 December 1918, US National Archives, Dept of State, Group 59, 861.00/3353
Mrs Page letter to daughter—5 December 1918, Nelson Page Papers, Earl Gregg Swem Library, College of William and Mary, Virginia, USA
US Embassy, London, report of Foreign Office attitude to Secretary of State, Washington—12 December 1918, US National Archives, Dept of State, Group 59, 861.00/3405

Page 93 Prince Lvov's statements—*La Tragédie Sibérienne*, by J. Lasies: Edition Française Illustrée, Paris 1920

Page 95 French report 5 December 1918—French Foreign Ministry document circulated by Commissariat Général des Affaires de Guerre Franco-Américaines
Janin report 29 January 1919—Foreign Ministry document no. 500/507

Page 96
Note 3

Kolchak's attitude:

After approving the appointment of Sokolov, Kolchak appears to have lost interest when the case became politically inconvenient. Diterikhs notes in April 1919 that, because the Admiral was wooing the socialists, "elucidation of the picture and circumstances of the assassination was absolutely unwelcome to him". It was right-winger Diterikhs who controlled the case from the moment it was entrusted to him. (Secret Order 111 April 10 1919—from Sokolov documents found in Paris.)

Chapter 8

Page 101

Sokolov foreword to interim report—Bulygin, p. 155

Page 103

Knox protest about Wilton and other correspondence by or about Wilton—*The Times* archives.

Knightley on Wilton; Knightley, *The First Casualty*. Deutsch, 1975, p. 162

Page 105

Sokolov conversation with Gilliard—Gilliard, *Le Tragique Destin,* p. 234

Chapter 9

Page 106
Note 4

Sokolov Sources:

To analyse Sokolov's conclusions we have drawn on his published work *Judicial Enquiry into the Assassination of the Russian Imperial Family* using the French and Russian language editions (see bibliography). We have also drawn on the 7 volumes of written evidence representing Sokolov's dossier until he left Russia in 1920. (Houghton Library, Harvard University.) Fuller copies of the dossier, including testimony gathered in exile, are filed at the Henry Ford Museum, Dearborn, Michigan.

A further valuable source of information has been the papers of Nikander Mirolyubov, one-time Prosecutor of the Kazan Court of Assize; these include a series of letters from Prosecutor Jordansky, appointed by Mirolyubov to keep a watching brief on the investigation. (Mirolyubov Papers, Hoover Institution on War, Revolution and Peace, Stanford University, California.)

We have also studied Sokolov's interim report for the Dowager Empress Marie (available in translation in the Harris Papers, Hoover Institution) and Soko-

Page 106   lov's short report sent to Mr Bannon, a British government official, in 1920 (PRO/FO 371/3977 Pt. II).

Tatiana's dog "Jemmy":

Note 5   Jemmy has generally been referred to in Romanov literature as Anastasia's pet. But the empress's confidante, Anna Vyrubova, makes it clear in her memoirs that the dog was in fact a gift from herself to the tsar's second daughter, Tatiana (Vyrubova, p. 53/4).

Page 112   Telegram handed over to Sergeyev 20 January 1919—Houghton, Vol. I, document 88

Telegram sent to Zlobin—Houghton, Vol. II, document 43

Telegram sent to Kulkov—Houghton, Vol. II, document 52

Page 114   Order to Sergeyev to transfer evidence 23 January 1919—Houghton, Vol. I, document 85

Chapter 10

Page 118   Medvedev testimony to Sergeyev—Houghton, Vol. II, document 86

Medvedev testimony to Alexeyev—Houghton, Vol. II, document 81

Page 122   Letemin testimony—Houghton, Vol. I, document 44

Proskuryakov testimony—Sokolov, Russian edition, chapter 23

Page 123   Yakimov testimony to Sokolov—Sokolov, Russian edition, chapter 23

Note 6   *Selected Discrepancies in Testimony:*

Last Words: Letemin says Yurovsky told the tsar, "Your life is finished". Proskuryakov said the tsar queried Yurovsky, saying "What?", to which Yurovsky replied, "Here's what!" and shot him. According to Yakimov, Yurovsky said, "Nicholas Alexandrovich, your relatives have tried to save you, but they did not succeed. And we ourselves must shoot you!" Medvedev's wife claimed he told her Yurovsky said, "The revolution is dying, and now you must die too!"

Confusion about the timetable of the night's events:
This is additionally complicated because the Bolsheviks had just advanced the clock two hours; witnesses often speak in terms of the old clock, and

then add the "new style" version as an afterthought. Even so, allowing for confusion, the testimony varies noticeably. Medvedev says the Romanovs were roused at midnight, while Yakimov is clear that it was after 2 am. This is an odd discrepancy, from witnesses whose stories were so detailed; whereas people might well be confused about the exact time of events during the early hours, they can usually distinguish between the small hours and the relatively reasonable hour of midnight. Similarly, Medvedev in a second version of his testimony said: "At 3 am everything was over", referring to the clean-up. Proskuryakov says he was not woken until 3 am to start the clean-up and specifies that a colleague checked the time on his watch. Sokolov quotes a neighbour and nightwatchman just across the street from the Ipatiev House; they said they were awake, and heard a truck departing not later than 3 am and possibly quite a while before. Now Medvedev says he called the guards, including Proskuryakov, to help carry out the bodies; but if we accept the firm evidence of the watch, then the bodies were still in the house *after* the truck had gone off down the road, and that does not make any sense.

Yakimov's remarkable memory: He specified: "In the centre of the room stood the tsar, the tsarevich on his right, seated on a chair, and to the right of the tsarevich stood Doctor Botkin. All three . . . were facing the door which led from the room . . . Behind them stood the tsarina with her daughters . . . On one side of the tsarina and her daughters, in the corner, stood the cook and the servant, and on the other side of them, also in a corner, stood Demidova . . ." and so on. Sokolov omits this part of Yakimov's evidence, given in May 1919, ten months after the events described.

The small print of the testimony contains its own unsatisfactory oddities. Medvedev denied he was actually in the murder room at the time of the shooting, claiming that he was sent outside to "listen whether the shots can be heard or not".

(A goonish chore this, as it would have been too late to make any difference.) But Medvedev's wife said Medvedev confided to her that he had actually taken part in the shooting. Similarly, Proskuryakov changed his testimony five times before giving his final statement. Perhaps both lied to save their skins, but where did the lying begin and end?

Medvedev speaks of his appointment to the guard of the Ipatiev House in mid-May, and tells how on the twenty-fourth "the former tsar with his family arrived". But the tsar had actually arrived at the end of April, and without most of the children! Similarly, Sokolov uses the testimony of another guard, Suetin, who joined the guard in April, stayed for just three days, and described seeing the entire family walking in the garden. Sokolov has Suetin describing all four daughters, and Alexei being carried by the doctor, but he could not have seen them, because he left the guard nearly three weeks *before* the arrival of the children. Medvedev speaks of calling ten men from the guardhouse to help clear up, and Proskuryakov says categorically that *all the guards* were roused to help in the operation. His exact words are "All the guards except those on guard duty"; but Yakimov contradicts this, stating that he and a considerable number of comrades slept until 4 a m when they were assembled to be told the murder story, but not asked to work on the clean-up at all.

Yakimov twice says the bodies were dragged out of the house wrapped up in white sheets, while Medvedev says stretchers were constructed using the shafts of two sledges as handles. This seems improbable—it would have taken a considerable time to produce such makeshift stretchers.

Page 124 Medvedev capture according to Alexeyev— Houghton, Vol. II document 81

Page 126 Description of interrogation by Sergeyev—letter from Ostroumov to Princess Xenia Georgievna of Russia in 1928

Diterikhs on Medvedev heart attack—*New York Times*, 1 August 1920

Page 127 Lasies on Medvedev death—Lasies, *op. cit.* p. 107

Page 127 Jordansky on Medvedev death—undated letter of
      late March 1919, Mirolyubov Papers, Hoover
      Institution on War, Revolution and Peace

Page 128 Sokolov states, in the Russian edition of his book,
Note 7   that other business deprived him "of the possibility
      of interrogating Medvedev myself. I found him ill
      with typhus." Would illness really have prevented
      him talking to such a key witness? Perhaps, in the
      light of everything else, the question is academic.
      Slaughter on Medvedev—quoted from lecture notes
      preserved by the Slaughter family

Page 129 *Witnesses:* An alternative theory has it that the
Note 8   captured guards, including Medvedev, were Bol-
      shevik stooges rather than White plants. Like
      Medvedev, Proskuryakov and Yakimov also de-
      fected. (Yakimov also allegedly died of illness—
      pneumonia, says the death certificate). Letemin
      turned up just when Sergeyev had been advertising
      for witnesses. John O'Conor (see bibliography)
      finds all this suspect. He notes that Medvedev and
      Letemin were Bolshevik party members, and that
      the first version of Sokolov quotes Yakimov too as
      styling himself as a Bolshevik. O'Conor suspects
      testimony was contrived by the Bolsheviks to fool
      the Whites, and to distract them from looking for
      the Romanov survivors. But the trick did not at
      first come off. Six months later the Whites were
      still looking for surviving Romanovs, so Medvedev
      and Yakimov were ordered to present themselves
      and tell their murder story, saving their own necks if
      possible by denying that they themselves were in-
      volved in the actual murders. It is an interesting
      scenario, although one wonders what inducement
      would make witnesses come forward to risk their
      lives in this way. But there is evidence that the
      Bolsheviks did go out of their way to spread false
      stories about the massacre. A Red soldier, Prokopy
      Kukhtenkov, had been manager of the Verkh-
      Isetsk Workmen's Club, and gave evidence
      (Houghton, Vol. 1, docs 51 & 59) of a curious visit
      in the morning of 18 July 1918, by a group of six
      leading Bolsheviks, including Commissar Yermakov.

Kukhtenkov said he heard the Communists speak of burying, exhuming and reburying the imperial victims. His account of the conversation reads like a bad film script:

Levatnikh:	When we came they were still warm, I myself felt the empress and she was warm . . . Now it is not a sin to die, for I have felt the Empress . . .
Krivtsov:	How were they dressed?
Partin:	Oh, they were all dressed in civilian clothes, and in their dresses were sewn jewels and diamonds . . . they were all in trousers.
Kostousov:	How many did you say there were?
Levatnikh:	I told you before that there were thirteen. The doctor was the thirteenth.
Yermakov:	Were they pretty?
Partin:	There was not a pretty face among them.
Unidentified Voice:	You cannot find beauty in the dead . . .

The conversation ended with everyone bursting out laughing.

One of the speakers included Anna Vyrubova amongst the victims. But of course there are supposed to have been eleven murder victims, not thirteen; there is no respectable evidence that the family were ever buried, and Anna Vyrubova, the close friend of the tsarina, was at the time hundreds of miles away. She survived and escaped to Finland in 1920. Commissar Yermakov had seen the family frequently and knew very well whether the girls were pretty. Either Kukhtenkov was primed to spread this nonsense, or was fooled into doing so—was it a first crude effort to disseminate a story that later deceived Sokolov and ultimately the world?

Chapter 11

Page 132   Varakushev story—Samoilov testimony: Houghton, Vol. I, document 39

Varakushev's girlfriend—Kotova testimony: Houghton, Vol. I, document 39

Lacher evidence—Hamburg (Vol. XXIX) Court transcript, Lacher, p. 48; hearings of 17/18 January 1966

Page 133   Sakovich testimony—Houghton, August 1918

Page 134   Death of Yurovsky—Diterikhs (*op. cit.*)

Yurovsky's career—McCullagh, p. 142

Major Sipek—Article in *New York Times Magazine*, 6 April 1919

Note 9   *Goloshchokin after Ekaterinburg:*

Goloshchokin survived, and was in Perm in the late winter of 1918. He went on to become an important Soviet administrator, until purged by Stalin. He is now said to have died in 1941.

Chapter 12

Page 137   Sokolov report to British Government—sent from Paris 15 November 1920 to Foreign Office official Bannon, PRO/FO 371/3977 Part II

Page 139   *Fuller List of Objects at the Mineshaft:*

Note 10   *Jewels:*

A cross of precious stones—emeralds, brilliants, and pearls, set in platinum. Damaged by fire. Had belonged to the tsarina.

A brilliant—again set in platinum, and damaged by fire. Identified as part of a pendant, again belonging to the empress.

An earring—pearl and brilliant set in platinum, with a gold fastening.

Parts of a pearl, and part of a broken gold ornament—smashed into splinters. Possibly the pair to the other earring.

Also fragments from another large pearl, and thirteen pearls which had been part of a string.

Part of a broken ornament—made up of brilliants set in pure silver and gold brazing.

Thirteen splinters of emerald apparently smashed with some heavy object.

Two splinters of sapphire.

Two brilliants, a ruby, two almandines, two adamants. The adamants came from a bracelet belonging to the tsarina.

Two gold safety chains from bracelets. All the
female members of the imperial family had such
bracelets.

Parts of a gold ornament, apparently part of a gold
ring.

A gold ornament with three diamonds.

Topazes.

A military badge. Said to have been on a bracelet
belonging to the empress.

Other Personal Effects:

Two matching jewelled shoe buckles—as on the
shoes of the grand duchesses and the tsarina.

Buckles, buttons and hooks and eyes—all damaged
by fire.

Buckle from an officer's belt—probably from the
tsar's belt.

Brass buckle from a boy's belt—bearing the imperial coat of arms. Identified as Alexei's.

Pieces of cloth—believed to come from Alexei's
overcoat.

Piece of khaki material—identified as part of the
tsarevich's knapsack.

Also lead foil, four nails, a used revolver bullet, and
two copper coins of two kopek denomination, believed to be Alexei's playthings.

A hairbrush and two lenses from a pince-nez—
thought to be Dr Botkin's.

Other male items—a collar button, a tieclasp,
seven men's buckles from underwear, male suspenders, a penknife, an iron plate from a bootheel,
high quality shoeleather, cork and cobblers' wax.

Various religious miniatures. A phial of salts and a
broken green phial such as the grand duchesses and
the tsarina carried when travelling.

An American suitcase key and parts of handbags.

Page 140   Doctor on bones—Belogradsky testimony—Sokolov,
Russian edition, chapter 22

Sokolov's doubt on ashes—Wilton, p. 113

Fesenko's story—Wilton, p. 113

Page 141 Leonov brothers (garage mechanics) testimony—Sokolov, Russian edition, chapter 21
Jacob Lobukhin (crossing-keeper) testimony—Sokolov, Russian edition, chapter 21

Page 142 Rednikov (forester) testimony—Sokolov, Russian edition, chapter 21
Vasily Lobukhin (crossing-keeper's son) testimony—Sokolov, Russian edition, chapter 21
Voikov order for acid—Sokolov, Russian edition, illustration no. 78
Kotenev testimony (on gasoline)—Sokolov, Russian edition, chapter 21

Chapter 13

Page 148 Sir Charles Eliot on blood—Report from Eliot to Balfour PRO/FO 371/3977
Carl Ackerman on blood—Ackerman, p. 104
Sokolov on blood—Sokolov, Russian edition, chapter 17
Captain Bulygin on blood—Bulygin, p. 239
Wilton on blood—Wilton, p. 97
General Diterikhs' reference to blood—Diterikhs, Vol. I, p. 27

Page 149 Gilliard on bullet holes (1st version)—Gilliard testimony: 5/6 March 1919: Houghton, Vol. II, document 55
Gilliard on bullet holes (2nd version)—Gilliard, *Le Tragique Destin*, p. 231
McCullagh on bullets—McCullagh, p. 138

Page 150 Letemin on state of room—Letemin testimony: Houghton, Vol. I, document 44

Page 152 Ackerman on corsets—Ackerman, p. 104
Note 11 *Confusion on where corsets were found:*
British military intelligence report (PRO/FO 800/205) refers to "corset ribs" being found at mine.

Page 153 Medvedev testimony on bracelets—Houghton, Vol. II, document 81

Page 155 Bulygin on bones—Bulygin, p. 158
Page 156 *The "Romanov" remains:*
Note 12 It is usually accepted that the relics—including the finger, bone fragments, epidermis, blood (capsules), etc., found at the Four Brothers—were brought to

Europe from the Far East in 1920 by the French General Janin, who was returning to France. (Previously, General Diterikhs had asked the British to transport the boxes, but turned to Janin when London refused.) Thus far, the story is confirmed by Janin's memoirs (*op. cit.*) and British Foreign Office files (PRO/FO 371/4047).

In France, Janin tried to give the boxes to Grand Duke Nikolai, the tsar's cousin, as Diterikhs had requested. When the grand duke refused, the boxes were taken to a Janin country home. But eventually they are said to have reached M. de Giers, doyen of the imperial Russian diplomatic corps, and in 1921 were allegedly back with Sokolov at his Paris hotel (Bulygin, p. 158). The orthodox version is that they have ever since remained in France, but this may not be so.

Lady Violet Kirkpatrick, who in 1920 worked at the British Foreign Office, has recalled an incident involving Miles Lampson, the British diplomat whom Diterikhs had initially approached in the Far East. In *The Times* (14.4.71) she wrote that in 1920, "Mr Lampson came into my room and left a leather bag with me. He returned later and told me he had a very painful thing to do. He was going straight to Marlborough House to give the box which was in the bag to Queen Alexandra, as it contained all the remains of the imperial family which were not destroyed by being burnt." Queen Alexandra's papers were destroyed on her death, and the royal archivist cannot confirm the handover. But Sir Thomas Preston says that when he was received by King George V in February 1921, the king told him the remains had reached Buckingham Palace. It seems they were not welcome there (see p. 171). Later Prince Yusupov said he had seen the relics at Buckingham Palace (BBC interview, Prince Sergei Obolensky, 1971) and as late as 1957 Prince Dmitry, the tsar's nephew, wrote that they were in Windsor Castle (*Picture Post* 11.2.67). However, Lady Violet understood the remains were destined to be given to the tsar's mother, Empress Marie, and there is evidence they were.

The empress's daughter, Olga, who accompanied Marie to Denmark, told her biographer that she "wept over the little box before it went to France, there to find its last resting place together with a few other relics in the Russian cemetery outside Paris". Enquiries at the cemetery today bring firm denials, as do enquiries at the Russian cathedral in Paris. Professor Pierre Kovalevsky says an exile group always has custody of the relics, and "whoever has them at the time simply keeps them on top of a cupboard". The man said to be in charge now, General Pozdnyshev, says only: "They are preserved in a state of inviolability". He may be referring to jewellery and ikons from Ekaterinburg, which are kept at the Russian church outside Brussels. But the location of the human remains is a mystery. The man who should know, Heir Assumptive Grand Duke Vladimir, says the box was in France till World War II, when it was removed from a Paris bank by the German Secret Service. Vladimir added: "There seems to be a mystery about what Sokolov brought back and I don't know why." (BBC interviews, 1971 and 1974.) German interest as late as World War II is fascinating, and may be linked to German bargaining with the Bolsheviks over the lives of the tsarina and her children (see chapter 23).

Page 157   Dr. Rich comment—BBC interview, 1971
Page 158   Voikov on destruction of bodies—Bessedovsky, p. 210
Yermakov on destruction of bodies—Halliburton, p. 143
Page 159   Wilton on removal of heads—Wilton, p. 146
Note 13   *The missing heads:*
The most extravagant story about the tsar's head comes from Russian monk and tall-story teller, Ilyodor. He wrote of visiting the Kremlin, "As I was walking down a dark corridor, my guide suddenly opened the door of a little hidden room. On the table, under a glass dome, was the head of Nicholas II. He had a deep wound in the left eye. I was rooted to the spot." The head had allegedly been returned to Moscow by the lover of one of the assassins, a task which drove her crazy. Eventually,

according to Ilyodor, she was shot for her pains. *cf. Essad Bey, p. 374.*

Chapter 14
Page 161   Discovery of dog according to Wilton—Wilton, p. 116
Page 162   Report of Alexander Sheremetevsky on pumping—Houghton, Vol. 5, document 5. Also report of Assistant Prosecutor Magnitsky—Houghton, Vol. I, document 77
Page 163   Dog autopsy report—Houghton, Vol. V, document 21 (see also Vol.V documents 13 and 14)
Page 165   Jordansky on corruption—Letter from Jordansky to Nikander Mirolyubov, Public Prosecutor, Kazan Court of Assize, 1919: Mirolyubov Papers, Hoover Institution on War, Revolution and Peace
Page 166   Magnitsky report on finding other bodies—Houghton, Vol. I, document 77
Page 167   Tsar and son in outdoor clothes ("soldiers' shirts")—Medvedev testimony to Judge Sergeyev 21 and 22 February 1919: Houghton, Vol. II, document 86

Chapter 15
Page 169   Sokolov's departures—Botkin, Gleb, *The Real Romanovs,* p. 229
            Sokolov quarrel with Diterikhs—Memorandum to Mirolyubov Papers by W. S. Sworakowski, Assistant Director, Hoover Institution, 15 August 1967
            Sokolov's nervousness—Botkin, Gleb, *The Real Romanovs,* p. 230
            Bulygin anecdote—Bulygin, p. 157
Page 171   British Foreign Office records and relics—PRO/FO 371/4047
            Preston and relics at Buckingham Palace—(a) letter from Preston to *Spectator*, February 1972; (b) Preston letter to British researcher, 22/7/65 (for full relics story see our note to p. 156)
Page 173   Sokolov and Henry Ford—memorandum in files, Office of American Naval Intelligence. Reg. No. 16406, 25 March 1924, Navy and Old Army Branch, Military Archives Division, US National Archives
Page 174   Orlov statement—*New York Times*, 6 February 1924
Page 176   Telegram from Denmark—Bulygin, p. 273
            Sokolov letter to Mirolyubov—letter 22 April 1922,

Page 176   Mirolyubov Papers, Hoover Institution
Sokolov letter to Bulygin—Bulygin, p. 159
Sokolov "mental patient"—Memorandum to Mirolyubov Papers by W. S. Sworakowski, Hoover Institution, 15 August 1967

Chapter 16

Page 178   *Izvestiya* report—Wilton, p. 102
Pravda report—Wilton, p. 102

Page 179   Bykov on bodies—Bykov, *The Last Days of Tsardom*,
p. 88

Page 181   Yermakov story—Halliburton, p. 101 *et seq.*
Note 14   *Yermakov interview according to Halliburton:*
The British writer, Marvin Lyons, has written that
he is absolutely convinced of its authenticity—"the
only first-hand account" of the massacre. But Halliburton's story is filled with discrepancies. Sokolov's
Medvedev, for example, quotes Yermakov as saying
explosives were used at the Four Brothers; Halliburton's Yermakov makes no mention of it. He
refers to a Bolshevik maid being shown out of the
murder room at the last moment, to save her life.
There was no such maid at the Ipatiev House. The
whole Halliburton account could have been filched
from existing sources.

Page 182   Voikov story—Bessedovsky, p. 201 *et seq.*
Bessedovsky "memoirs"—Bessedovsky exposed as
forger in series of articles in *Est et Ouest*, published
by Bulletins d'Association d'Etudes et d'Informa-
tions Politiques Internationales 14, Nos. 88, 89, 106,
121, 128, 135, 139, 141, 144, 151, 153, 154, 163,
196, 212, 253, 263

Note 15   *Voikov:*
While still ambassador to Poland, Voikov was shot
and killed by a teenage monarchist exile on Warsaw
railway station. Ironically, the boy claimed it was
revenge for the massacre of the imperial family, and
was dubbed "The Assassin's Assassin".

Chapter 17

Page 187   Wrangel anecdote—Wrangel, p. 203
Page 188   Swedish bandleader—*Svenska Dagbladet*, 28 August
1918
Obolensky—*Giornale d'Italia*, 15 March 1919

Page 189	French secret service report—5 December 1919, document 277; French Foreign Ministry, Russia 15 Serie Z Carton 608 Dossier 3
Page 190	Uspensky story—*New York Times*, 20 July 1922
	Vladivostok "sighting"—*Gazette de Lausanne*, 24 May 1920
	Tsar as "oiler"—*New York Times*, 6 June 1920
	Tsar "on Riviera"—*New York Times*, 29 September 1926
	Berlin Mass—Smirnoff, p. 242
Page 192	*Marga Boodts:*
Note 16	Mrs Boodts claims the Kaiser asked Frau von Schevenbach, the daughter of a friend, to look after her. This arrangement was interrupted by the war in 1939, and "Olga" was in penury after Frau von Schevenbach's death. After Prince Sigismund recognized her in 1957, he introduced her to the Hereditary Grand Duke of Oldenburg, a godson of the tsar. He took a keen interest and supplied Mrs Boodts with funds until his own death in 1970.
	Alexei "Sighting in Altai"—Gilliard, *Le Tragique Destin*, p. 237
Page 193	Edmond's story—Letter to the authors, 1972
Page 194	*Goleniewski:*
Note 17	Richard Deacon, authoritative author on intelligence affairs, says that before his defection, Goleniewski's information had been treated with reserve. Only after he came west was he credited with providing vital clues about double-agent Kim Philby, and Russian spy George Blake. Deacon suggests that Goleniewski may be an example of KGB disinformation techniques. His persistent claims that the CIA was infiltrated by Russian agents may be a Soviet ploy to instill alarm in enemy ranks.
	Goleniewski's claim:
	Goleniewski says rescue followed a secret deal between the Kremlin and Emperor Yoshihito of Japan. He says he was smuggled out in a trunk, and travelled to Poland with his parents and sister Maria. In Poland the whole family was re-united. The tsarina allegedly died in 1924, the tsar in 1952.
	In 1965 a man describing himself as a retired

CIA identification expert, Herman Kimsey, declared that Goleniewski was indeed the tsarevich, saying he had seen dental charts, blood specimens etc. which proved it. He referred to comparisons with Alexei's fingerprints taken in London in 1909. (Richards, *Imperial Agent*, p. 259.) Alexei did not come to London in 1909, or ever.

Page 194   Goleniewski confrontation with Mrs Smith—Guy Richards, *Imperial Agent*, pp. 253–256

Page 195   Fleming review—the *Spectator*, 20 March 1971

Note 18   *"Hunt for the Czar"*:

Richards's second Romanov work devotes much space to analysing a book published anonymously in 1920 in America—*Rescuing the Czar*. It purports to be the record kept of the "rescue" by two special agents. Richards established the author was William McGarry, who had done some work for the State Department, and hinted that McGarry knew of the rescue and left his book as an allegory for future generations to unravel. But the story McGarry tells is of comic strip quality. We checked McGarry's private archives in Florida, and they reveal that money was an important motive in the production of *Rescuing the Czar*.

Note 19   *"Romanoff File"*:

In his book, *Hunt for the Czar*, Richards's claim that there is still a secret "Romanoff File" is based largely on a 1927 embassy despatch about an Alexei impostor. (US National Archives, Dept. of State, Group 59 861.0011/14.) This document is indeed marked "Romanoff File". We investigated this, and traced the owner of the initials "RFK" on the despatch—a retired State Department official called Robert Kelley, formerly chief of the Division of Eastern European Affairs. On 26 May 1975, he wrote: "We undoubtedly had a Romanov file ... It certainly was not secret ... neither I nor anyone in my Division gave any credence to stories about 'survivors of the massacre'." The explanation of the lone document is that DEEA papers were dispersed according to geographical source in the late thirties. Officials of the National Archives confirm Kelley's explanation.

Page 196

Note 20

Parliamentary question:

Bessell asked "Why Her Majesty's Government have refused to release for research or publication, official documents relating to the assassination of Tsar Nicholas II and his family, in view of the thirty year rule policy on such papers."

The PM replied: "All the documents in the possession of Her Majesty's Government relating to the assassination of Tsar Nicholas II and his family were opened to the public with other records relating to the first world war on 10 February 1966." (Hansard, 14 May 1970.)

Bessell and Brest–Litovsk claim—*Observer* Colour Magazine, 7 March 1971

Bessell claims about Allied rescue—formal Bessell statement for press agencies, 27 April 1971

Note 21

American papers allegedly seen by Bessell:

According to Bessell, many of the documents he saw were still in code. They were messages between American agents and the 1918 Secretary of State, Lansing, and a series of notes between Lansing and the White House. The papers showed that the massacre was faked and the Romanovs removed to a safe house near Ekaterinburg by an American-Japanese force. Months later they were taken south to Odessa and put aboard a British ship. Bessell said the operation's code-name was "Chivers".

Page 197

Bessell letter to Jeremy Thorpe, MP—20 June 1972

Thorpe Parliamentary question—Hansard, 14 May 1973

Thorpe letter to Foreign Secretary—18 May 1973

Sir Alec Douglas-Home letter to Thorpe—30 May 1973

Note 22

The Hardinge letter:

This purports to show Lord Hardinge, then Permanent Under-Secretary of State at the Foreign Office, reporting to George V on the journey of the tsar and three daughters from Odessa to "Wroclau". It is full of errors: the salutation on the letter is not as Hardinge would have addressed the king; there is a reference to the "Chargé d'Affaires" in Vienna, but the post did not exist in June 1919. The letter refers to Wien, rather than "Vienna"—highly improbable in a letter from one Englishman to another. Lord Hardinge's signature is not as he usually styled himself.

Note 23   *US "Escape Papers" as disinformation:*
The documents Bessell spoke of may conceivably have been like the Sisson Papers, other famous forgeries created as black propaganda in 1918. Sisson, a US official, brought the documents out of Russia and sincerely believed them to be genuine. Only later did it emerge that they were fakes created by the Russian right-wing to smear the Bolsheviks as German lackeys. Passages in the Bessell documents show the tsar speaking of the Kaiser with affection. An improbable attitude, but one which would have successfully smeared the Romanovs in Russian eyes if published.

Note 24   *Existence of US state papers on Romanov rescue:*
(1) Dr Kissinger's aide, Ambassador Robert Anderson, had research done specifically for us in 1975. The result, we were informed, was that "the rumour that the US government holds documents concerning the fate of the Romanovs is totally without foundation . . . Dr Kissinger has no knowledge of any documents that would support the claim that the Romanovs were removed from Ekaterinburg."

(2) Loy Henderson, retired senior State Department official who worked on secret material concerning Russia for twenty years, told us on 25 May 1975: "I did not find any hint or indication whatever that the Department might have any secret files relating to the fate of the Romanov family. I do not believe that any such files existed . . ."

(3) In response to an application under the US "Freedom of Information Act" the FOI Co-ordinator, Robert Young, said on 16 May 1975: "Please be advised that this agency does not have any files pertaining to Russia from the period of 1917 through 1919 that originated in the offices of the Counsellor of the Department of State. Nor does this agency have any files of the Secret Intelligence Bureau dealing with Russia for the same period."

Chapter 18
Page 198   We thank Brien Purcell Horan, BA Hist., Amherst
             College, Mass., for help in planning this chapter,
             drawing on extensive research and personal contact
             with the claimant and other principal witnesses.
                 A primary source on "Anastasia" has been the
             court record of Anderson *v.* Duchess Christian
             Ludwig of Mecklenburg, Hamburg Court of
             Appeal 1967. The originals are kept at Hamburg
             and we refer to documents from this source as
             "Hamburg", followed by the page reference.
                 See also special bibliography for main published
             works used in the chapter on "Anastasia."
Page 200   1967 Verdict—Hamburg (Vol. XXXVII) 6949
Page 201   Police bulletin—*I, Anastasia*, p. 89
Page 202   *Roumanian story:*
Note 25   This has been taken up as "evidence" against the
             claimant. A Soviet source (quoted by V. Alexandrov
             in *The End of the Romanovs*, 1966) explains the whole
             Anastasia matter thus—a deserter from the Ipatiev
             House guard went to Roumania from Ekaterin-
             burg, taking with him a deranged Polish girl. He
             approached the Polish Secret Service who agreed
             to use her for political ends and obtain recognition
             for her as Anastasia. But then, "after the setback
             suffered by Pilsudski's expedition and the signing
             of the Peace at Riga, the 'Anastasia intrigue' lost
             all interest". The soldier was killed in a brawl, and
             his Polish mistress jumped into the Landwehr
             Canal on 17 February 1920. She was rescued, and
             became the Anastasia claimant.
                 This Soviet version is clearly tailored to fit the
             history of Anna Anderson. But it gets the dates
             wrong. The rescue from the canal was indeed on 17
             February 1920, but Pilsudski's campaign did not
             even start till April. The Peace of Riga was not
             signed till 18 March 1921.
Page 203   Doctor's report—note of Dr T. Schiler; files of
             Edward Fallows
Page 204   Rathenau note—Hamburg [Beiakte 2K83 (Tsch) 45]
             Andrei correspondence with S. Botkin, President
             of White Russian Association in Berlin; Hoover
             Institution.

Page 205
Note 26

Martin Knopf:
In a wry sequel to this episode, Knopf turned up two years later, this time offering to write an exposé of his own earlier activities, if the claimant's lawyers would pay him $5,000.
Doctor on sanity—report by Dr Wahrendorff; files of Edward Fallows

Page 208

News of the World—report 4 September 1932

Page 209

Tsar's money in Germany—letter of Mendelssohn Bank to claimant 8 February 1938; Hamburg (Vol. X) 1764. The authors have not given space to the perennial rumour that a vast Romanov fortune awaits a successful claimant. No such claim has been made by Anna Anderson.

Page 210
Note 27

£1,000 left in Mendelssohn Bank:
Grand Duchess Xenia, the tsar's sister, had left her share almost untouched in the account.

Page 211

Mayer affair—files of the lawyer, Dr Vermehren.

Page 214

Romanov declaration—Gilliard, *La Fausse Anastasie*, p. 9

Page 215

Olga memoirs—Vorres, p. 176
Olga letter to Zahle—Hamburg (Vol. XIII 2291)

Page 216

Prince report—US National Archives, Dept. of State Group 59, 861.0011/12
Rudnev—note in Fallows files dated March 1926

Page 217

"short" & "stout"—Gibbes testimony 1 July 1919; Wilton, p. 255
The "malachite room":
The former head of the Court Chancery was Alexander Mossolov. He wrote of the room five years after the claimant first mentioned it. (A. Mossolov, *At the Court of the Last Tsar*, Methuen, London 1935 (trans. from French)
Andrei on Gilliard—correspondence with S. Botkin, Hoover Institution
Princess Heinrich—statement 31 July 1925; Hamburg, Bln III, 185

Page 218

Anderson on "Ernie"—statement of Amy Smith; cf. Hamburg (Vol. XXXVII) 6855

Page 219

Cecile statement—Hamburg (Vol. XXIV) 4696
Ferdinand statement—Hamburg (Vol. XXXI) 5826
Galitzin statement—Hamburg cf. (Vol. XXXVII) 6955
Thurn and Taxis statement—Hamburg (Vol. XVIII) 3658

Page 220	Pilar von Pilchau statement—Hamburg (Bln VII) 299
Note 28	*Witness of Hesse Mission in Finland:* Colonel Dmitry von Lar-Larsky stated in 1949— "In 1915 and 1916 I had to be treated [for war wounds] at a sanatorium, Raula, on Lake Soima, not far from the Imata Waterfall. It was there one evening that I had the opportunity to notice a 'foreign dignitary' passing through, in whom I at once recognized the Grand Duke Ernst Ludwig of Hesse-Darmstadt; he was accompanied by the tsar's aide-de-camp, Colonel Mordvinov. The tsarina's brother was well known to me . . . When Mordvinov saw that I had recognized the Grand Duke he asked me not to let it be noticed, and to keep quiet about it. He confided in me that the tsarina's brother was travelling incognito, indeed under the name of a Prince Thurn and Taxis . . ." Hamburg (Vol. I) 186.
	Von Unruh statement—Hamburg (Vol. XX) 3932
Page 223	Andrei letter to Olga 1928—Hamburg (Vol. XVII) 3119
	Andrei letter to Olga 1950—Hamburg (Vol XIV) 2549
	Andrei letter 1928—Andrei correspondence with S. Botkin; Hoover Institution.
	Andrei attitude 1956—statement of Princess Kira; Hamburg (Vol. XXVI) 5003
	Kschessinska interview—published verbatim *Le Figaro* 21 September 1967
Page 224	Princess Xenia statement—Hamburg (Vol. IV) 749
Page 225	Sigismund statement—Hamburg, loose folder
	Cecile first statement—Hamburg (Vol. XXIII) 4412
	Cecile second statement—Hamburg (Vol. XXIII) 4412
Page 226	Von Braun statement—Hamburg (Vol. XXIV) 6304
Page 228	Dassel description—Dassel *op. cit.*
	Von Dehn statement—Hamburg (Vol. I) 28
Page 229	Tatiana Botkin statement—Rathlef-Keilmann, p. 137
Page 230	Kostritsky quoted—Gilliard, *La Fausse Anastasie*, p. 164

Page 232   Olga on feet—Hamburg (Vol. VII) 1300
            Cornelius Institute report—Hamburg (Vol. XXXI)
            5827
Page 233   Becker statement—Hamburg (Vol. X) 1890; (Vol.
            XI) 1909
            Dr Nobel—Rathlef-Keilmann, p. 242
            Dr Bonhoeffer—Hamburg, loose folder; (Vol. XIV)
            2389
Page 234   Buchholz statement—Hamburg (Bln IV) 98
            Dassel statement—Hamburg (Vol. II) 331; 352 *et seq.*
            Gilliard statement—Gilliard, *La Fausse Anastasie*,
            p. 71
Page 235   Tatiana   Botkin   statement—Rathlef-Keilmann,
            p. 143
            Gibbes quote—testimony 1 July 1919 to Sokolov,
            cited Wilton, p. 255
Note 29   *Attitude of the English tutor, Gibbes:*
            Gibbes met Anna Anderson in Paris, in 1954, and
            like other witnesses, at first expressed no firm con-
            clusion. He told a friend, Michael Scott, that he
            would need to meet the claimant again before
            reaching a final decision. He never did, but signed
            a deposition against her in 1958, saying that she
            had not recognized him, and clearly spoke neither
            English nor Russian. It is not surprising the
            claimant did not recognize Gibbes—since 1918 he
            had become a Russian Orthodox priest, and was
            now an old man with a long white beard. To the
            ordinary observer, his photographs in this role
            appear totally different from those of the close-
            shaven young tutor of 36 years earlier. As for the
            language question, overwhelming evidence shows
            that Anderson could understand Russian; and
            English has been her everyday language since at
            least 1928.
            Bischoff conclusion—Gilliard, *La Fausse Anastasie*,
            p. 159
Page 236   Baron von Eickstedt conclusion—Hamburg, loose
            folder
            Reche conclusion—Hamburg (Vol. IX) 1648,
            1653 *et seq.*
            Furtmayr conclusion—report 17 May 1971, pri-
            vately submitted.

Page 237   *Story of escape to Roumania:*
Note 30   Some other clues suggest there is a grain of truth to
            at least the final lap of the escape story. In 1953, a
            former German intelligence officer in the Ukraine,
            Lt. Col. Werner Hassenstein, testified that in late
            1918 he was approached on behalf of "Grand
            Duchess Anastasia", said to be lying wounded in a
            peasant cart. The German commander at Nikolaiev
            had then allowed her to pass on her journey west-
            wards. Other evidence suggests she was subsequently
            lodged in the grounds of the German Embassy in
            Bucharest. Hassenstein's date, "mid-September",
            may be wrong. The claimant herself has talked of
            snow during the journey.

Page 238   Zahle comment—Prince Frederick of Saxe Alten-
            burg.
            Dr Bock statement—Hamburg (Vol. XX) 3929

Chapter 19

Page 243   Grand Duke Andrei comments—correspondence
            of Andrei with S. Botkin, President of White
            Russian Association in Berlin; Hoover Institution

Page 244   Letter on occasion of tsar's marriage—Massie,
            p. 68
            George V telegram to deposed tsar (sent through
            Lord Stamfordham)—PRO/FO 800/205 (Folio 53)
            Provisional Government concern about King
            George telegram—reported by Sir George Buchanan
            25 March 1917 PRO/FO 371/2998

Page 245   Lord Mountbatten on asylum—BBC interview 1971
Page 246   Waters consulted—Waters, p. 245
            Foreign Office warning 19 March 1917—FO tele-
            gram to Sir George Buchanan, PRO/FO 371/2998
            Buchanan's "encouraging conversation"—telegram
            from Buchanan to Foreign Office; PRO/FO
            371/2995

Page 247   Sir George Buchanan on Milyukov's assumption of
            British co-operation—telegram Buchanan to Foreign
            Office 20 March 1917, PRO/FO 371/2998
            Milyukov formally requests British asylum for tsar
            —telegram from Buchanan to Foreign Office 21
            March 1917, PRO/FO 371/2998
            British offer asylum—two telegrams from Foreign
            Office to Buchanan 22 March 1917

1. PRO/FO 371/2998
2. PRO/FO 371/3008
Foreign Office chaser—telegram from Foreign Office to Buchanan 23 March 1917, PRO/FO 371/2998

Page 248 George V first expresses doubts about asylum—letter from Lord Stamfordham to Balfour 30 March 1917, PRO/FO 800/205 (F.63)
Balfour reply—letter from Balfour to Stamfordham 2 April 1917, PRO/FO 800/205 (F.65)

Page 249 King George "regards matter settled"—letter from Stamfordham to Balfour, 3 April 1917, PRO/FO 800/205
Letters to King from Lord Carnock and Lord Beresford—information supplied by royal archivist, 1975

Page 250 Two royal objections to asylum on same day—letters from Stamfordham to Balfour 6 April 1917, PRO/FO 800/205 and Lloyd George Papers F3/2/19 (Beaverbrook Library)
Lloyd George discusses asylum doubts in Cabinet—Minute 118 for war cabinet meeting 11.30 am 13 April 1917, PRO/Cab 23/2, war cabinet 118

Page 251 Buchanan asked to avoid asylum question from now on—Foreign Office to Buchanan 13 April 1917, PRO/FO 800/205
Hardinge to Bertie—private letter 17 April 1917, Hardinge Papers, Cambridge University Library
Stamfordham to Bertie—letter from Windsor Castle 18 April 1917, PRO/FO 800/191 (Papers of Lord Bertie)
Bertie to Hardinge—letter 22 April 1917 (draft copy), Papers of Lord Bertie (Beaverbrook Library F51/4/20)
Britain makes denial of asylum quite clear—letter from Buchanan to Hardinge 21 May 1971 reporting discussion with Minister Tereshchenko. Hardinge Papers 1917 Vol. IV, Cambridge University Library

Page 252 Provisional Government again request British co-operation summer 1917 and British reaction—Article by Kerensky, *Evening Standard*, 4 July 1932 and Kerensky, *La vérité sur le Massacre des Romanov*, p. 166

Page 252 — Foreign Office correspondence over Kerensky allegations—various documents, PRO/FO 370/273; 1003/50/405
Meriel Buchanan counters official version—Buchanan, M., *The Dissolution of an Empire*

Chapter 20

Page 253 — Major Hardinge speaks of "gaps in the record"— Hardinge letters from Buckingham Palace to Gaselee at Foreign Office, 10 July, 19 July 1932

Page 255 — *Gibbes letter to Jackson (ghosted for tsarina):*
Note 31 — One of the heavy hints in the letter to Miss Jackson was "I hear that David is back from France, how are his father and mother . . .?" David was the family name for the Prince of Wales. The original draft of the letter is still held by Gibbes's adopted son, George (Gibbes/Trewin, p. 90)

Page 256 — Jonas Lied diary—The papers of Jonas Lied, Norsk Sjofartsmuseum, Oslo

Page 258 — *Lied scheme:*
Note 32 — In an autobiography 25 years later (*op. cit.*, chap. I), Lied spoke briefly of the Romanov rescue plot, and said it was his plan. The diary entries in question are not the original ones but were compiled after the war from surviving notes, papers and memory. On inspection, it has clearly been heavily edited. Lied's friend Hewins is certain that the version he was given verbally is the correct one, and that Lied watered down his diary and book versions to avoid contemporary scandal.

Page 259 — Mountbatten on King George V role—BBC interview 1971

Chapter 21

Page 261 — Solovyov episode—Markov, S. V., p. 160 *et seq.* Rasputin M. *The Real Rasputin*, p. 184 *et seq.*

Page 263 — Yakovlev arrival—Kobylinsky testimony: Houghton, Vol. III, document 29

Page 264 — Yakovlev's behaviour during departure—Volkov testimony—Sokolov French edition, chap. 6.

Page 266 — Soviet account of Yakovlev—Bykov, *op. cit.*, p. 66

Page 267 — Kobylinsky on Yakovlev route—Melnik, Tatiana née Botkin, p. 56

Page 268   Gleb Botkin on Yakovlev—Botkin, Gleb, *op. cit.*,
                  p. 194
                  Tatiana Botkin on Yakovlev—Melnik, Tatiana née
                  Botkin, p. 56
Page 269   Yakovlev's career—Alexandrov, V., (p. 205) writes
Note 33   that, according to Maslovsky, a former senior official
                  in the Kerensky regime, Yakovlev was the son of a
                  Lithuanian engineer called Zarrin, who adopted
                  the name Yakovlev in 1905, on deserting from the
                  imperial navy. He was in Canada till 1917, allegedly
                  under British influence, and is said to have returned
                  with British backing at the time of the tsar's
                  abdication.
                  Yakovlev press interview—*Uralskaia Jisn*, Russian
                  newspaper cited by Jacoby, p. 294
Page 270   Counter-intelligence report on Yakovlev's disap-
                  pearance—Houghton, Vol. IV, document 49
Note 34   King George's eventual activity on 3 May 1918. King
                  George contacted the Foreign Office through Lord
                  Cromer. He was distressed at news of the imperial
                  family's conditions at Tobolsk, and proposed the
                  Foreign Office ask Bruce Lockhart, British consul
                  in Moscow, to take up the matter with Trotsky.
                  The request was sent, but nothing further is re-
                  corded in the files (Telegram no. 109 PRO/FO
                  371/3329).
Note 35   *Yakovlev's intentions:*
                  Another theory, put forward by the Japanese
                  historian and former diplomat, Toshikazu Kase, is
                  that "Yakovlev himself had the special intention
                  of taking the family further east from Omsk, making
                  contact with the White army, and sending them on
                  to Japan." (Kase, *The Russian Revolution by a
                  Witness*, Shin Chosha, Tokyo, 1968.) It is a plausible
                  theory, but the question remains—who were
                  Yakovlev's masters?
Page 271   Observation of Ipatiev House—Ackerman, p. 100
                  Foreigners watch Ipatiev House—Smirnov, p. 118/
                  120
                  British officer in plain clothes—Preston, p. 110
Page 272   George V diary entry—extract for 10 February
                  1921, by gracious permission of HM the Queen.
                  King George conviction that all Romanovs dead—

letter from King to Marchioness of Milford Haven
1 September 1918.

Kaiser's attitude to British role—memorandum by
imperial liaison officer to German Foreign Office,
21 July 1918; document A31003 Russland Nr 82,
no. 1.

Note 36   Our main source for the German diplomatic record
has been from German Foreign Office archives
filed at US National Archives. These cover 1 June
1918–24 July 1918 (Bd. 66), and 25 July 1918–
30 September 1918 (Bd. 67), under main title
*Auswärtiges Amt. Abteilung A. Akten betreffend: die
russische Kaiserfam.* Also studied is a microfilm reel
from Bonn entitled: *Gr. Hauptquartier, Russland A.-Z.
Russische Kaiserfamilie: Ermordung des Zaren 16.7.1918.*
All documents from German official files subsequently quoted refer to these sources, and numbers
refer to the US Archives record, except where the
sender is Supreme Headquarters, when the source
is Bonn.

Chapter 22

Page 274   Nicholas's break with Wilhelm—Massie, p. 297
Page 276   Kaiser's claim of readiness to help in 1917—Waters,
p. 255 *et seq.*
German promise—Kerensky writing in Bulygin,
p. 118. Story confirmed by Kurt Jagow of German
Foreign Ministry, Bulygin, p. 389
Page 277   Mirbach reassurance—Bulygin, p. 202
German overtures at Brest-Litovsk—Wilton memor-
andum to British Foreign Office; PRO/FO 371/
3310
Page 278   Kaiser message to King of Denmark—German
Foreign Office document A.S. 1356 (draft). Also
Kerensky, *La Vérité sur le Massacre des Romanov*,
p. 210
Mirbach rebuff to monarchists—A. Krivoshein
testimony, Sokolov French edition, chapter 9
Page 279   German representations over princesses of German
blood—series of German Foreign Office documents
May 1918; souce as note to p. 272
Mirbach report 10 May 1918—telegram to Berlin,
German Foreign Office document A. 19964

Page 279   Concern in May/June—Mirbach report 21 June
            1918; German Foreign Office telegram no. 338
Page 281   Grand Duke of Hesse's approach to tsar—letter of
            Grand Duke Andrei to Sergei Botkin 8 December
            1927; Hoover Institution
Note 37   *German plan for puppet control in the east:*
            The scheme was to safeguard the eastern frontier by
            setting up a chain of monarchies with a pro-
            German orientation. It began to take shape on
            5 November 1916 when the "independent" king-
            dom of Poland was proclaimed. On 10 August 1918
            the Lithuanian diet voted to offer the throne of
            Lithuania to a Duke of Urach, who accepted the
            nomination and announced he would be known as
            Mendowe II. There were also plans to offer the same
            throne to a prince of Saxony, and the throne of the
            Ukraine to a prince of Prussia. Prince Friedrich
            Karl of Hesse Kassel was actually designated King
            of Finland. In the event the scheme never came off.
            General Waters's papers—letter from Lt. Col. L.
            Taylor to Sir Owen Morshead, 18 October 1945
Page 282   Report of Kaiser's concern—report by British
            ambassador, Berne, to Foreign Office, 19 June 1918
            PRO/FO 370/3328
            Reports of German plot to save tsar: report by
            British Consul, Geneva, following visit by White
            Russian representatives 18 July 1918 PRO/FO
            371/3328
            Swatowski's original letter to Balfour—17 July 1918
            PRO/FO 371/3328
            Telegram from British ambassador, Berne to
            Foreign Office 21 July 1918 and London minute
            PRO/FO 371/3335
Page 284   Deuxième Bureau report—French Foreign Office
            Archives
            Poznanski and Swatowski—report by British am-
            bassador, Berne, to Foreign Office 23 July 1918
            PRO/FO 371/3328
Page 285   Alvensleben briefing—Dolgorukov testimony to
            Sokolov 5 February 1921. Sokolov papers in Ford
            Archives, Henry Ford Museum, Dearborn, Michi-
            gan

Page 286   German presence in Ekaterinburg—Buxhoeveden, *Left Behind*, p. 77

Note 38   *Alvensleben incident:*
According to General Dolgorukov, six officers were selected following Alvensleben's request. Two pairs were sent to Moscow and Kotelnich respectively. A third pair set off for Ekaterinburg, Captain Karangozov and Captain Karasov. They heard of the tsar's execution en route, at Moscow, but never obtained conclusive evidence.
German "Red Cross" in Ekaterinburg—Wilton, p. 151
American Intelligence Report enclosure to report of Ambassador Francis to Dept. of State 26 August 1918; US National Archives, Dept. of State, Group 59, 861.00/2888

Page 287   *Copenhagen requiem incident:*
Note 39   Report from French Minister in Denmark, M. Conty, to Paris 3 August 1918: French Foreign Ministry Archives—Russia 15 série Z, Carton 608 dossier 3, Questions Dynastiques et Cour I.

Page 290   Report of "military execution"—telegram from British ambassador, Berne to Foreign Office 24 July 1918 PRO/FO 371/3335
Kaiser's vision—Müller, Admiral, *Regiert der Kaiser?* p. 396

Chapter 23
Page 291   Central Executive discusses tsar—Trotsky, *Diary in Exile 1935*, p. 80
Page 292   Berzin Telegram—Houghton, Vol. II, document 66
Page 293   Telegraph operators' testimony—report no. 1497 of Criminal Investigation Division 3 February 1919; Houghton, Vol. III, document 12
Lenin denies execution rumours—article in *National Tidende* 5 July 1918 quoting *People's Daily*, (Moscow)
Telegram from Chairman of Ural Soviet—telegram no. 4558 Houghton, Vol. I, document 30
Page 294   Lenin speech on 23 February—addressed to Central Committee, Wheeler-Bennett, *op. cit.* p. 257
Page 295   Lenin reaction to death of Mirbach—Wheeler-Bennett, *op. cit.* p. 340
Page 296   Sverdlov on German threat—Sverdlov's telegraph

dialogue with Ural Regional Soviet 20 July 1918
—Sokolov Russian edition, chapter 25

Page 297 — Lenin attitude to Brest-Litovsk—Wheeler-Bennett, *op. cit.* p. 276
German Embassy enquiry 19 July—German Foreign Ministry document A. 30727
Visit to Radek—German Embassy message 20 July 1918 German Foreign Ministry document A. 30764
German approval of approaches. Berlin to German Embassy message 520, 20 July 1918. German Foreign Ministry document A. 30727 (minute) and Sokolov Russian edition, p. 272

Page 298 — Riezler visit to Chicherin—German Embassy message 551, 23 July 1918. German Foreign Ministry document A. 31165 Sokolov Russian edition, p. 272
Riezler visit to Chicherin—German Embassy message 561, 24 July 1918 German Foreign Ministry document A. 31329

Page 299 — Radek's suggestion—German Foreign Ministry document 6399

Page 300 — German Consulate message 10 September 1918—German Foreign Ministry document A. 37912

Page 301 — Telegram from Sweden, stating Romanov family alive—Broadlands Archives
Magener and Cornel working for Grand Duke of Hesse and statement by grand ducal court steward Carl Herrmann lodged in files of Hamburg Appeal Court (Anastasia case) (Vol. Bln III) 168

Page 302 — Markov testimony—March/April 1921, Sokolov Russian edition, p. 100/101

Note 40 — According to Markov, Magener had also seen Joffe, Bolshevik ambassador in Berlin, and Radek, German specialist at the Bolshevik Foreign Ministry in Moscow; in line with what they were telling German diplomats in the autumn they had "categorically stated" the Romanov women were alive.
Milyutin account of tsar's execution news: Milyutin—quoted in Bykov, *op. cit.*, p. 82

Note 41 — It is interesting that the leadership wanted the delegates, like the outside world, to believe the execution decision had been taken not in Moscow, but Ekaterinburg. Yet all other evidence shows that

Moscow really held the reins throughout July. The nature of the announcement may have been mere expediency, to shift the blame away from the leadership. Or—and this is hypothesis—the tsar alone may have been executed as a result of pressure within the Ural Soviet (see pp. 316/317).

Page 303　　Trotsky accounts—Trotsky, *Diary in Exile 1935*, p. 81 and Trotsky, *Stalin*, p. 414
Chicherin on survival of females—British report repeated in *New York Times* 20 September 1918
Chicherin statement at Genoa—*The Times* 25 April 1922
Dzerzhinsky on survival of women—Essad Bey, *op. cit.* p. 373
Litvinov on survival of family—article in *Revue des Deux Mondes* 1 August 1920

Page 304　　Zinoviev on survival of family—*San Francisco Sunday Chronicle*, 11 July 1920

Chapter 24

Page 307　　Ackerman original draft from Ekaterinburg—Carl Ackerman papers, Library of Congress, Washington D.C. (All Ackerman letters and documents in this chapter are from same source)

Page 310　　Kobylinsky on Chemodurov—Houghton, Vol. III, document 29

Page 311　　Gibbes on Chemodurov—Houghton, Vol. V, document 31
Gilliard on Chemodurov—Houghton, Vol. II, document 55

Note 42　　The fact that, according to Gilliard, the valet included the emperor amongst those removed alive, should not lessen the impact of Chemodurov's statements. In his remarks to both Gibbes and Kobylinsky, Chemodurov referred only to the family surviving, indicating he assumed the tsar was shot. Gilliard probably misquoted Chemodurov, or was himself misquoted.

Page 312　　Slaughter account—Military Intelligence Division report, filed from Ekaterinburg 12 December 1918. US National Archives, Navy and Old Army Branch, Military Archives Division, document 184/123

Page 314   Mikulova testimony—Houghton, Vol. I, document
            67
Page 315   *Pravda* account—quoted in *Svenska Dagbladet* 24
            July 1918 and other European newspapers
Page 319   Proskuryakov on Sednev—Proskuryakov testimony:
            Houghton, Vol. III, document 18

Note 43   *Destination immediately after Ekaterinburg:*
            In February 1919, the minister of justice with the
            White government at Omsk, Starynkevich, wrote:
            "A series of prisoners testify that the family was not
            shot, but was transferred from Ekaterinburg to
            Perm, *or to Verkhoturye.*" (French Foreign Ministry
            archive document 17 February 1919) Verkhoturye
            was mentioned as a possible destination by Captain
            Voitkevich, the Polish officer cited earlier, and also
            in several CID reports. Lydia Sitnikova testified that
            her brother, an armoured car driver at Ekaterinburg,
            told her the tsar was being taken to Verkhoturye
            (Houghton, Vol. I, document 39). The town also
            crops up in reports from agents working behind Com-
            munist lines (Houghton, Vol. I, document 39) and in
            a report from the British Embassy in Peking (PRO/
            FO 371/3335). But the Verkhoturye stories seem
            implausible—they refer to travel by both car,
            troika, and train, are usually second-hand, and
            differ from all other sources in saying the tsar was
            still alive and with his family. Verkhoturye was
            possibly a piece of deliberate Bolshevik disinforma-
            tion, designed to cover not the massacre of the
            family (there were too many clues to that already)
            but to confuse those still looking for the Romanovs
            elsewhere. As we show, the family was almost
            certainly at Perm, the logical destination.

Chapter 25
Page 321   Mutnykh testimony 8 March 1919—Houghton,
            Vol. IV, document 5
Page 323   Shamarin statement—Shamarin testimony, Hough-
            ton, Vol. VI, document 2
Page 324   Karnaukovaya testimony—Houghton, Vol. V, docu-
            ment 27
Page 325   Rimashevsky testimony—Houghton, Vol. IV, docu-
            ment 7

Page 326   Krivopdenova statement—Mirolyubov-Jordansky correspondence. Mirolyubov Papers, Hoover Institution

Page 327   Mutnykh testimony (final) undated (approx 1–7 April 1919)—Houghton, Vol. IV, document 5

Page 328   Mutnykh testimony 2 April 1919—Houghton, Vol. IV, document 5

Page 329   Girschfeld statement—17 February 1919, Houghton, Vol. IV, document 5

Sibiryev testimony 3 February 1919—Houghton, Vol. III, document 12

Sokolova testimony—17 March 1919, Houghton, Vol. IV, document 5

Page 330   Glafyra Malysheva testimony 30 March 1919—Houghton, Vol. IV, document 5

Glafyra Malysheva testimony 2 April 1919—Houghton, Vol. IV, document 5

Page 331   Yevdokiya Malysheva testimony 30 March 1919—Houghton, Vol. IV, document 5

Page 332   Telegram 4852—published V. Alexandrov, illustration no. 55; orig. neg. held at *Opera Mundi*, Paris

Page 334   Grigoryev testimony 23 March 1919—Houghton, Vol. IV, document 5

Sitnikova testimony 24 March 1919—Houghton, Vol. IV, document 5

Page 335   Sitnikov testimony 28 March 1919—Houghton, Vol. IV, document 5

Kuklin, Kuklina, Ryabov, Varankina, testimonies. Also Houghton, Vol. IV, document 5

Note 42   *Utkin testimony*—Dr Utkin testified twice, first to Kirsta on 10 February 1919, then to Sokolov on 14/15 June 1919. (For 10 February testimony, see Houghton, Vol. IV, document 5; for 14/15 June testimony, see Vol. V, document 7.) The Utkin testimony we have quoted at length is from 14/15 June.

Page 342   Sergei Smirnov anecdote—Smirnov, p. 153

Podorova testimony 20 January 1919—Houghton, Vol IV, document 5

Page 343   Bonde anecdote—formal letter by Count Bonde during Anastasia hearings: 15 October 1952

Page 344   Shilova testimony—7 March 1919, Houghton, Vol. IV, document 5

Note 44 *Fate of Anastasia at Perm:*
Apart from those who simply assumed that Anastasia died or was killed after her escape bid, one witness in the dossier does refer specifically to a "secret burial at 1.00 am near the racecourse". But we know from other sources that during White enquiries into Bolshevik atrocities at Perm, the place mentioned was thoroughly excavated. Only male bodies were found.

Page 347 Solovyov testimony—29 March, Houghton, Vol. IV, document 5

Page 348 Kirsta report to Gaida 7 April 1919—Houghton, Vol. IV, document 5

Page 350 Bykov on Kirsta—Bykov, *op. cit.*, p. 88

Page 351 Tikhomirov statement—2 April 1919, Houghton, Vol. IV, document 5

Page 352 German consulate message 15 September 1918— German Foreign Ministry; document A 38734
Attitude of Joffe—German Foreign Ministry; document A. 38420

Note 45 *Eventual Radek version:*
According to a German Foreign Office memorandum in January 1920, Radek produced an "explanation" of events which clashes with all other Soviet versions. He said that in mid-July 1918, a people's commissar was taking the Romanovs from Ekaterinburg to Moscow by train, but the party was attacked by Czechs en route. The Communist escort decided to shoot all the Romanovs. Their corpses were later dug up, photographed and reburied in zinc coffins, at Ekaterinburg. (German Foreign Ministry archives; document A. 1275.)

Page 354 Gaida on Romanov case—Gaida, p. 166/167
Grand Duke Andrei's restriction—statement as told to Prince Frederick of Saxe Altenburg by Vladimir, son of Grand Duke Andrei.

BIBLIOGRAPHY

ACKERMAN, Carl W.: *Trailing the Bolsheviki*, Charles Scribner, New York, 1919

ALEXANDER, Grand Duke: *Once a Grand Duke*, Cassell, London, 1932

ALEXANDROV, Victor: *The End of the Romanovs*, Hutchinson, 1966

ALFERIEFF, Eugene E.: *Letters of the Tsar's Family from Captivity* (in Russian)—Holy Trinity Monastery, Jordanville, New York, 1974

ALMEDINGEN, E. M.: *The Romanovs. Three Centuries of an Ill-Fated Dynasty*, Bodley Head, London, 1966

BADIA, Gilbert: *Le Spartakisme. Les dernières années de Rosa Luxemburg et de Karl Liebknecht, 1914–1919*, Paris, 1967

BAEDECKER, Karl: *Russia (Handbook for Travellers)*, Facsimile of 1914 Edition, Arno Press, USA, 1971

BALFOUR, Michael: *The Kaiser and His Times*, Crescent Press, London, 1964

BARTON, George: *Celebrated and Famous Mysteries of the Great War*, Page, Boston, 1919

BATTISCOMBE, Georgina: *Queen Alexandra*, Constable, London, 1969

BENTINCK, Lady N.: *The Ex-Kaiser in Exile*, Hodder & Stoughton, London, 1921

BERGAMINI, David: *Japan's Imperial Conspiracy*, William Heinemann, London 1971

BESSEDOWSKY, Grigory: *Im Dienste Der Sowjets*, Grethlein, Leipzig, 1930

BEY, Essad: *Devant la Revolution. La vie et la règne de Nicolas II*, Payot, Paris, 1935

BLACK, M. L.: *My Seventy Years*, Thomas Nelson, London, 1938

Le Bolchevisme en Russie (Livre Blanc Anglais), Berger-Levrault, Paris, 1919

BOTKIN, Gleb: *The Real Romanovs*, Fleming H. Revell, New York, 1931

BOTKIN, Pyotr Sergeyevich: *Les Morts Sans Tombes*, Paris, 1922

BOUCHARD, Robert: *Les Dessous de l'Espionage Anglais*, Les Editions de France, Paris, 1929

BRINKLEY, George A.: *The Volunteer Army and Allied Intervention in*

South Russia, 1917–1921, University of Notre Dame Press, Notre Dame, Indiana, 1966

BRUCE LOCKHART, Sir Robert: *Diaries*, Macmillan, London, 1973
—— *Memoirs of a British Agent*, Putnam, London, 1932

BRUCE LOCKHART, Robin: *Ace of Spies*, Hodder & Stoughton, London, 1967

BUCHANAN, Meriel: *The Dissolution of an Empire*, John Murray, London, 1932
—— *Ambassador's Daughter*, Cassell, London, 1958

BULYGIN, Captain Paul: *The Murder of the Romanovs*, Hutchinson, London, 1935

BUXHOEVEDEN, Baroness Sophie: *Left Behind: Fourteen Months in Siberia During the Revolution,* Longmans, London, 1928
—— *The Life and Tragedy of Alexandra Feodorovna, Empress of Russia*, Longmans, New York, 1928

BYKOV, Paul Mikhailovich: *The Last Days of Tsardom*, Martin Lawrence, London, 1934
—— Article in *Arkhiv Russkoi Revolyutsii XVII*, Berlin
—— Article attributed to American Naval Intelligence Report, 28 June 1923, Document 20978–321, Navy & Old Army Branch, Military Archives Division, US National Archives

CARR, E. H.: *History of Soviet Russia—The Bolshevik Revolution, 1917–1923*, Macmillan, London, 1964

COWLES, Virginia: *The Romanovs*, Collins, London, 1971

CHURCHILL, Winston: *The World Crisis, 1911–1916*, Thornton Butterworth, London, 1921–1923

DALLIN, David J.: *The Rise of Russia in Asia,* Hollis & Carter, London, 1950

DEACON, Richard: *A History of the British Secret Service*, Muller, London, 1972
—— *A History of the Russian Secret Service*, Muller, London, 1972

DEHN, Lili: *The Real Tsaritsa*, Little, Brown, Boston, 1922

DENIKIN, A. I.: *Ocherki Russkoi Smuty*, 5 vols, Paris, 1921–1926

DITERIKHS, General Mikhail Konstantinovich: *Ubiistvo tsarskoi sem'i i chlenov Doma Romanovykh na Urale*, 2 vols, Vladivostok, Military Academy, 1922

ELIOT, John: *Fall of Eagles*, BBC, London, 1974

ENEL (pseud.), (Mikhail Vladimirovich Skaryatin): *Sacrifice*, Brussels, 1923

EVANS, Rowland, & Robert D. Novak: *Nixon in the White House*, Davis Poynter, London, 1972

FLEMING, Robert Peter: *The Fate of Admiral Kolchak*, Rupert Hart-Davis, London, 1963

GAIDA, Rudolf: *Moje Paměti*, Vesmir, Prague, 1924

GILLIARD, Pierre: *Thirteen Years at the Russian Court*, Hutchinson, London, 1921

—— *Le Tragique Destin de Nicolas II et de sa Famille*, Payot, Paris, 1921

GOULEVITCH, A.: *Czarism and Revolution*, Omni Publications, California, 1962

GOURKO, General: *Russia in 1914–1917*, John Murray, London, 1918

GRAVES, William S.: *America's Siberian Adventure, 1918–1920*, Jonathan Cape, London, 1931

GREY, Ian: *The Romanovs. The Rise and Fall of a Russian Dynasty*, David & Charles, Devon, 1971

GRIGG, John: *The Young Lloyd George*, Eyre Methuen, London, 1973

HALLIBURTON, Richard: *Seven League Boots*, Unwin, London, 1936

HARCAVE: *Years of the Golden Cockerel*, Robert Hale, London, 1970

HARDINGE, Lord: *Old Diplomacy* (Lord Hardinge's Memoirs), John Murray, London, 1947

HASKELL, Arnold: *Dancing in Petersburg, The Memoirs of Kschessinska*, Gollancz, London, 1960

HILL, Captain George: *Go Spy the Land*, Cassell, London, 1932

HOFFMANN, Max: *War Diaries and Other Papers*, Martin Secker, London, 1929

HOUGH, Richard: *Louis and Victoria, The First Mountbattens*, Hutchinson, London, 1974

JACOBY, Jean: *Tsar Nicolas et la Révolution*, Arthur Fayard, Paris, 1931

JAGOW, Kurt: "Die Schuld am Zarenmord", chapter in *Berliner Monatshefte 13*, 1935

JAMES, Admiral Sir William: *The Eyes of the Navy*, Methuen, London, 1955

JANIN, General Maurice: *Ma Mission en Sibérie*, Payot, Paris, 1933

KAHN, David: *The Codebreakers. The Story of Secret Writing*, Weidenfeld, London, 1961

KATKOV, George: *Russia 1917. The February Revolution*, Longmans, London, 1967

KENNAN, G. F.: *Soviet-American Relations, 1917–1920*, 2 vols, Faber, London, 1958

KERENSKY, Alexander: *The Crucifixion of Liberty*, Arthur Barker, London, 1935

—— *The Road to the Tragedy*, Hutchinson, London, 1935

—— *La Vérité sur le Massacre des Romanov*, Payot, Paris, 1936

KNIGHTLEY, Phillip: *The First Casualty*, Deutsch, London, 1975

KOKOVTZOFF, Comte: "*La Verité sur la Tragédie d'Ekaterinbourg*", *Revue des Deux Mondes*, 1 October 1929; "Les Responsabilités", *Revue des Deux Mondes*, 15 October, 1929

KYRIL Vladimirovich, Grand Duke of Russia: *My Life in Russia's Service—Then and Now*, Selwyn & Blount, London, 1939

LASIES, Joseph: *La Tragédie Sibérienne*, L'Edition Française Illustrée, Paris, 1920

LIED, Jonas: *Return to Happiness*, Macmillan, London, 1943

LUCKETT, Richard: *The White Generals*, Longmans, London, 1971

LUDENDORFF, E.: *My War Memories, 1914–1918*, Hutchinson, London, 1919

LYONS, Marvin: *Nicholas II, The Last Tsar*, Routledge & Kegan Paul, London, 1974

MADER: *Who's Who in the CIA*, Mader, Berlin, 1968

MARKOV, S. V.: *How We Tried to Save the Tsaritsa*, Putnam, London, 1929

MASSIE, Robert K.: *Nicholas and Alexandra*, Gollancz, London, 1968

MAXIMILIAN, Alexander F. W.: *The Memoirs of Prince Max of Baden*, 2 vols, Constable, London, 1928

McCULLAGH, Francis: *A Prisoner of the Reds*, John Murray, London, 1921

MELGUNOV, S.: *Sudba Imperatora Nikolaya II posle otrecheniya*, Editions La Renaissance, Paris 1931

MELNIK, Tatiana: *Vospominaniya o Tsarskoi sem'i*, Stephanovich, Belgrade, 1921

MONTGOMERY HYDE, H.: *Stalin, The History of a Dictator*, Rupert Hart-Davis, London, 1971

MOOREHEAD, Alan: *The Russian Revolution*, Collins, London, 1958

NICHOLAS II: *The Letters of Tsar Nicholas and the Empress Marie*, Nicholson & Watson, London, 1937

NICOLAI, Colonel Walter: *The German Secret Service*, Stanley Paul, London, 1924

NICOLAS II: *Journal Intime de Nicolas II*, Payot, Paris, 1925

NICOLSON, Harold: *George the Fifth. His Life and Reign*, Constable, London, 1952

NIKOLAI II: *Dnevnik Imperatora Nikolaya II*, Berlin, 1923

NULL, Gary: *The Conspirator Who Saved the Romanovs*, Pinnacle Books, New York, 1973

O'CONOR, John F.: *The Sokolov Investigation*, Souvenir Press, London, 1972; Robert Speller & Sons, New York, 1971

ORLOV, Vladimir: *Assassins, Faussaires, Provocateurs*, Brucken Verlag, Berlin, 1929

PAGE, Russell: *Thomas Nelson Page*, Charles Scribner, New York, 1923

PALÉOLOGUE, Maurice: *An Ambassador's Memoirs*, 3 vols, Hutchinson, London, 1923–1925

PARES, Sir Bernard: *A History of Russia*, Cape, London, 1927

PAYNE, Robert: *Life and Death of Lenin*, W. H. Allen, London, 1964
—— *The Rise and Fall of Stalin*, W. H. Allen, London, 1965

POGGENPOHL, Nicholas de Berg: "Le Crime d'Ekaterinburg, 1916–1917", *Revue des Deux Mondes*, Paris

PONSONBY, Sir Frederick: *Recollections of Three Reigns*, Eyre & Spottiswoode, London, 1951

POPE-HENNESSY, James: *Queen Mary*, Allen & Unwin, London, 1959

POSSONY, Stefan T.: *Lenin. The Compulsive Revolutionary*, Allen & Unwin, London, 1965

PRESTON, Sir Thomas: *Before the Curtain*, John Murray, London, 1950

PRIDHAM, Vice-Admiral Sir Francis: *Close of a Dynasty*, Allen Wingate, London, 1956

RADZIWILL (Princess Catherine): *Secrets of Dethroned Royalty*, John Lane, New York, 1920
—— *Nicholas II, The Last Tsar*, Payot, Paris, 1933

RANSOME, Arthur: *Six Weeks in Russia in 1919*, Allen & Unwin, London, 1919

RASPUTIN, M.: *Rasputin*, John Long, London, 1929
—— *My Father*, Cassell, London, 1934

RICHARDS, Grant: *The Last of the War Lords*, London, 1918

RICHARDS, Guy: *Imperial Agent. The Goleniewski-Romanov Case*, Devin Adair, New York, 1966
—— *Hunt for the Czar*, Peter Davies, London, 1971
—— *The Rescue of the Romanovs*, Devin Adair, Old Greenwich, Connecticut, 1975

RIEDEL, W.: *Die Ermordung des Zaren Nikolaus II und seiner Familie*, Leipzig, 1921

RIIS, Sergius M.: *Yankee Commissar*, Robert Speller, New York, 1933

RODNEY, William: *Joe Boyle, King of the Klondike*, McGraw-Hill, New York, 1974

RODZIANKO, Colonel Paul: *Tattered Banners*, Seeley Service, London, 1939

ROOT, Jonathan: *Halliburton, The Magnificent Myth*, Longmans, Toronto, 1965

ST PIERRE, Michel de: *Le Drame des Romanovs*, Robert Laffont, Paris, 1967

SAKHAROV, K. V.: *Belaya Sibir*, Munich, 1923

SALISBURY, Harrison E.: *Russia*, Atheneum, New York, 1965

SAVINKOV, Boris: *Memoirs of a Terrorist*, A. & C. Boni, New York, 1931

SCHAPIRO, Leonard: *The Communist Party of the Soviet Union*, Methuen, London, 1960

Scott, J. D.: *Vickers—A History*, Weidenfeld, London, 1963

"The Secret Documents of Sydney Reilly": article in *Evening Standard*, May 1931

Semenov, G. M.: *Memoirs (Vospominaniya o Sebe, Mysli i Vyvody)*, Harbin, 1938

Seraphim, Dr E.: *Die Tragödie der Zarenfamilie*, Königsberg, 1927

Seymour, Charles: *The Intimate Papers of Colonel House*, Ernest Benn, London, 1926

Shub, David: *Lenin*, Doubleday & Co., New York, 1948

Smirnoff, Serge: *Autour de l'assassinat des Grands-Ducs*, Payot, Paris, 1928

Smythe, J. P.: *Rescuing the Czar*, California Printing Co., San Francisco, 1920

Sokoloff, Nicolas: *Enquête judiciaire sur l'Assassinat de la Famille Impériale Russe*, Payot, Paris, 1924

Sokolov, N.: *Ubiistvo tsarskoi sem'i*, Slowo, Berlin, 1925

Speranski, Valentin: *La Maison à Destination Spéciale,* Ferenczi et Fils, Paris, 1929

Theen, Rolf, *Lenin*, Quartet Books, London, 1974

Thompson, Sir Basil: *The Scene Changes*, Gollancz, London, 1939

Tisdall, E. E. P.: *The Dowager Empress*, Stanley Paul, London, 1957

Tokoi, Oskari: *Sisu, Even Through a Stone Wall*, Robert Speller, New York, 1957

Trewin, J. C.: *Tutor to the Tsarevich*, Macmillan, London, 1975

Trotsky, Leon: *Stalin*, Hollis & Carter, London, 1947

—— *Trotsky's Diary in Exile*, Harvard University Press, 1953

—— *The History of the Russian Revolution*, Gollancz, London, 1932–3

Troufanov, Sergei (Iliodor): *The Mad Monk of Russia*, Century, New York, 1918

Tschebotarioff, Gregory: *Russia, My Native Land*, McGraw-Hill, London, 1964

Varneck and Fisher: *The Testimony of Kolchak and Other Siberian Materials,* Stanford University and London, 1935

Viktoria Luise, Herzogin von Braunschweig: *Ein Leben als Tochter des Kaisers*—Göttinger Verlagsanstalt, 1965

Viroubova, Anna: *Souvenirs de ma Vie*, Payot, Paris, 1927

Volkov, A. A.: *Okolo tsarskoi semi*, Paris, 1928

Walls, H. J.: *Expert Witness: My Thirty Years in Forensic Science*, Long, London, 1972

Wallworth, Arthur: *Woodrow Wilson*, 2 vols, Longmans, London, 1958

Walsh, Edmond: *The Fall of the Russian Empire*, Williams & Norgate, London, 1929

WATERS, General Hely-Hutchinson Wallscourt: *Potsdam and Doorn*, John Murray, London, 1935

WHEELER-BENNETT, John W.: *Brest-Litovsk, The Forgotten Peace, March 1918*, Macmillan, London, 1963

WILLIAM II: *The Kaiser's Letters to the Tsar*, Hodder & Stoughton, London, 1921

—— *My Memoirs, 1878–1918*, Cassell, London, 1922

—— *My Early Life*, Methuen, London, 1926

WILTON, Robert: *The Last Days of the Romanovs*, Thornton Butterworth, London, 1920

WRANGEL, General Baron Peter: *Always with Honour*, Robert Speller, New York, 1957

XYDIAS, Jean: *L'Intervention Française en Russie 1918–1919*, Editions de France, Paris, 1927

YUSUPOV, F. F.: *Lost Splendour*, Cape, London, 1953

Books Specifically on "Anastasia"

AUCLÈRES, Dominique: *Anastasia Qui êtes-vous?*, Hachette, Paris, 1962

KRUG VON NIDDA, Roland (Ed.): *I, Anastasia*, Michael Joseph, London, 1959

BOTKIN, Gleb: *The Woman Who Rose Again*, Fleming H. Revell, New York, London, 1937

DASSEL, Felix: *Grossfürstin Anastasia Lebt*, Verlagshaus für Volksliteratur und Kunst, Berlin, 1928

DECAUX, Alain: *L'énigme Anastasia*, La Palatine, Paris, 1961

ESCAICH, René: *Anastasie de Russie, la Morte Vivante*, Editions Plantin, Paris, 1955

GILLIARD, Pierre: *La Fausse Anastasie (Histoire d'une prétendue grande-duchesse de Russie)*, Payot, Paris, 1929

NOGLY, Hans: *Anastasia*, Methuen, London 1959

RATHLEF-KEILMANN, Harriet von: *Anastasia*, Payson & Clarke, New York, 1929

INDEX

by

Michael Gordon

Bold figures indicate a description of person or place. *See also* Cast of Main Characters, pages 21–5.
Ekat. = Ekaterinburg   I.H. = Ipatiev House
Mine = Four Brothers mine

Abaza, Lt A., and code breaking, 113
Ackerman, Carl (*New York Times*): reports from Ekat., 93, 148, 152; on tsar rescue, 271; on "Domnin", 307–10, 311
Alexander II, Russian Emperor, 32
Alexander III, Russian Emperor, 32–3, 273–4
Alexander Mikhailovich, Grand Duke, and "Anastasia", 214
Alexandra Feodorovna, Russian Empress (Princess Alix of Hesse): marriage and children of, 34–5: and Rasputin, 36; **43, 274**; *see also* Romanovs
Alexei (tsarevich): haemophilia of, **35**; **43–4**; impersonators of, 192–5, 375n; and abdication, 279–80; executed?, 318–19; *see also* Romanovs
Alexeyev, S. (White official), 118, 124–6
Allied intervention in Russia, 83
alphabet, revised Russian, 14
Alvensleben, Count Hans Bodo von, 285–9
Anastasia, Grand Duchess (tsar's daughter), **44**; escape at Perm?, 333–45, 353, 393n;

claimant (Mrs Eugenia Smith), 194–5; *see also* "Anastasia" *and* Romanovs
"Anastasia" claimant (Mrs Manahan; form. "Anna Anderson"; alias "Tschaikowsky"): claim investigated, 198–239; in mental homes, 201–2, 207, 208; legal action over, 209–14; *evidence on :* teeth, 230–1; feet, 231–2; handwriting, 232–3; sanity, 233; speaking of Russian, 233–5; photographs, 235–6; survival story of, 202, 237–8, 382n; *also* 126, 132, 273, 378n
Anderson, Robert, 377n
"Anderson, Anna", *see* "Anastasia"
Andrei Vladimirovich of Russia, Grand Duke, and "Anastasia", 204–5, 214, 217, 221–4, 234, 243, 280–1, 354; son, Vladimir, of, 222–4; wife, Mathilde Kschessinska, of, 223
Andrew of Greece, Prince, 259
Andrew of Greece, Alice, Princess (sister of Lord Mountbatten), and "Anastasia", 211
Avdeyev, Alexander (first commandant at I.H.), **45, 46, 47, 67, 293**

Bainsmith, Capt. Bruce, protects Sokolov, 170

Balfour, Arthur (Br. Foreign Sec.), 84; and tsar rescue, 245–52 *passim*, 257

Barbara, Duchess Christian Ludwig of Mecklenburg, and "Anastasia", 211, 378n

Barker, Sir Francis, and Lied,257

Batchelor, Dr Tony (mining lecturer), 162–3

Battenberg, Prince Louis of, 92; *see also* Mountbatten, Earl

Becker, Minna (graphologist), 232–3

Beloborodov, Alexander (chairman of Ural Soviet): telegram to Sverdlov, 106–17; on replacement of Avdeyev, 293; *also* 47, 49, 130, 212, 266, 315, 317–18, 326–7, 328, 347

Belotserkovsky, Capt. Nikolai, and Medvedev's death, 127

Benckendorff, Count Pavel, and tsar rescue, 278

Bernstein, Herman (*New York Tribune*), interviews Sergeyev, 89, 94; 173

Bernstorff, Count Albrecht, 209

Bertie, Lord (Br. Amb. in Paris), and tsar rescue, 251

Berzin, General Jan, on Romanovs' fate, 292–3

Bessedovsky, Grigory, "memoirs" of, 181–2, 303

Bessell, Peter (former Br. M.P.), and "secret Romanov files", 195–7, 376n, 377n

Bethmann-Hollweg, Herr von (German Chancellor), and tsar rescue, 275

Bezak, Fyodor, and tsar rescue, 285–9

Biron, alleged killer of tsar, 95

Bischoff, Prof. Marc-Alexis (anthropologist), and "Anastasia", 235

"black bag" documents: discovery of, 61–2; 127–8, 322

Bock, Dr Günther, 238

Bolsheviks, 39

Bonde, Count Carl (Swedish Red Cross), and Anastasia's escape from Perm?, 343

Bonhoeffer, Dr Karl, and "Anastasia", 206–7; 70–1, 268

Boodts, Marga, claims to be Grand Duchess Olga, 192, 374n

Borodigan and Henry Ford, 174

Botkin, Gleb (son of Dr), 70–1, 268; and "Anastasia", 206–7

Botkin, Tatiana (Mme Melnik; d. of Dr), and "Anastasia", 204, 229, 234–5; 268

Botkin, Dr Yevgeny, 44, 77, 78, 85, 89, 121, 154, 165, 268, 310–11, 363n

Boyle, Col. Joe, interviews Marie, Dowager Empress, 92

Brasol, Boris, 173, 174

Brassova, Countess, 209

Braun, Baron Magnus von, 226–7

Brest-Litovsk, Treaty of, 277–80, 294, 295, 296–7

Bronard (Fr. agent), 262

Browning, Col. Frederick, 256

Buchanan, Sir George (Br. Amb. in St Petersburg), and tsar rescue, 246–52 *passim*

Buchholz, Erna (nurse) and "Anastasia", 234

Buivid, Viktor (peasant witness at Ekat.), 31–2

Bulygin, Capt. Pavel (Asst to Sokolov), 102, 169–70, 172; death of, 176

Buxhoeveden, Baroness Sophie ("Isa"), 46, 172; and "Anastasia", 201–2, 214

Bykov, Pavel, *The Last Days of Tsardom* by, 179–80, 350–1

Camps, Prof. Francis, forensic investigation by, 146–60

Cecil, Lord Robert, and tsar rescue, 257

Cecile, German Crown Princess, Duchess of Mecklenburg (d.-in-law of Kaiser), and "Anastasia", 203, 218–19, 225–6; and tsar rescue, 281–2

Cheka (Soviet secret police), 49, 119–20; terror by, 352

Chemodurov, Terenty Ivanovich, 44, 45, 66–8, 77, 87; alias "Domnin"?, 307–12 *passim*, 390n

Chicherin, Georgy (Soviet Commissar for Foreign Affairs), 238, 295, 298, 300; on Romanovs' fate, 303, 351–2

Christian X, King of Denmark, and tsar rescue, 278, 287

Chutskayev, S. (dep. to Beloborodov), 49

CID (Whites' Criminal Investigation Division), 323, 329, 331, 345, 349, 351; *see also* Kirsta, Alexander

Cockerill, Brig. Gen., 102

Cornel (German spy), 301

corsets, evidence of bullets and, 151–2

Cumming, Mansfield, 256

Czechs, 49

Dassel, Felix, and "Anastasia", 227–8, 234

Deacon, Richard, and Goleniewski, 374n

Dehn, "Lili" von (friend of tsarina), and "Anastasia", 228

Demidova, Anna, 44, 89, 123, 139, 310, 363n

Denikin, Gen. Anton, 307

Deryabin, Nikita (I.H. guard), 123

Deverenko, Dr Vladimir, 41, 56, 66, 67, 70–1, 77, 154, 172

Diterikhs, Gen. Mikhail, 80, 88, 90–1, 96–7, 103, 104–5, 110, 114, 126–7, 138, 140, 148–9, 165, 168, 169, 170, 270, 340, 349, 350, 361n, 370n

Dmitry Alexandrovich of Russia, Prince, 370n

Dobrynin, Konstantin (I.H. guard), 123

Dogert, Gen., and tsar rescue, 307

dogs: Alexei's spaniel, Joy, 52–3, 164; Tatiana's Jemmy, found in mine, 141, 161–5, 361n

Dolgorukov, Prince Alexander, 285–8

Dolgorukov, Prince Vassily, 41, 267–8

"Domnin, Parfen", alias for Chemodurov?, *q.v.*

Domontovich, Gen. Sergei (Military Governor at Ekat.), 138, 164–5

dossier, *see under* Sokolov, Nikolai

Dutov, Gen. Alexei, and tsar rescue, 307, 308

Dzerzhinsky, Felix (founder of Soviet secret police), on Romanovs' fate, 303

Edmonds, Cecil, and "Alexei", 193

Edwards, Middleton (Br. Consul in Geneva), 282

Eickstedt, Prof. Egon, Baron von (Mainz Univ.), and "Anastasia's" photos, 235–6

Ekaterinburg: **42**; encircled, falls to Whites, 49, 56, 166; climate of, 162–3; falls to Reds, 349–50

Eliot, Sir Charles (Br. High Commissioner for Siberia), investigates at Ekat., 80, **82–3**, 83–7, 108, 132, 148–50, 165, 272, 318, 319

Elisabeth Feodorovna, Grand Duchess Sergei of Russia, Princess of Hesse (sister of tsarina), 279, 339, 359n

Ernst Ludwig of Hesse, Grand Duke (tsarina's brother): and "Anastasia", 205, 209, 217, 273; and visit to Russia?, 218–21, 226–7, 273, 380n; and tsar rescue, 280–1, 353; on tsarina's and children's survival, 301

Fallows, Edward, and "Anastasia" case, 206

Feodora, Princess Heinrich XXX Reuss, J. L. (Princess of Saxe Meiningen), and "Anastasia", 226

Fesenko, I. A. (mining engineer), 140–1

Ford, Henry, meets Sokolov, 173–5

Foreign Office, British, and missing files, 253–5

Four Brothers mine: Sheremetevsky investigates, 65–6; Nametkin investigates, 66; Sokolov investigates, 138–45; dog discovered at, 161–5; climate at, 162–3; corpses at, 166–8; tsar executed at?, 314–15

Frederick of Saxe Altenburg, Prince, protects "Anastasia", 208, 209, 218, 239

Freiberg, Col., Sokolov robbed at house of, 179

French secret service: at Ekat., 47, 95; on Romanovs' survival, 189; on tsar rescue, 284

Friedrich Karl of Hesse Kassel, Prince, 387n

Fryd, Maxwell (forensic documents expert), 115–16

Fullerton (*Times* correspondent), 173

Furtmayr, Moritz, and "Anastasia" photos, 236

Gaida, Gen. Rudolf (Czech), orders investigation at Perm, 323, 348–9, 350, 354

Galitzin, Prince Dmitry, and Hesse visit to Russia, 219

Ganin Pit, *see* Four Brothers mine

George V, King; meets tsar, 36, 244; accepts tsar's death, 80–2, 272, 301; and tsar rescue plans, 243–5, 259–60, 270; 86, 92, 171–2, 275, 385n

George of Greece, Prince, and "Anastasia", 216

Gibbes, Sydney (Romanovs' tutor), 41–2, 46, 77, 85, 311; and "Anastasia", 235, 381n; and letter seeking aid for tsar, 255, 384n

Giers, Mikhail de, 370n

Gilliard, Pierre (Romanovs' tutor): on Sokolov, 105, and bullets at I.H., 149; in Paris, 172; death of, 176; and "Alexei", 192–3; and "Anastasia", 203–4, 214, 217, 230–1, 234, 235; *The False Anastasia* by, 217; 41–2, 46, 77–8, 310, 311, 390n

Gilliard, Alexandra ("Shura", wife of Pierre, form. Tegleva, Romanovs' nursemaid), 139; and "Anastasia", 203–4, 231–2, 234

Girschfeld, Ivan (Perm witness), 329

Goleniewski, Michal, claims to be Alexei, 193–5, 374–5n

Goloshchokin, Chaya (member of Ural Soviet), 41, 49, 103, 108, 130, 134, 145–6, 167, 212, 266, 293, 317–18, 329; announces tsar shot, 55

Gorbunov, Nikolai, 107

Gorshkov, Fyodor (witness on I.H.), 67, 79, 123

Gracheva, Anastasia, and Anastasia's escape at Perm, 342

Graves, Gen. William, 312

Grigoryev, Maxim (signalman at Ekat.), 333–4, 341–2

guards at Ipatiev House, *see under* Ipatiev House

Gulyayev (Rail Commissar at Ekat.), 55

Gurko, Gen. Vassily (Chief of Russ. Imp. Gen. Staff), 189

Guseva, Lydia (nurse at Perm), 125–6

Hall, Sir Reginald (Dir. of Br. Naval Intelligence), and tsar rescue, 257

Halliburton, Richard, claims interview with Yermakov, 180–1, 373n

Hardinge, Charles, Lord, and tsar rescue, 197, 247, 282, 376–7n

Hardinge, Major A. (George V's sec.), 253

Harvard University, Houghton Library at, and Sokolov dossier, 61

Hassenstein, Lt Col. Werner, 382n

Heine, Heinrich, quotation from, 75–6

Heinrich of Prussia, Prince (Kaiser's brother): and "Anastasia", 224; and tsar rescue, 281

Heinrich of Prussia, Princess (Princess Irene of Hesse, tsarina's sister), 92; and "Anastasia", 203, 214, 217–18, 221

Helen of Serbia (Yelena Petrovna), Princess Ioann Konstantinovich of Russia (Princess of Serbia), at Perm, 342

Henderson, Loy, 377n

Hesse, *see* Ernst Ludwig *and* Friedrich Karl, *and* Marianne

Hewins, Ralph, and Jonas Lied, 558–9, 384n

Hill, Brigadier George (Br. agent in Russia), 102

Hoffmann, Gen. Max: and Hesse visit to Russia, 219–20; on "Anastasia", 226–7, 273

Hoover Institution on War, Revolution and Peace, and Sokolov "black bag", 61

"Huntingdon, Countess of" (Jill Cossley-Batt), and "Anastasia", 207

Hüttenhain, Dr Erich (code expert), 111–12

Ilyodor (Russian monk), and tsar's head, 371

Ipatiev House, **42**; Nametkin investigates, 67–9; Sergeyev investigates, 72–7; Sokolov investigates, 136–7; Professor Camps on evidence at, 146–60; guard's evidence on, 67, 79, 118–32, 135, 150, 153, 319, 362–6n

Irene of Hesse, Princess, *see* Heinrich of Prussia, Princess

Italy, Queen Helena of, believes Romanovs alive, 92

Ivanov, Fyodor (barber at Ekat.), 55–6

Izvestya reports (1918) tsar's exhumation, 178

Jackson, Miss Margaret, and letter seeking aid for tsar, 255, 384n

Jacob, Sir Ian, (Dir. Gen. BBC), 213

Jacoby, Jean (French historian), 270

Janin, General P. T. C. Maurice (C.-in-C. Allied forces in Siberia), 95, 98, 110, 112; and Romanov "remains", 370n

Jemmy, *see under* dogs

Jennings, Annie B., hostess to "Anastasia", 206–7

jewels, Romanovs', 65–6, 78, 138, 367–8n; gemmologist on, 152–4

Jews: inscription at I.H., 76–7, 83–4; anti-semitism, 97, 103, 173–5, 340

Jogiches, Leo, and exchange with Romanovs?, 299

Joffe, Adolf (Soviet Amb. in Berlin), 297, 352

Jordansky, Prosecutor Valery, 62, 91, 164–5, 176, 322; and Medvedev's death, 127–9

Joseph of Austria, Archduke, and Hesse visit to Russia, 220

Juliana of the Netherlands, Queen, 238

Kanevstev, Konstantin (Cheka official), and tsar execution, 313–14

Kaplan, Dora, shoots Lenin, 299

Karakhan, Lev (deputy foreign commissar), 53

Karnaukovaya, Vera (witness at Perm), 324

Kerensky, Alexander (Min. of Justice, later P.M. of Russian Provisional Govt.), **39–40**; and tsar rescue, 245, 251–2, 276

Kharitonov, Ivan (Romanovs' cook), 44

Kimsey, Herman, 375n

Kirkpatrick, Lady Violet, and Romanov "remains", 370–1n

Kirsta, Alexander, investigation by, 326, 329–52 *passim*

Kissinger, Henry, 196, 197, 377n

Kleist, Baron Arthur von, and "Anastasia", 202

Kleshchov, Ivan (I.H. guard), 123

Knightley, Phillip (*Sunday Times*), 104

Knopf, Martin (private detective), and "Anastasia", 205, 379n

Knox, General Sir Alfred, M.P. (chief of Br. military mission to Siberia), and asylum for tsar, 252

Kobylinsky, Col. Yevgeny, and tsar rescue, 262, 263–4, 267; on Chemodurov's story, 310

Kolchak, Admiral Alexander (White Russian "Supreme Ruler"), 90, 96, 169, 269, 349, 350, 361n

Komsomolskaya Pravda repeats (1966) "Romanovs killed" story, 180

Konstantin Konstantinovich of Russia, Grand Duke: three sons' bodies found, 359n

Kostina, Anna, at Perm, 327, 331–2

Kostritsky, Dr Serge (Court dentist), on "Anastasia", 230–1

Kovalevsky, Prof. Pierre, 371n

Krivopdenova, Alexandra (witness at Perm), 325–6

Krokaleva, Maria, see nuns

Kschessinska, Mathilde, 223

Kukhtenkov, Prokopy (Red soldier), on burials at Ekat., 365–6

Kuklin, Ivan (switchman at Perm), 335, 340, 343

Kuklina, Matrena (witness at Perm), 335, 340, 343

Kuli-Mirza, Prince (White garrison cdr. at Ekat.), 71

Kulkov, A. N. (chief of Whites' code dept.), 112

Kutuzov, Alexander (Asst. Public Prosecutor at Ekat.), 67, 71, 176

Kyril Vladimirovich of Russia Grand Duke, and claim to throne, 91

Lacher, Rudolf (P.O.W. at Ekat.), 132–3

Lampson, Miles (later Lord Killearn; Br. chargé d'affaires in Siberia), 171–2; and Romanov "remains", 370n

Lar-Larsky, Col. Dmitry, and Hesse visit to Russia, 380n

Lasies, *Commandant* Joseph, 103–4, 127, 128

Left Social Revolutionaries, 179, 295, 296; see also Social Revolutionary Party

Lenin, 33, 39; and Brest-Litovsk, 276–7; and Romanovs' fate, 291–304 *passim*, 317, 352–3; attempted assassination of, 299

Lerche, Robert von, exposes Mayer, 212

Letemin, Mikhail (guard at I.H.), 122, 124, 150, 362–4n

"Letts" (foreign soldiers serving Bolsheviks), 48, 120

Leuchtenberg, Duke George of, and "Anastasia", 205, 238

Leuchtenberg, Duke Nicholas of, and tsar rescue, 282, 284

Leverkuehn, Dr Paul, and legal case for "Anastasia", 209

Liebknecht, Karl, and exchange with Romanovs, 299, 352

Lied Jonas, and tsar rescue, 255–60, 384n

Litvinov, Maxim (deputy foreign commissar), and Romanovs' fate, 303

Lloyd George, David (Br. P.M.): and tsar's death, 244,

Lloyd George—*cont.*
245; and tsar rescue, 246, 250, 252, 259
Lobov (Bolshevik at Perm), 336
Lockhart, Robert Bruce (Br. Consul General at Moscow), 53, 54
Louise, Queen of Sweden (sister of Lord Mountbatten), 211
Lukoyanov, Fyodor Nikolay-evich (Cheka chairman), 324
Lvov, Prince Georgy (first P.M. of Russian Prov. Govt.), 93–4, 98
Lydig, Col. (U.S.), 173
Lyons, Marvin, 373n
Lyukhanov, Sergei (truck driver at Ekat.), 121

McCullagh, Captain Francis (Br. Intelligence Officer), 149–50
Mackworth-Young, Robert (Br. royal archivist), 253
Magener, Adolf (German agent), 301–2
Magnitsky, N. N. (Asst. Prosecutor at Ekat.), 166
Malinovsky, Capt., 67, 69, 168, 273
Malkov (Bolshevik at Perm), 336
Malysheva, Glafyra and mother-in-law (witnesses at Perm), 329–31
Malyshev, Rafael (husband of Glafyra), 330–1, 345
Manahan, Dr John (husband of "Anastasia"), 198–9
Maria of Russia, Grand Duchess (tsar's daughter), 44; imper-sonator of, 195

Marianne, Princess Wilhelm of Hesse Philippsthal (Princess of Prussia), and "Anastasia", 226
Marie, Russian Dowager Em-press (Princess Dagmar of Denmark; tsar's mother), 91–2, 102, 104, 175–6, 360n; and "Anastasia", 203, 206; death of, 215; and Romanov "remains", 370–1n
Markov, Lt Sergei, and tsar rescue, 280–1, 301, 389n
Maslovsky, Sergei, 385n
Max of Baden, Prince, says tsar executed, 289–90, 315
Mayer, Hans Johann ("Ivan Leopoldovich"), gives evi-dence against "Anastasia", 211–13
Mecklenburg, *see* Barbara, Duchess *and* Cecile, German Crown Princess
Medvedev, Pavel (sgt. of I.H. guard), 118–22, 124–29, 153; his wife interrogated, 130, 362–4n, 365n
Melnik, Mme, *see* Botkin Tatiana
Mensheviks, **39**
Mikhail Alexandrovich of Russia, Grand Duke (tsar's brother), 38
Mikhail Mikhailovich of Russia, Grand Duke (tsar's cousin), 257–8
Mikulova, Zinaida (witness at Ekat.), 313–14
Milford Haven, Marchioness of (form. Princess Victoria of Hesse; tsarina's sister): and Romanovs' survival, 81–2, 272, 300–1; and tsar rescue,

Milford Haven—*cont.*
257; and "Anastasia", 209, 214

Milner, Lord (Br. Sec. of State for War, 1918), 81

Milyukov, Pavel (Foreign Min. of Russian Prov. Govt.), and tsar rescue, 245–6, 247

Milyutin, Vladimir, on tsar's execution, 302

mine at Ekat., *see* Four Brothers mine

Mirbach, Count Wilhelm von (German Amb. in Moscow), 276–9, 285, 294–5; murder of, 295–6

Mirolyubov, Prof. Nikander, and "black bag", 61–2, 322; 127, 176

Mordvinov, Anatoly, 380n

Moshkin, Alexander (Avdeyev's asst), 47

Mossolov, Alexander, 379n

Mountbatten of Burma, Louis, Earl, 44, **92**, 182–3, 245, 259–60; and "Anastasia", 211, 213–14; and BBC, 213; and tsar rescue, 259–60

Mrachkovsky, Sergei, (Bolshevik Commissar at Ekat.), 131–2

Mutnykh, Natalya and Vladimir (witnesses at Perm), 321, 326–9, 331, 333, 341, 345

Nametkin, Alexander (Ekat. investigator), 57–8, 66–70, 72

New York Times, The, 93, 94, 134; and Romanovs' survival, 190, 191

News of the World, The, apologises to "Anastasia", 208

Nicholas II, Russian Emperor: accession, marriage and reign of, **35–8**; **43**; abdication of, 38, 278–9; executed?, 53–6, 212, 289, 292–3, 307–10, 313–15, 317–18, 362–4n, 389–90n; *see also* Romanovs

Nikiforov, Col. (White Intelligence Officer), 325–6, 349

Nikolai Nikolayevich of Russia, Grand Duke, 174, 175, 370

Nikulin, Prokopy (asst. to Yurovsky), 49, 52

Nobel, Dr Lothar, and "Anastasia", 233

nuns at Ekat., 46, 51, 52, 144

Obolensky, Prince, on Romanovs' survival, 188–9

O'Conor, John, *The Sokolov Investigation* by, 107–8, 365n

Oldenburg, Hereditary Grand Duke of, 374n

Olga of Greece, Queen (Grand Duchess Olga Konstantinovna of Russia), 281–2

Olga Alexandrovna of Russia, Grand Duchess (tsar's sister; Anastasia's godmother): and "Anastasia", 203, 204, 209, 214, 215–16, 221, 231–2; and Romanov "remains", 371n

Olga Nikolayevna of Russia, Grand Duchess (tsar's daughter), 44; claimant, 192, 374n

Omsk, White military H.Q. at, **90**; and Romanov deaths, 90–8 *passim*; *see also* Diterikhs, General Mikhail

Orlov, Prince Nikolai (ed. of Russian edition of Sokolov's book), 113, 173–4

Ostroumov Nikolai (asst. prosecutor at Ekat.), 90, 127, 128, 176

Page, Mr and Mrs Nelson (Amb. in Rome), 92
Palmer, Henry (U.S. Consul in Ekat.), 312
Pavel Alexandrovich, Grand Duke: son's body found, 359n
Perm: Romanovs taken to?, 56, 131, 298, 321–54, 391n; trial of tsar "killers" reported at, 178–9; taken by Whites, **322**; taken by Bolsheviks, 349
Peuthert, Clara, and "Anastasia", 201
Pichon, Stephen (French foreign minister), 93, 94
Pilar von Pilchau, Baroness Marie, and Hesse visit to Russia, 220
Pilsudski, Josef, (Cdr. Polish armies), 378n
Podorova, Stefanida, 342
Poole, Gen. Frederick, 81
Postnikov (White Regional Controller), and corruption, 165
Pozdnyshev, Gen. S., 60, 371n
Poznanski, Maurice, and tsar rescue, 284
Pravda: reports trial of tsar's murderers, 178–9; on tsar's execution, 315–17
Preston, Thomas (later Sir; Br. Consul at Ekat.), 31, 46, 82, 83, 86–7, 127, 171, 271–2, 316, 322–3, 370n
Prince of Wales, Edward David, and Lied, 257, 384n
Prince, John (U.S. envoy in Denmark), 216

Proskuryakov, Philip (guard at I.H.), 122–4, 130, 133, 362–4n, 365n
Proteau, Gilbert, 223–4
Prussia, Prince and Princess of, *see* Heinrich, Prince and Princess *and* Sigismund, Prince
Ptitsin, Grigory (White officer), on I.H., 98

Rachmaninov, Sergei (pianist), 206
Radek, Karl, 295, 297, 298–9, 300, 351–2; on Romanovs' fate, 393n
Rasputin, Grigory, 36, 37–8, 261
Rathenau, Dr. (Prussian official), and "Anastasia", 204
Reche, Prof. Otto, and "Anastasia" photos, 236
Ree, Poul (Danish vice-consul in Perm), on tsar's death, 314–15, 316
Reilly, Sidney (spy), 258
Rich, Dr Edward (of West Point), 157–8
Richards, Guy, *Imperial Agent* and *The Hunt for the Tzar* by, 195; *The Rescue of the Romanovs* by, 197, 375n
Riezler, Dr Kurt (Counsellor at German Embassy in Moscow), 209, 297–8
Rimashevsky, Vitold (White commandant at Perm), 324–5
Rodzyanko, Col. Pavel (officer with Br. mission in Siberia), 87
Romanovs: confined at Tsarskoe Selo, 38–9; at Tobolsk, moved to Ekat., 40–1; children, **43–4**; last service at I.H. for, 149–51; report—tsar shot, family sent to safer place, 52–6;

Romanovs—*cont.*
reported taken to Denmark, 71; rescue plans for, 245–90 *passim*, 299, 301, 317, 352; alleged post-war sightings of, 187, 190, 191; fate of "remains" of, 156, 369–71n; *see also* individual Romanovs *and* Ipatiev House *and* jewels *and* Perm

Rudneff, Prof. Sergei, and "Anastasia", 218

Ryabov, Vassily (witness at Perm), 335

Safarov, Georgy (member Ural Soviet), 103

Sakovich, Dr Nikolai (at Ekat.), 133–4

Saxe-Weimar, Hereditary Grand Duke of, 238

Schanzkowska, Franziska, identified with "Anastasia"?, 205, 232–3

Schevenbach, Frau von, 374n

Schoenaich Carolath, Prince Ferdinand of, and Hesse visit to Russia, 219

Schwabe, Capt. Nikolai von, and "Anastasia", 201

Scott, Michael, 381n

Sednev, Leonid (Romanovs' kitchen boy), 44, 50, 319

Semyonov, Ataman Grigory (White warlord), 170

Sergei Mikhailovich, Grand Duke, body found of, 359n

Sergeyev, Judge Ivan: investigation at Ekat. by, 71, 72–9, 83–9, 126; believed tsarina and children not shot at I.H., 89; dismissal of, 89–91; character smeared, 97;

executed?, 89; *et seq. passim*

Shackleton, Ernest, and Lied, 257

Shamarin (Perm district prosecutor), 176, 323, 391

Sheremetevsky, Alexander, 162

Sheremetevsky, Lt Andrei, 65–6

Shilova, Klavdiya (witness at Perm), 344

Shlenov (Bolshevik at Perm), and Anastasia's escape, 336, 339

Sibiryev (Perm witness), 329

Sigismund of Prussia, Prince, and "Anastasia", 192, 224–5, 374n

Simpson, Prof. Keith (Br. Home Office pathologist), 163–4

Sipek, Jan (Czech officer in Ekat.), and Goloshchokin, 134

Sitnikova, Tatiana and son, Fyodor, on Anastasia's escape at Perm, 334–5, 341–2

Sivkov, Alexander (guard at Perm), 345

Skoropadsky, Gen. Pavel (Hetman of Ukraine; aide to tsar), and tsar requiem service, 287

Slaughter, Major Homer, on Medvedev, 128, **311–13**, 365–6n

Smirnov, Sergei (Serb at Perm), 342

Smith, Amy, and "Anastasia", 218

Social Revolutionary Party (Left and Right), 96, 176, 179, 295, 296, 299

Sokolov, Nikolai: judicial enquiry by, 59–60, 106 *et seq. passim*; his research dossier found, 60–1; "black bag"

Sokolov, Nikolai—*cont.*
found, 61–2; and Sergeyev's evidence, 88; appointed investigator, **98–9, 101,** 102–5; and telegram, 106–17; and guards' testimony, 118–35, 362–4n; and I.H., 136–7, 146–51; and mine, 138–45, 151–65; sacked?, 169–71; in Paris, 172; visits Henry Ford, 173–5; death of, 175–6; robbed, 179–80; anti-German, 288; 361n, 365n

Sokolova, Yevgeniya (witness at Perm), 329–30, 333, 344, 345–6

Solovyov, Boris, and tsar rescue, 261–2, 268

Solovyov, Mikhail, on Romanovs at Perm, 346–7

Soviet Foreign Ministry and Romanovs' fate, 180, 238–9

Stalin accused by Trotsky of ordering Romanovs' execution, 303

Stamfordham, Lord (George V's sec.), 247–50

Starynkevich, S. (White Minister of Justice), intervenes for Sergeyev, 90–1; 391n

Stephan, Otto, exposes Mayer, 212

Stoneman, William (corr. of *Chicago Daily News*), on Halliburton, 181

Storozhev, Father, **46;** and last Romanov service, 49–51

Strekotin, Andrei (guard at I.H.), 122

Suetin, Gregory (guard at I.H.), 364n

sulphuric acid and corpse disposal, 142–4, 145, 157–60

Sverdlov, Yakov (Soviet head of state): announces tsar shot, 53–4; on tsar's execution, 302; 103, 107–8, 263, 293, 295–6, 317

Swatowski, and tsar rescue, 284

Syromolotov, Fyodor (member of Ural Soviet), 103, **293**

Tatiana of Russia, Grand Duchess (tsar's daughter), **44,** escape at Perm of?, 333

Tatishchev, Gen. Ilya (aide to tsar), 41, 91

Tegleva, *see* Gilliard, Mme Alexander

telegram, "Beloborodov", examined, 106–17

Thomas, Arthur (asst. to Br. Consul at Ekat.), 31

Thorpe, Jeremy, M.P., 196–7

Thurn and Taxis, Elisabeth, Princess of, and Hesse visit to Russia, 219

Tikhomirov (Perm Dist. Prosecutor), 349, 351

Tobolsk, Romanovs at, 41, 91

Tolmachev, Georgy (guard at Perm), 345

Tomashevsky, Mikhail (Whites Court Investigator), 67

Trinkina, Antonina, *see* nuns

Trotsky, Lev, 39, 53, 291; and Romanov deaths, 303

Trupp, Alexei (Romanovs' servant), 44, 310

Tsarskoe Selo, Romanovs confined at, **38–9**

Tschaikowsky, Alexander, and rescue of "Anastasia"?, 202

tutors to Romanovs, *see* Gibbes, Sydney *and* Gilliard, Pierre

typhus epidemic, 126–7, **134**

Ulyanov, Alexander (Lenin's brother), 33

Unruh, Fritz von, on Hesse visit to Russia, 220

Urach, Duke of, 387n

Uritsky, Moisei, murdered, 299 *bis*

Utkin, Dr Pavel Ivanovich, and Anastasia's escape at Perm, 335–41, 344

Valdemar of Denmark, Prince (brother of Marie, Dowager Empress), 215, 287, 360n

Varakushev, Alexander (guard at I.H.), 130–2, 135, 319

Victoria, Queen, 35

Victoria of Hesse, Princess, *see* Milford Haven, Marchioness of

Vladimir Andreyevich, *see under* Andrei Vladimirovich

Vladimir Kyrilovich of Russia, Prince (assumptive Grand Duke and pretender to the Russian throne), 253, 260, 360n, 371n

Voikov, Commissar Pyotr, 103, 142, 158–9; on Romanov murders, 181–2

Voitkevich, Capt. (Polish off. with Nametkin), 80–1, 391n

Volkov, Alexei (tsar's servant), 203

Vorobtsov (Bolsh. at Perm), 336

Vyrubova, Anna (tsarina's friend), 260, 366n

Waters, Gen. Wallscourt, and tsar rescue, 246, 275–6, 281

Webster, Robert (consultant gemmologist), 152–3

Weinstein, S. L. (Commissar), 239

Wilhelm II, Kaiser: and relations with tsar, 36–7, 69, 274–5; sends wife, Hermine, to "Anastasia", 208, 226, 273; and tsar rescue, 267, 272–90 *passim*, 317, 353; exiled, 352

Wilton, Robert (of *The Times*), 60, 102–4, 148, 159, 161–2, 172; death of, 176; and Brest-Litovsk, 277–8

Wrangel, Gen. Baron Pyotr (C.-in-C. White forces in Crimea), 187

Xenia Alexandrovna of Russia, Grand Duchess (tsar's sister), and "Anastasia", 203, 209, 214; 379n

Xenia Georgievna of Russia, Princess (Mrs W. B. Leeds), and "Anastasia", 205–6, 224

Yakimov, Anatoly (guard at I.H.): describes tsar and tsarina, 43; 79, 84, 122–4, 362–4n, 365n; sister's testimony, 79

Yakovlev, Vassily, and tsar rescue attempt?, 262–72 *passim*, 385n

Yermakov, Pyotr (member of Cheka), 119–20, 121, 144, 158–9; on Romanov killings, 181, 365–6n

Young, Robert, 377n

Yurganova-Baranova, Iraida, guards Anastasia at Perm?, 344

Yurovsky, Yakov (commandant of I.H.), **47–8,** 51, 52, 54,

Yurovsky, Yakov —*cont.*
103, 118, 119–22, 132–3, 134, 140, 159, 167, 295, 317–19, 362–4n
Yusupov, Prince Felix, 370n

Zahle, Herluf (Danish Minister in Berlin), 203, 204, 208, 215–16, 238
Zaicek, Col., and Yakovlev, 270
Zarnekau, Countess de, and Romanovs' survival, 190–1
Zimin, collects sulphuric acid at Ekat., 142
Zinoviev, Grigory, 238; and Romanovs' fate, 303–4, 327, 331, 332; *see also* Kostina, Anna
Zlobin, Col. (chief of White Military Intelligence), 112
Zvezda, and tsar's execution, 180
Zykov family (peasants at Four Brothers), 65

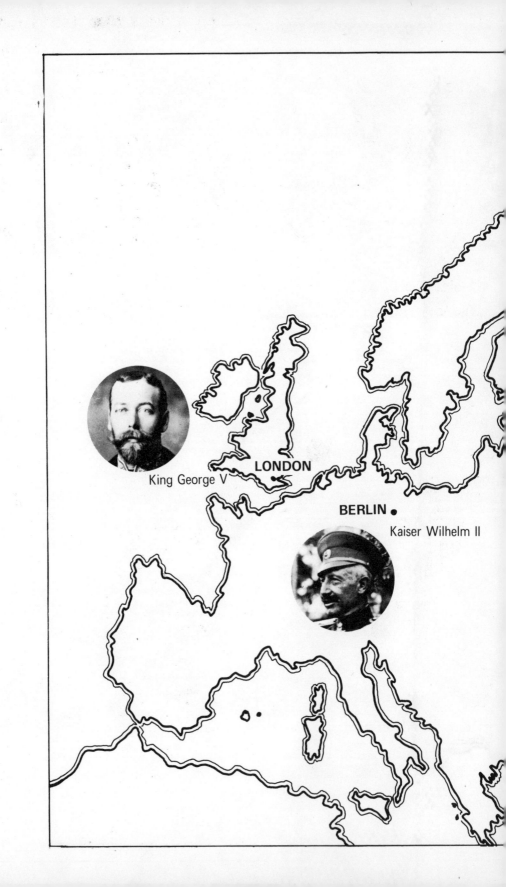

King George V

LONDON

BERLIN •

Kaiser Wilhelm II